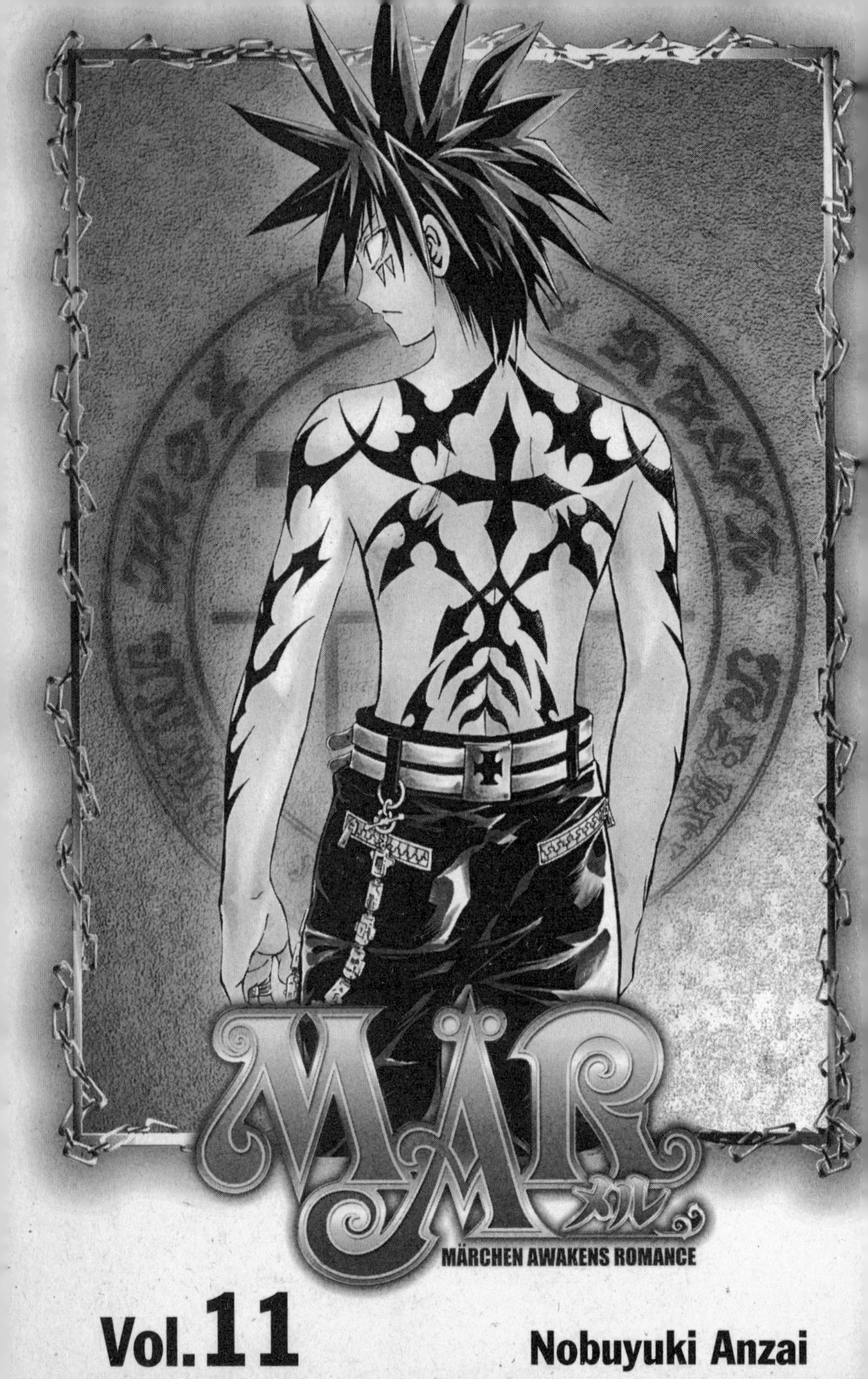

MÄR
MÄRCHEN AWAKENS ROMANCE

Vol. 11

Nobuyuki Anzai

Characters

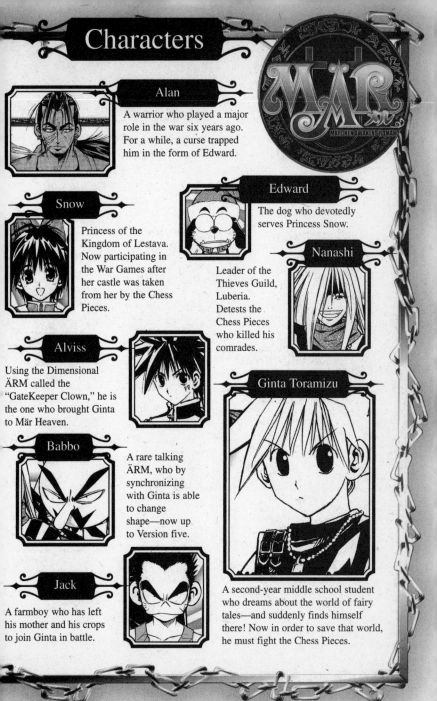

Alan

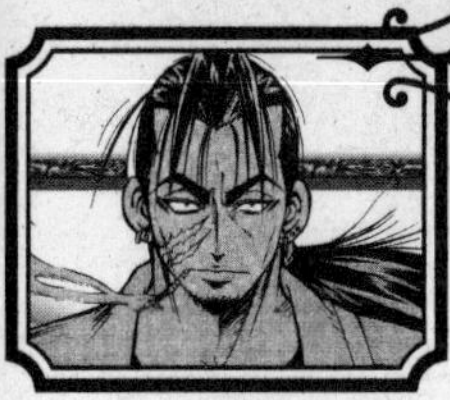

A warrior who played a major role in the war six years ago. For a while, a curse trapped him in the form of Edward.

Edward

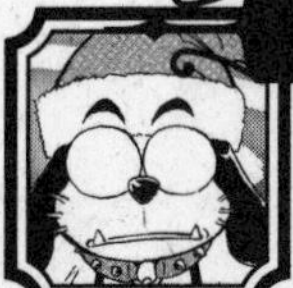

The dog who devotedly serves Princess Snow.

Snow

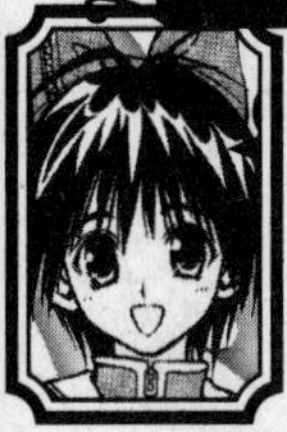

Princess of the Kingdom of Lestava. Now participating in the War Games after her castle was taken from her by the Chess Pieces.

Nanashi

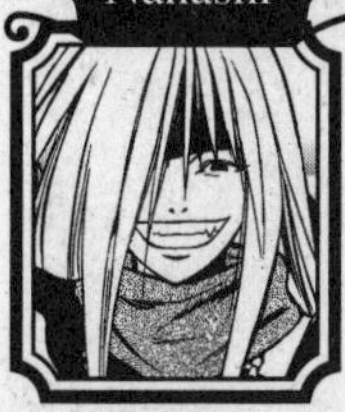

Leader of the Thieves Guild, Luberia. Detests the Chess Pieces who killed his comrades.

Alviss

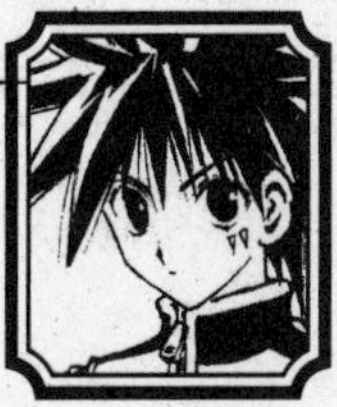

Using the Dimensional ÄRM called the "GateKeeper Clown," he is the one who brought Ginta to Mär Heaven.

Ginta Toramizu

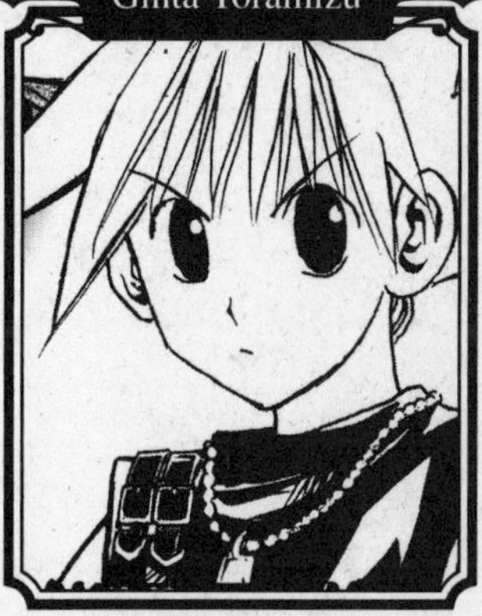

A second-year middle school student who dreams about the world of fairy tales—and suddenly finds himself there! Now in order to save that world, he must fight the Chess Pieces.

Babbo

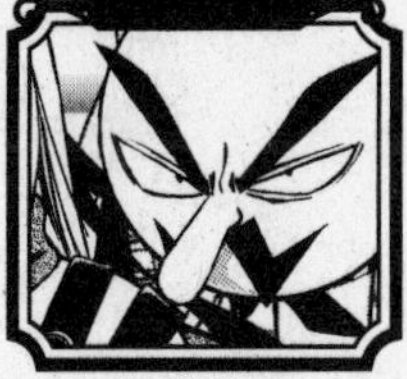

A rare talking ÄRM, who by synchronizing with Ginta is able to change shape—now up to Version five.

Jack

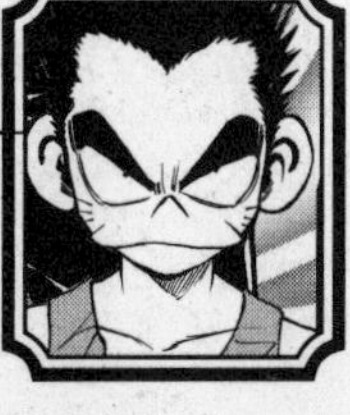

A farmboy who has left his mother and his crops to join Ginta in battle.

Previous Volume

Ginta jumps through a "door" that suddenly appears in his classroom, and finds himself in the magical world of his dreams. Now, at the "request" of the Chess Pieces, the War Games have begun—and Ginta and his eight friends, calling themselves "Mär," must battle the Chess warriors. Mär has managed to win the first five battles—but the match pitting Nanashi against Galian, the past and present leaders of Luberia, has become almost unendurably suspenseful!!

Phantom

A Chess Knight. The most powerful in the group and the leader of its combat force.

Galian

The former Leader of thieves who was lured away to the Chess Pieces by the temptation of power. A lightning-wielding Knight.

Diana

Queen of the Chess, Dorothy's older sister and Snow's stepmother

Rapunzel

A Chess Knight, and a woman of terrible cruelty who has dealt fatal punishments to her own teammates.

Ian

A mere Rook among the Chess. As a penalty for unauthorized behavior, he loses something very important to him.

Dorothy

A witch from Caldia, Kingdom of Magic. She has accepted the painful duty of killing the Queen of the Chess—her own sister

CONTENTS

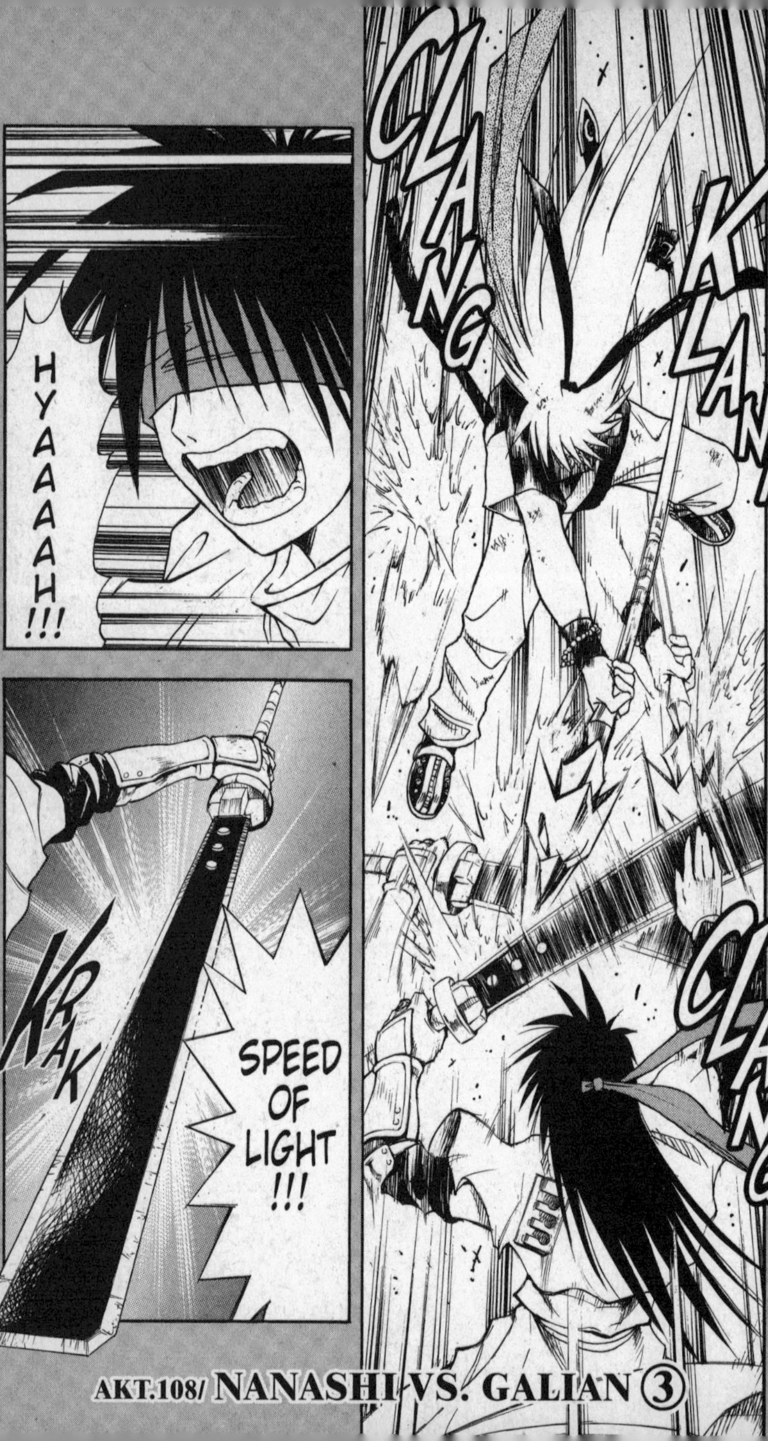
CLANG
KLANK
CLANG
HYAAAAAH!!!
KRAK
SPEED OF LIGHT!!!

AKT.108/ NANASHI VS. GALIAN ③

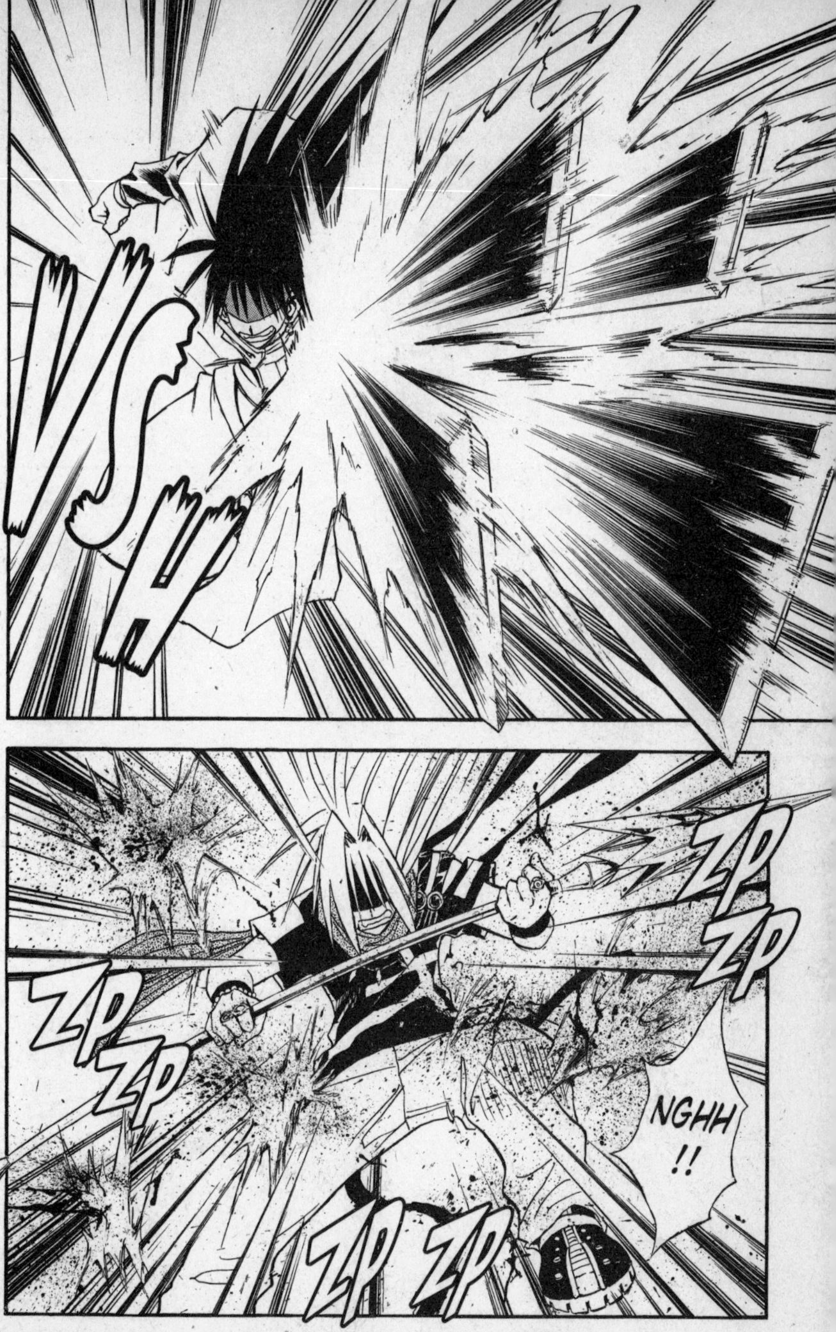
VSH
ZP ZP
ZP ZP
NGHH !!
ZP ZP

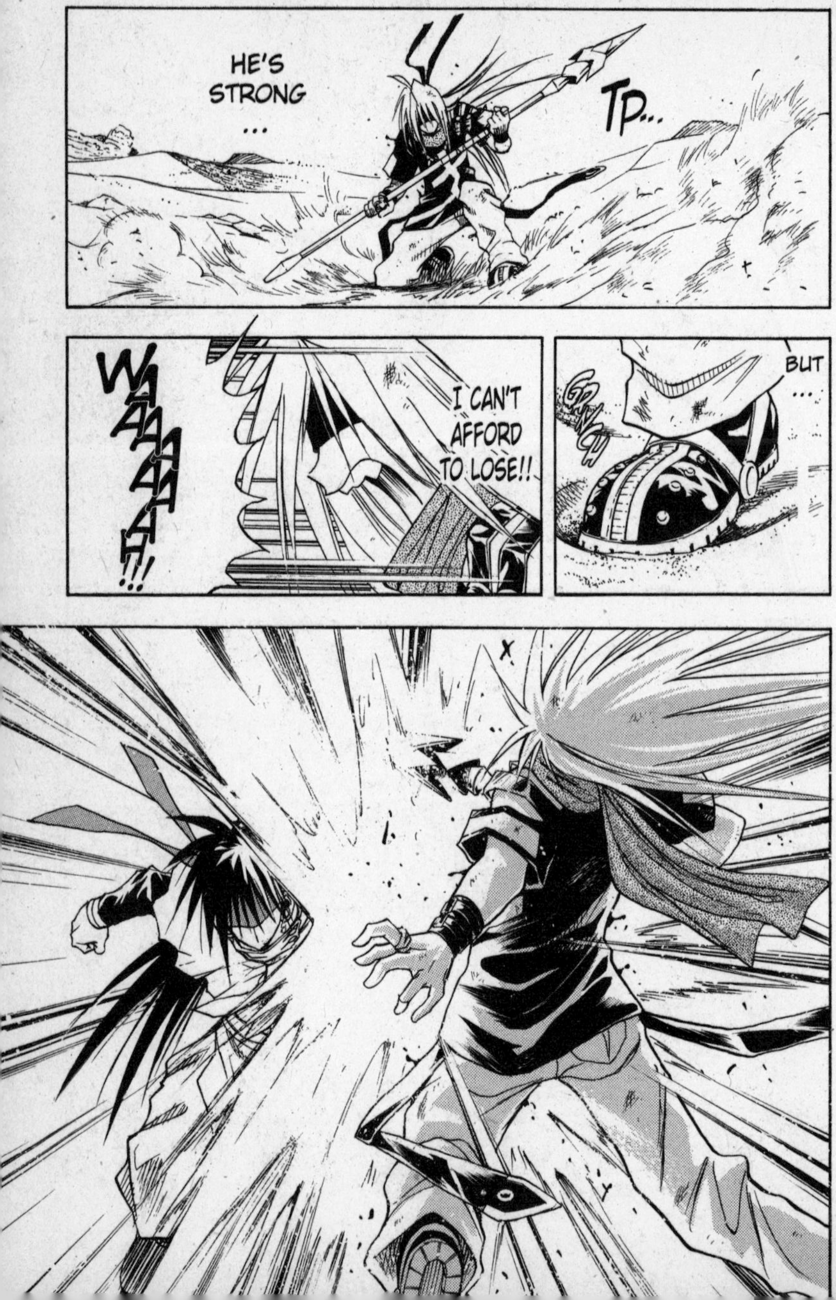
HE'S STRONG ...
TP...
BUT ...
I CAN'T AFFORD TO LOSE!!
WAAAAAAH!!!

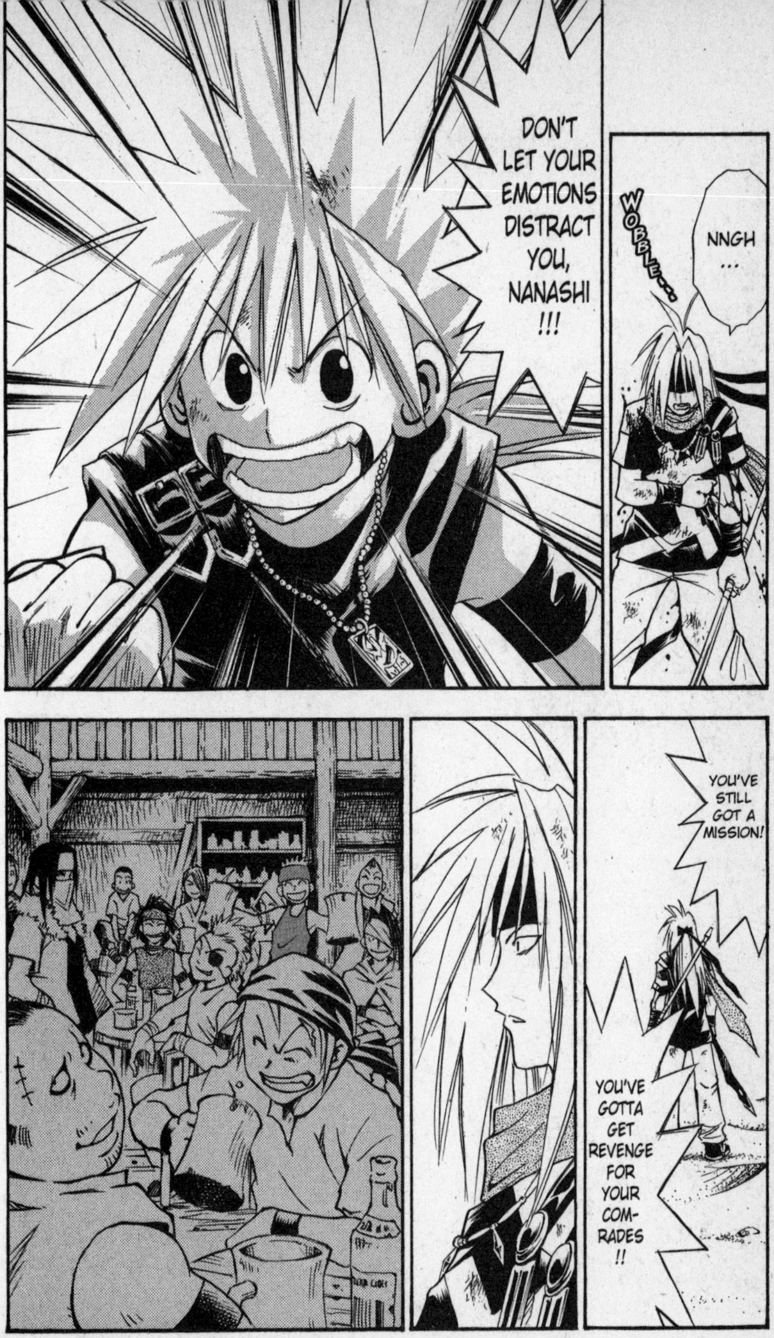
NNGH ...
WOBBLE...
DON'T LET YOUR EMOTIONS DISTRACT YOU, NANASHI !!!
YOU'VE STILL GOT A MISSION!
YOU'VE GOTTA GET REVENGE FOR YOUR COM-RADES !!

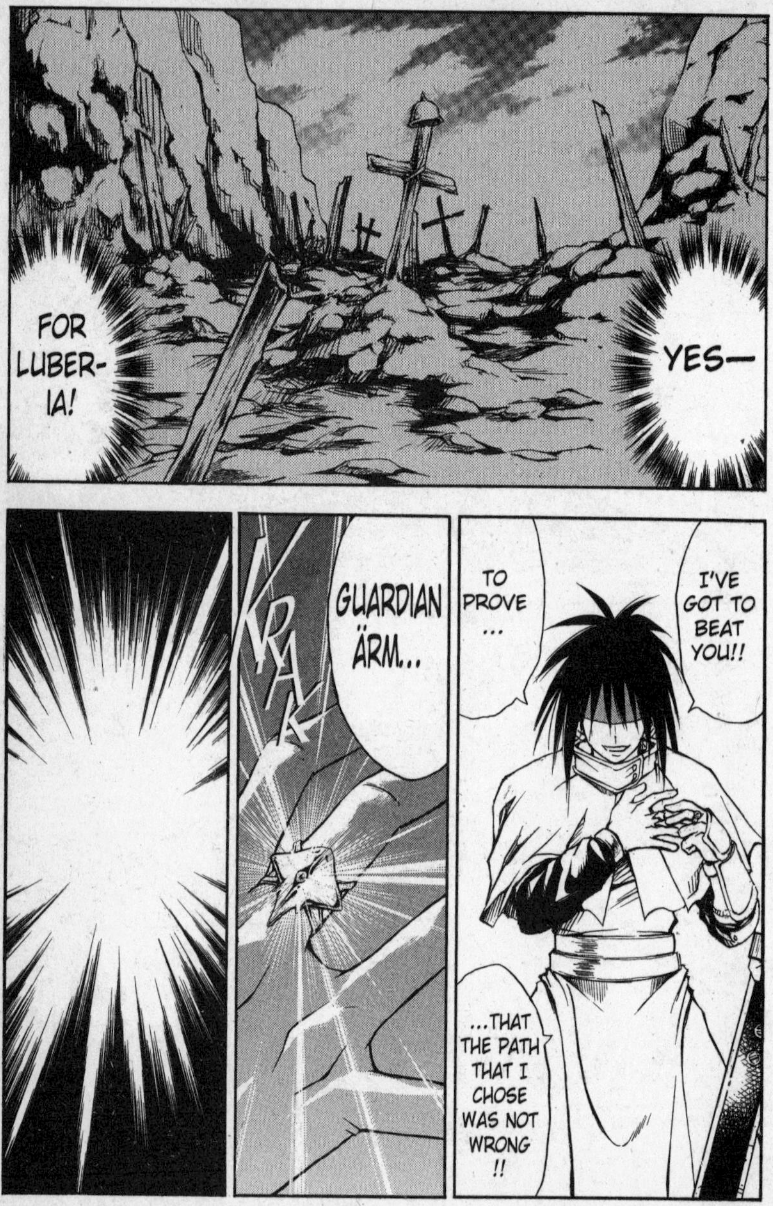
YES—
FOR LUBER-IA!
I'VE GOT TO BEAT YOU!!
TO PROVE...
...THAT THE PATH THAT I CHOSE WAS NOT WRONG!!
GUARDIAN ÄRM...
KRAK

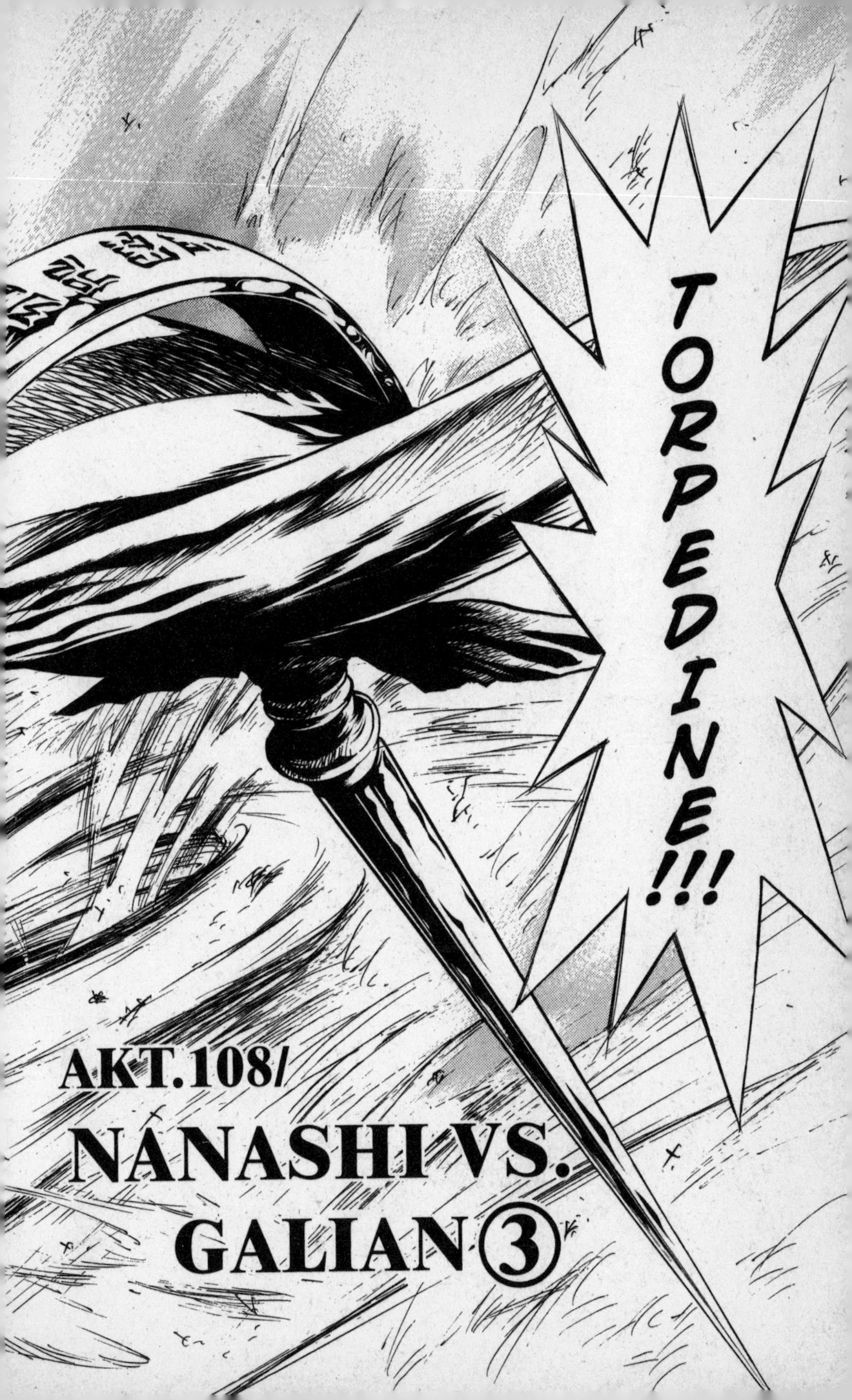
TORPEDINE!!!
AKT.108/
NANASHI VS.
GALIAN③

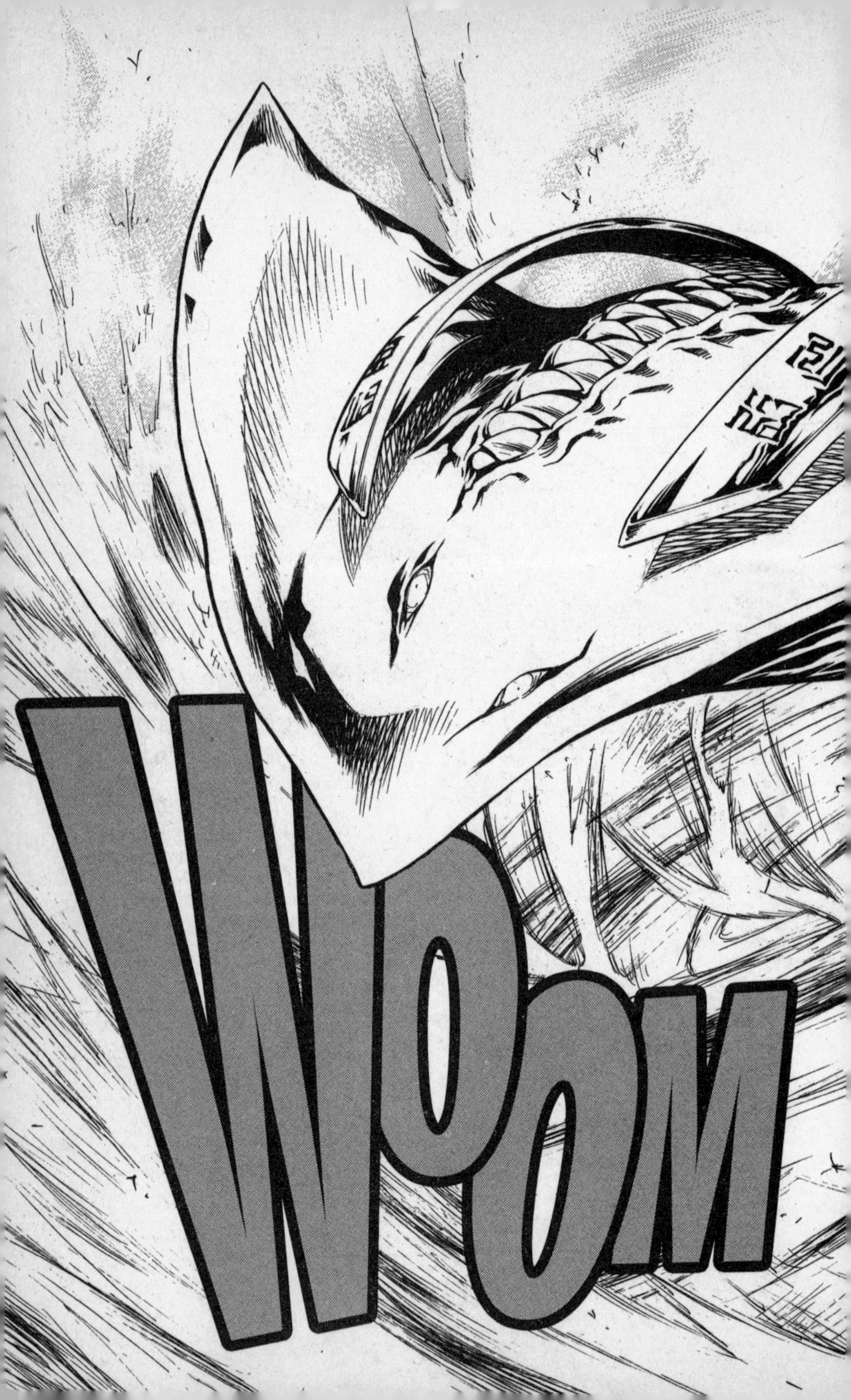
WOOM

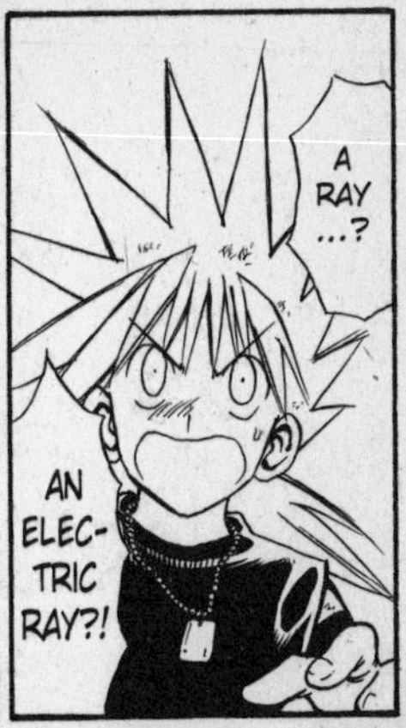
A RAY ...?
AN ELEC-TRIC RAY?!
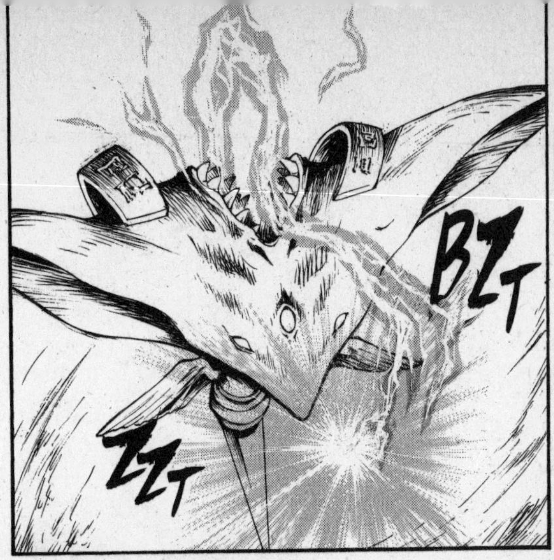
BZZT
ZZZT
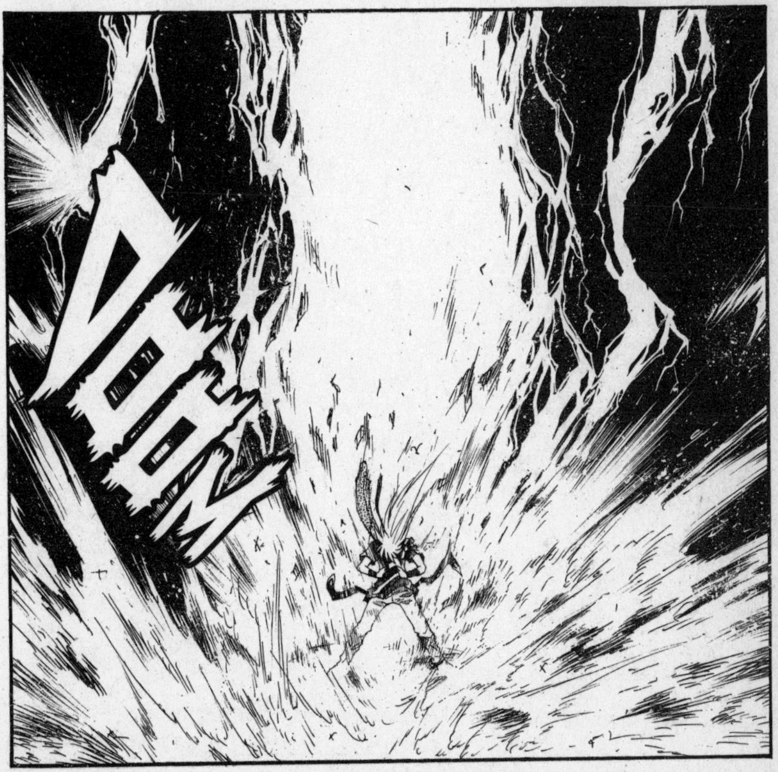

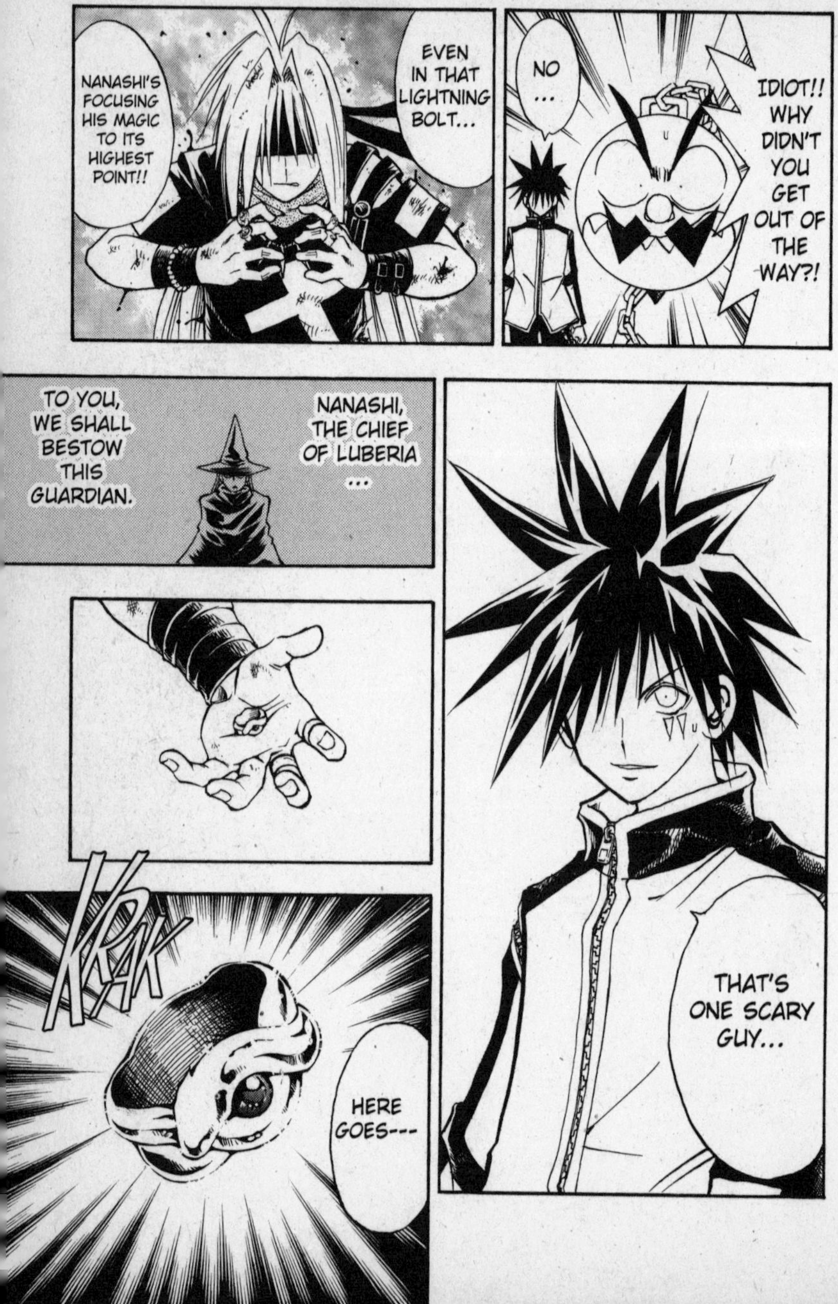
NO ...
IDIOT!! WHY DIDN'T YOU GET OUT OF THE WAY?!
EVEN IN THAT LIGHTNING BOLT...
NANASHI'S FOCUSING HIS MAGIC TO ITS HIGHEST POINT!!
THAT'S ONE SCARY GUY...
NANASHI, THE CHIEF OF LUBERIA ...
TO YOU, WE SHALL BESTOW THIS GUARDIAN.
KRAK
HERE GOES---

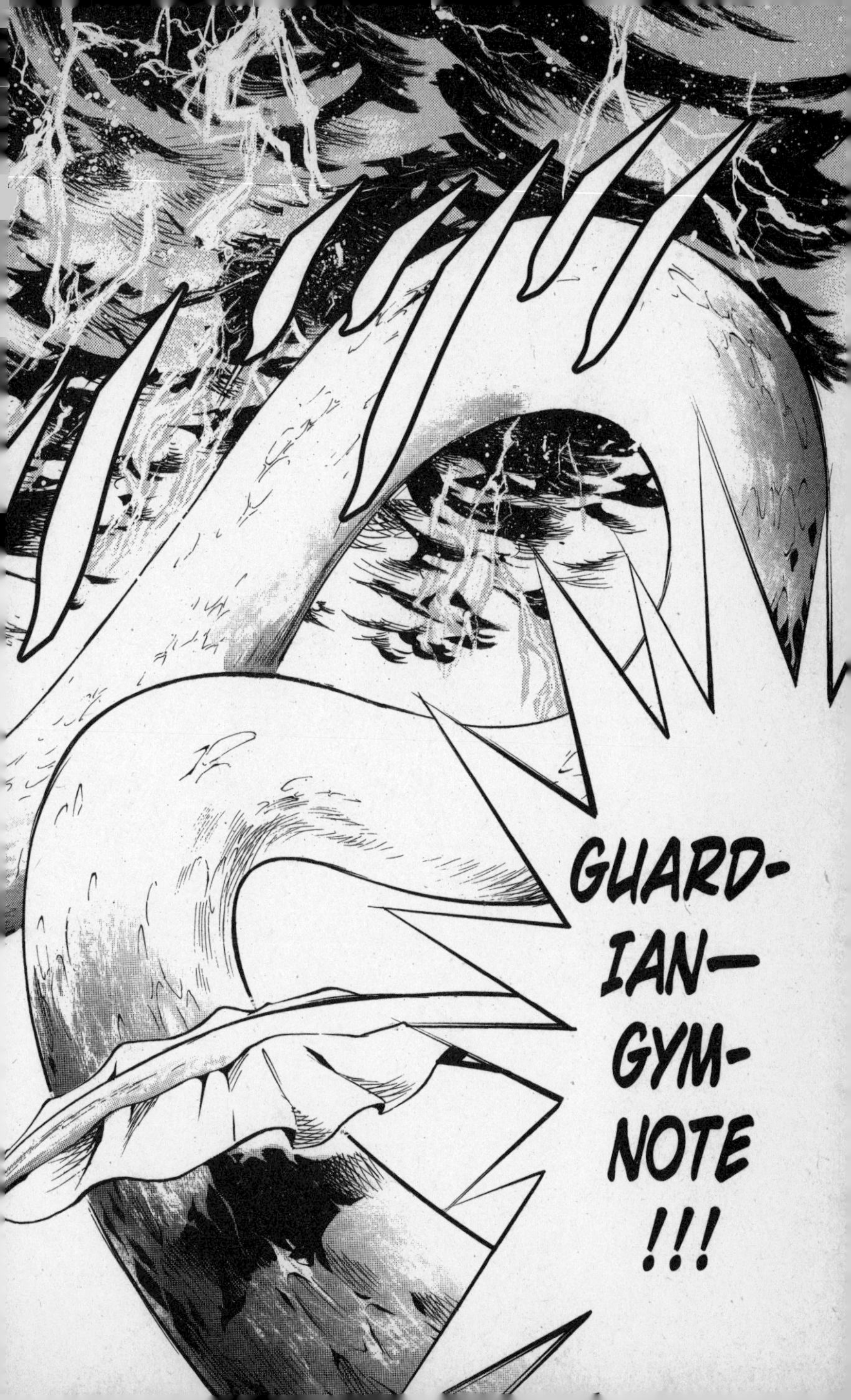
GUARD-
IAN-
GYM-
NOTE
!!!

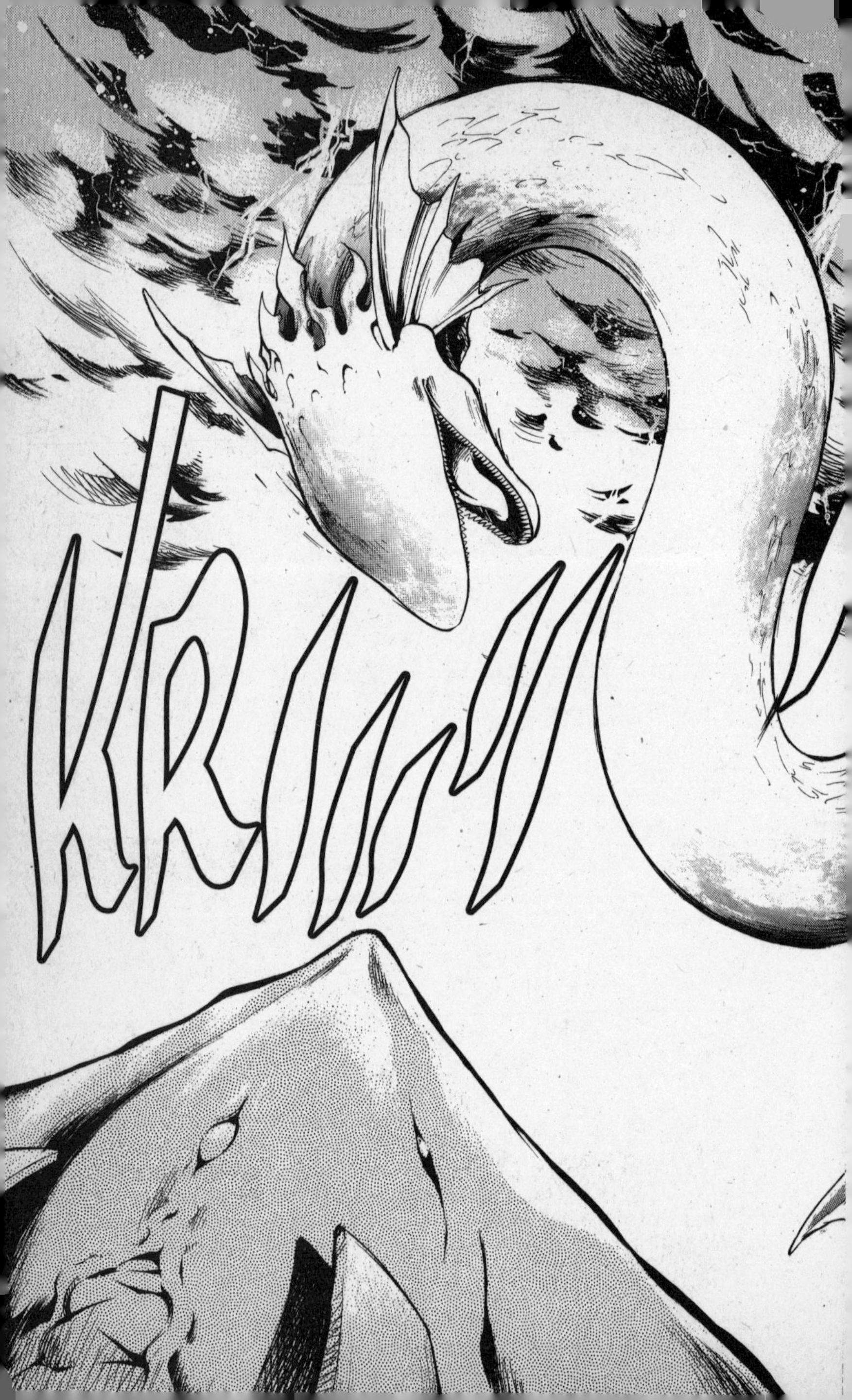
KRIIII

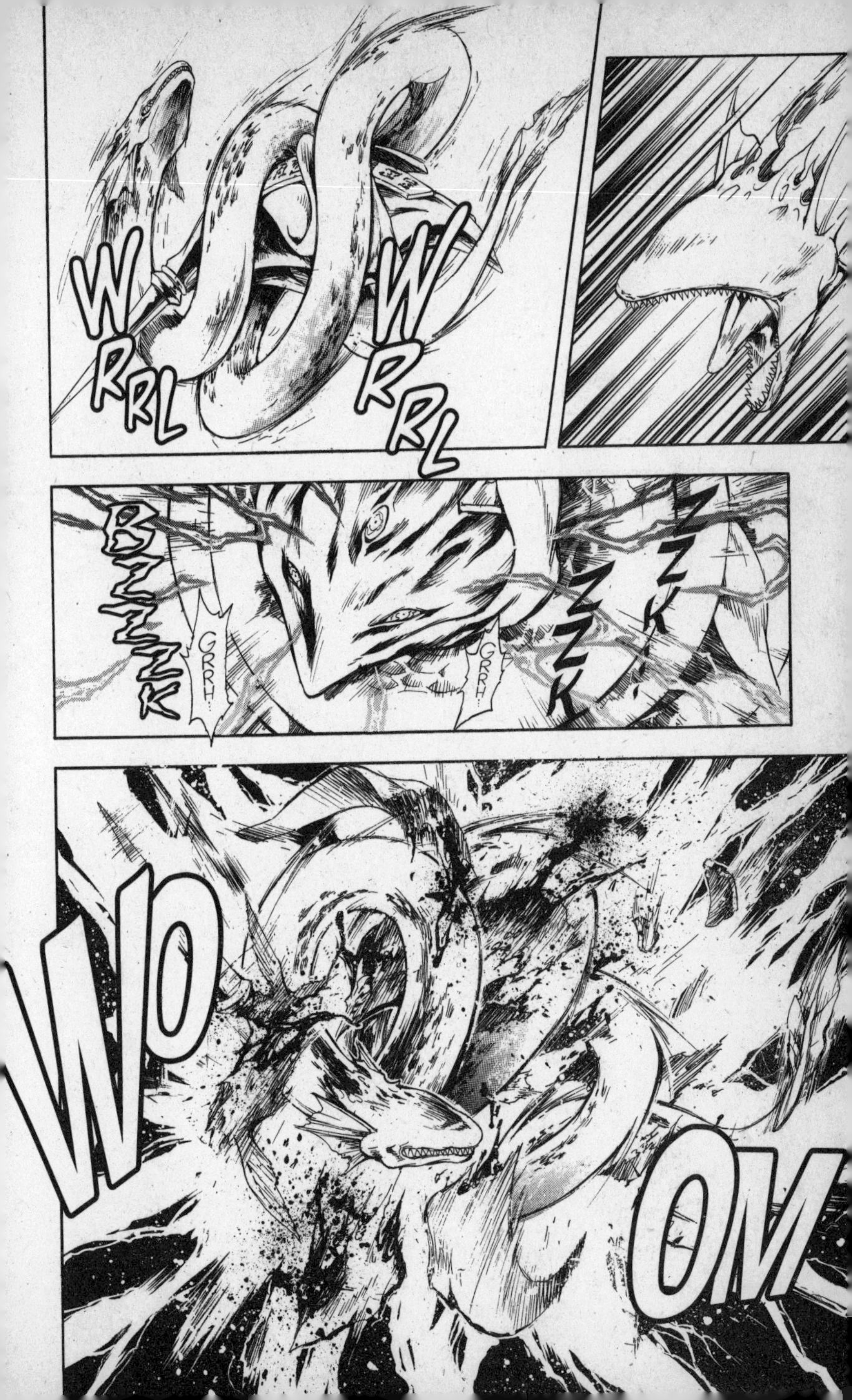
WRRL
WRRL
ZZK
ZZZK
GRRH
GRRH
BZZZZK
WOOM

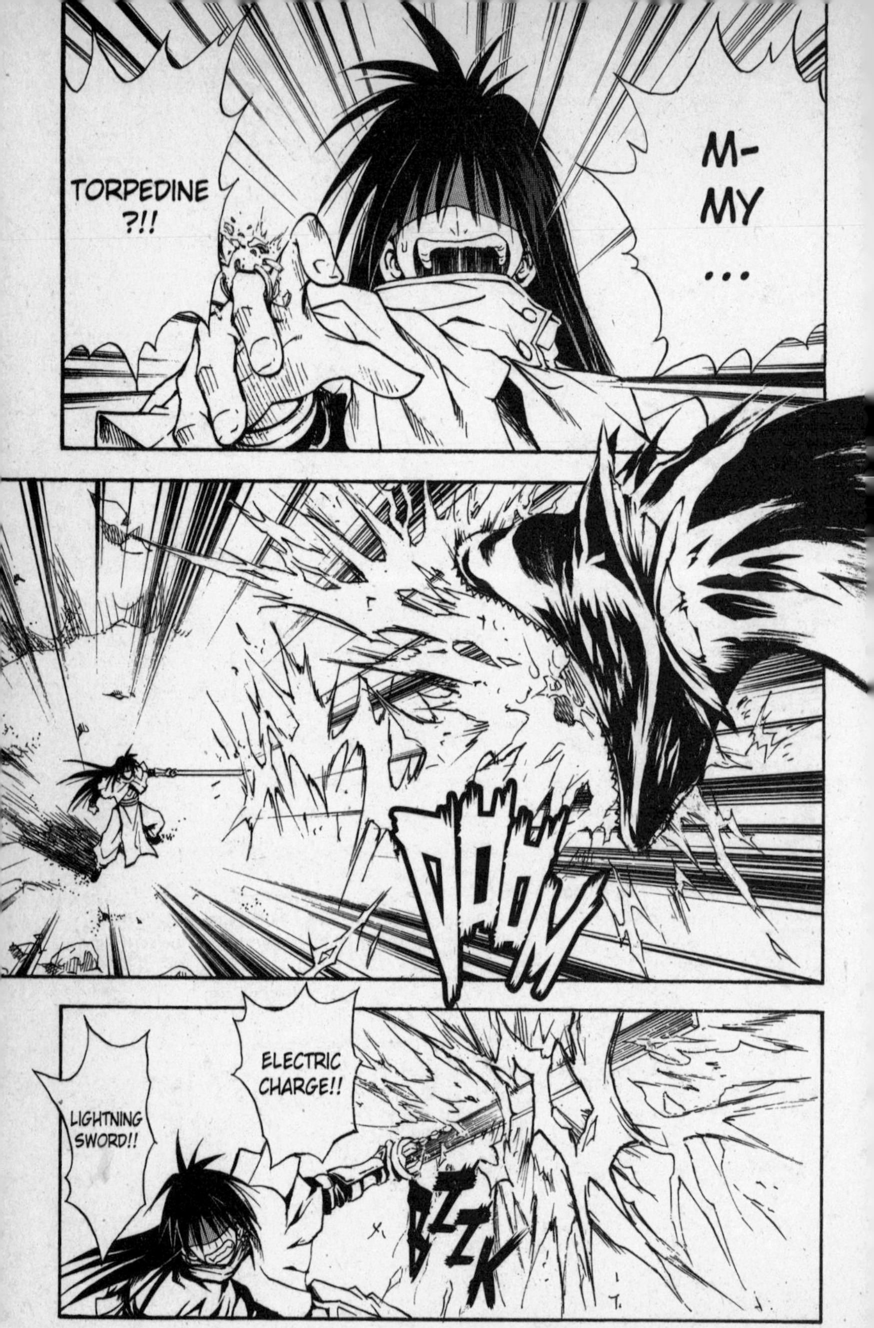
M-MY...
TORPEDINE ?!!
ELECTRIC CHARGE!!
LIGHTNING SWORD!!
BZZK

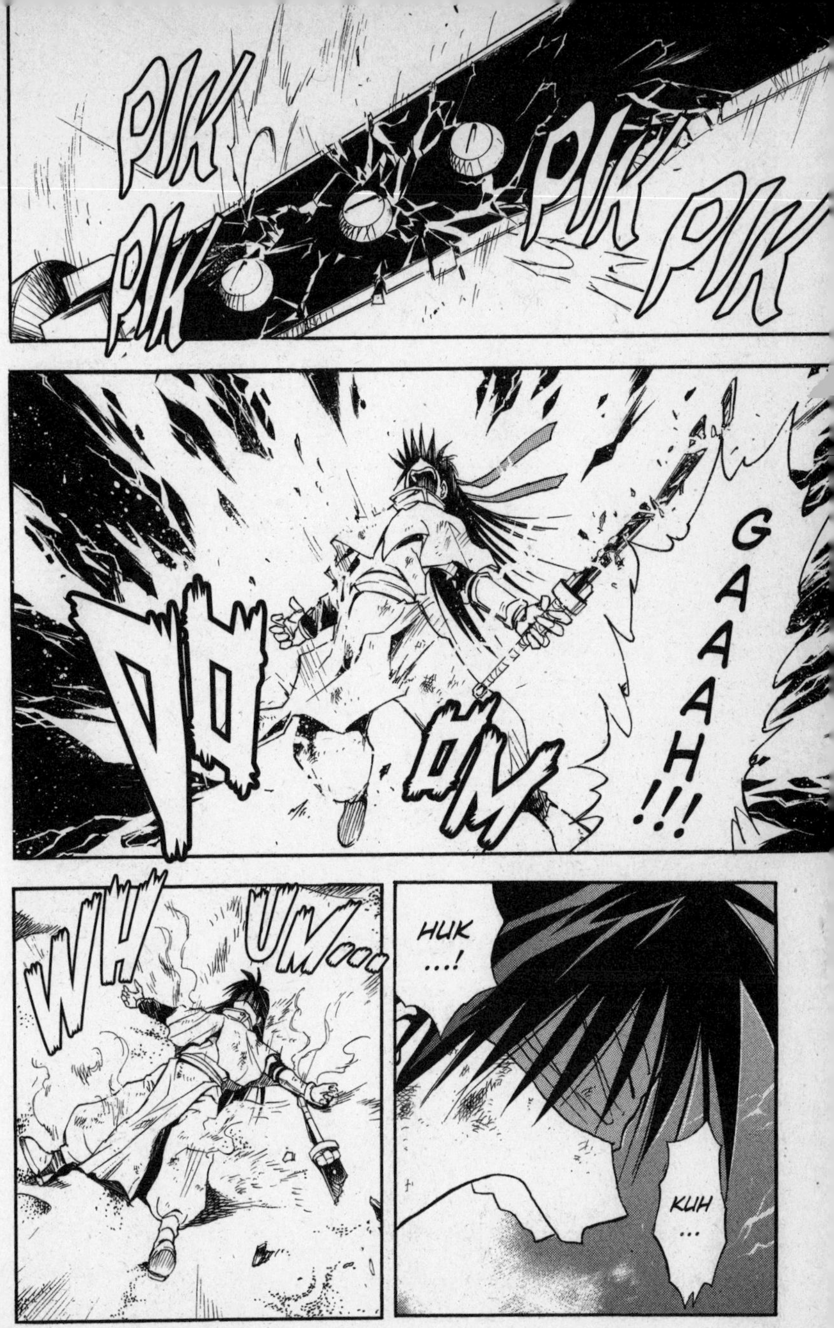
PIK
PIK
PIK
PIK
GAAAAH!!!
HUK ...!
KUH ...
WHUM...

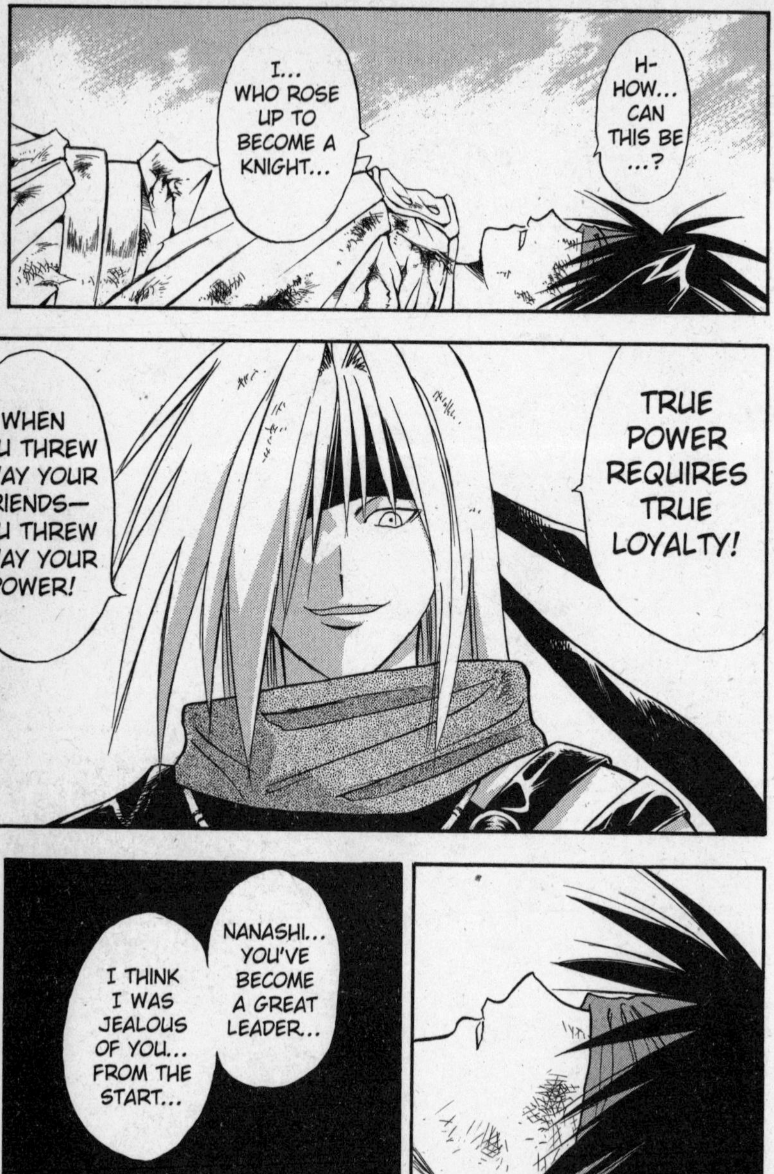
H-HOW... CAN THIS BE ...?
I... WHO ROSE UP TO BECOME A KNIGHT...
TRUE POWER REQUIRES TRUE LOYALTY!
WHEN YOU THREW AWAY YOUR FRIENDS— YOU THREW AWAY YOUR POWER!
NANASHI... YOU'VE BECOME A GREAT LEADER...
I THINK I WAS JEALOUS OF YOU... FROM THE START...

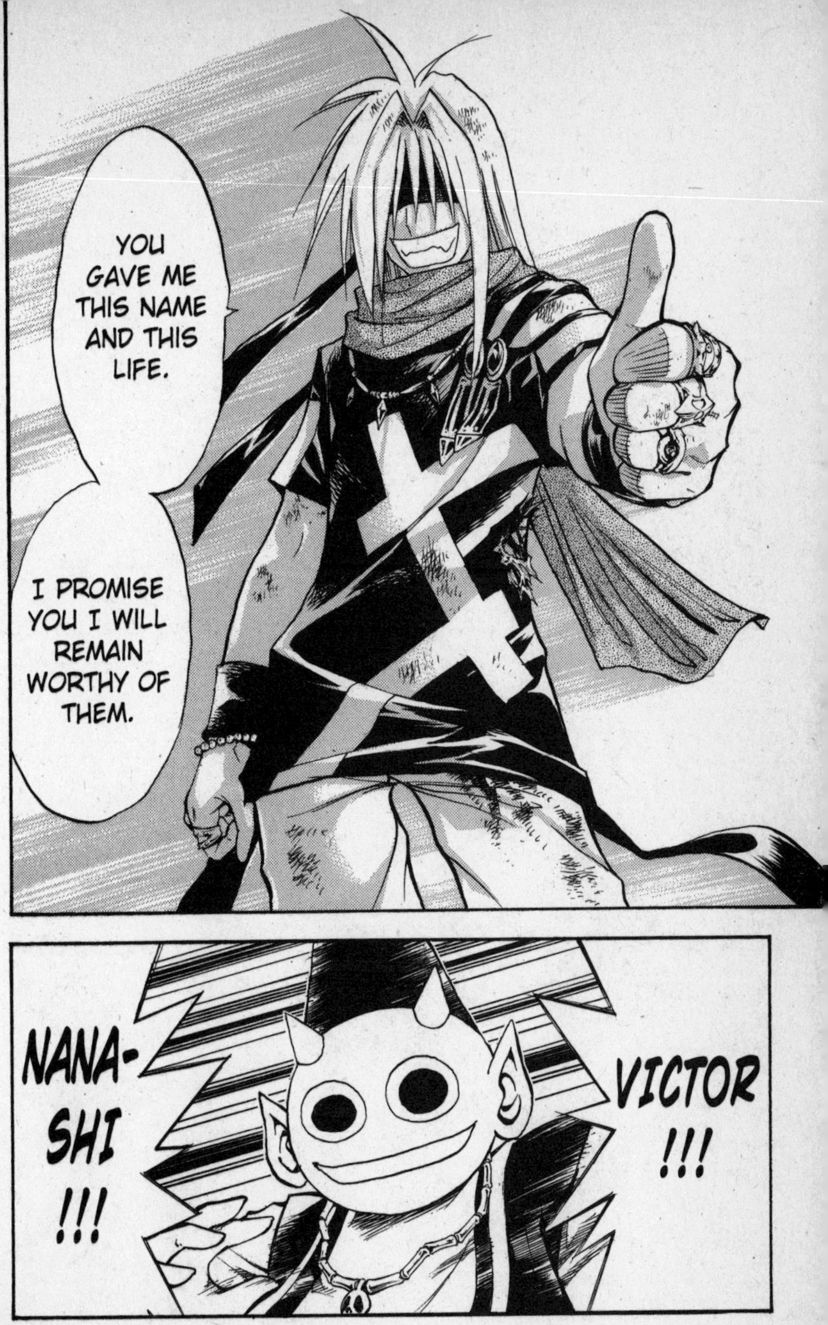
YOU GAVE ME THIS NAME AND THIS LIFE.
I PROMISE YOU I WILL REMAIN WORTHY OF THEM.
VICTOR !!!
NANA-SHI !!!

AKT.109/ A NEW MEMBER OF THE ZODIAC

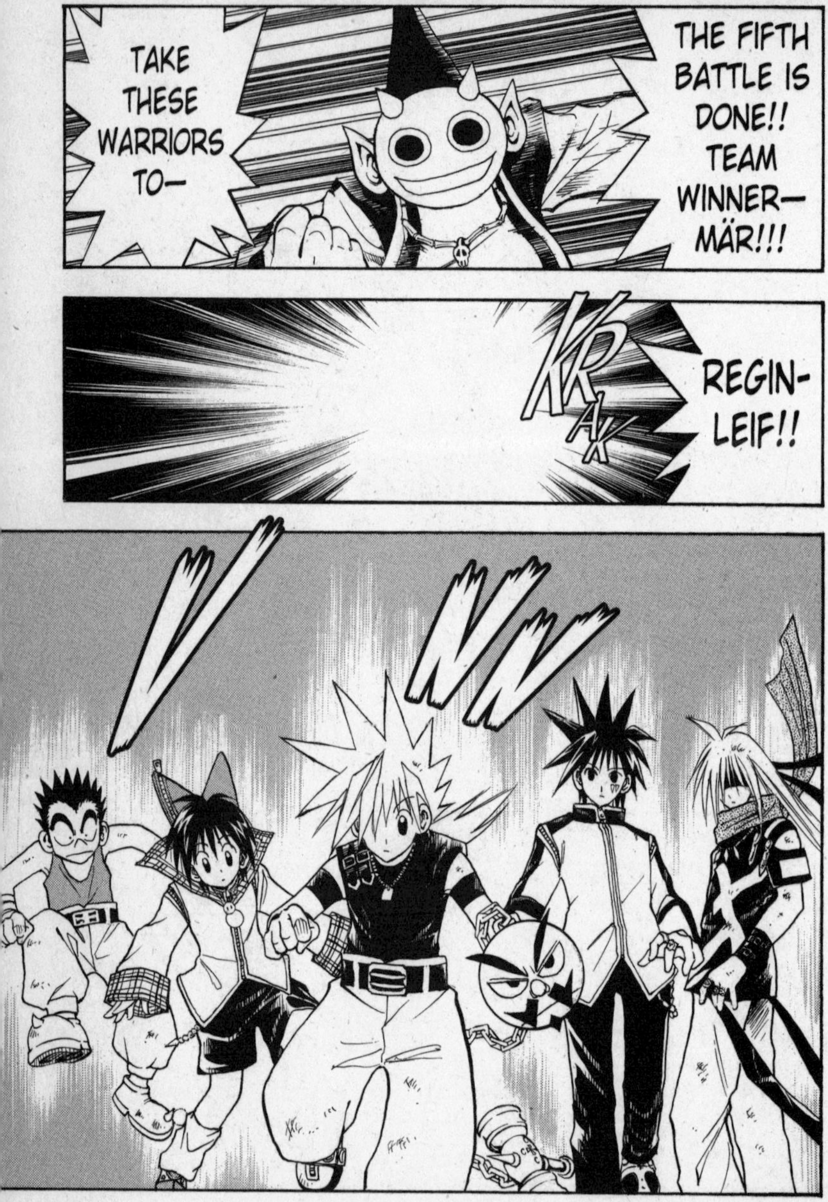
THE FIFTH BATTLE IS DONE!! TEAM WINNER-MÄR!!!
TAKE THESE WARRIORS TO—
REGIN-LEIF!!
KRAK

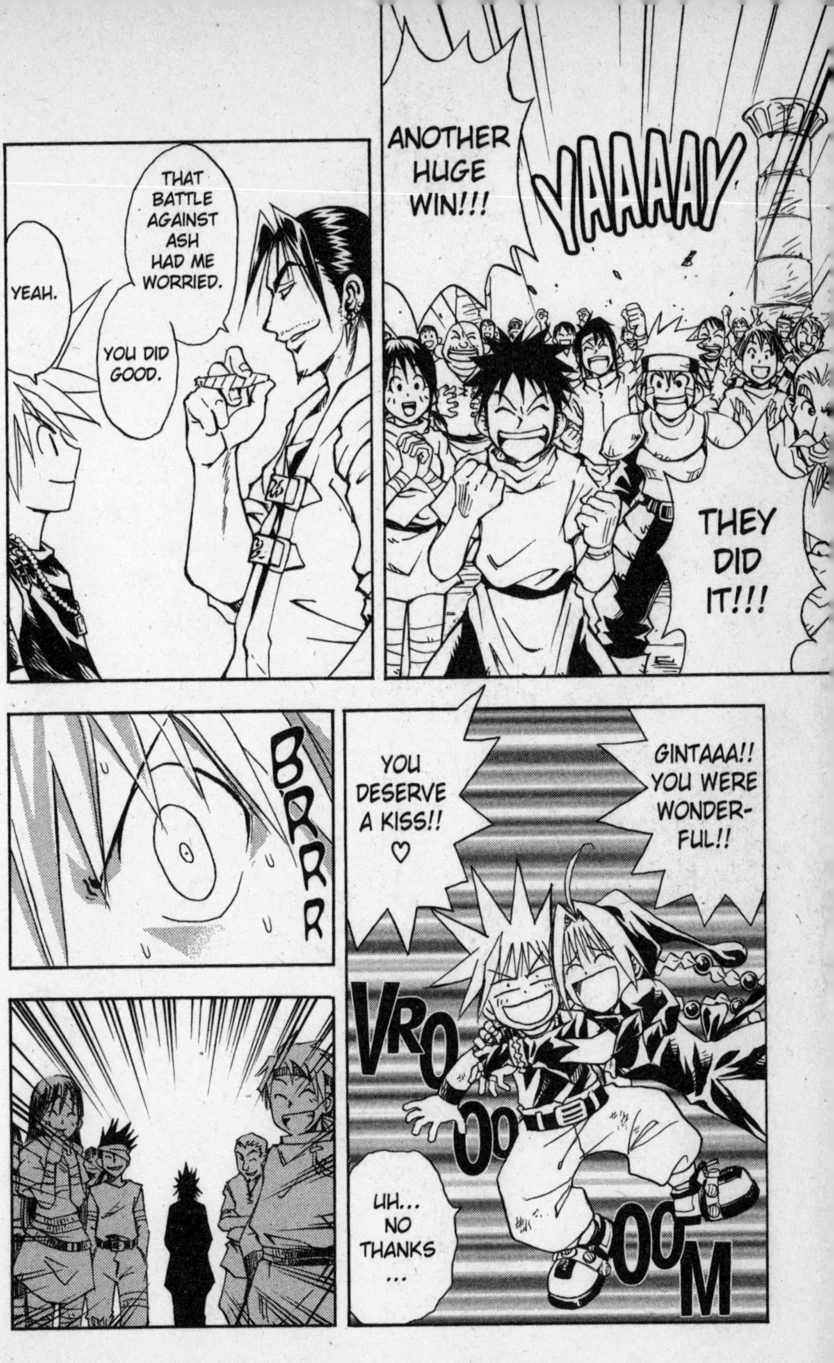
ANOTHER HUGE WIN!!!
YAAAAY
THEY DID IT!!!
THAT BATTLE AGAINST ASH HAD ME WORRIED.
YEAH.
YOU DID GOOD.
GINTAAA!! YOU WERE WONDER-FUL!!
YOU DESERVE A KISS!! ♡
VROOOOOOM
UH... NO THANKS ...
BRRRR

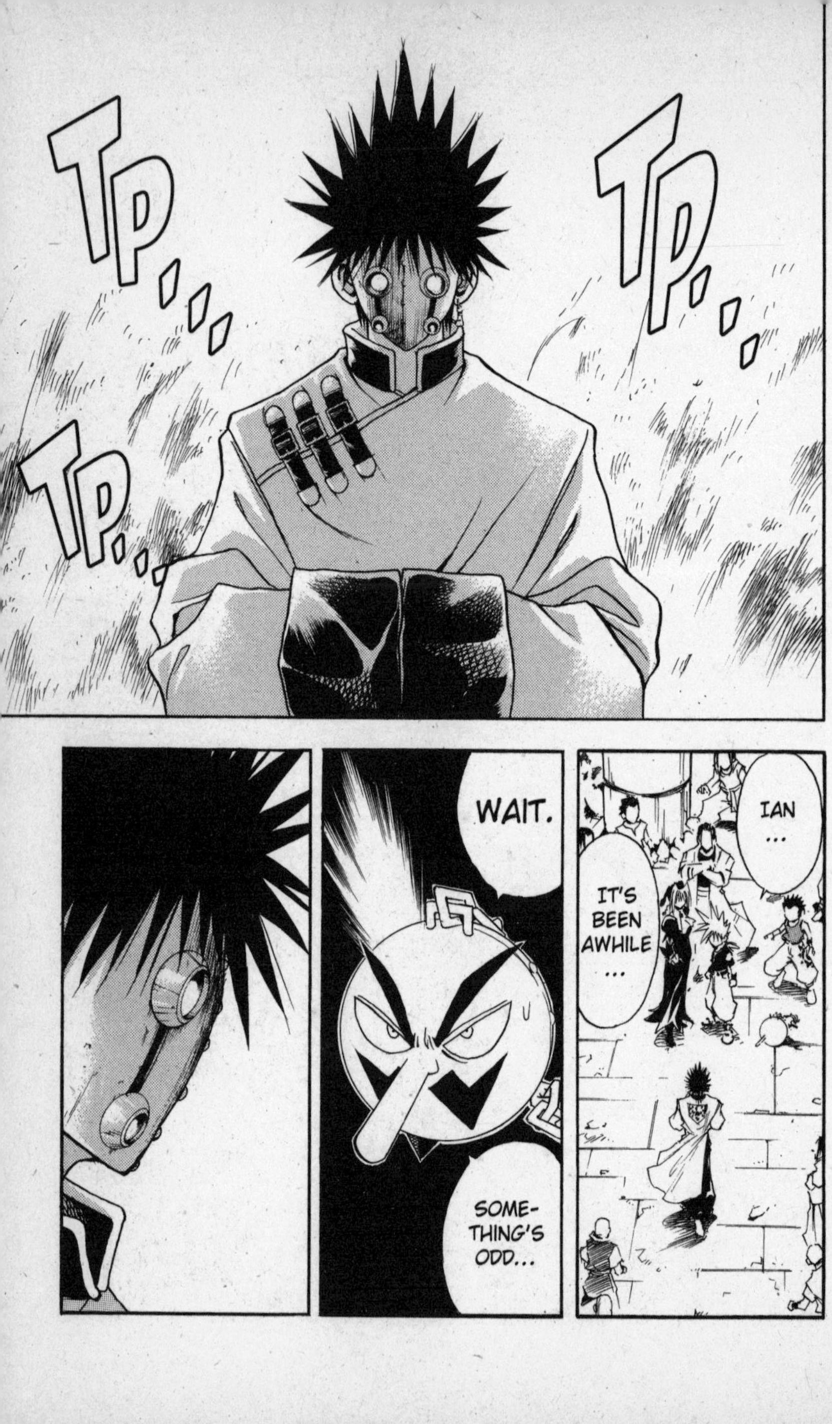
TP...
TP...
TP...
IAN ...
IT'S BEEN AWHILE ...
WAIT.
SOME-THING'S ODD...

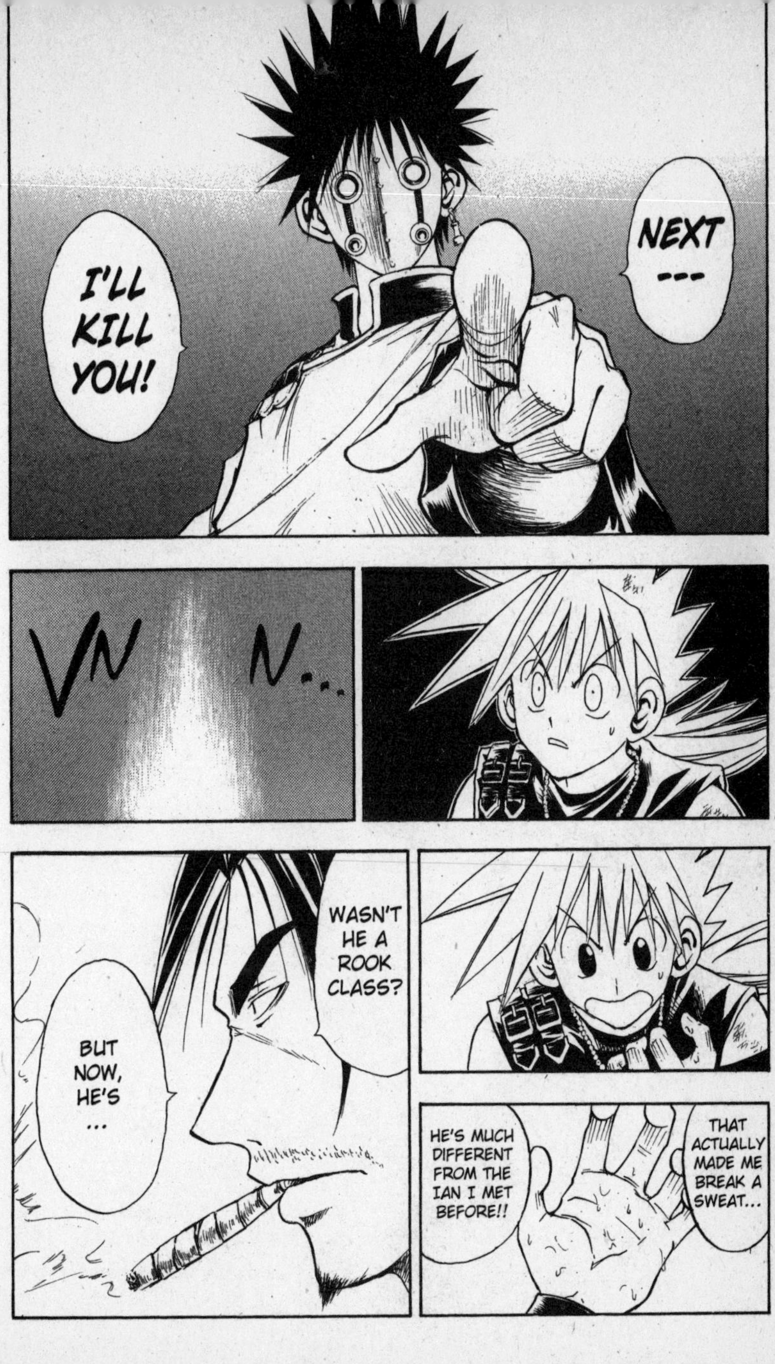
NEXT ---
I'LL KILL YOU!
VN N...
THAT ACTUALLY MADE ME BREAK A SWEAT...
HE'S MUCH DIFFERENT FROM THE IAN I MET BEFORE!!
WASN'T HE A ROOK CLASS?
BUT NOW, HE'S ...

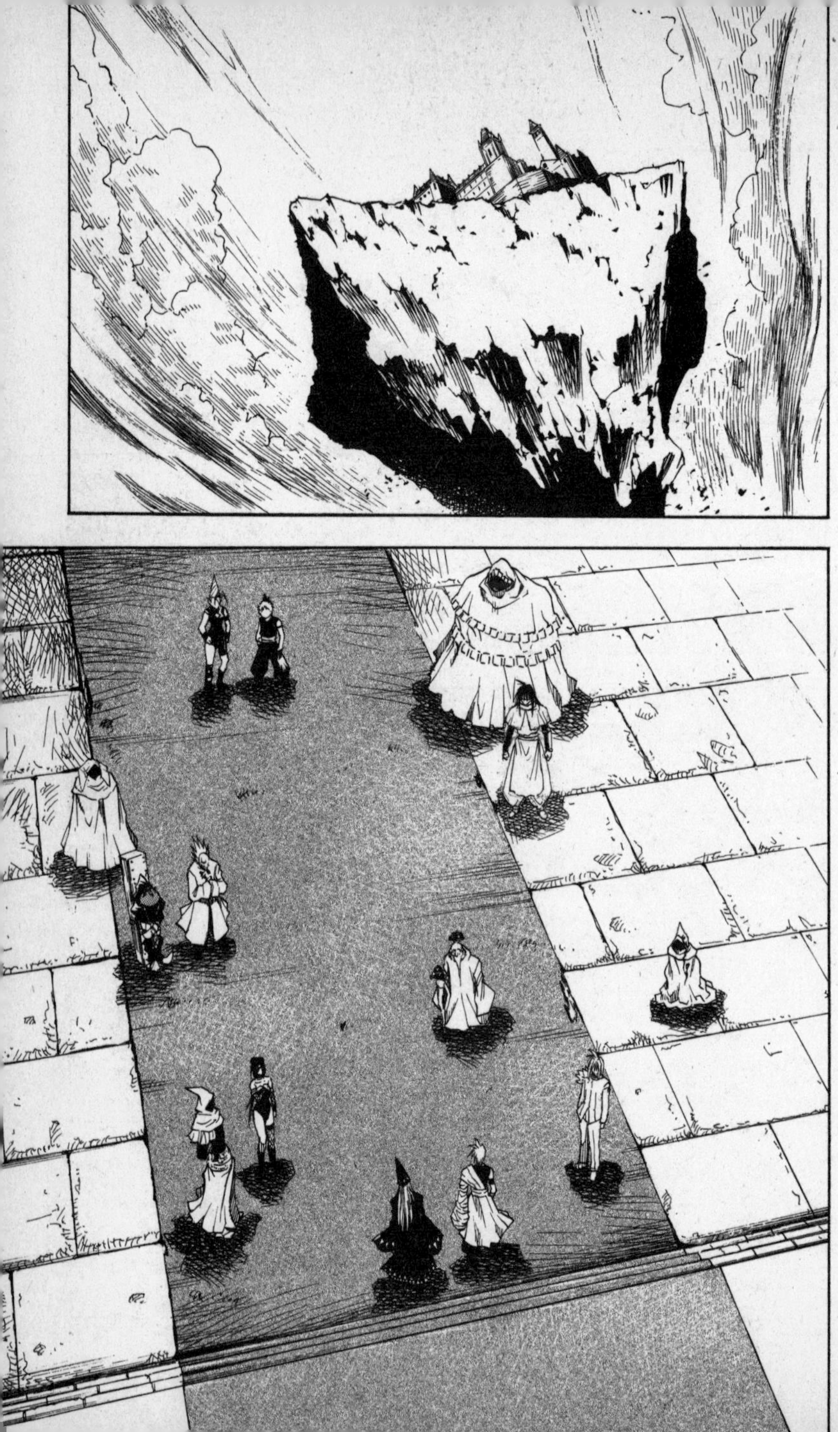

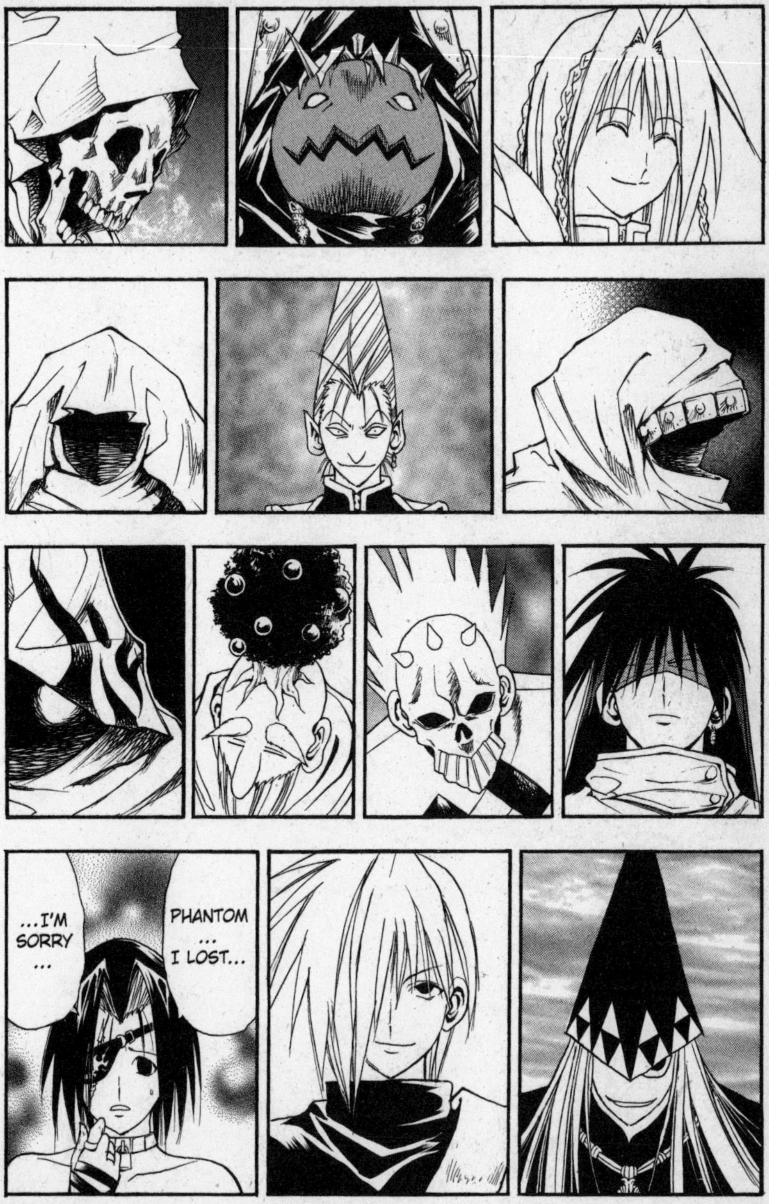
PHANTOM ... I LOST...
...I'M SORRY ...

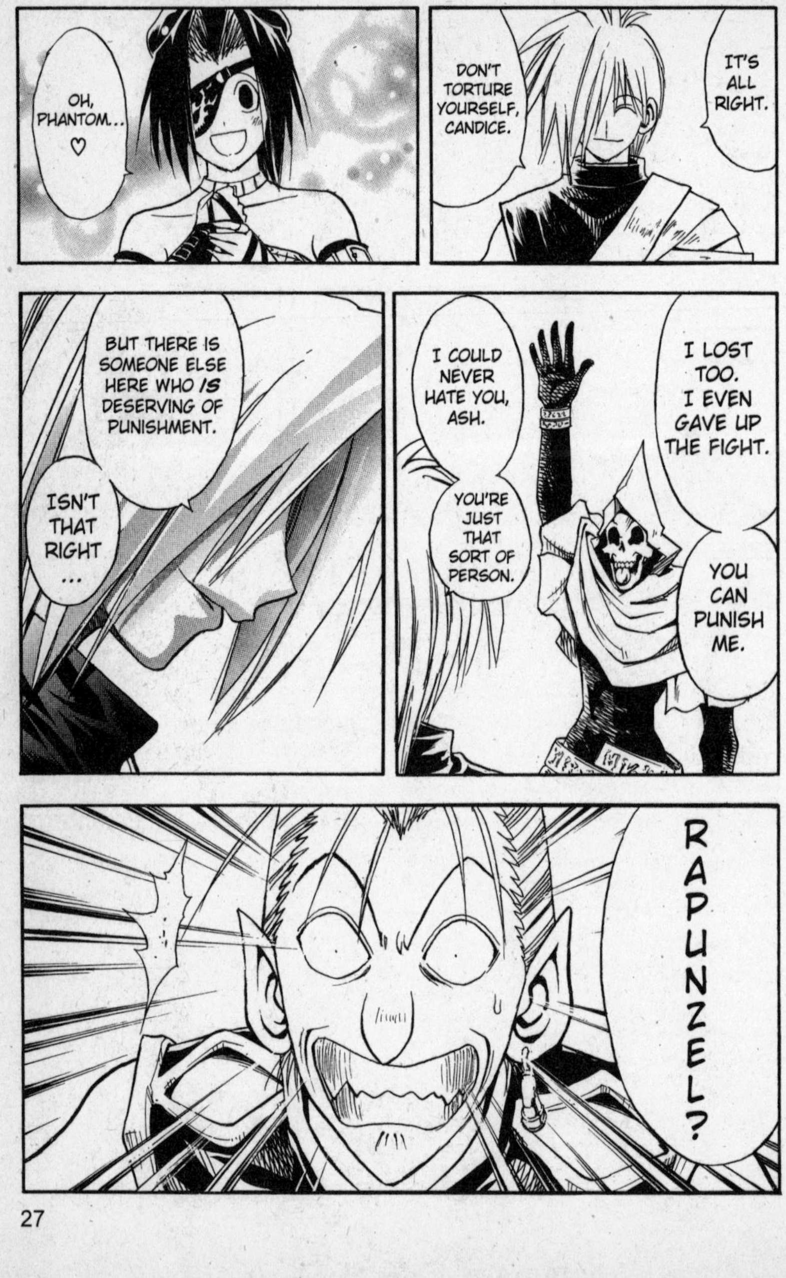
IT'S ALL RIGHT.
DON'T TORTURE YOURSELF, CANDICE.
OH, PHANTOM... ♡
I LOST TOO. I EVEN GAVE UP THE FIGHT.
YOU CAN PUNISH ME.
I COULD NEVER HATE YOU, ASH.
YOU'RE JUST THAT SORT OF PERSON.
BUT THERE IS SOMEONE ELSE HERE WHO *IS* DESERVING OF PUNISHMENT.
ISN'T THAT RIGHT...
RAPUNZEL?

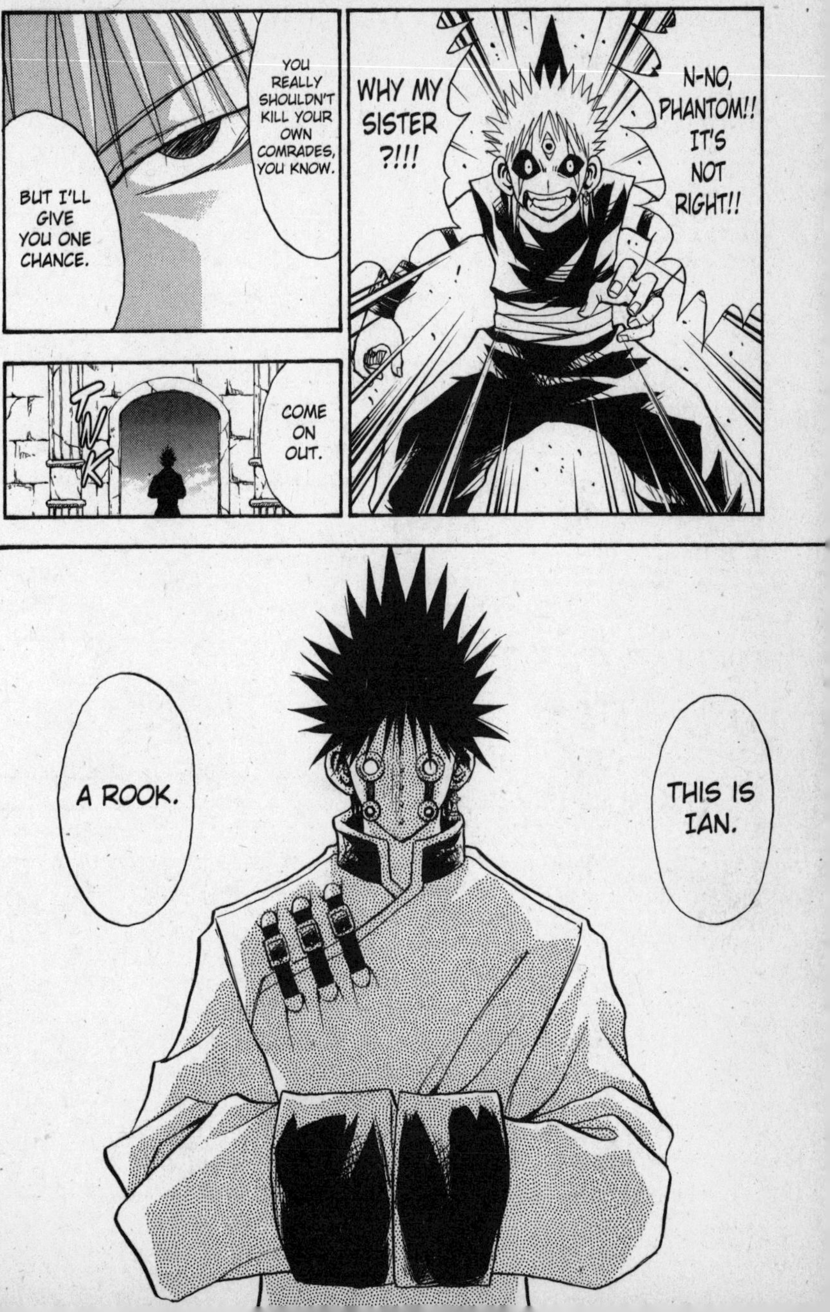
N-NO, PHANTOM!! IT'S NOT RIGHT!!
WHY MY SISTER ?!!!
YOU REALLY SHOULDN'T KILL YOUR OWN COMRADES, YOU KNOW.
BUT I'LL GIVE YOU ONE CHANCE.
COME ON OUT.
TNK
THIS IS IAN.
A ROOK.

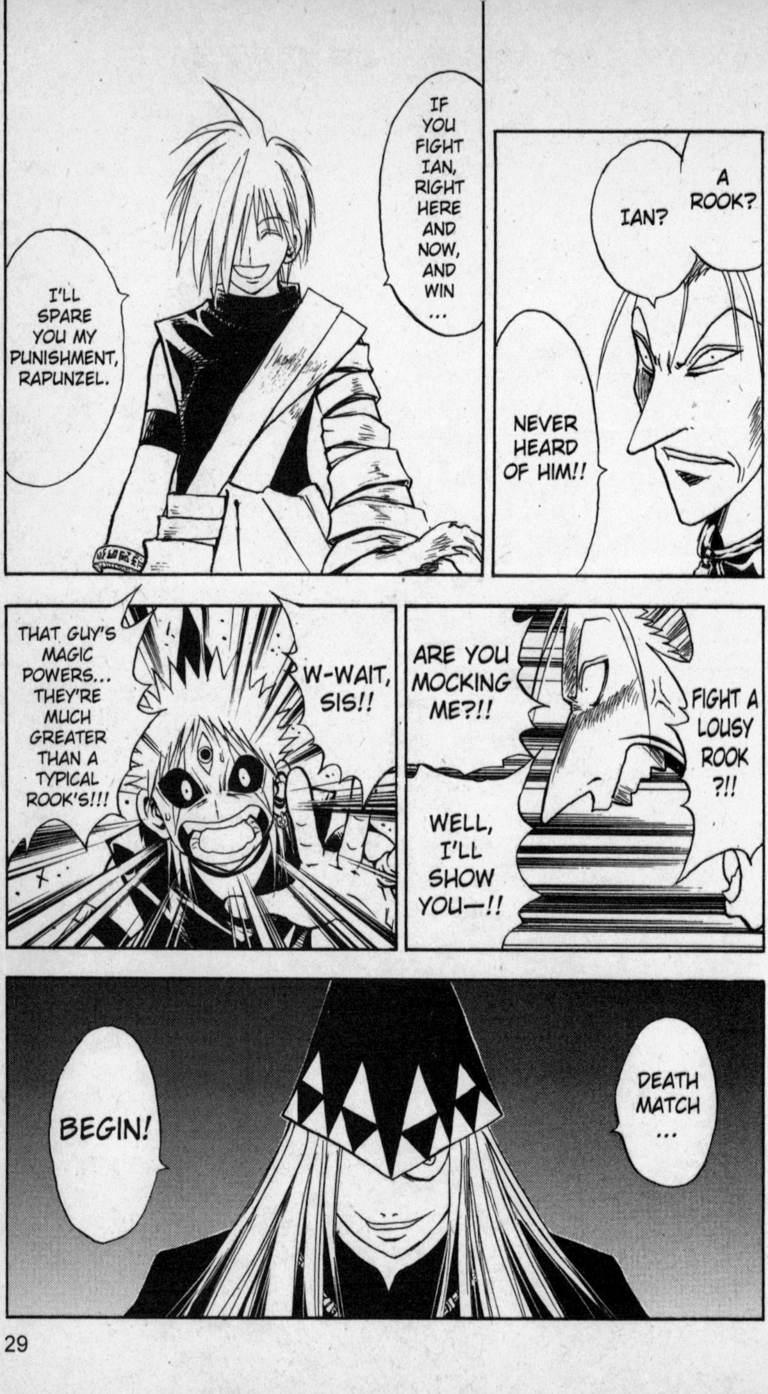

IF YOU FIGHT IAN, RIGHT HERE AND NOW, AND WIN...
I'LL SPARE YOU MY PUNISHMENT, RAPUNZEL.
IAN?
A ROOK?
NEVER HEARD OF HIM!!
W-WAIT, SIS!!
THAT GUY'S MAGIC POWERS... THEY'RE MUCH GREATER THAN A TYPICAL ROOK'S!!!
ARE YOU MOCKING ME?!!
FIGHT A LOUSY ROOK?!!
WELL, I'LL SHOW YOU—!!
DEATH MATCH...
BEGIN!

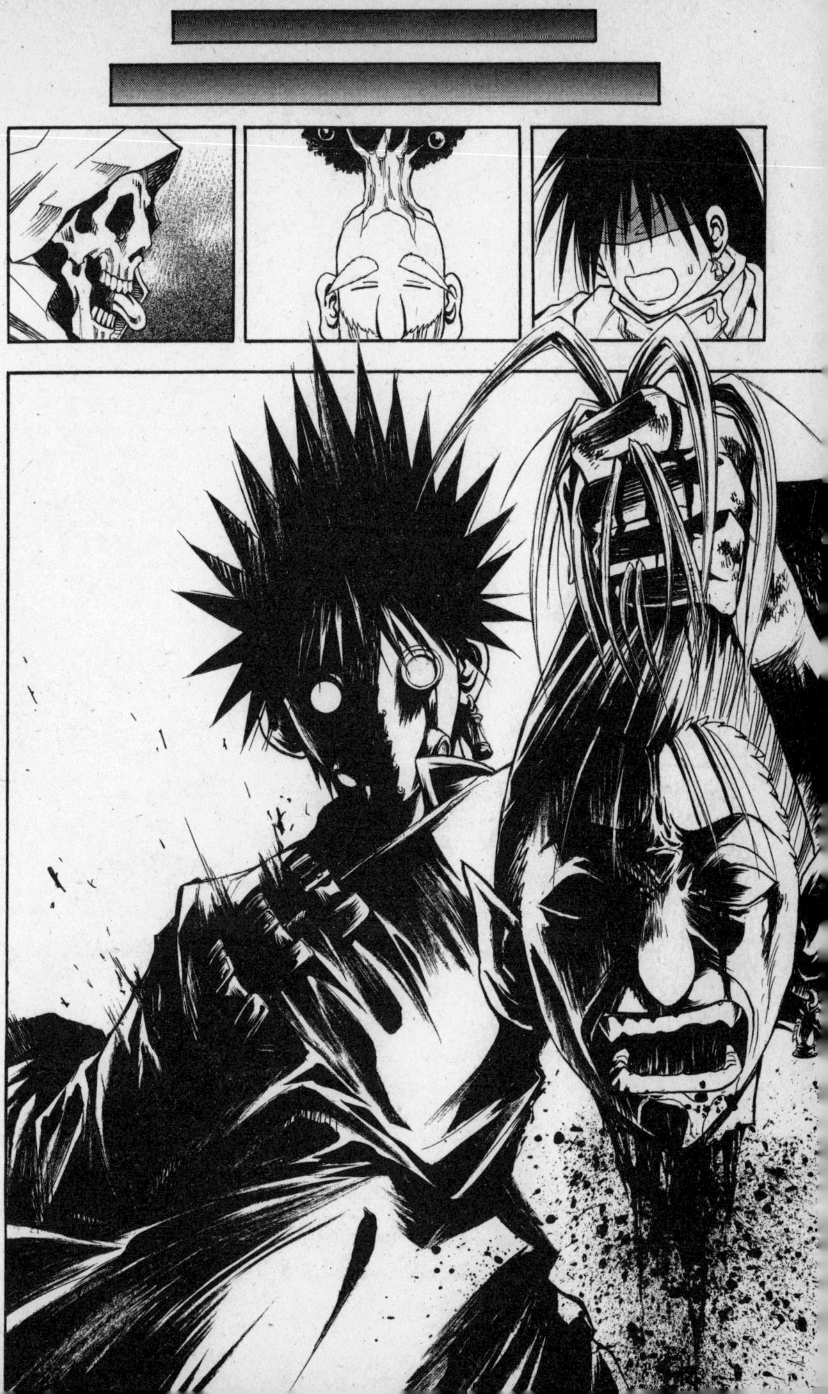

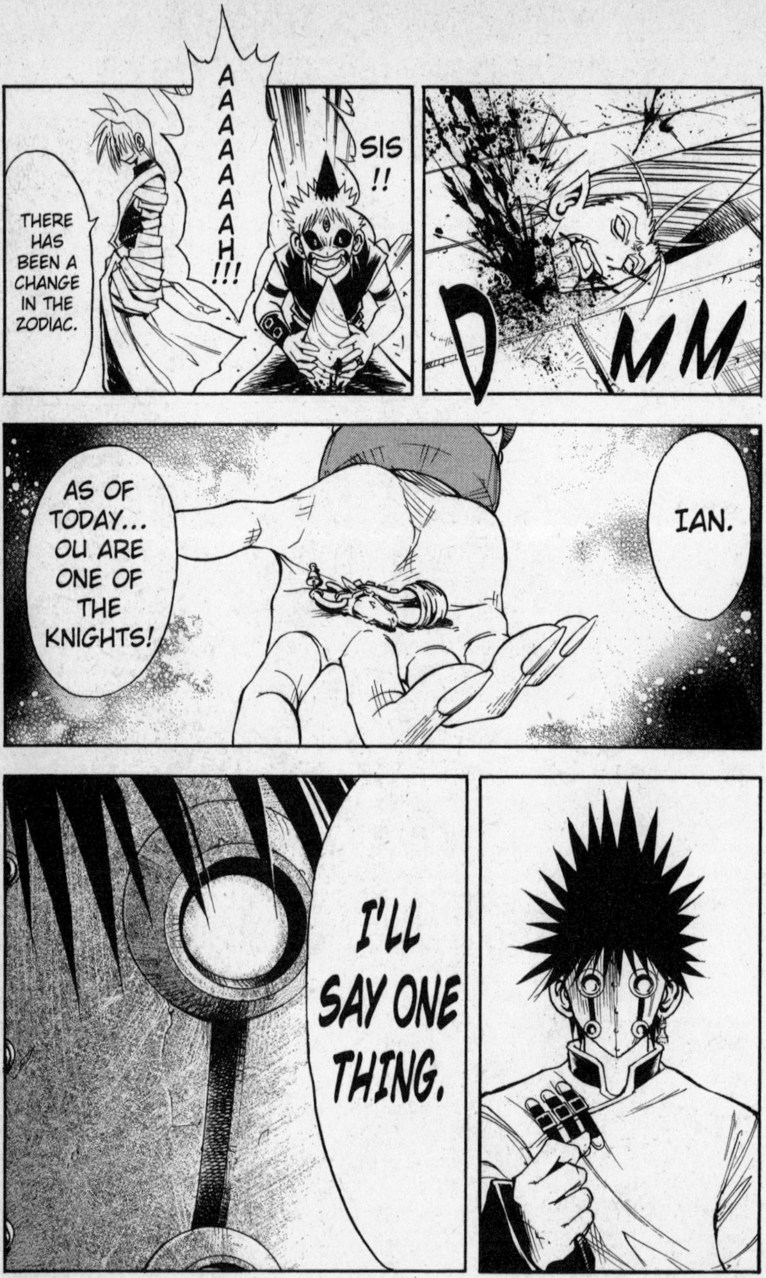
DMM
SIS!!
AAAAAAAAAH!!!
THERE HAS BEEN A CHANGE IN THE ZODIAC.
IAN.
AS OF TODAY... OU ARE ONE OF THE KNIGHTS!
I'LL SAY ONE THING.

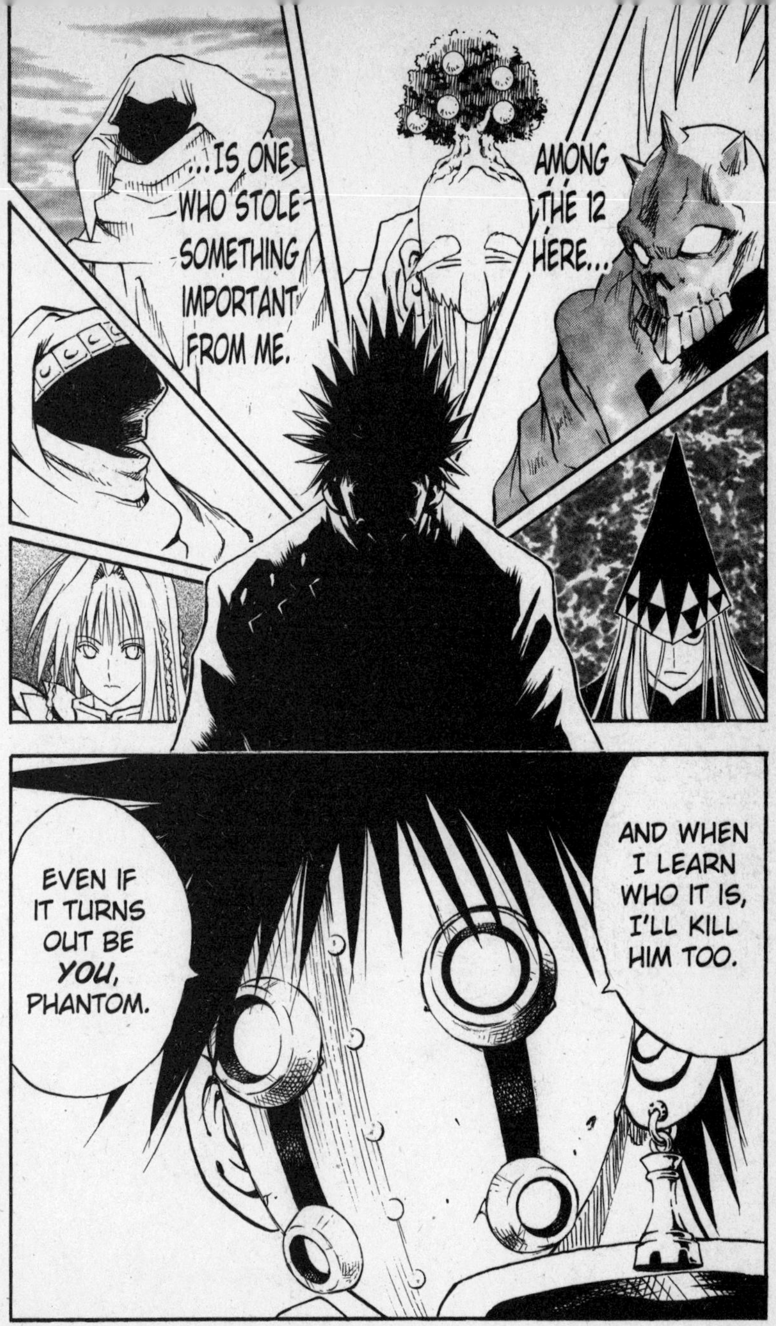
AMONG THE 12 HERE...
...IS ONE WHO STOLE SOMETHING IMPORTANT FROM ME.
AND WHEN I LEARN WHO IT IS, I'LL KILL HIM TOO.
EVEN IF IT TURNS OUT BE *YOU*, PHANTOM.

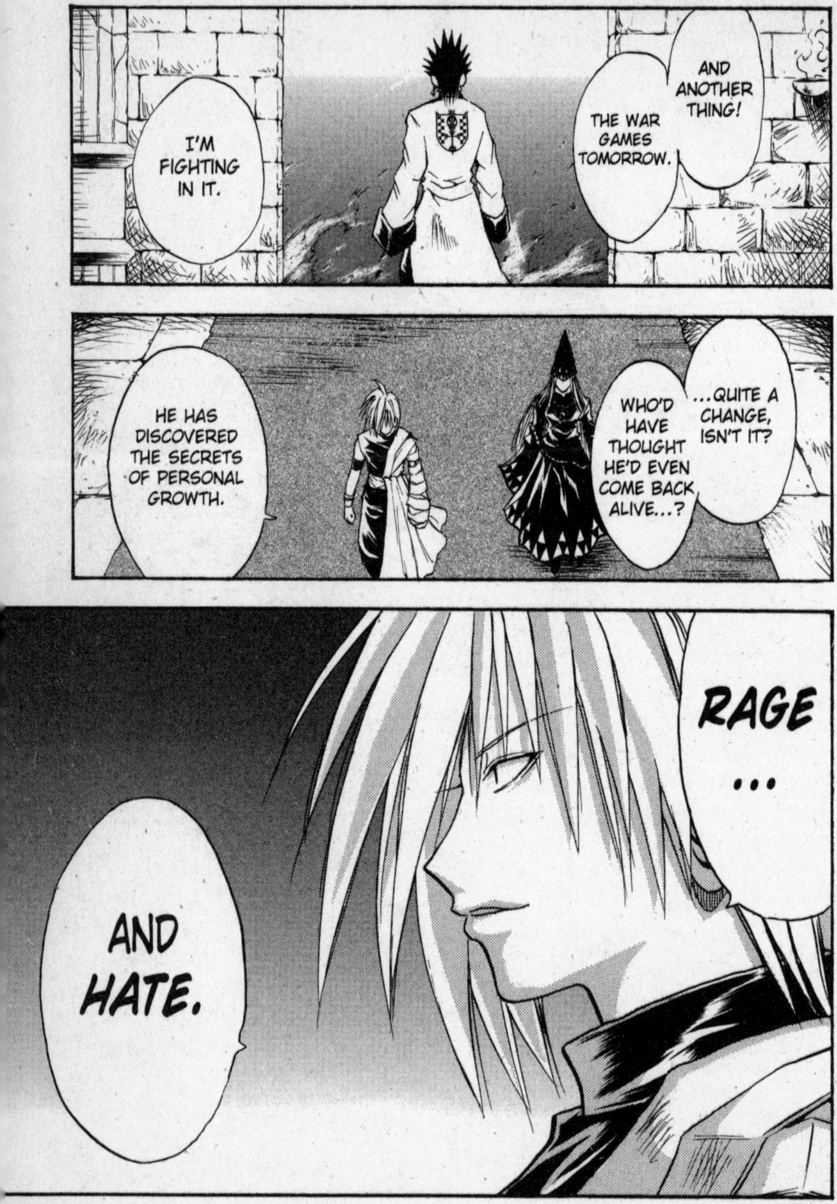
AND ANOTHER THING!
THE WAR GAMES TOMORROW.
I'M FIGHTING IN IT.
...QUITE A CHANGE, ISN'T IT?
WHO'D HAVE THOUGHT HE'D EVEN COME BACK ALIVE...?
HE HAS DISCOVERED THE SECRETS OF PERSONAL GROWTH.
RAGE...
AND HATE.

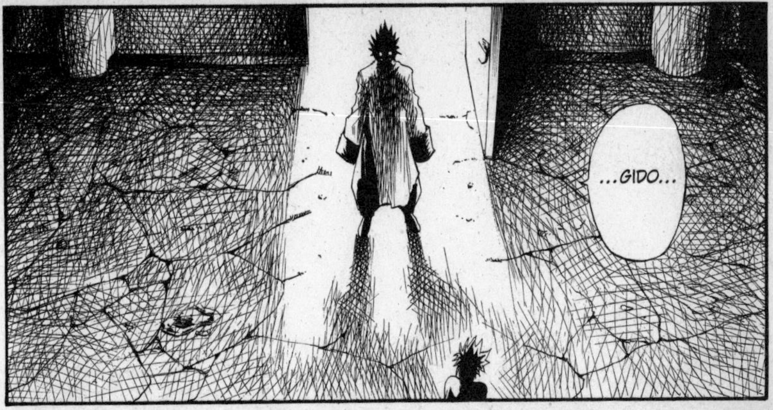
...GIDO...
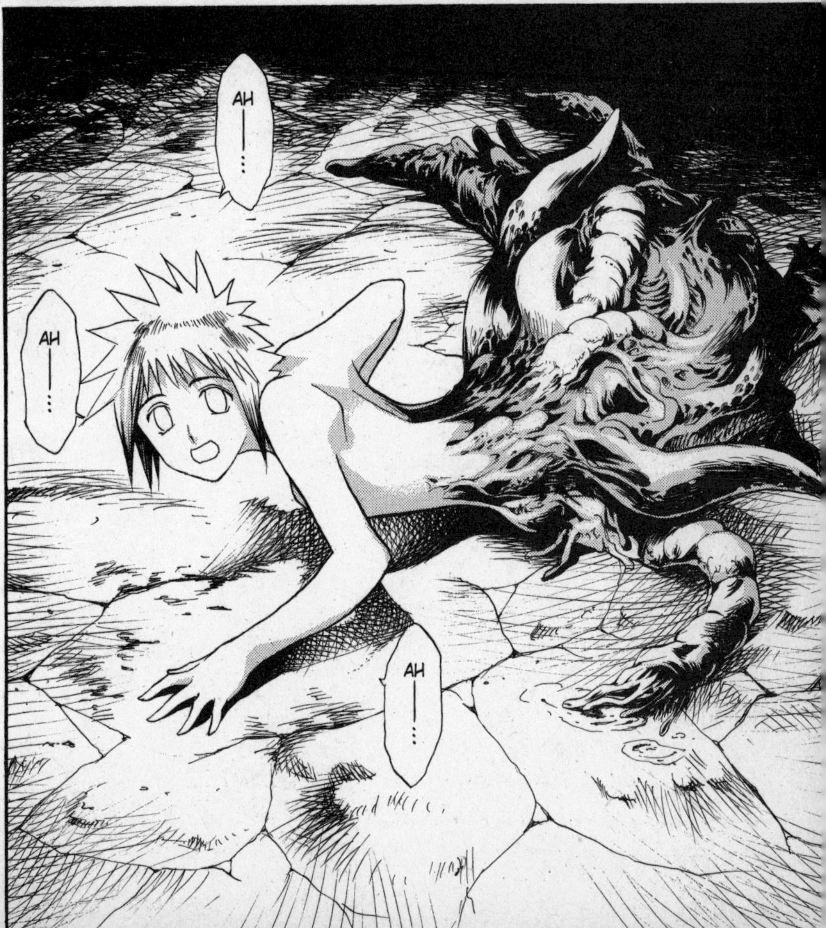
AH—...
AH—...
AH—...

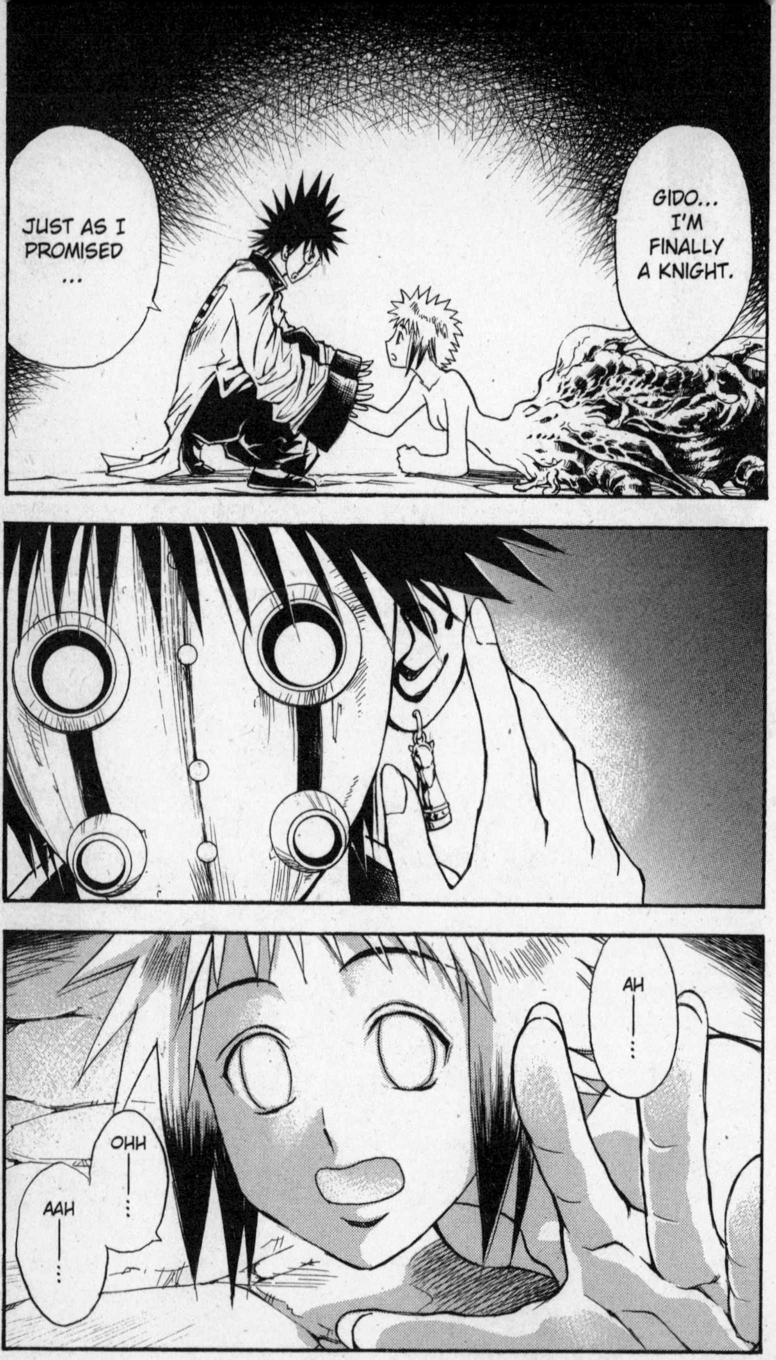
GIDO... I'M FINALLY A KNIGHT.
JUST AS I PROMISED ...
AH—...
OHH—...
AAH—...

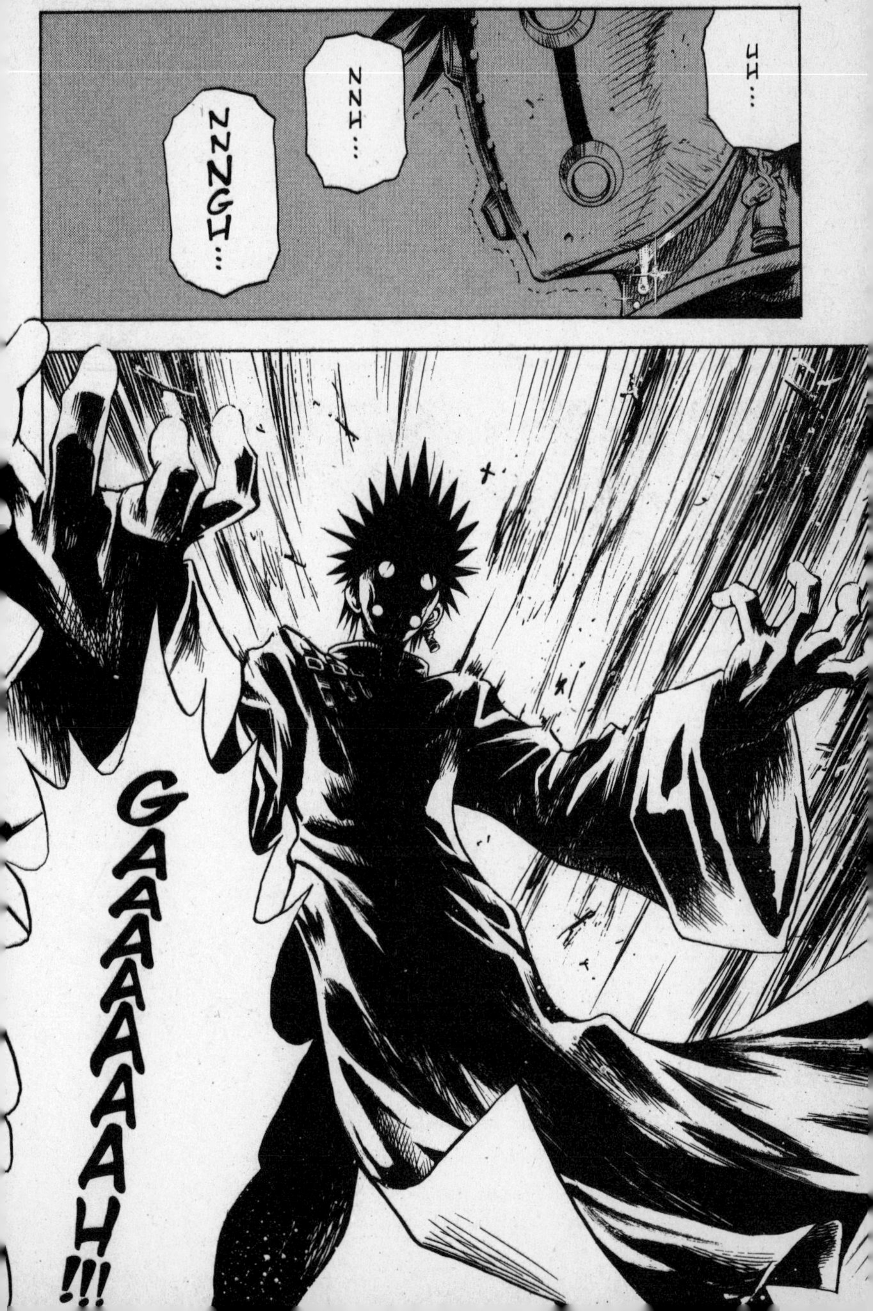
UH...
NNH...
NNNGH...
GAAAAAAAH!!!

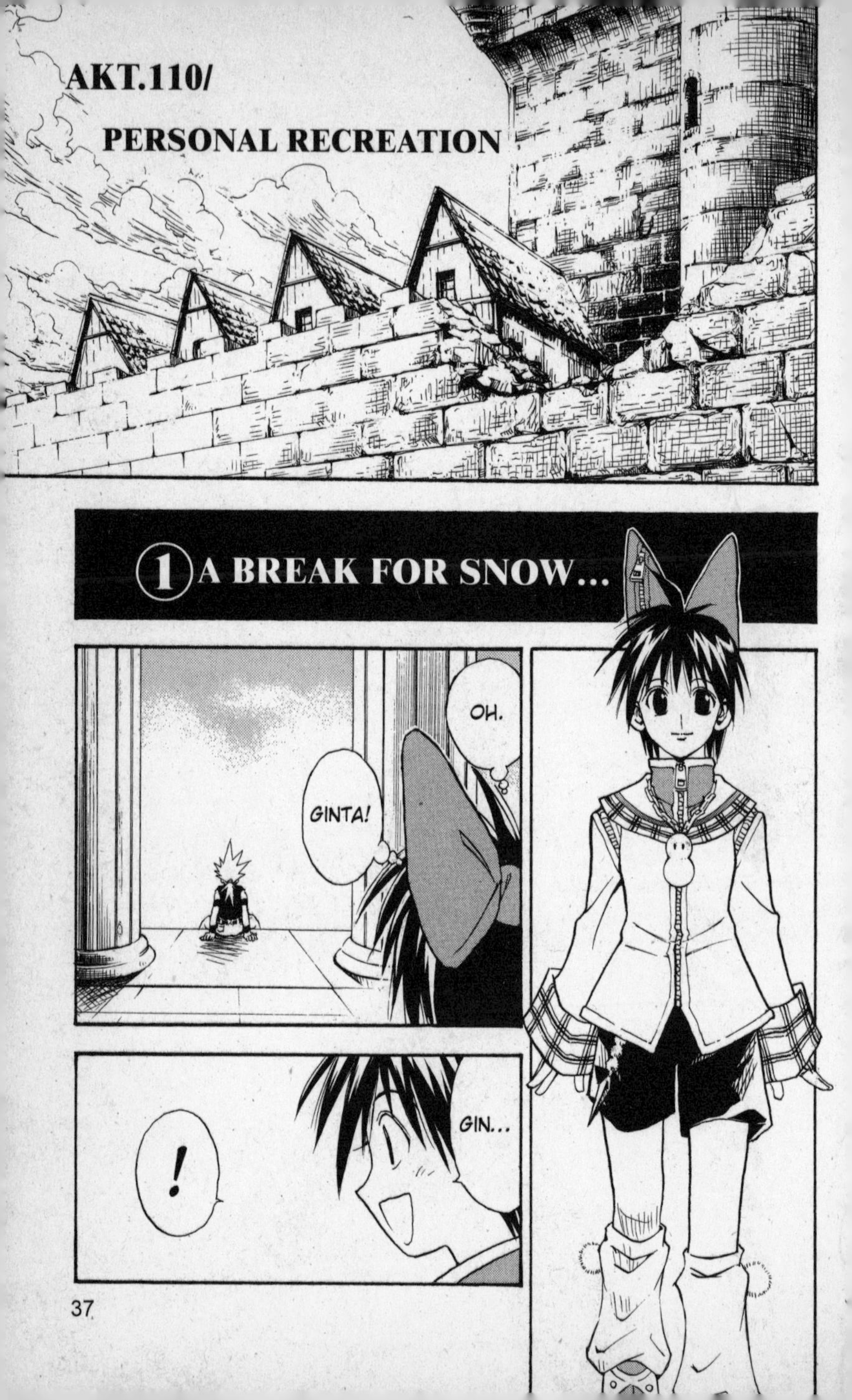
AKT.110/
PERSONAL RECREATION
1 A BREAK FOR SNOW...
OH.
GINTA!
GIN...
!

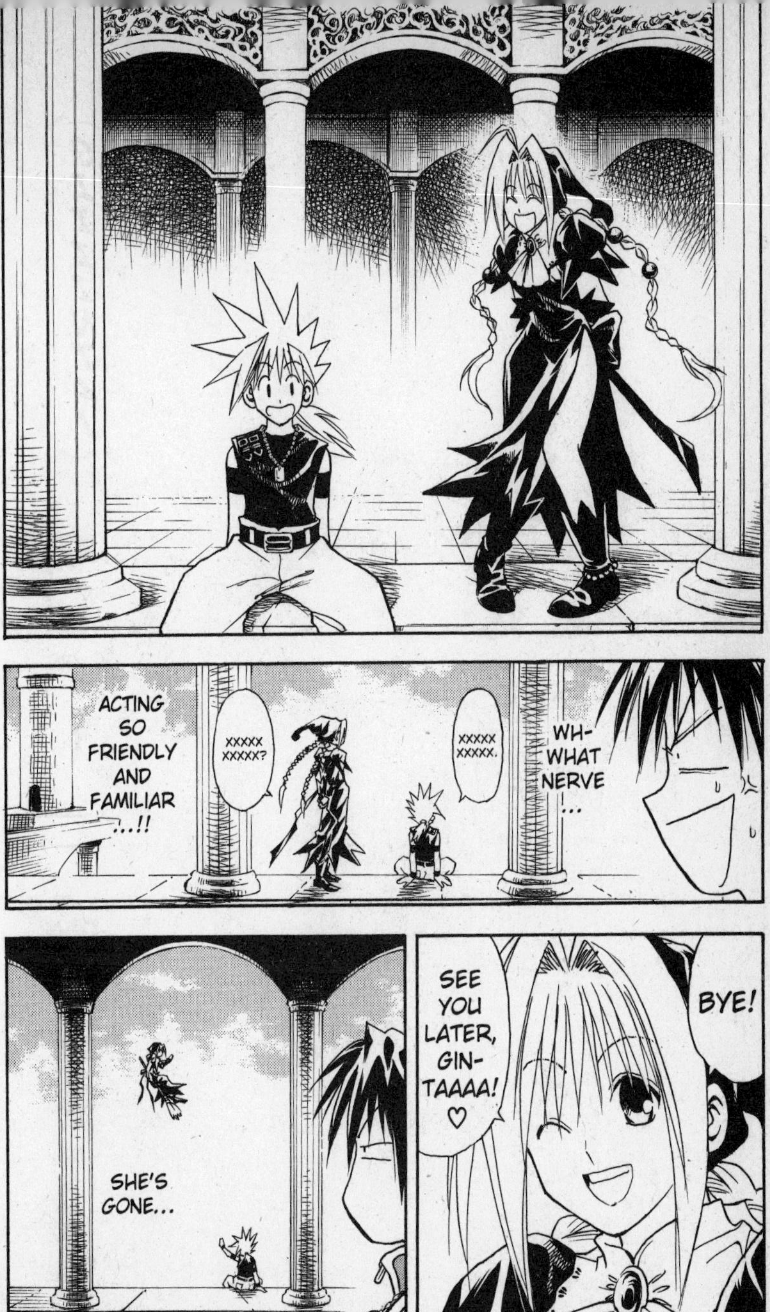
WH- WHAT NERVE...
XXXXX XXXXX.
XXXXX XXXXX?
ACTING SO FRIENDLY AND FAMILIAR...!!
BYE!
SEE YOU LATER, GIN-TAAAA! ♡
SHE'S GONE...

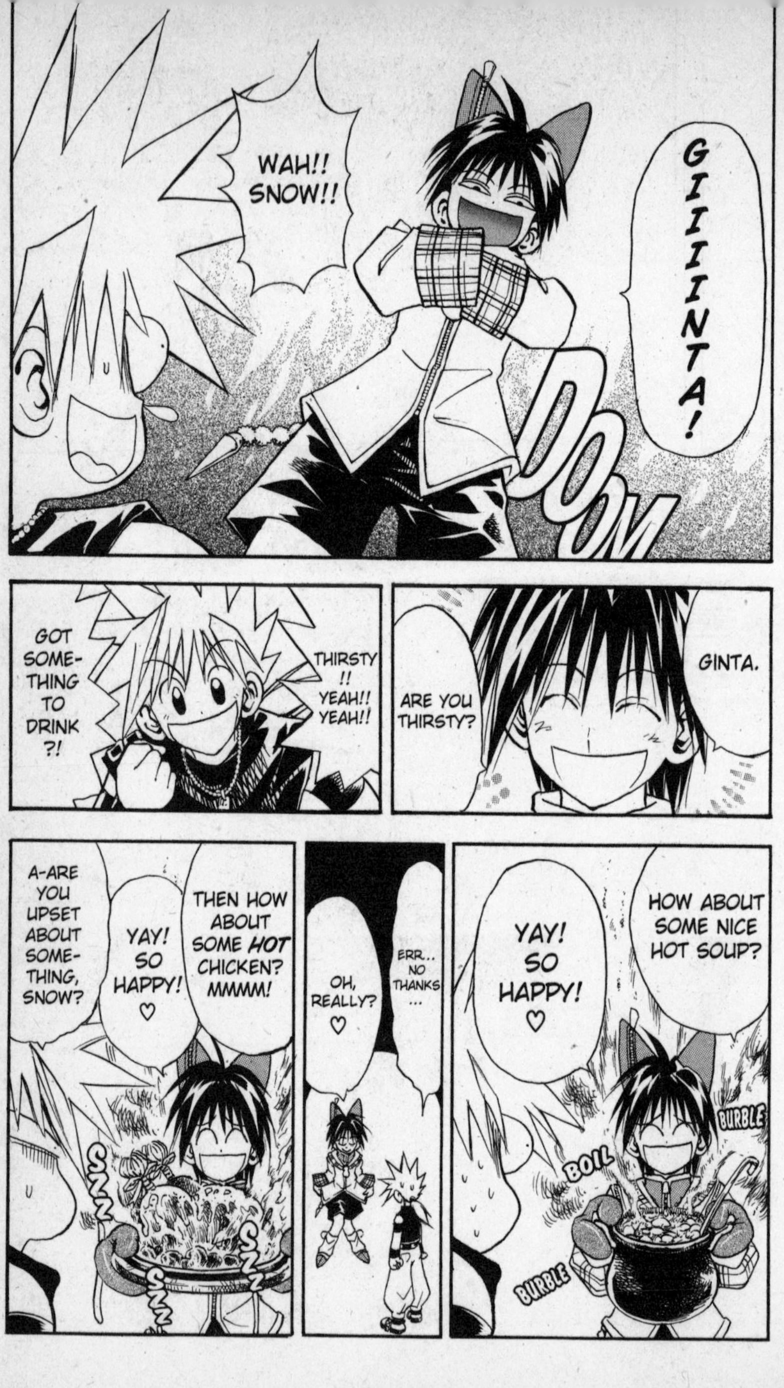
GIIIINTA!
DOOM
WAH!! SNOW!!
GINTA.
ARE YOU THIRSTY?
THIRSTY!! YEAH!! YEAH!!
GOT SOMETHING TO DRINK?!
HOW ABOUT SOME NICE HOT SOUP?
YAY! SO HAPPY! ♡
BURBLE
BOIL
BURBLE
ERR... NO THANKS...
OH, REALLY? ♡
THEN HOW ABOUT SOME *HOT* CHICKEN? MMMM!
YAY! SO HAPPY! ♡
A-ARE YOU UPSET ABOUT SOMETHING, SNOW?
SZZ
SZZ
SZZ

②ALVISS AND BELL...

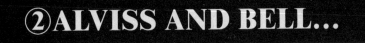

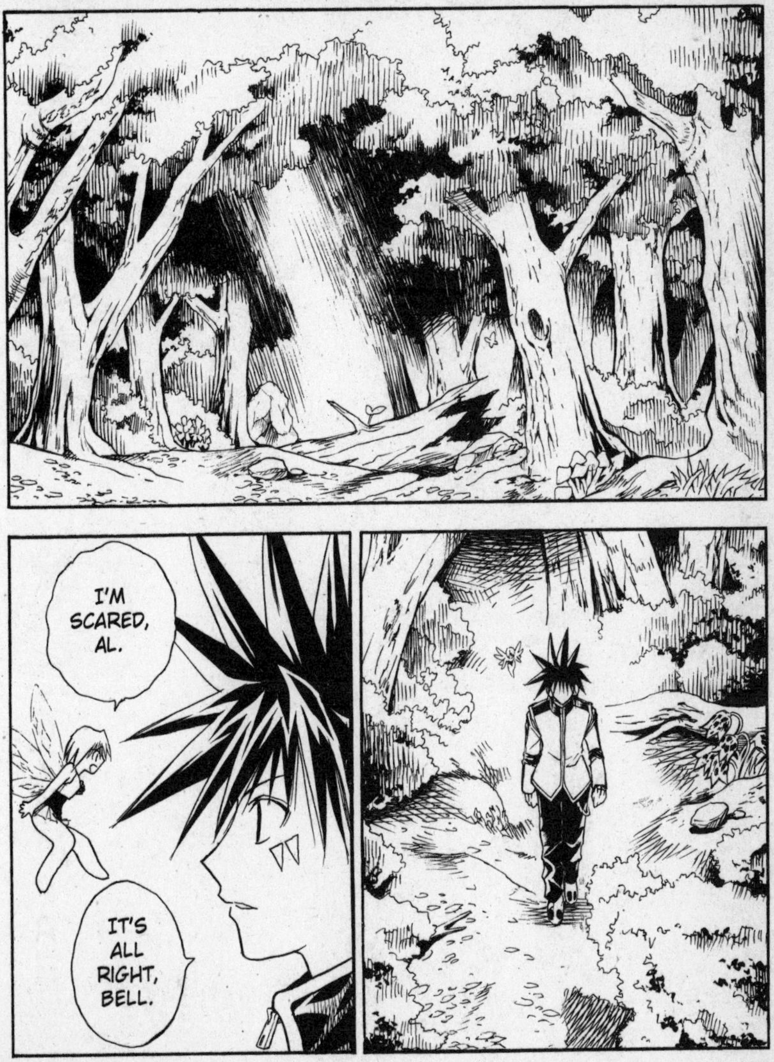
I'M SCARED, AL.
IT'S ALL RIGHT, BELL.

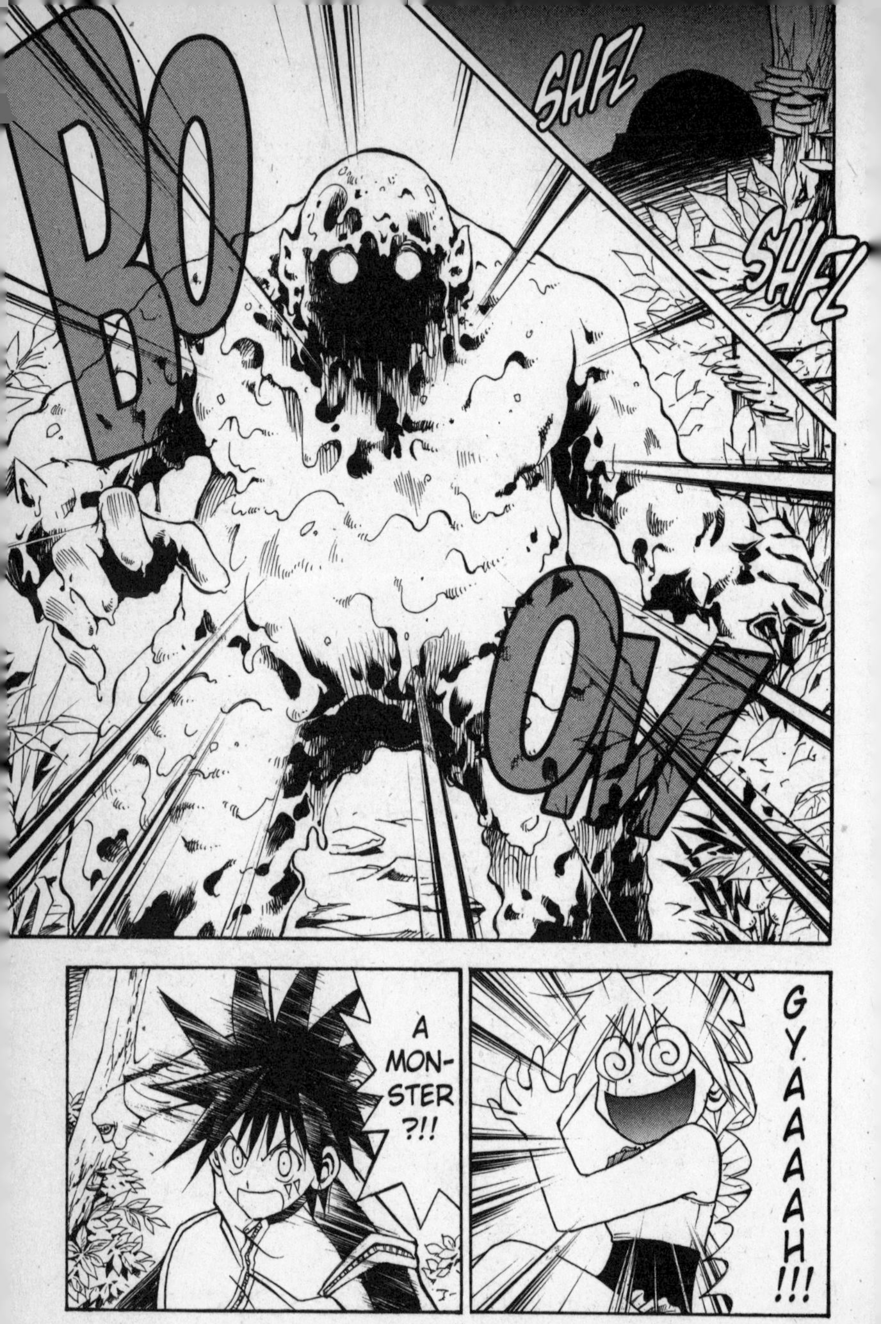
SHFL
SHFL
DO
D
OM
GYAAAAAH!!!
A MONSTER?!!

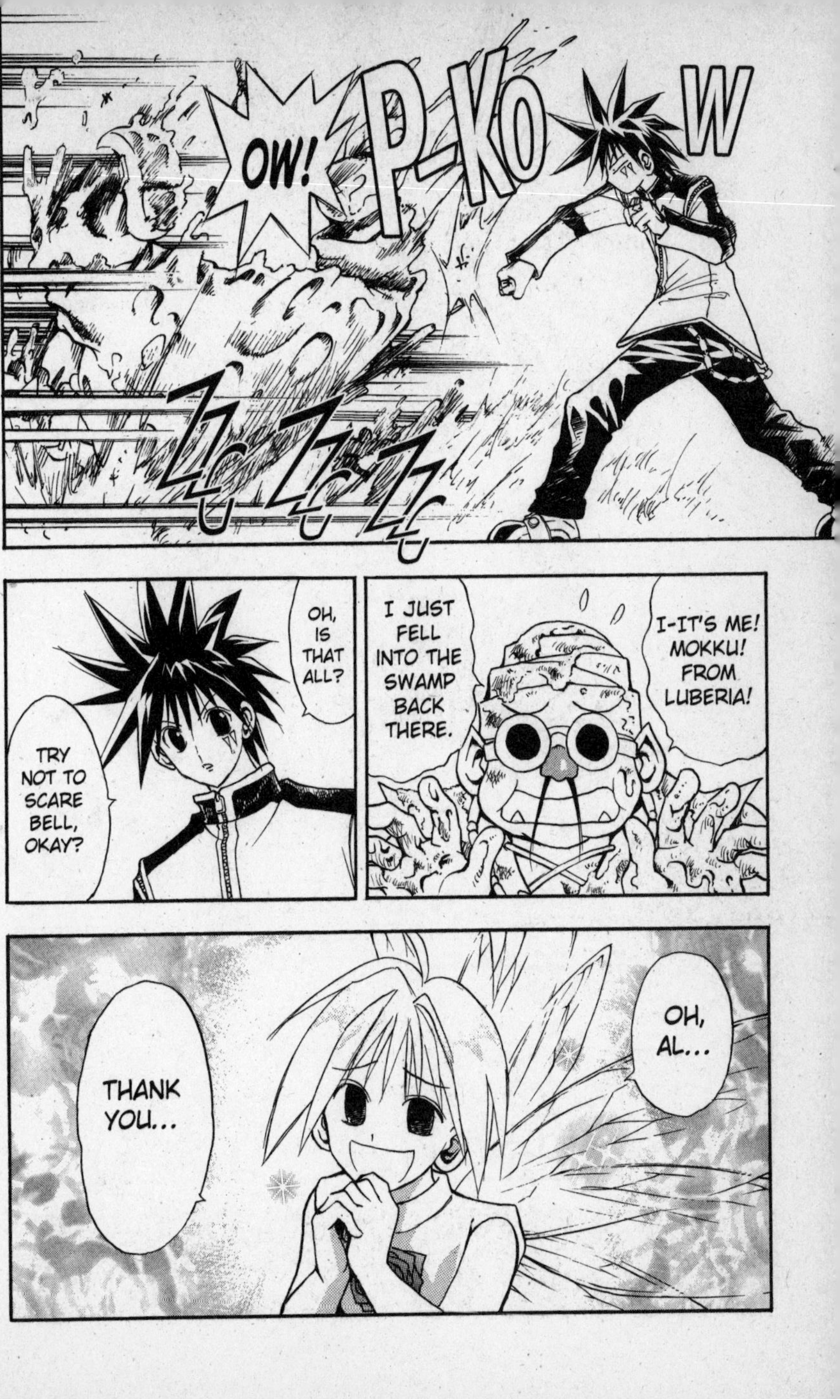
P-KOW
OW!
I-IT'S ME! MOKKU! FROM LUBERIA!
I JUST FELL INTO THE SWAMP BACK THERE.
OH, IS THAT ALL?
TRY NOT TO SCARE BELL, OKAY?
OH, AL...
THANK YOU...

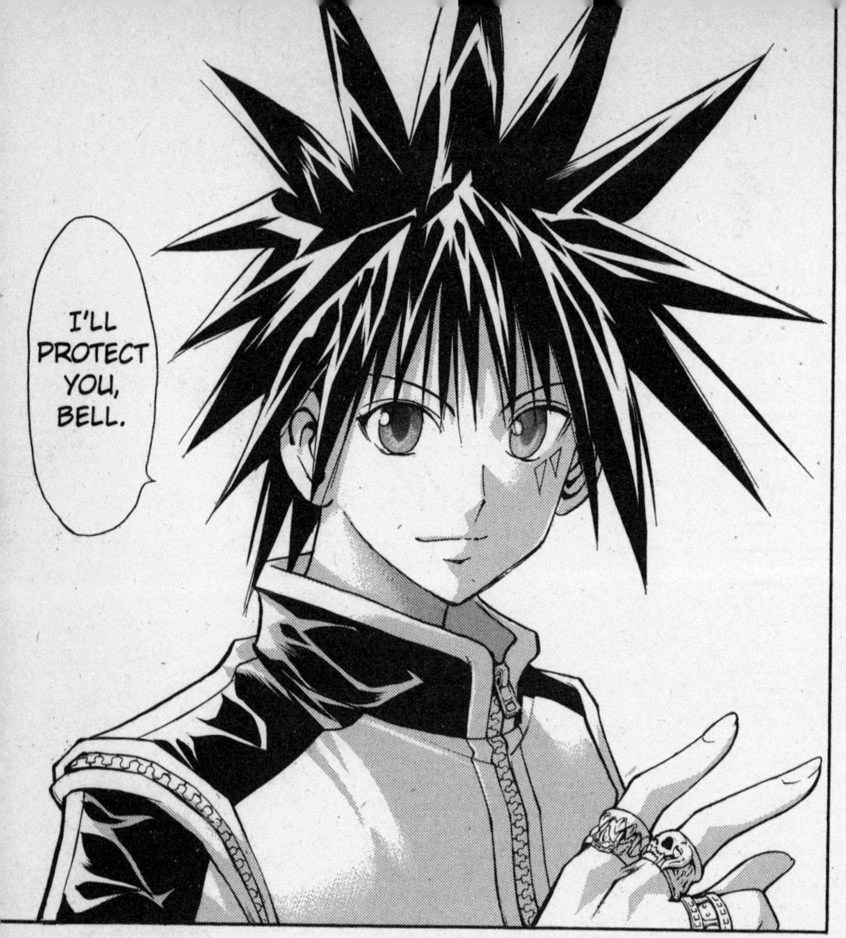
I'LL PROTECT YOU, BELL.

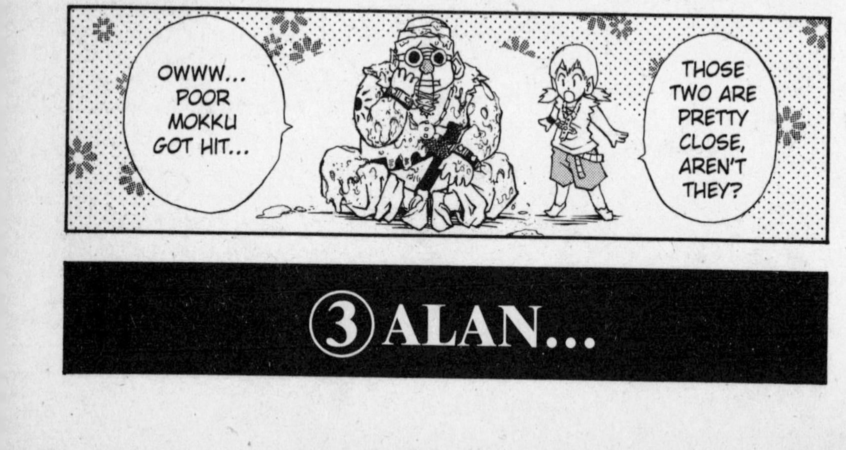
THOSE TWO ARE PRETTY CLOSE, AREN'T THEY?
OWWW... POOR MOKKU GOT HIT...

③ ALAN...

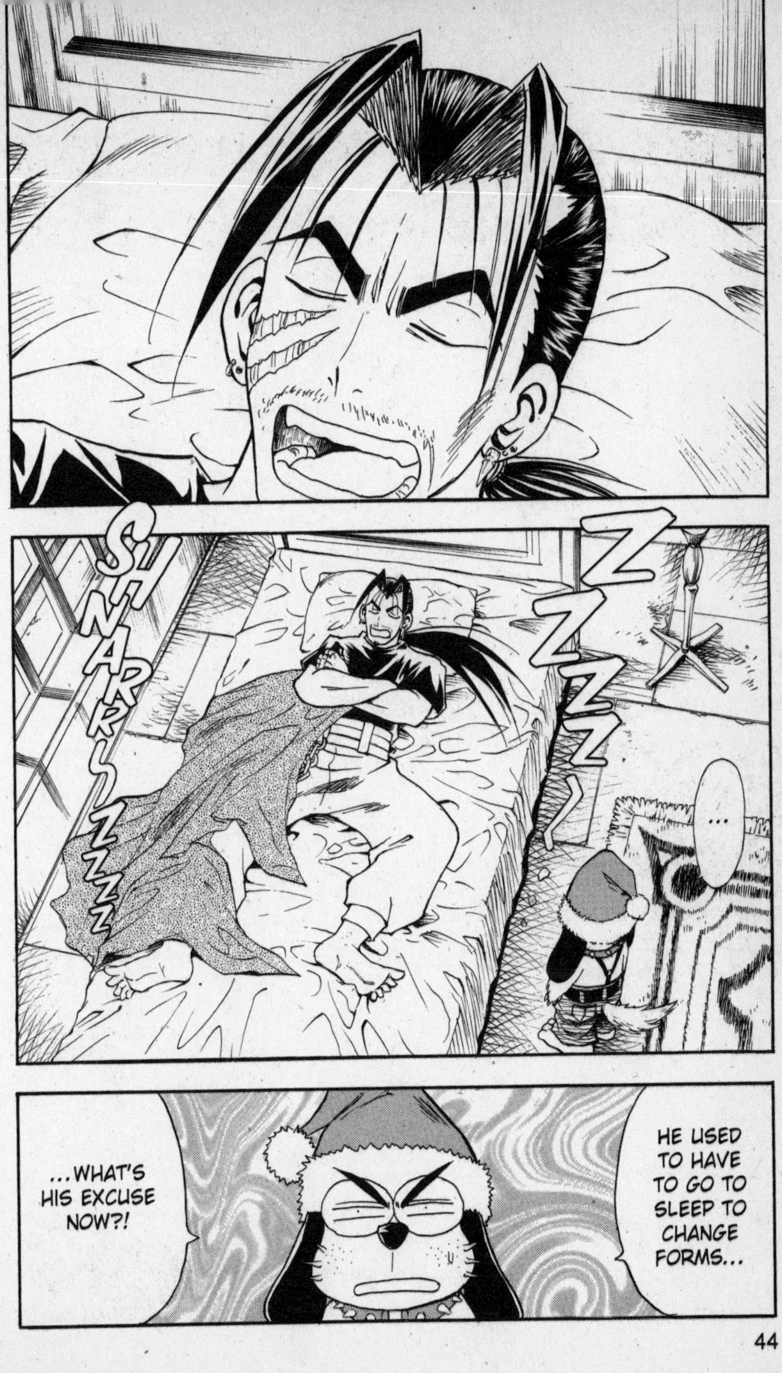
ZZZZZ
SHNARRRSZZZZ
...
HE USED TO HAVE TO GO TO SLEEP TO CHANGE FORMS...
...WHAT'S HIS EXCUSE NOW?!

④ FOR NANASHI...

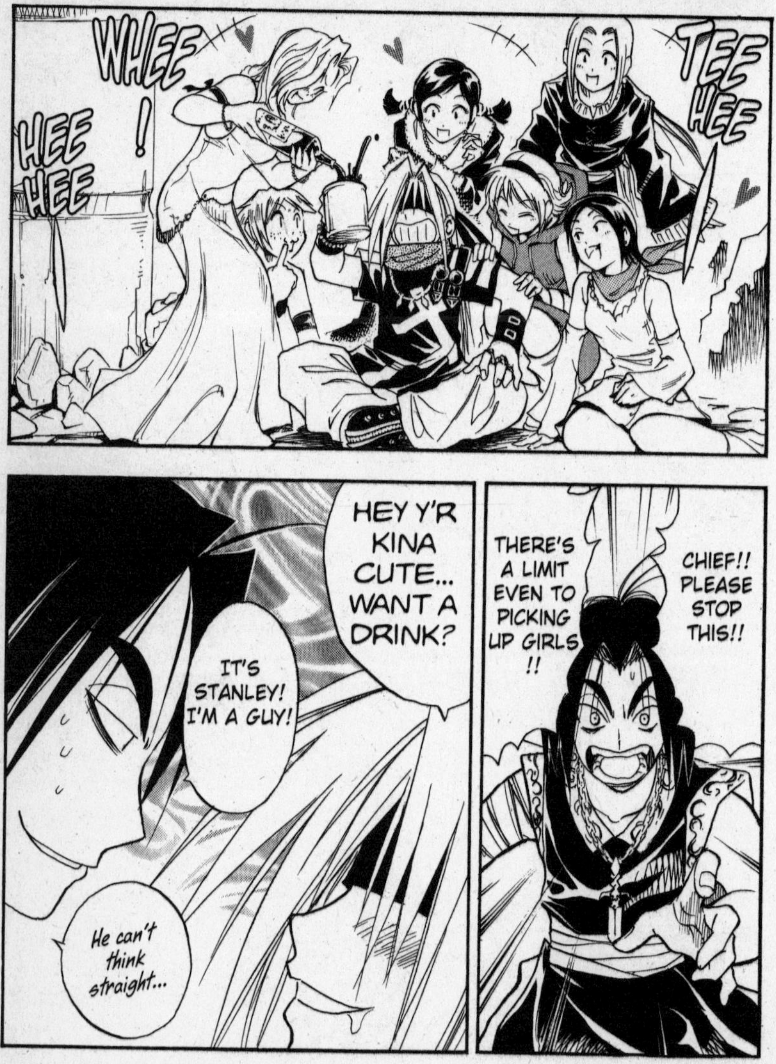
TEE HEE
WHEE!
HEE HEE
CHIEF!! PLEASE STOP THIS!!
THERE'S A LIMIT EVEN TO PICKING UP GIRLS !!
HEY Y'R KINA CUTE... WANT A DRINK?
IT'S STANLEY! I'M A GUY!
He can't think straight...

⑤ DOROTHY...

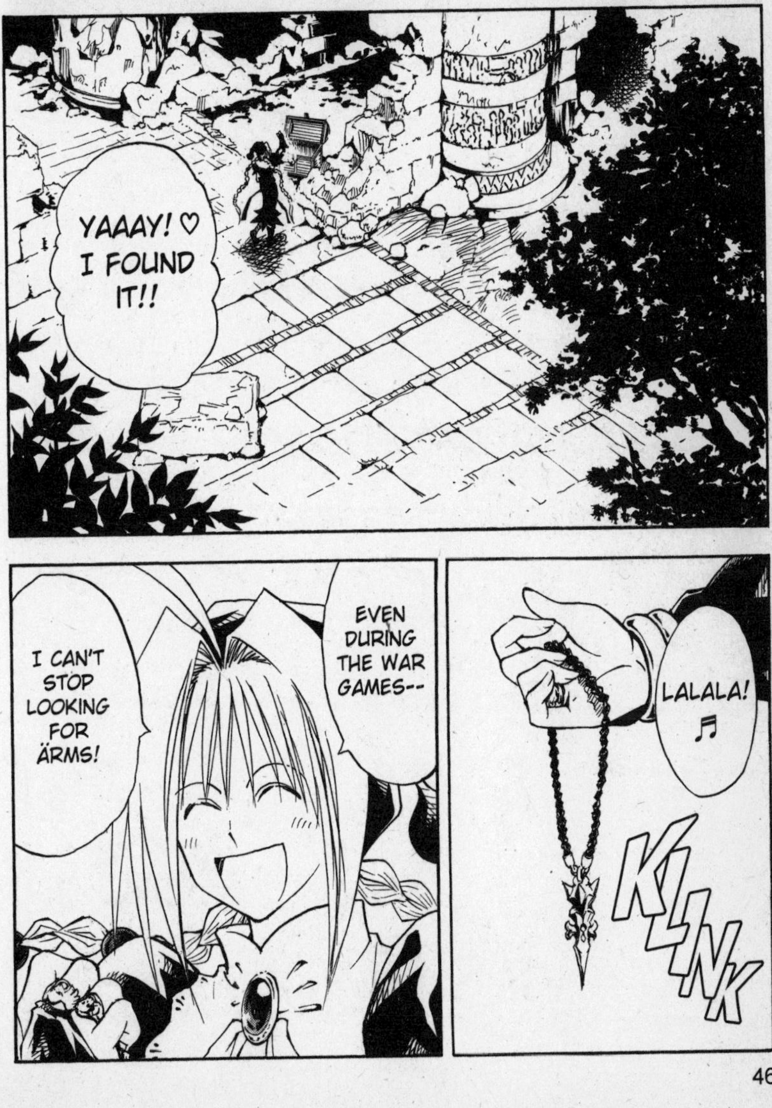
YAAAY! ♡ I FOUND IT!!
LALALA! ♬
KLINK
EVEN DURING THE WAR GAMES--
I CAN'T STOP LOOKING FOR ÄRMS!

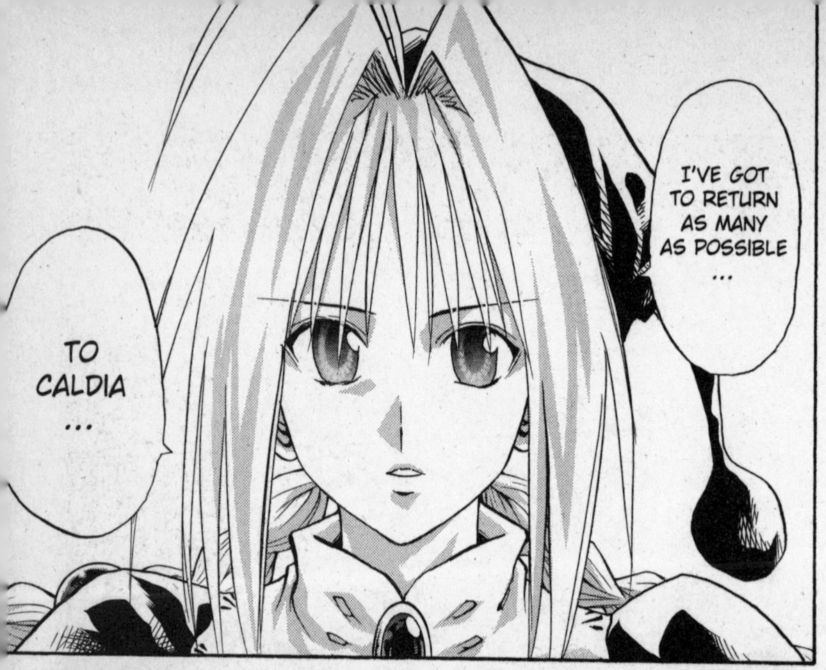
I'VE GOT TO RETURN AS MANY AS POSSIBLE ...
TO CALDIA ...

⑥ BABBO...

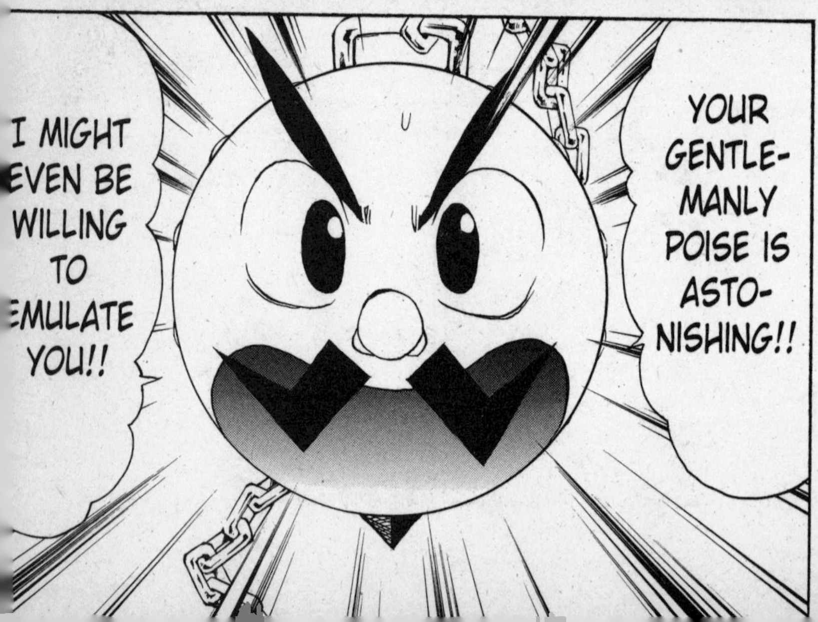
YOUR GENTLE-MANLY POISE IS ASTO-NISHING!!
I MIGHT EVEN BE WILLING TO EMULATE YOU!!

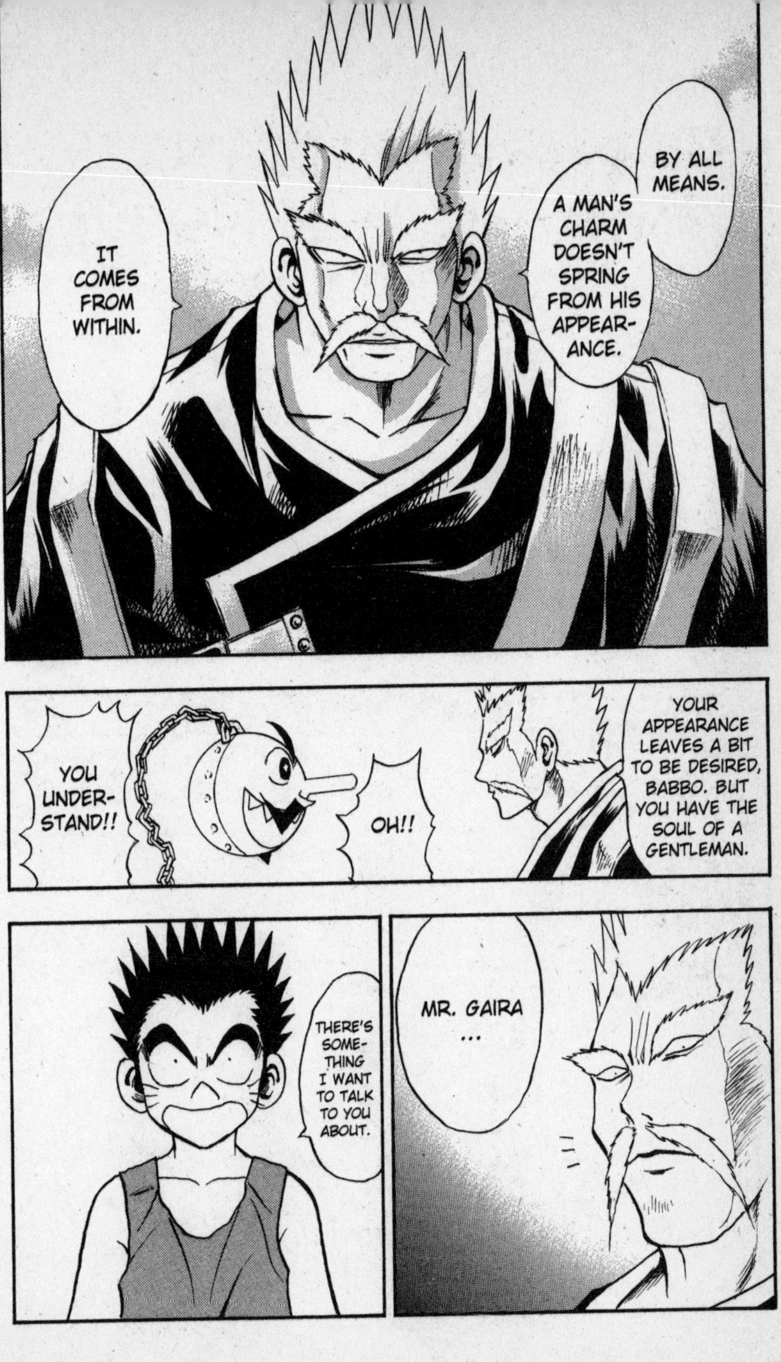
BY ALL MEANS.
A MAN'S CHARM DOESN'T SPRING FROM HIS APPEARANCE.
IT COMES FROM WITHIN.
YOUR APPEARANCE LEAVES A BIT TO BE DESIRED, BABBO. BUT YOU HAVE THE SOUL OF A GENTLEMAN.
OH!!
YOU UNDER-STAND!!
MR. GAIRA ...
THERE'S SOME-THING I WANT TO TALK TO YOU ABOUT.

⑦ JACK AND GAIRA...

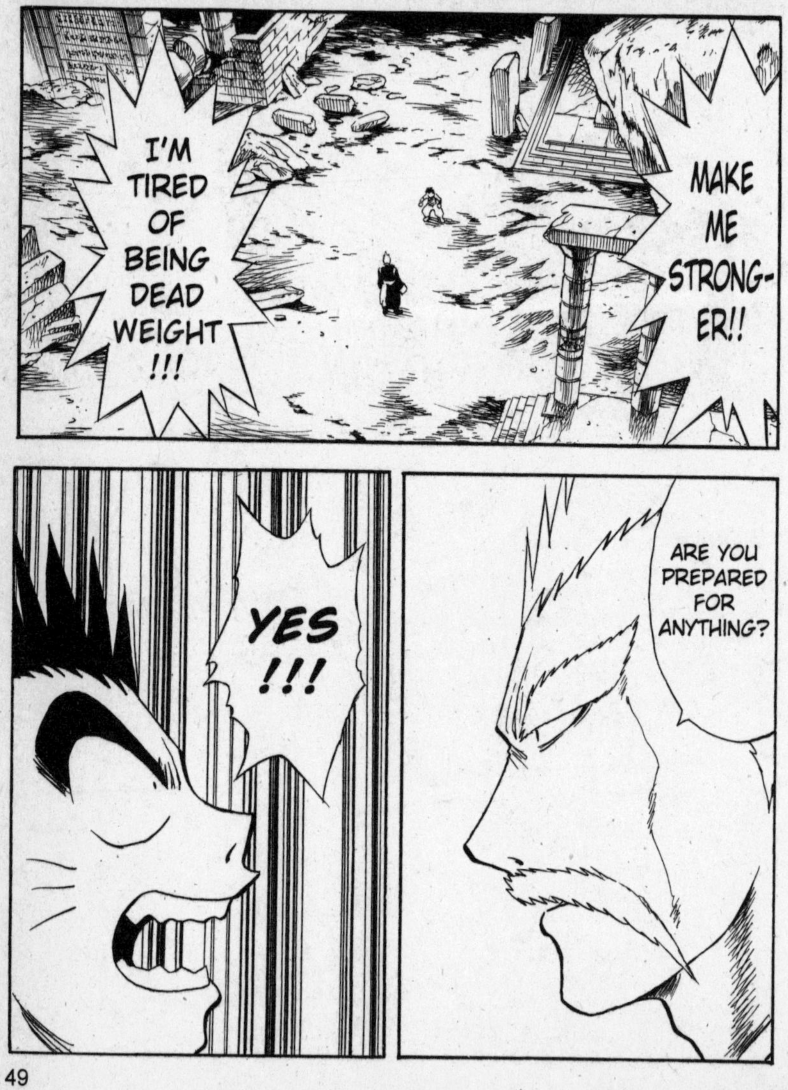
MAKE ME STRONGER!!
I'M TIRED OF BEING DEAD WEIGHT!!!
ARE YOU PREPARED FOR ANYTHING?
YES!!!

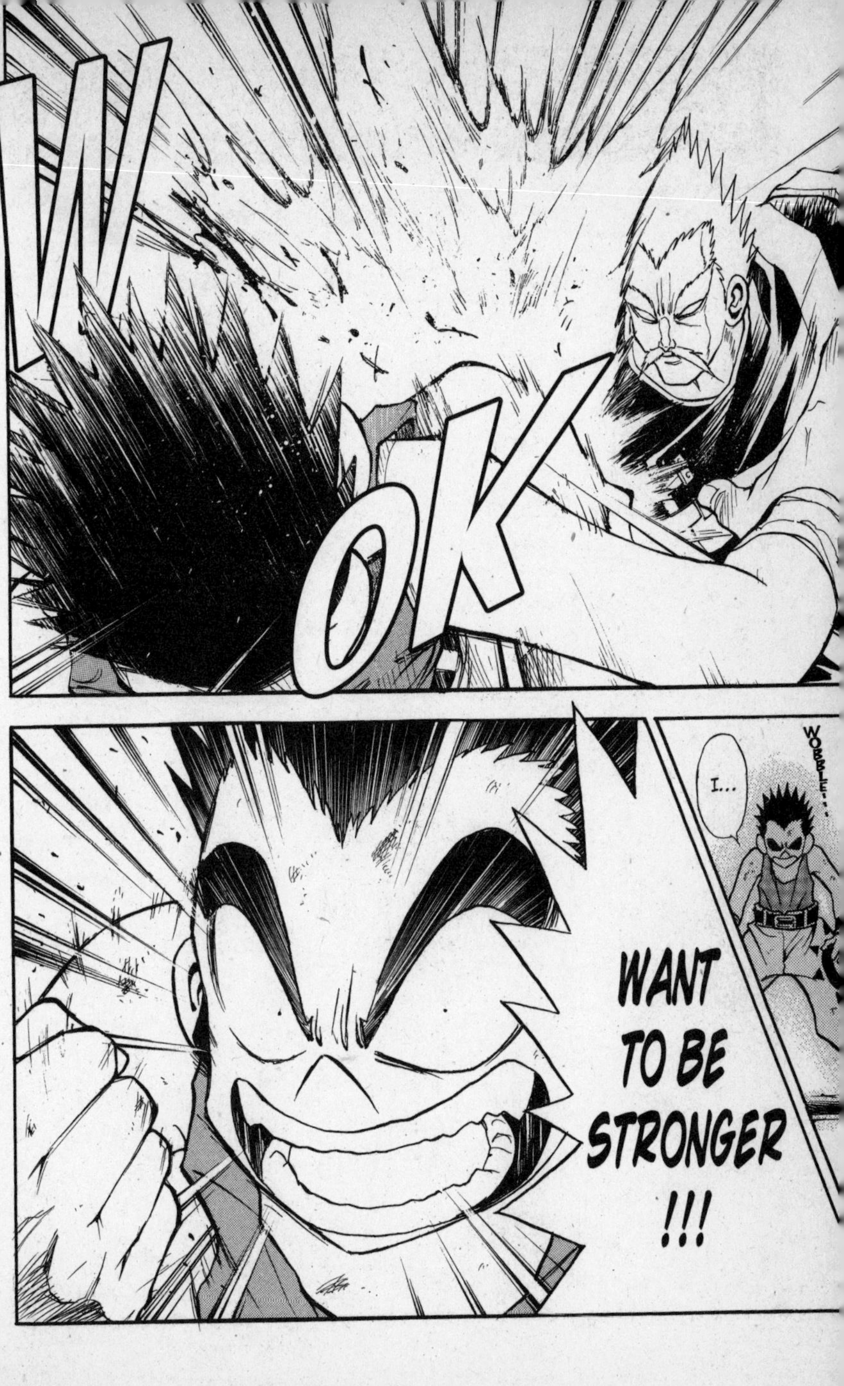
WOK
WOBBLE...
I...
WANT TO BE STRONGER !!!

⑧...AND FINALLY GINTA.

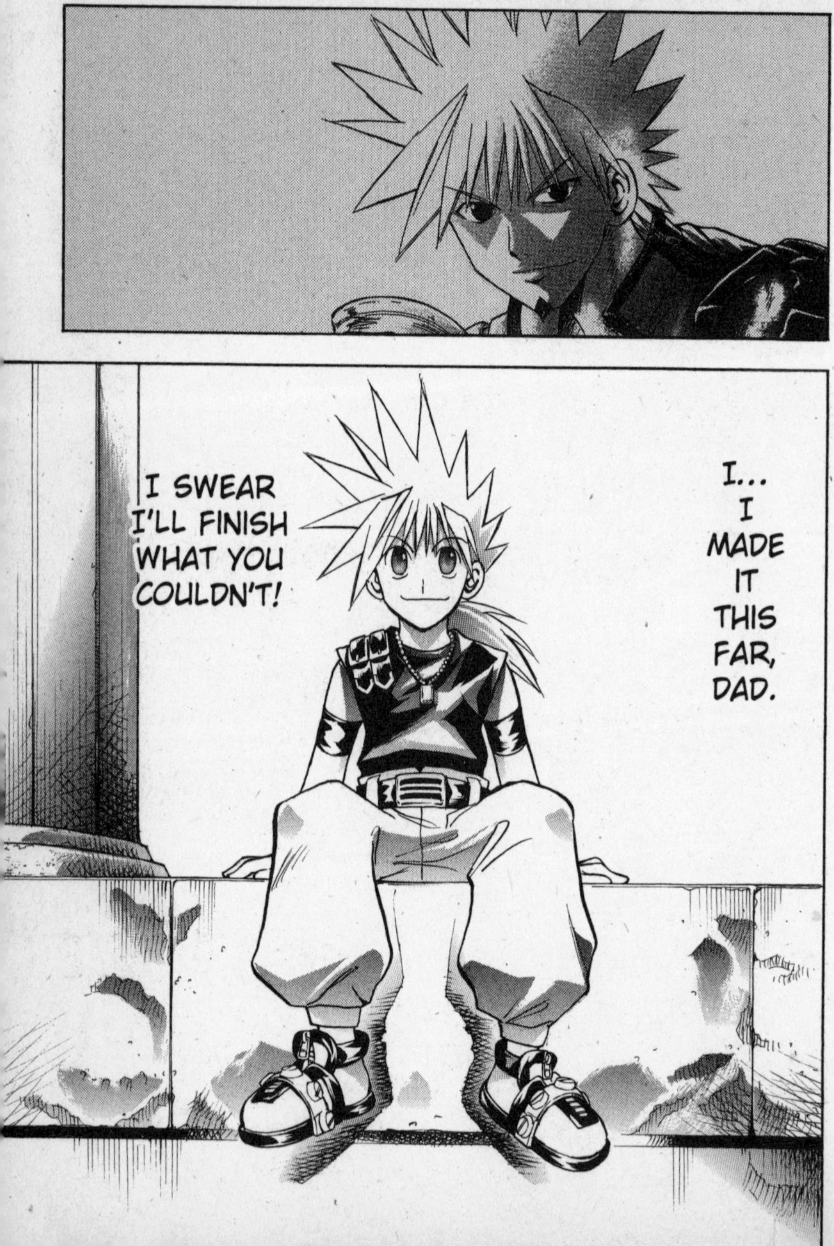
I... I MADE IT THIS FAR, DAD.
I SWEAR I'LL FINISH WHAT YOU COULDN'T!

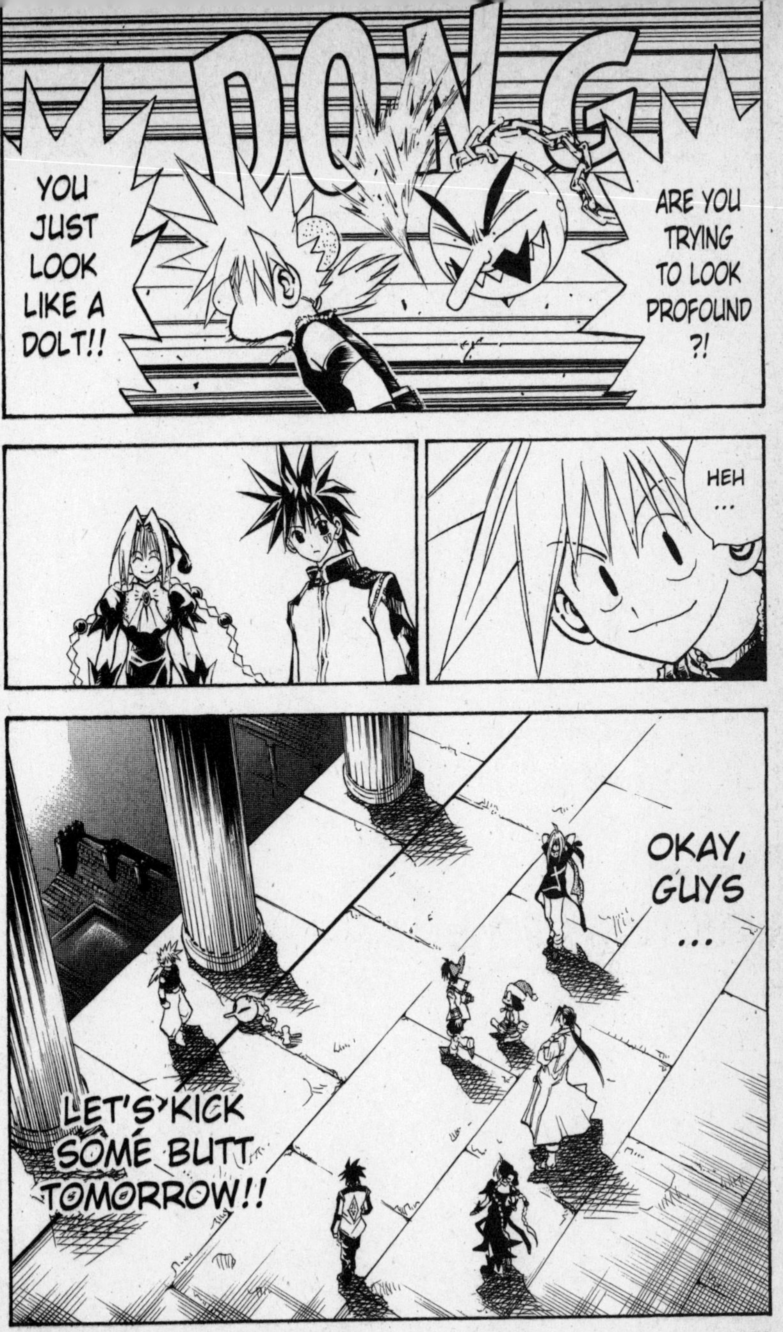
DONG
ARE YOU TRYING TO LOOK PROFOUND?!
YOU JUST LOOK LIKE A DOLT!!
HEH...
OKAY, GUYS...
LET'S KICK SOME BUTT TOMORROW!!

AKT.111/ ALAN VS. CHATON ①

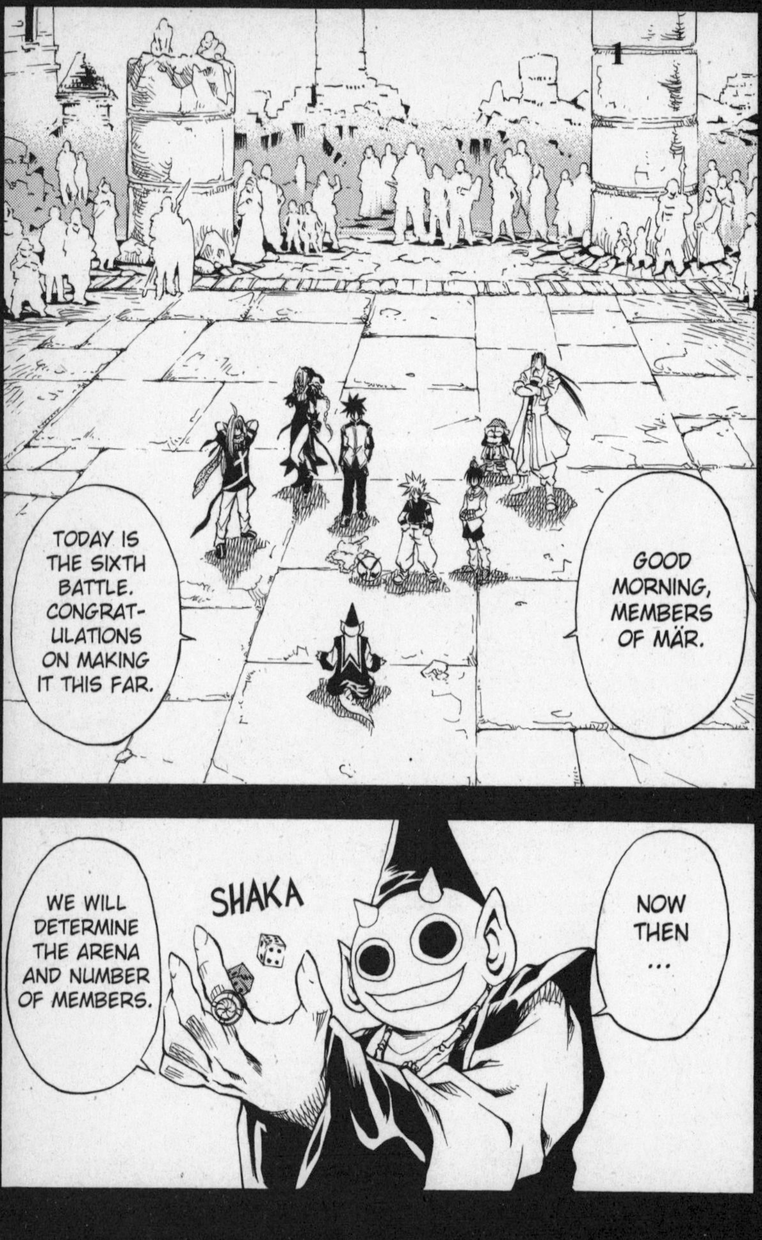
GOOD MORNING, MEMBERS OF MÄR.
TODAY IS THE SIXTH BATTLE. CONGRATULATIONS ON MAKING IT THIS FAR.
NOW THEN ...
SHAKA
WE WILL DETERMINE THE ARENA AND NUMBER OF MEMBERS.

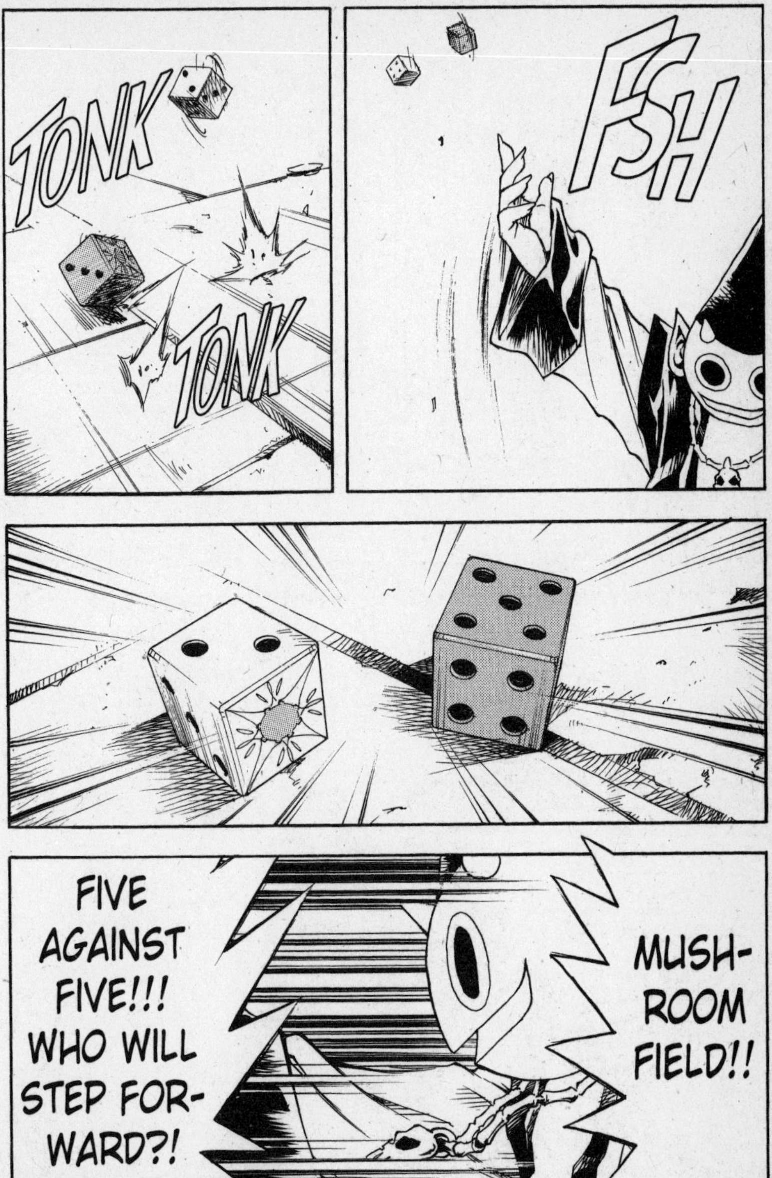
FSH
TONK
TONK
MUSH-ROOM FIELD!!
FIVE AGAINST FIVE!!! WHO WILL STEP FOR-WARD?!

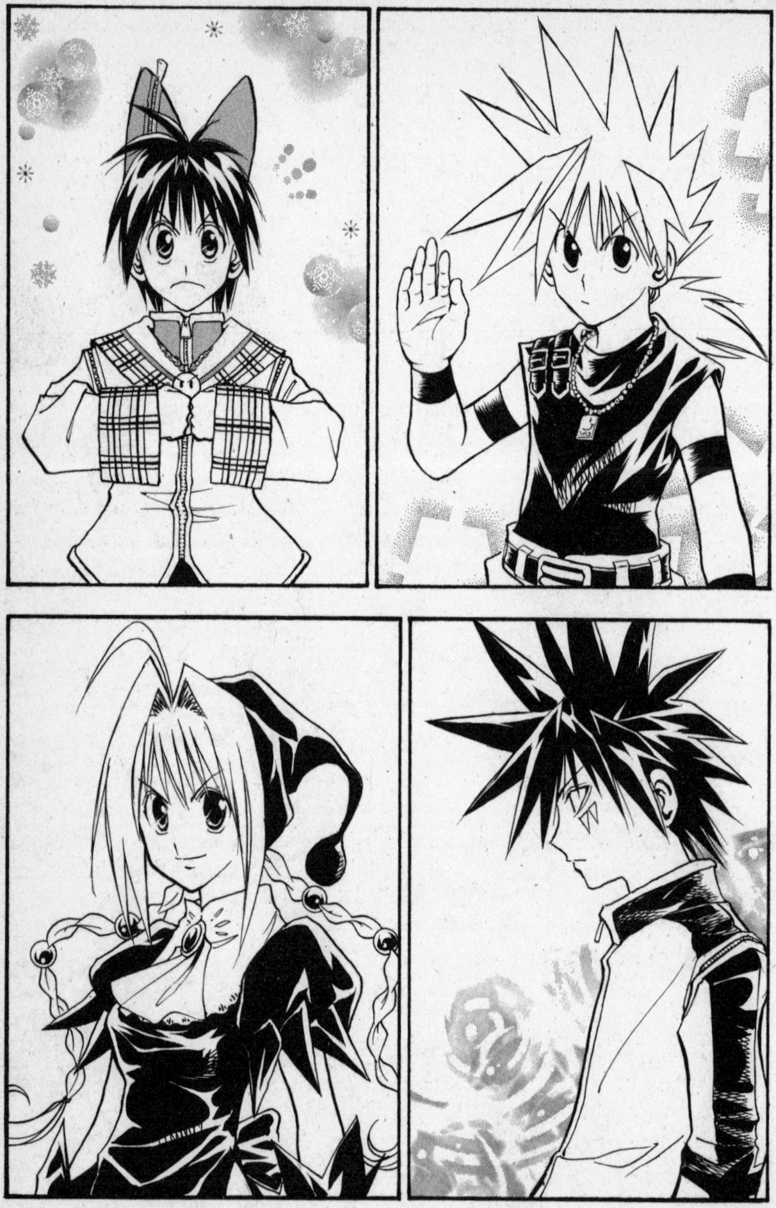

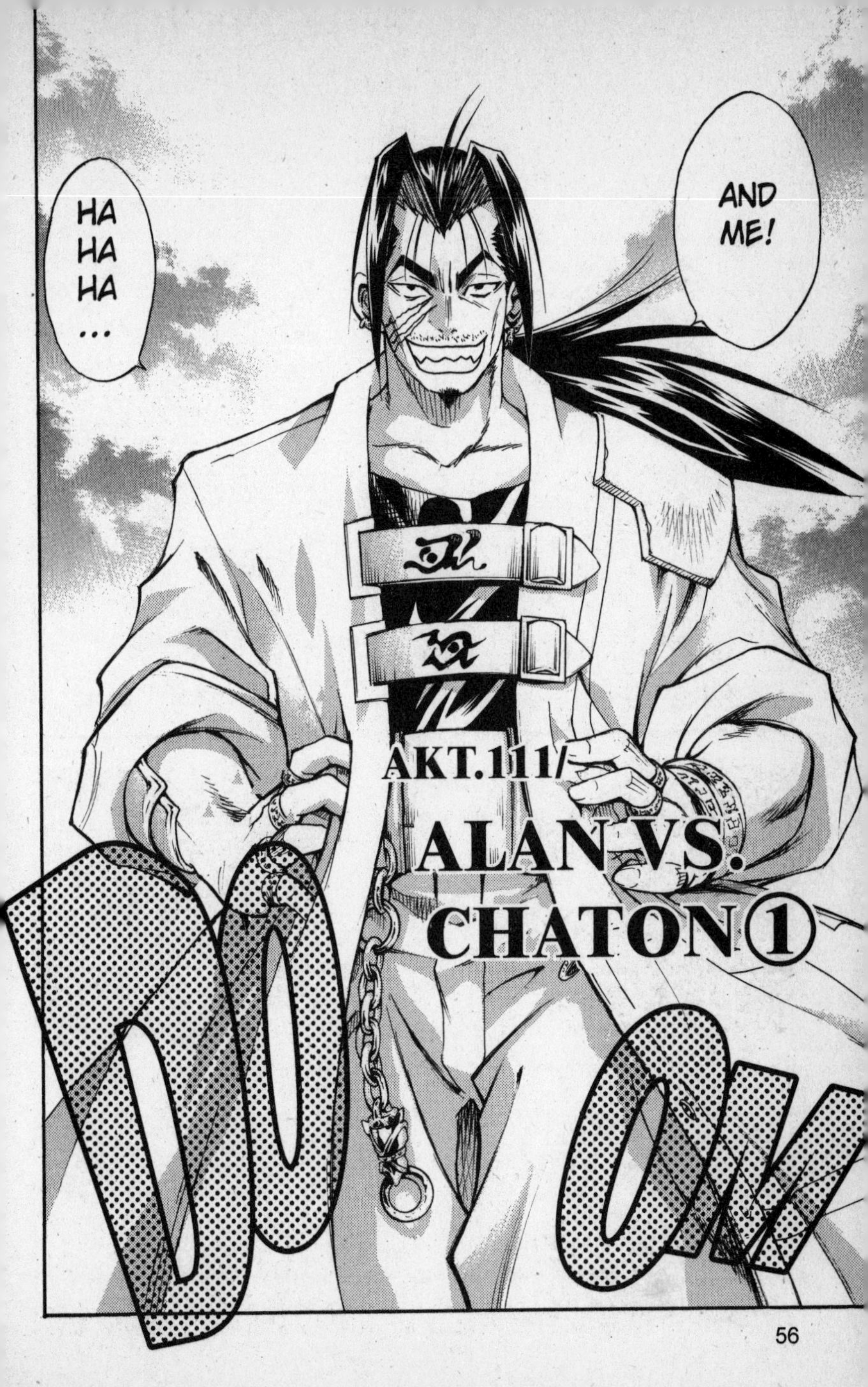
AND ME!
HA HA HA ...
AKT.111/
ALAN VS. CHATON ①
DOOOM

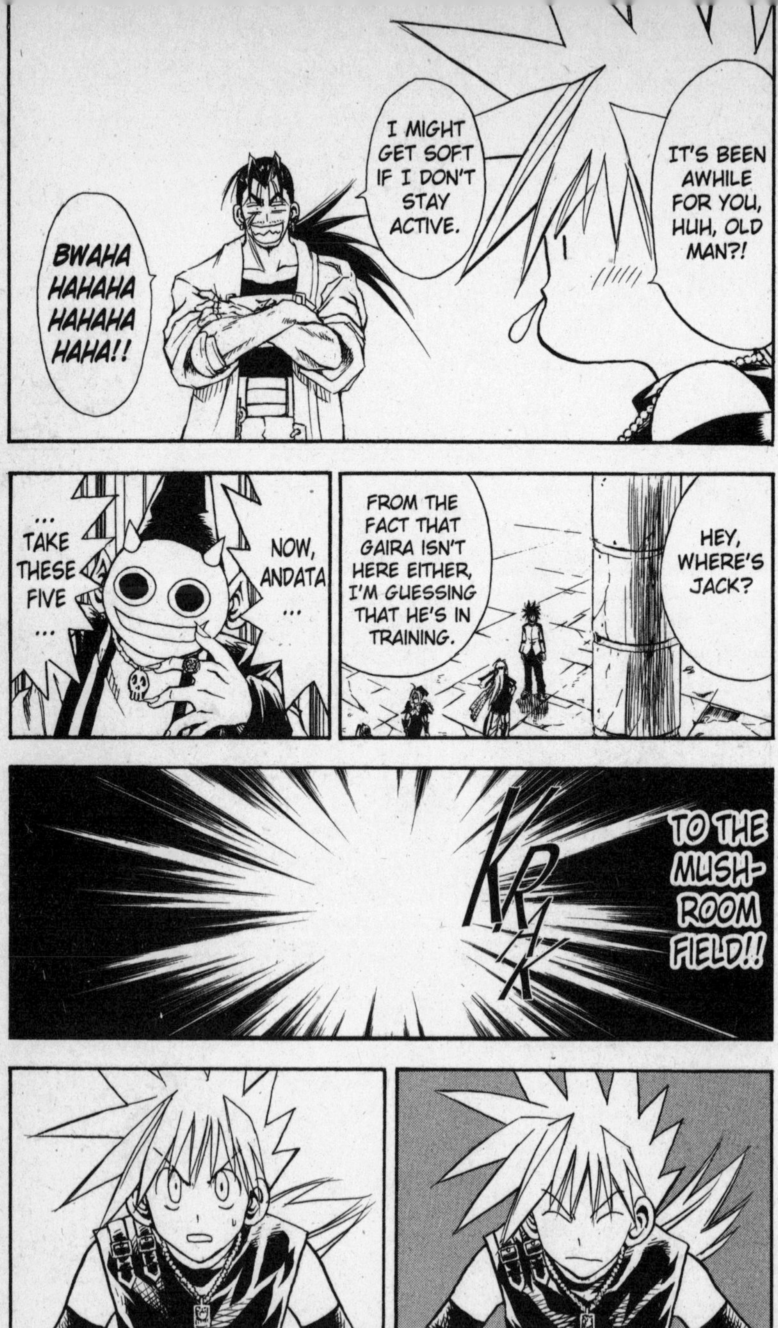
IT'S BEEN AWHILE FOR YOU, HUH, OLD MAN?!
I MIGHT GET SOFT IF I DON'T STAY ACTIVE.
BWAHA HAHAHA HAHAHA HAHA!!
HEY, WHERE'S JACK?
FROM THE FACT THAT GAIRA ISN'T HERE EITHER, I'M GUESSING THAT HE'S IN TRAINING.
NOW, ANDATA ...
... TAKE THESE FIVE ...
TO THE MUSH-ROOM FIELD!!
KRAK

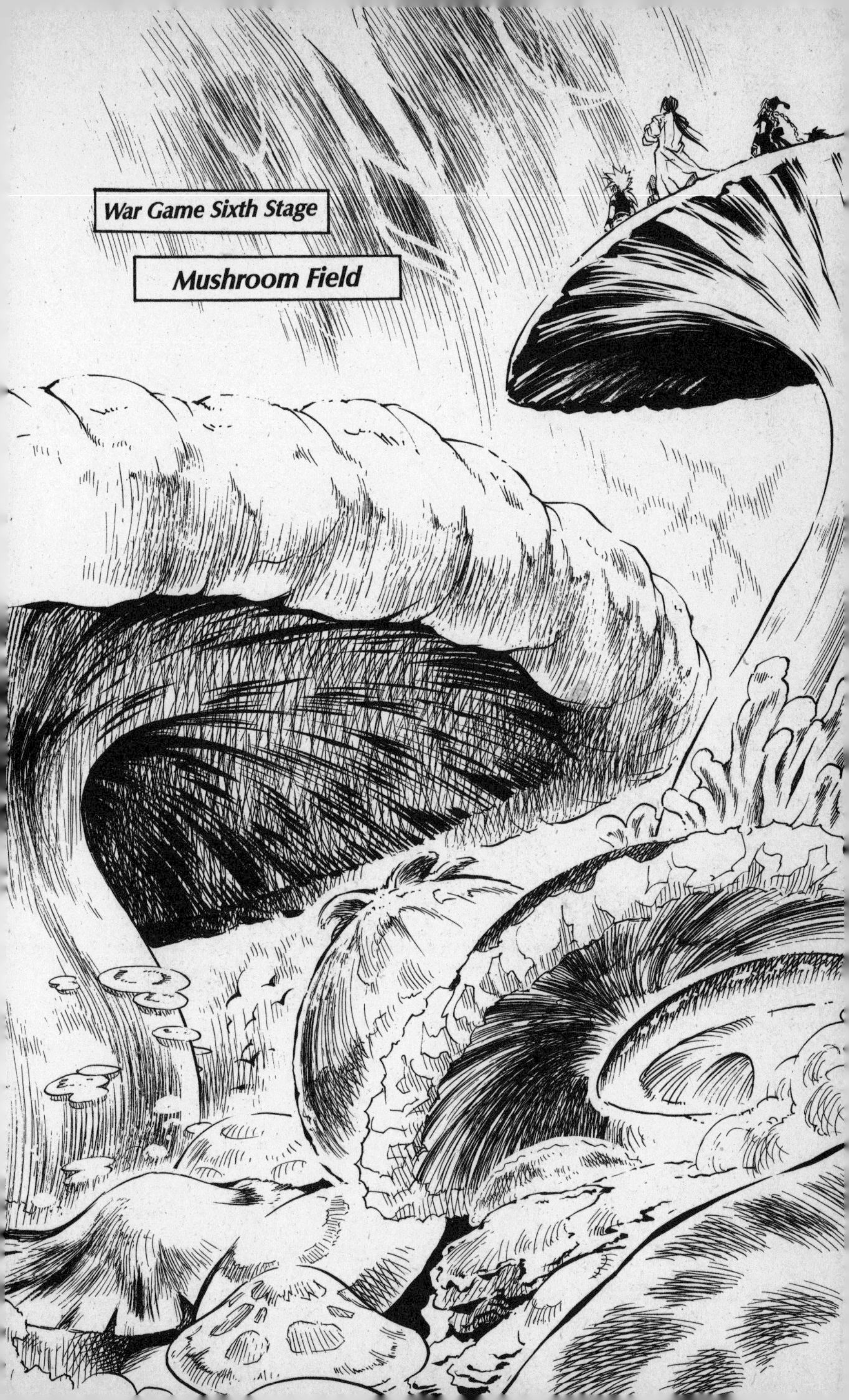
War Game Sixth Stage
Mushroom Field

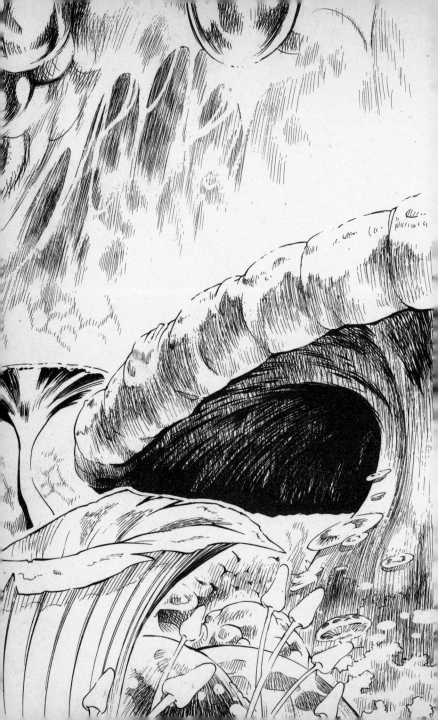

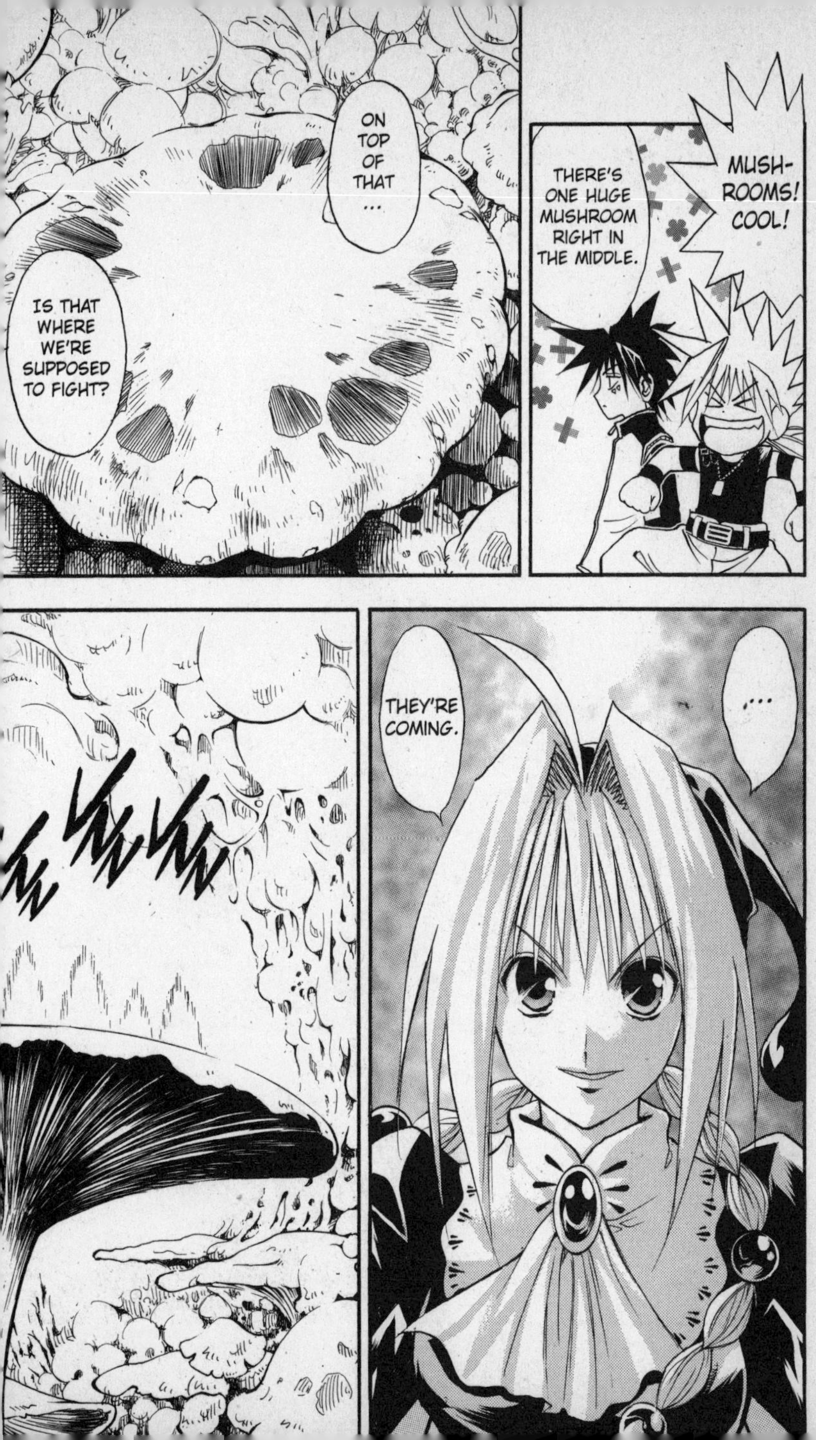
MUSH-ROOMS! COOL!
THERE'S ONE HUGE MUSHROOM RIGHT IN THE MIDDLE.
ON TOP OF THAT ...
IS THAT WHERE WE'RE SUPPOSED TO FIGHT?
...
THEY'RE COMING.

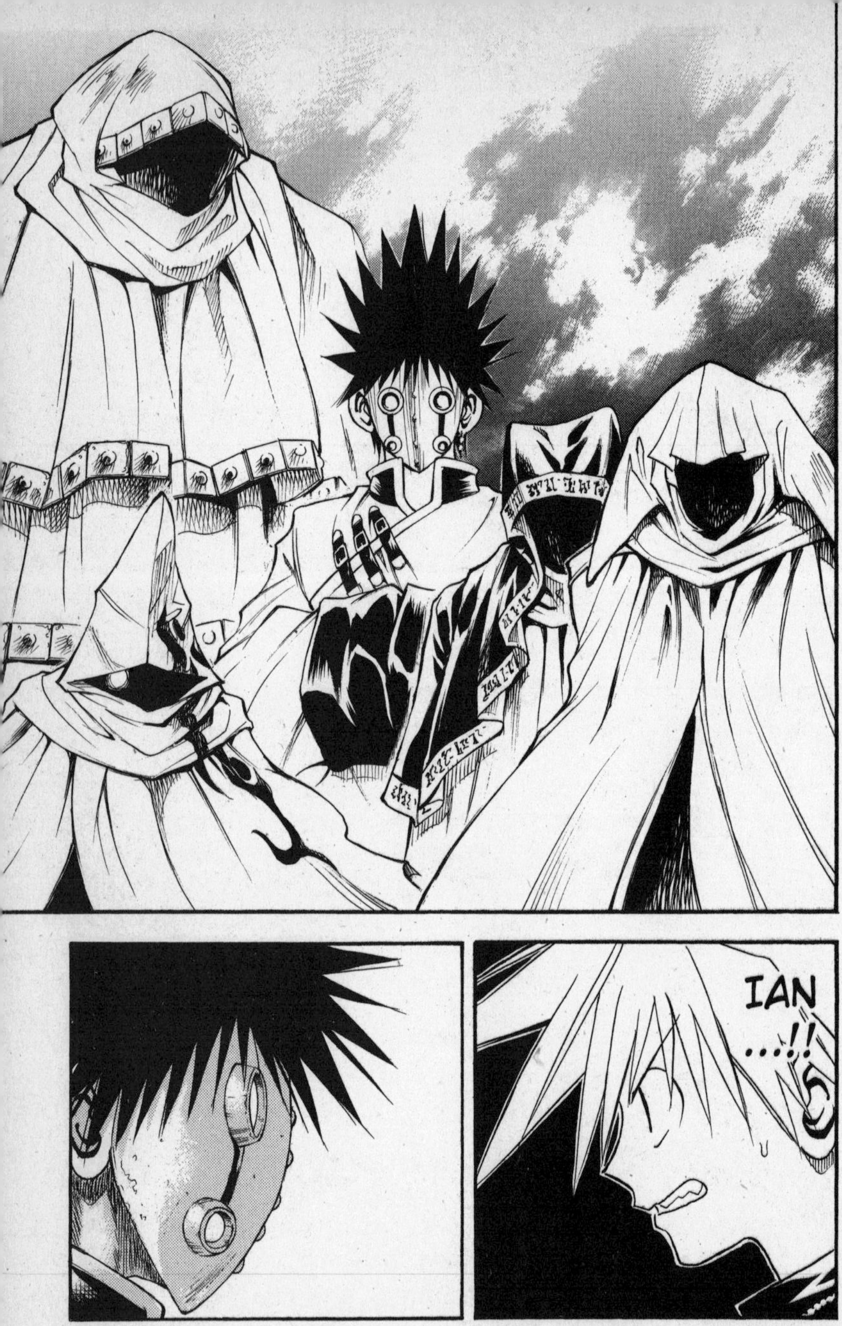
IAN
...!!

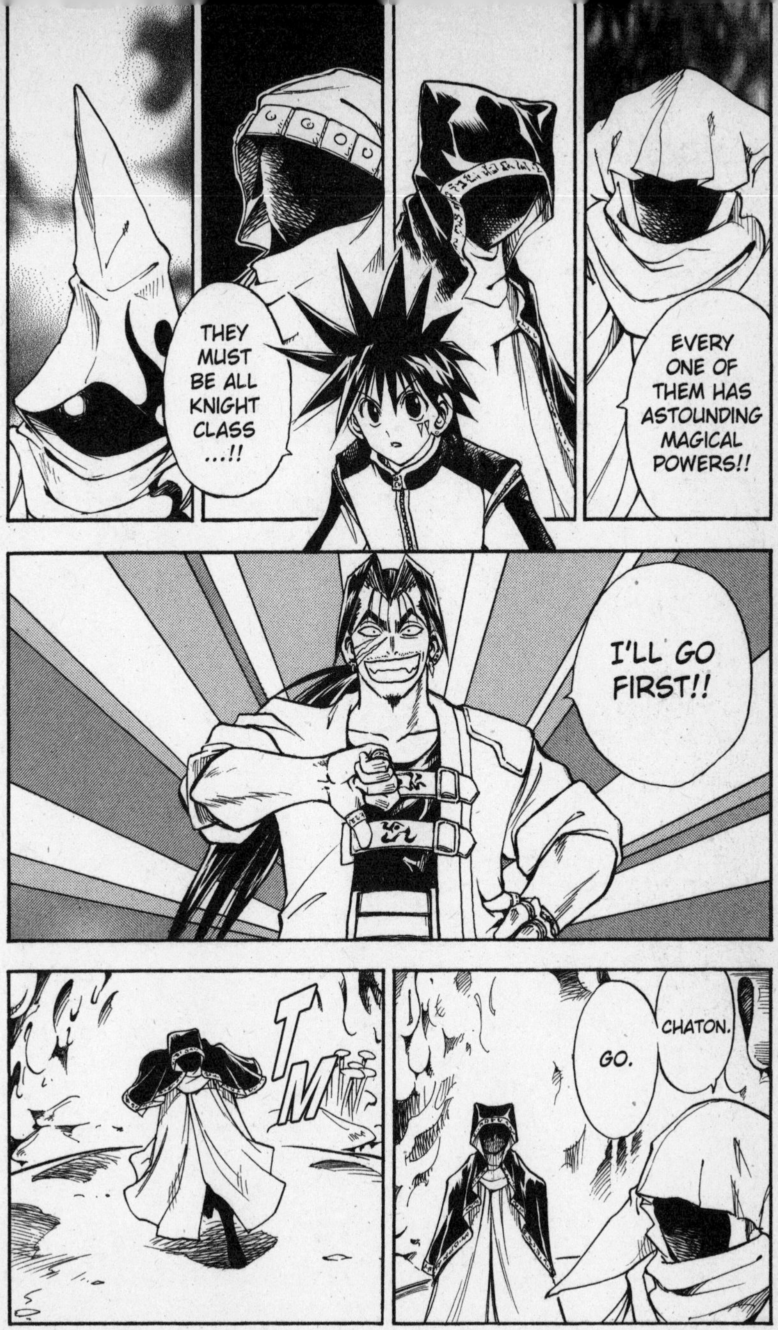
EVERY ONE OF THEM HAS ASTOUNDING MAGICAL POWERS!!
THEY MUST BE ALL KNIGHT CLASS ...!!
I'LL GO FIRST!!
CHATON.
GO.
TM

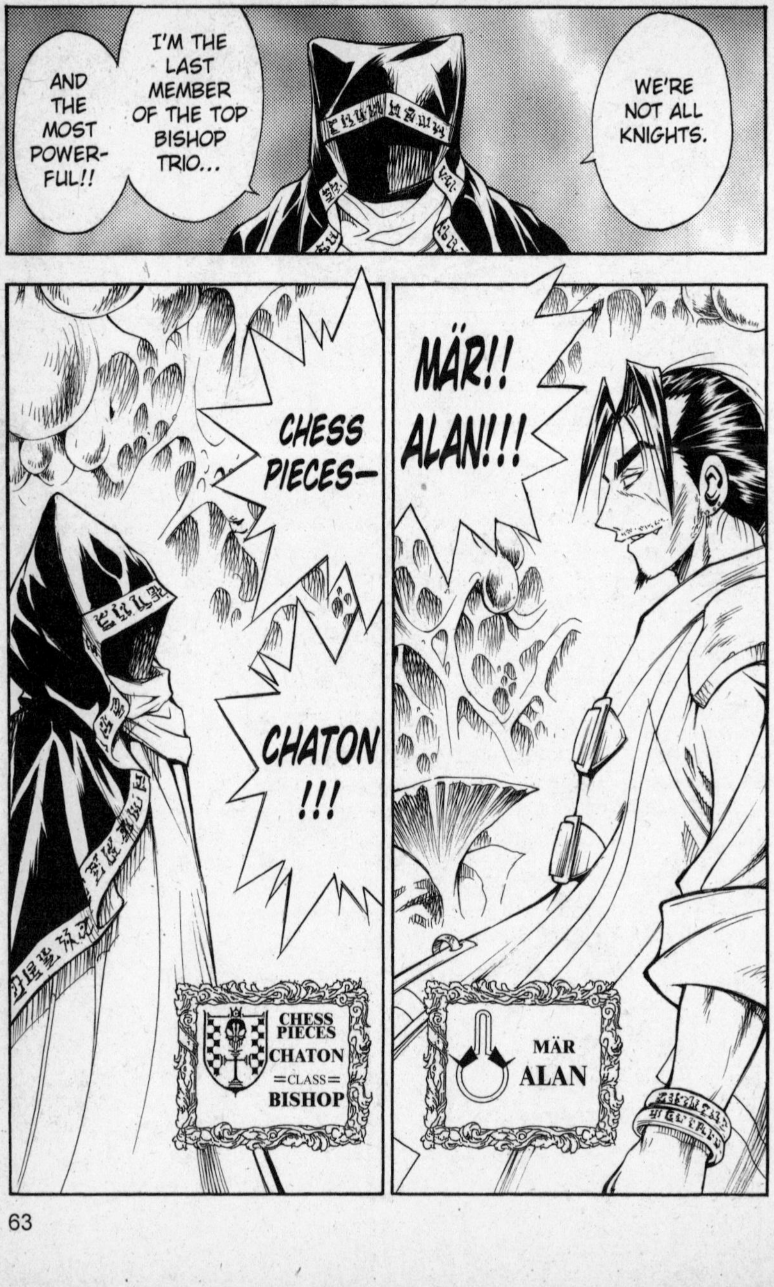
WE'RE NOT ALL KNIGHTS.
I'M THE LAST MEMBER OF THE TOP BISHOP TRIO...
AND THE MOST POWER-FUL!!
MÄR!! ALAN!!!
MÄR ALAN
CHESS PIECES— CHATON!!!
CHESS PIECES CHATON =CLASS= BISHOP

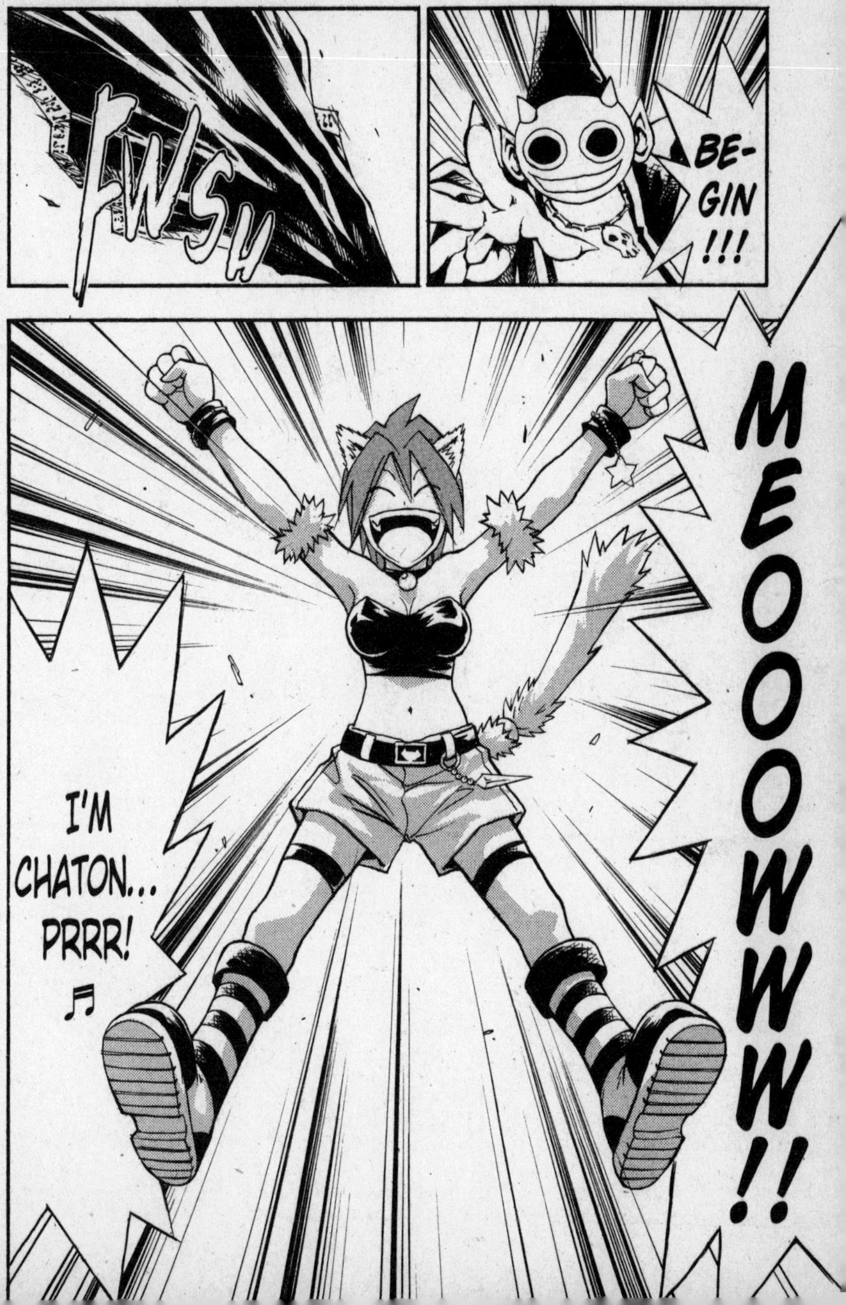
BE-
GIN!!!
FWSH
MEOOOWWW!!
I'M CHATON... PRRR! ♬

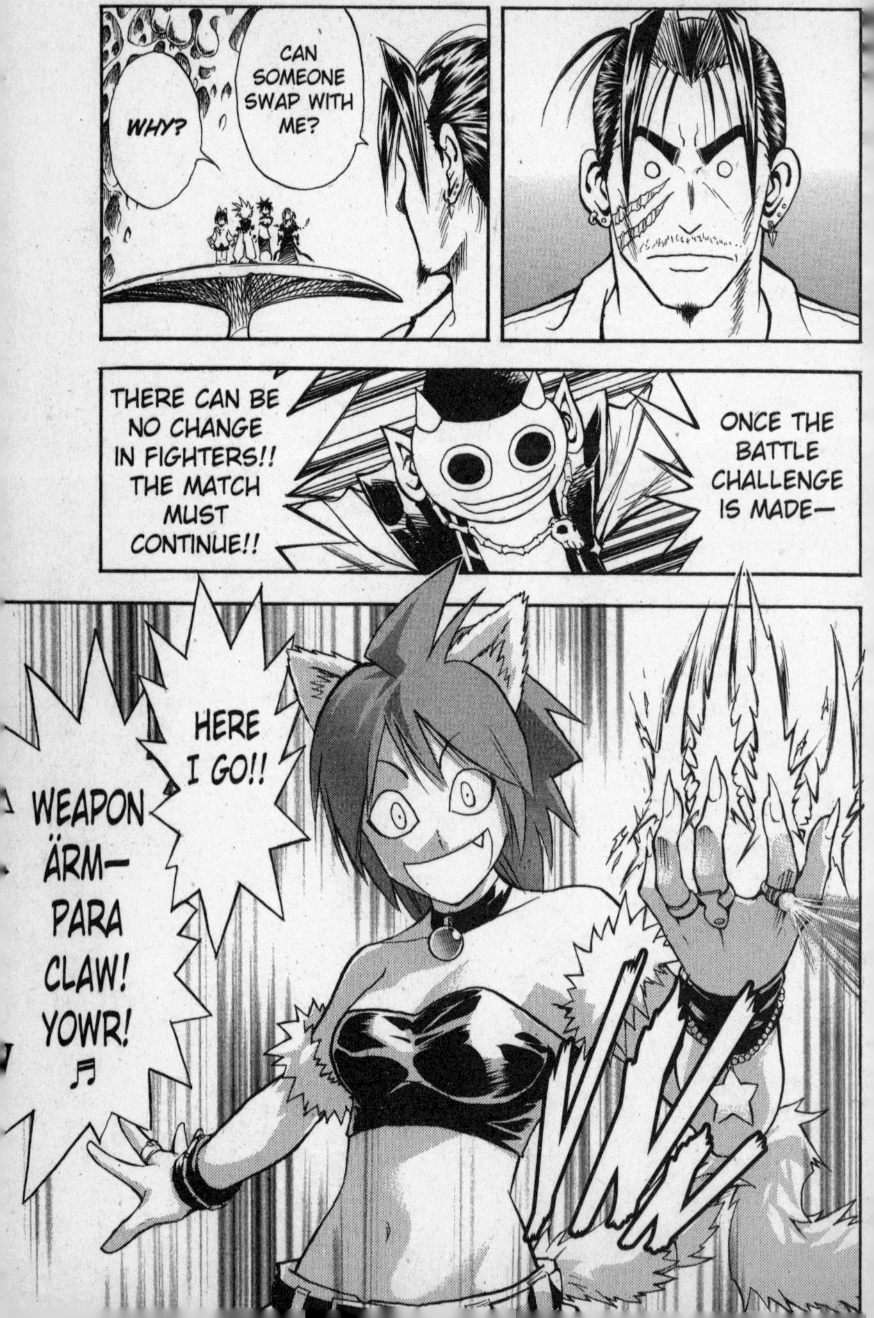
CAN SOMEONE SWAP WITH ME?
WHY?
ONCE THE BATTLE CHALLENGE IS MADE—
THERE CAN BE NO CHANGE IN FIGHTERS!! THE MATCH MUST CONTINUE!!
HERE I GO!!
WEAPON ÄRM-PARA CLAW! YOWR! ♬

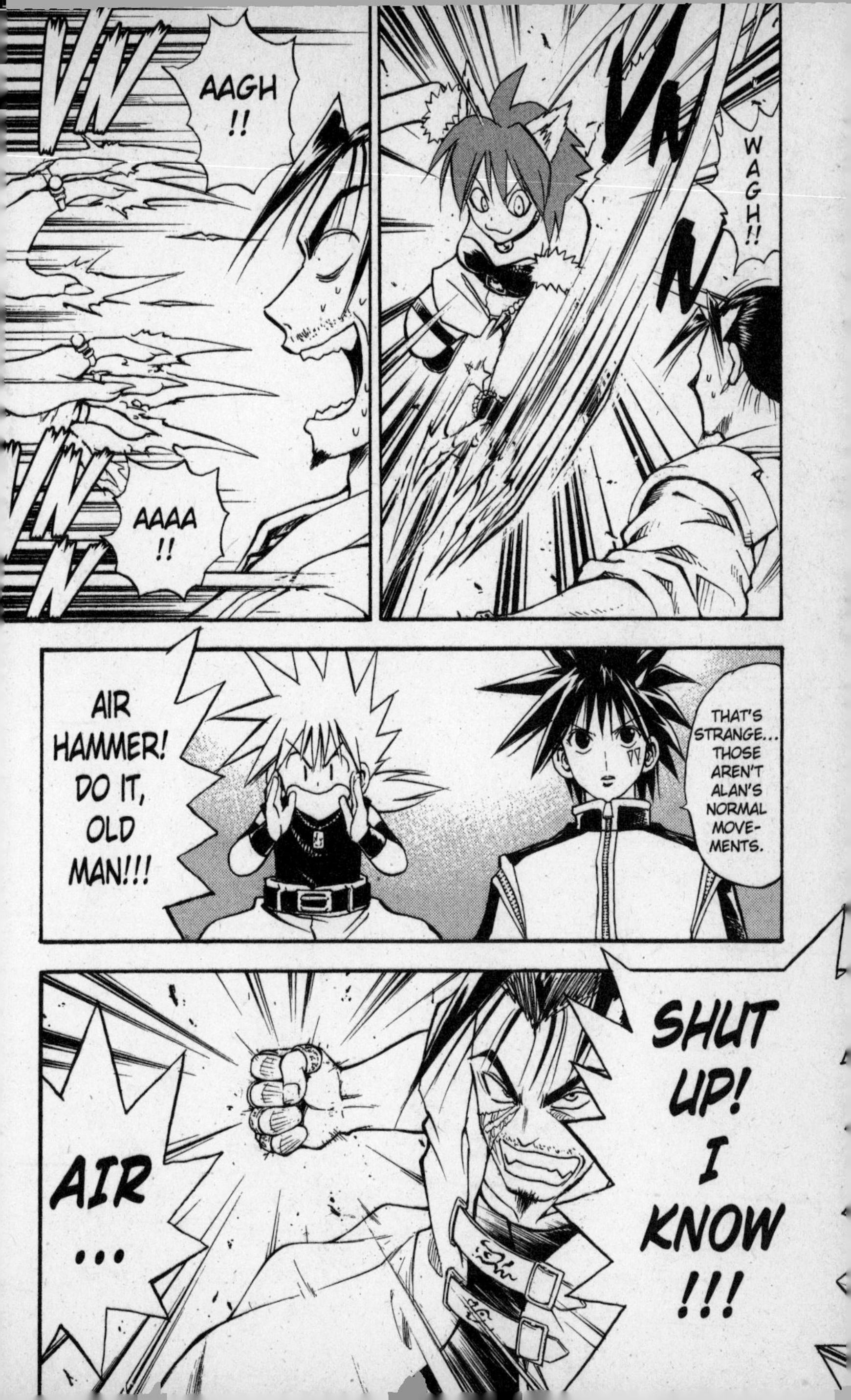

WAGH!!
AAGH!!
AAAA!!
THAT'S STRANGE... THOSE AREN'T ALAN'S NORMAL MOVEMENTS.
AIR HAMMER! DO IT, OLD MAN!!!
SHUT UP! I KNOW!!!
AIR...

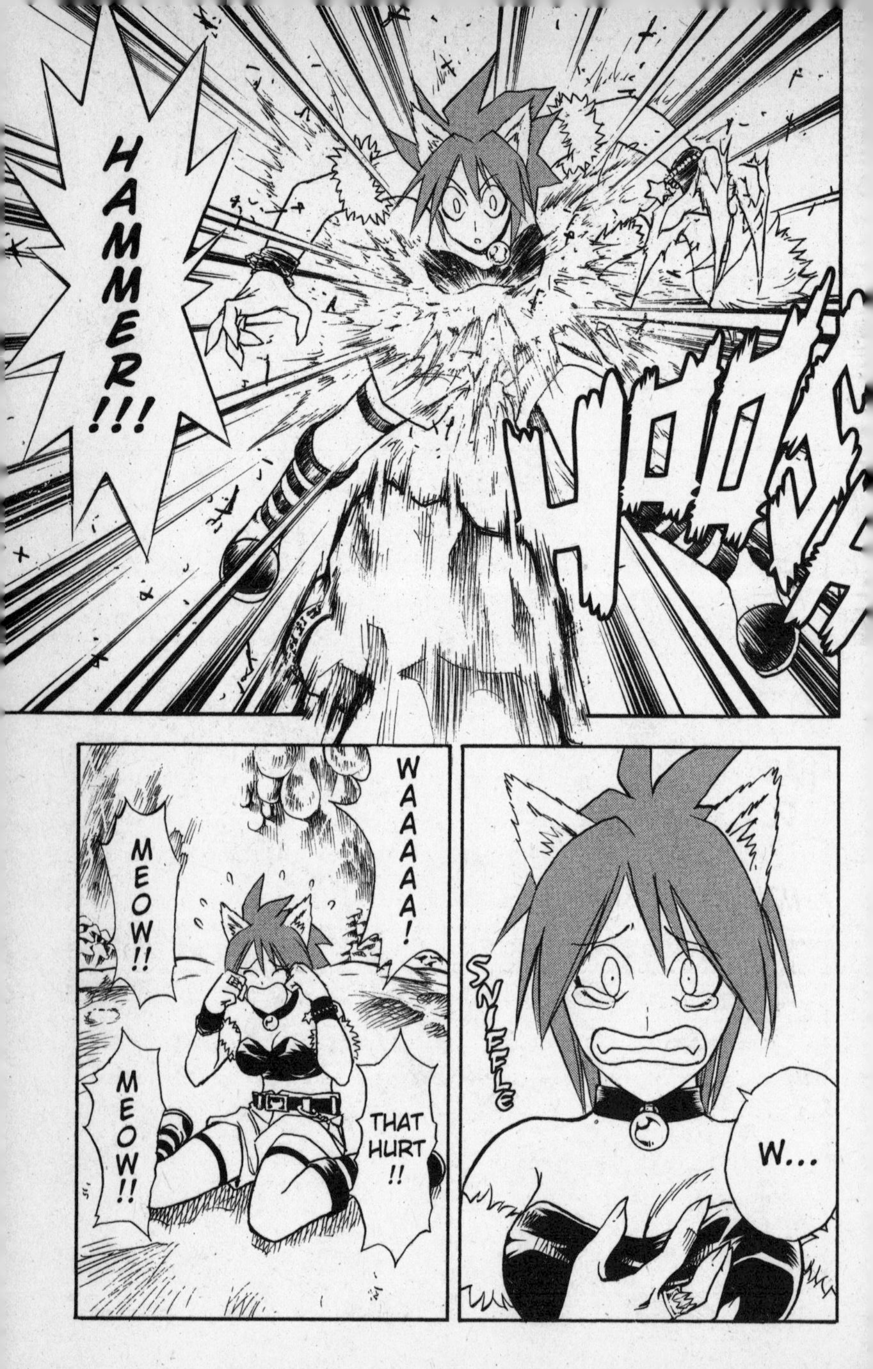
HAMMER!!!
SNIFFLE
W...
WAAAAAA!
MEOW!!
THAT HURT!!
MEOW!!

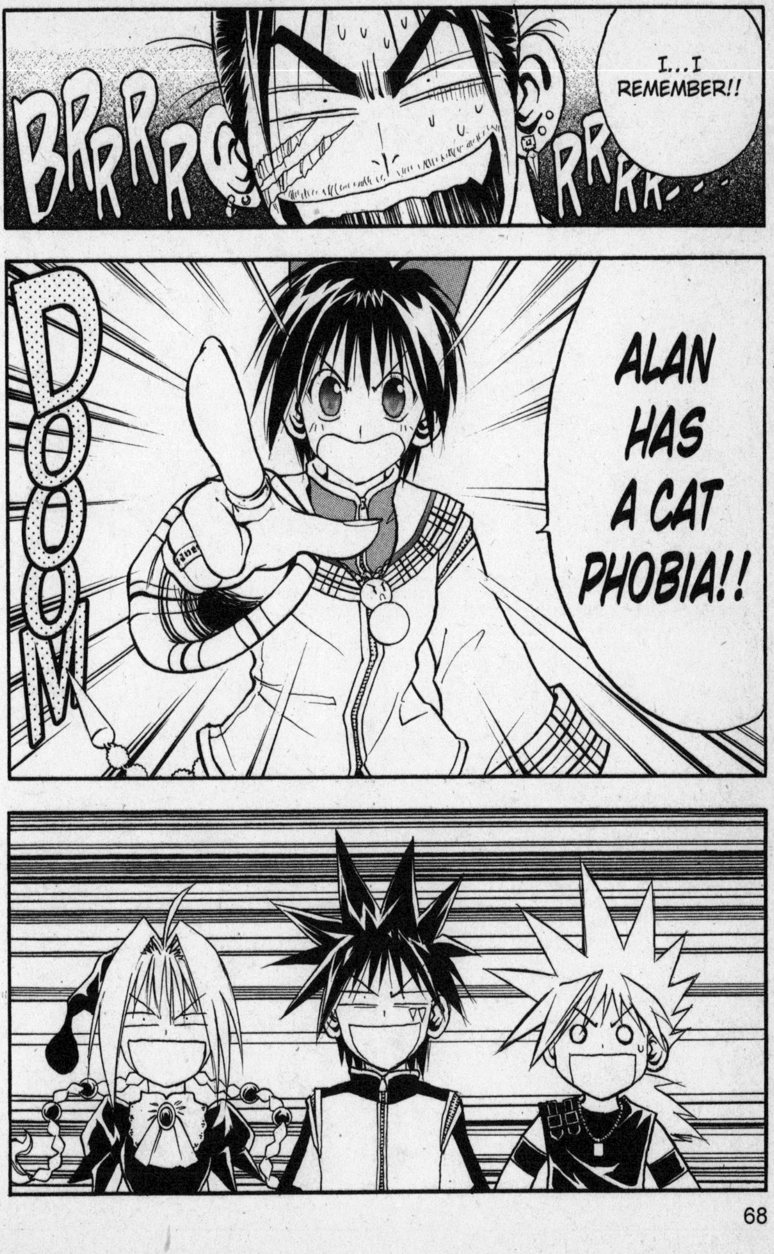
I...I REMEMBER!!
BRRRRO
RRKK...
ALAN HAS A CAT PHOBIA!!
DOOOOM

AKT.112/ ALAN VS. CHARON ②

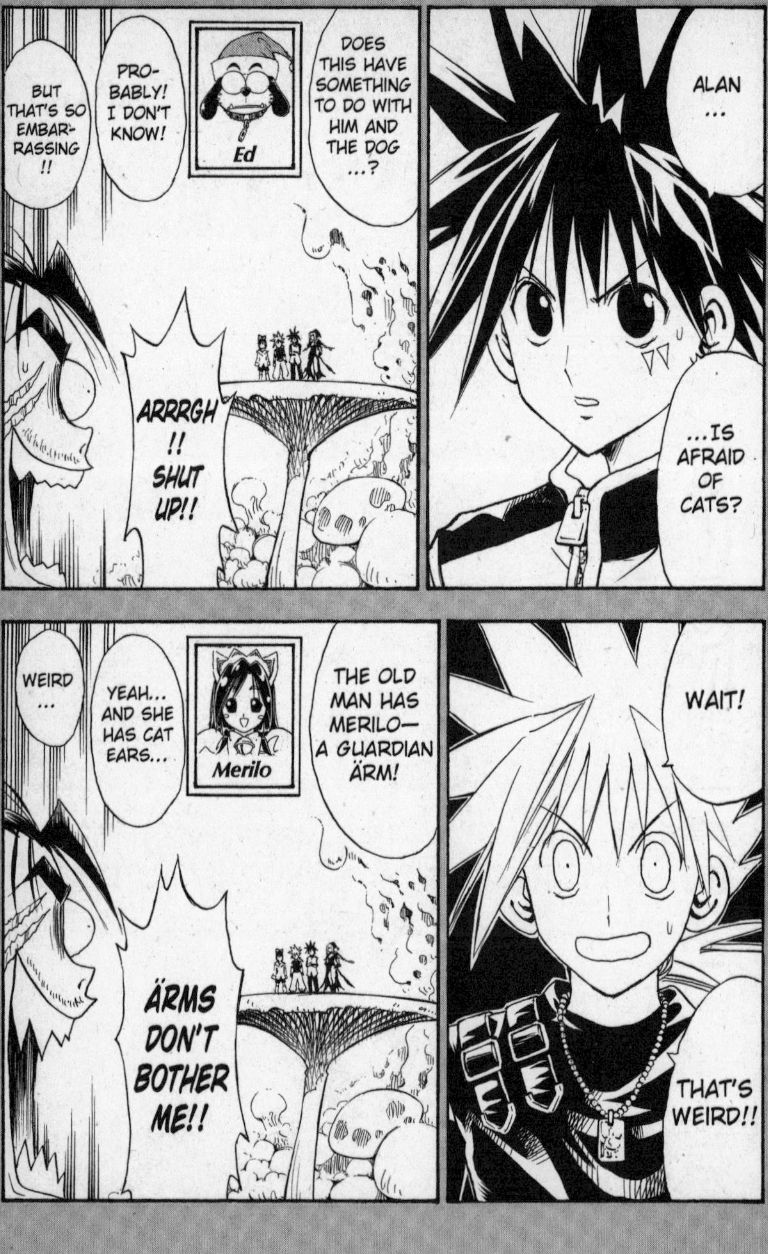
ALAN ...
...IS AFRAID OF CATS?
DOES THIS HAVE SOMETHING TO DO WITH HIM AND THE DOG ...?
Ed
PRO-BABLY! I DON'T KNOW!
BUT THAT'S SO EMBAR-RASSING !!
ARRRGH !! SHUT UP!!
WAIT!
THAT'S WEIRD!!
THE OLD MAN HAS MERILO— A GUARDIAN ÄRM!
Merilo
YEAH... AND SHE HAS CAT EARS...
WEIRD ...
ÄRMS DON'T BOTHER ME!!

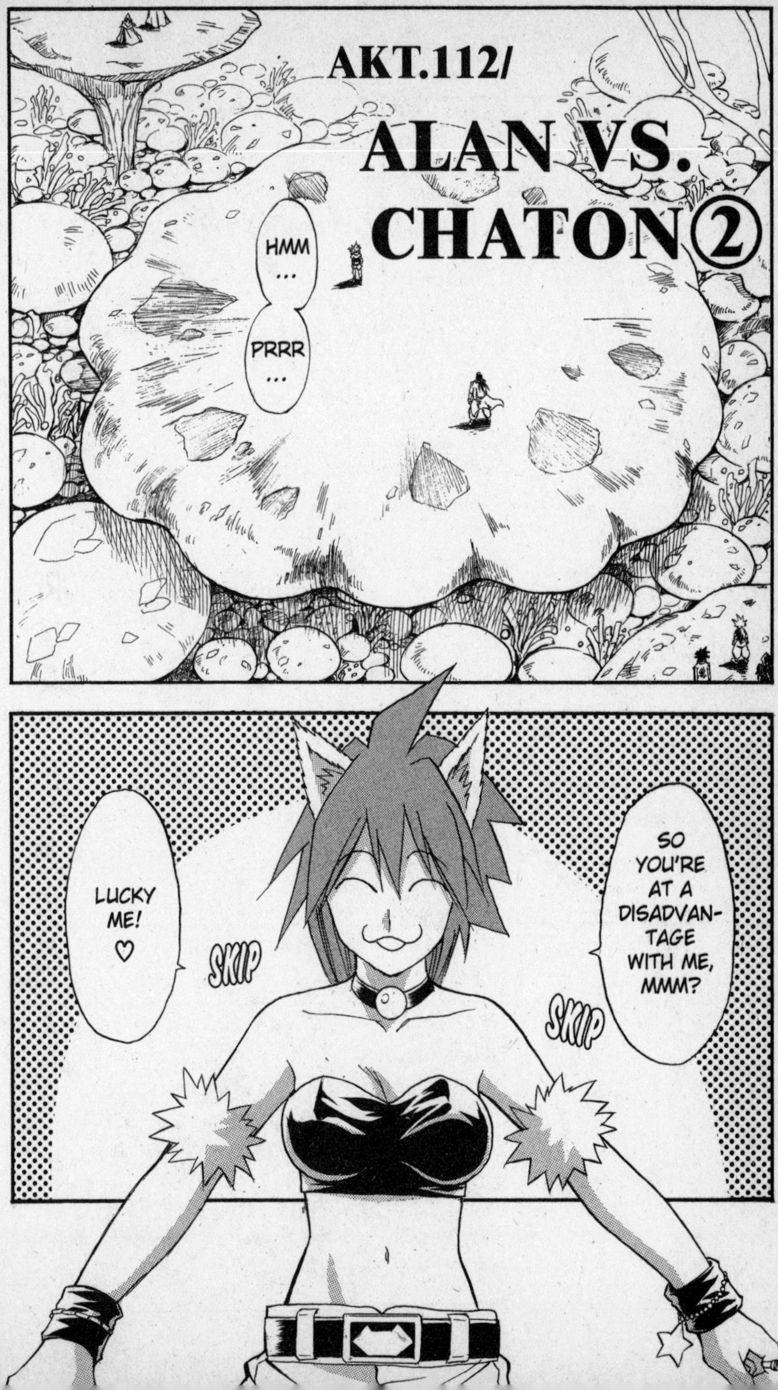
AKT.112/
ALAN VS. CHATON②
HMM...
PRRR...
SO YOU'RE AT A DISADVANTAGE WITH ME, MMM?
SKIP
SKIP
LUCKY ME! ♡

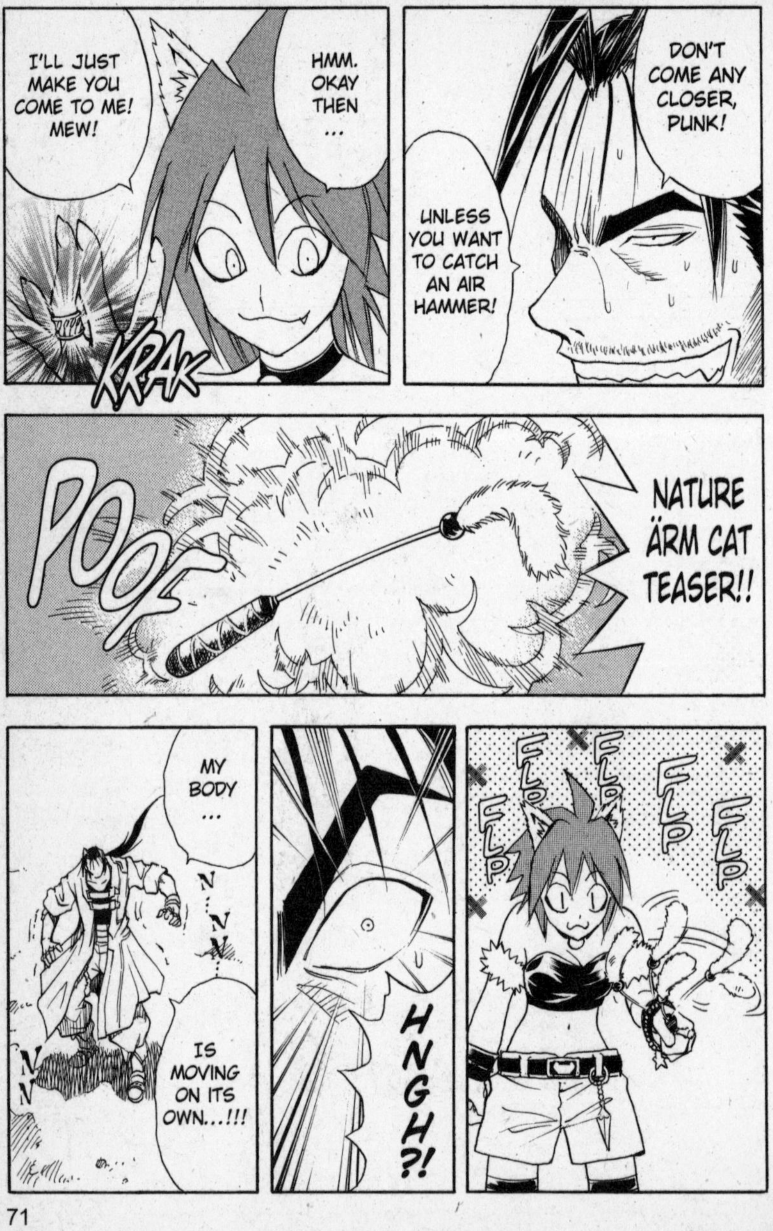
DON'T COME ANY CLOSER, PUNK!
UNLESS YOU WANT TO CATCH AN AIR HAMMER!
HMM. OKAY THEN ...
I'LL JUST MAKE YOU COME TO ME! MEW!
KRAK
NATURE ÄRM CAT TEASER!!
POOF
FLP FLP FLP FLP FLP
HNGH?!
MY BODY ...
N...NN...
IS MOVING ON ITS OWN...!!!
NN

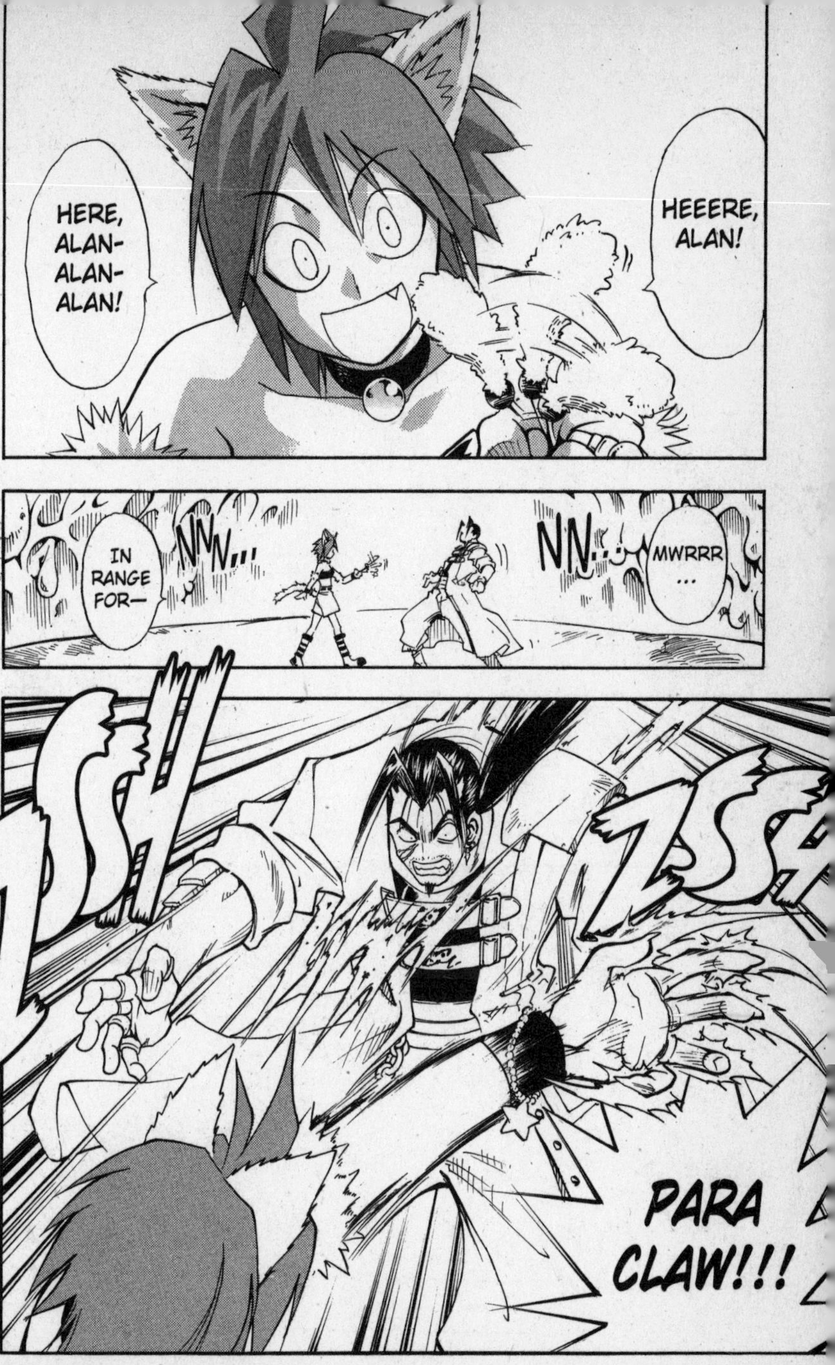
HEEERE, ALAN!
HERE, ALAN-ALAN-ALAN!
MWRRR ...
NN...
NNN...
IN RANGE FOR—
ZSH
ZSH
PARA CLAW!!!

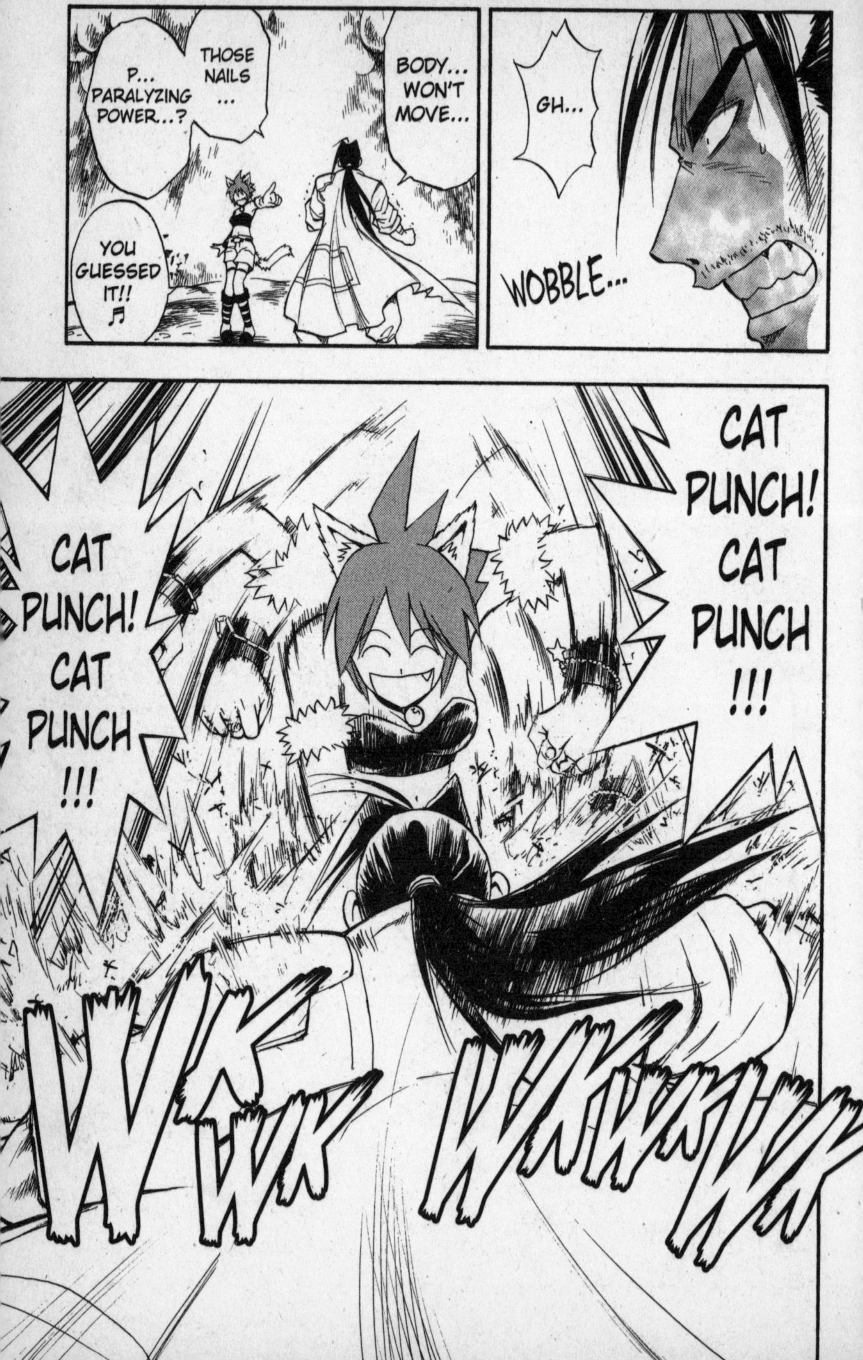
GH...
WOBBLE...
BODY... WON'T MOVE...
THOSE NAILS ...
P... PARALYZING POWER...?
YOU GUESSED IT!! ♫
CAT PUNCH! CAT PUNCH !!!
CAT PUNCH! CAT PUNCH !!!

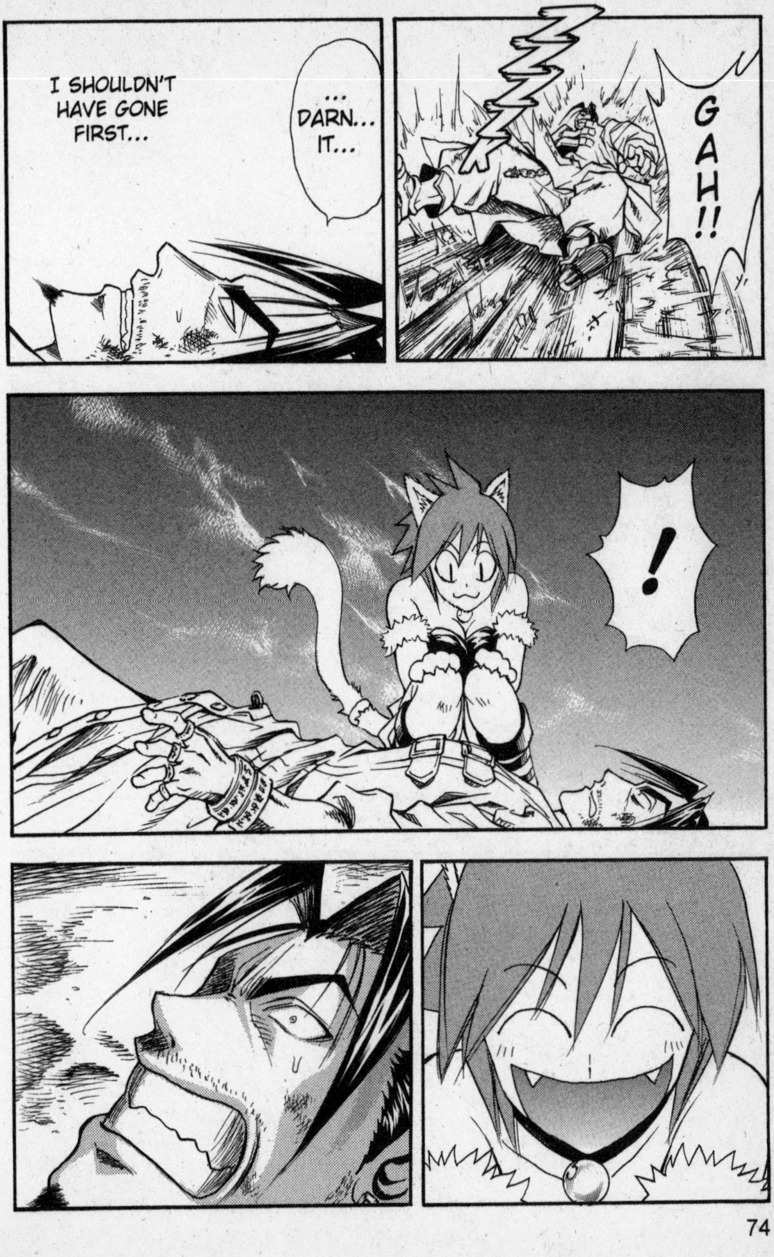
GAH!!
... DARN... IT...
I SHOULDN'T HAVE GONE FIRST...
!

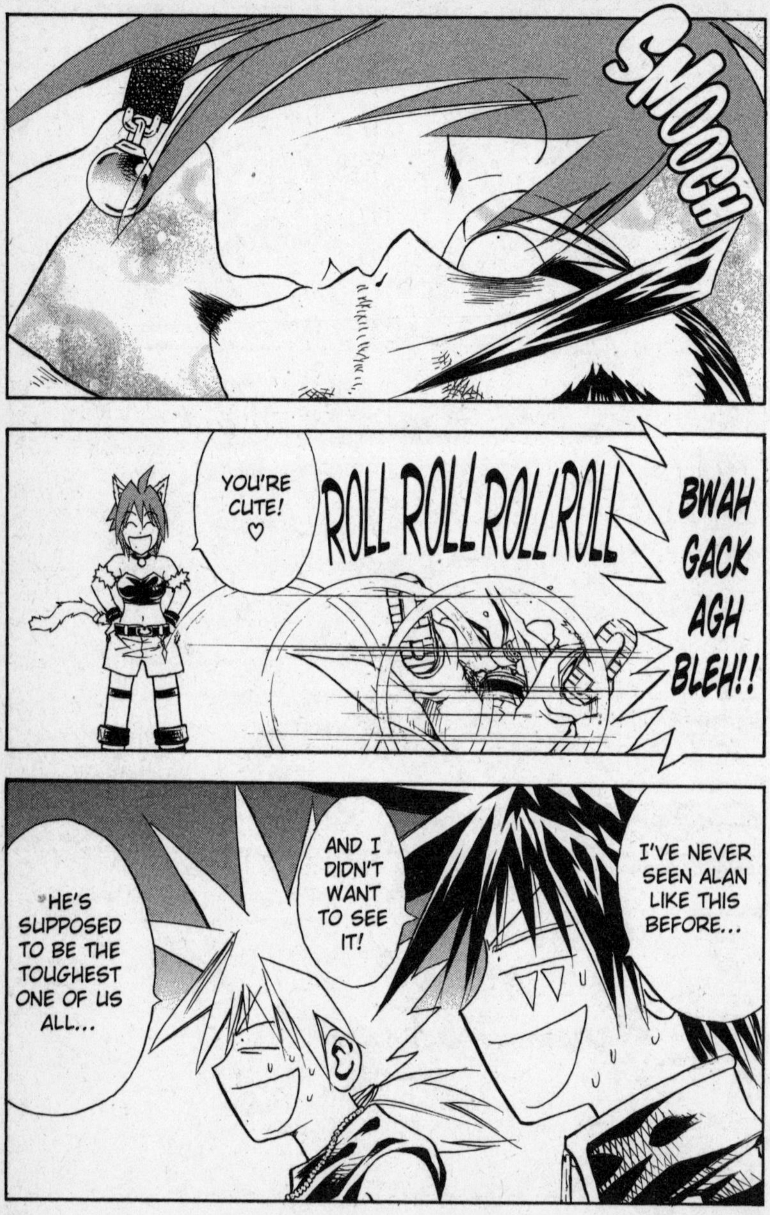
SMOOCH
BWAH GACK AGH BLEH!!
ROLL ROLL ROLL ROLL
YOU'RE CUTE! ♡
I'VE NEVER SEEN ALAN LIKE THIS BEFORE...
AND I DIDN'T WANT TO SEE IT!
HE'S SUPPOSED TO BE THE TOUGHEST ONE OF US ALL...

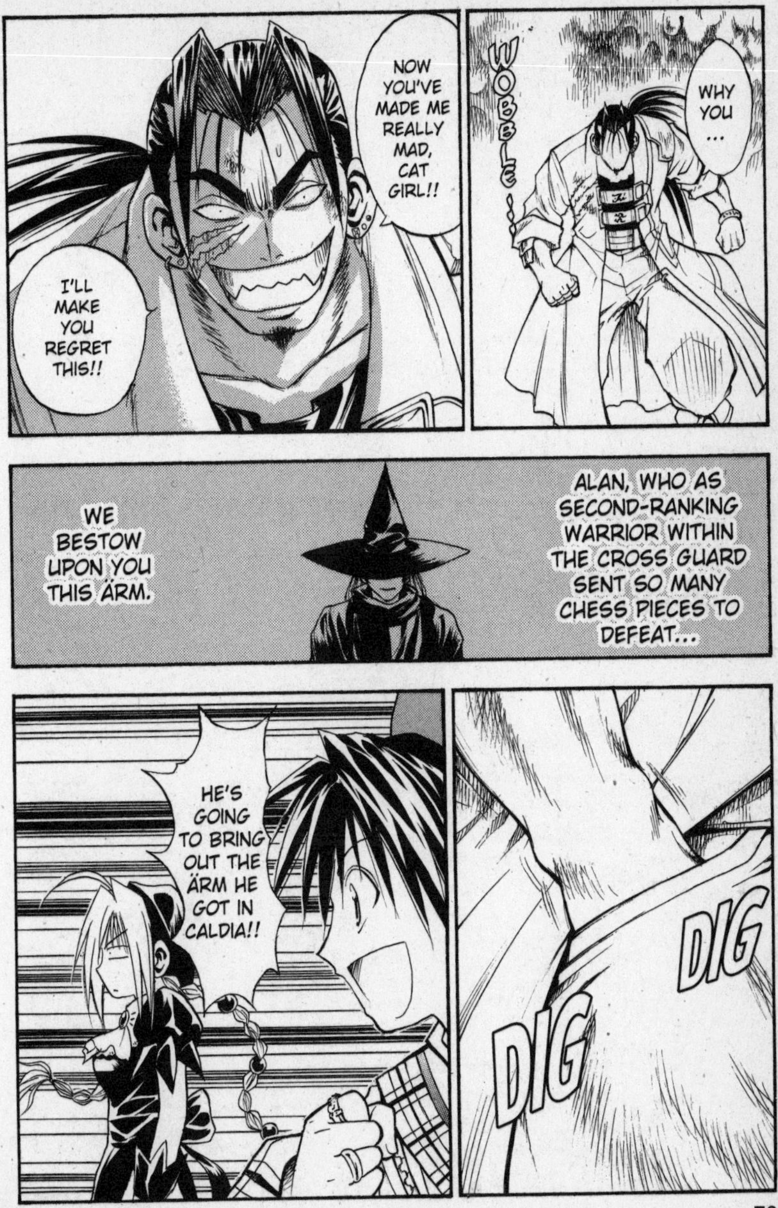
WOBBLE
WHY YOU...
NOW YOU'VE MADE ME REALLY MAD, CAT GIRL!!
I'LL MAKE YOU REGRET THIS!!
ALAN, WHO AS SECOND-RANKING WARRIOR WITHIN THE CROSS GUARD SENT SO MANY CHESS PIECES TO DEFEAT...
WE BESTOW UPON YOU THIS ÄRM.
DIG
DIG
HE'S GOING TO BRING OUT THE ÄRM HE GOT IN CALDIA!!

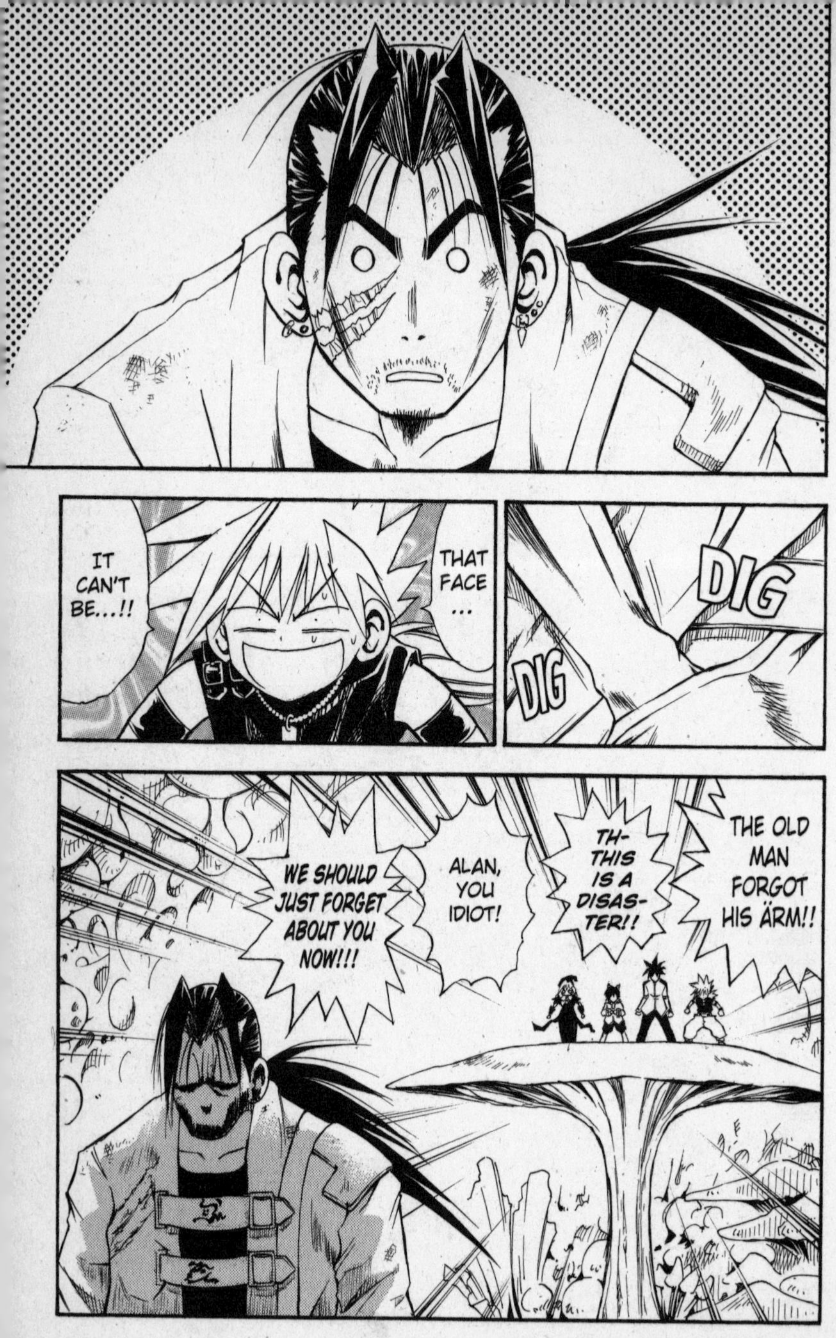
DIG
DIG
THAT FACE...
IT CAN'T BE...!!
THE OLD MAN FORGOT HIS ÄRM!!
TH-THIS IS A DISASTER!!
ALAN, YOU IDIOT!
WE SHOULD JUST FORGET ABOUT YOU NOW!!!

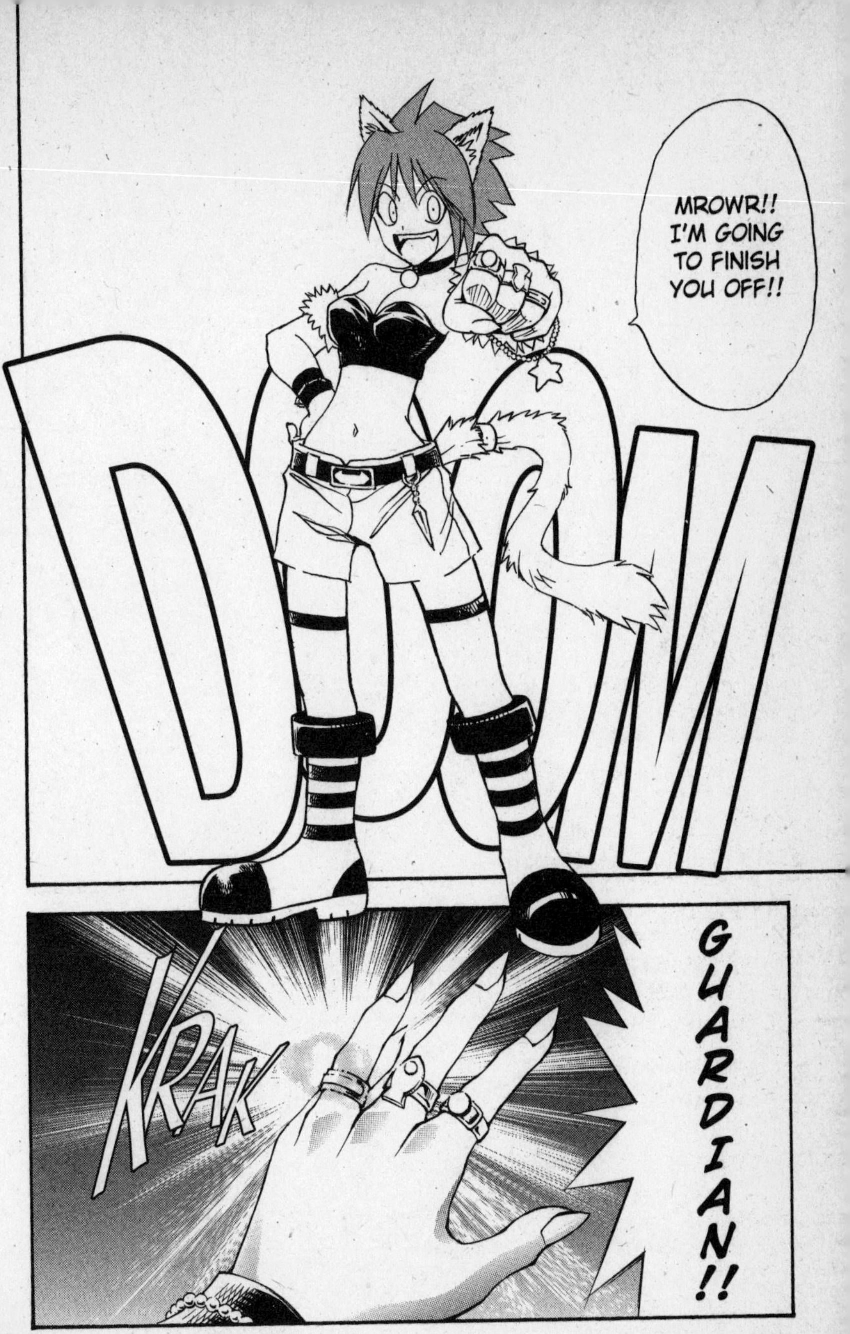
MROWR!! I'M GOING TO FINISH YOU OFF!!
DOOM
GUARDIAN!!
KRAK

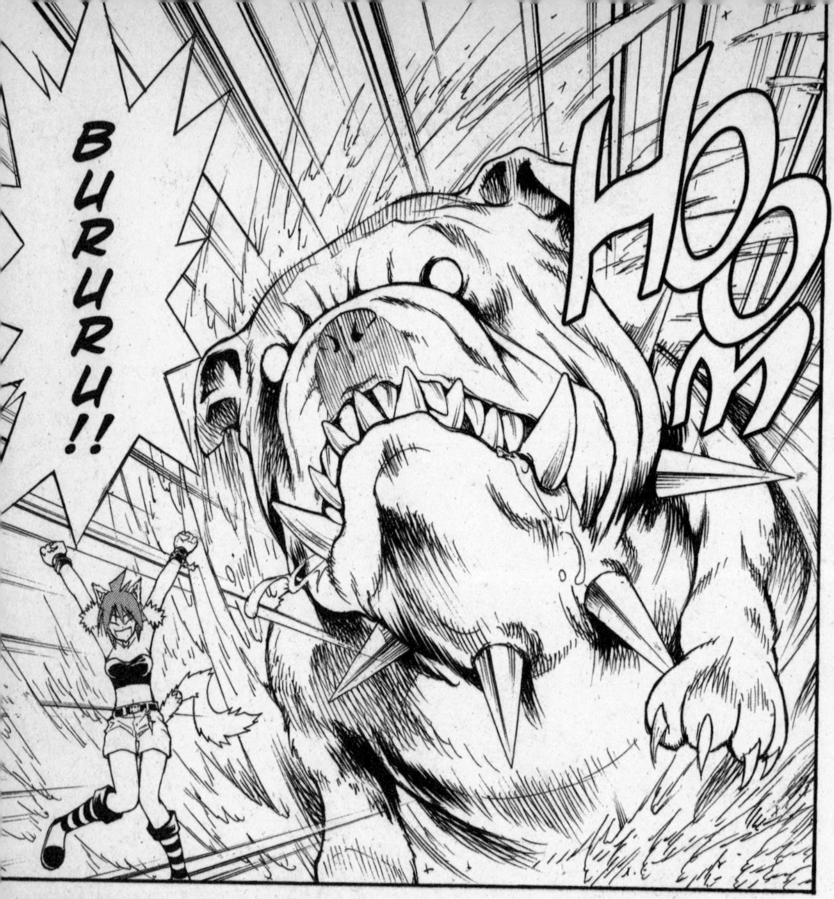
HOON
BURURU!!
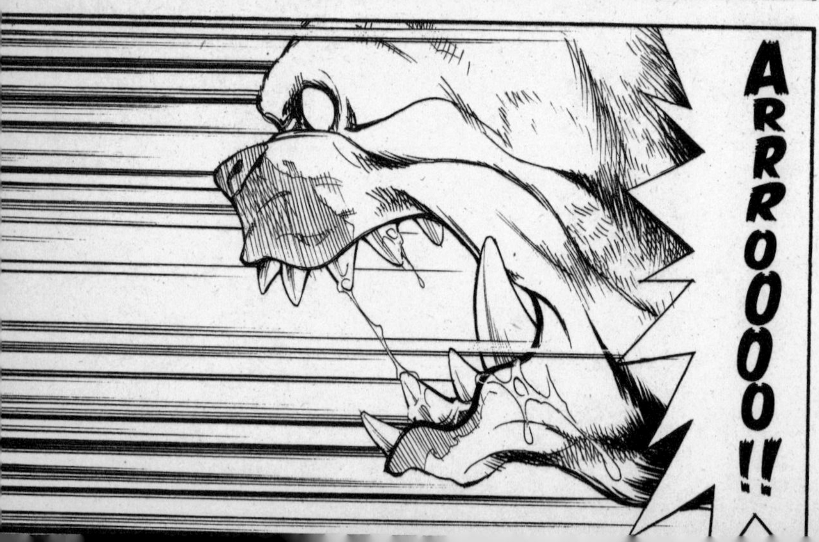
ARRROOOO!!

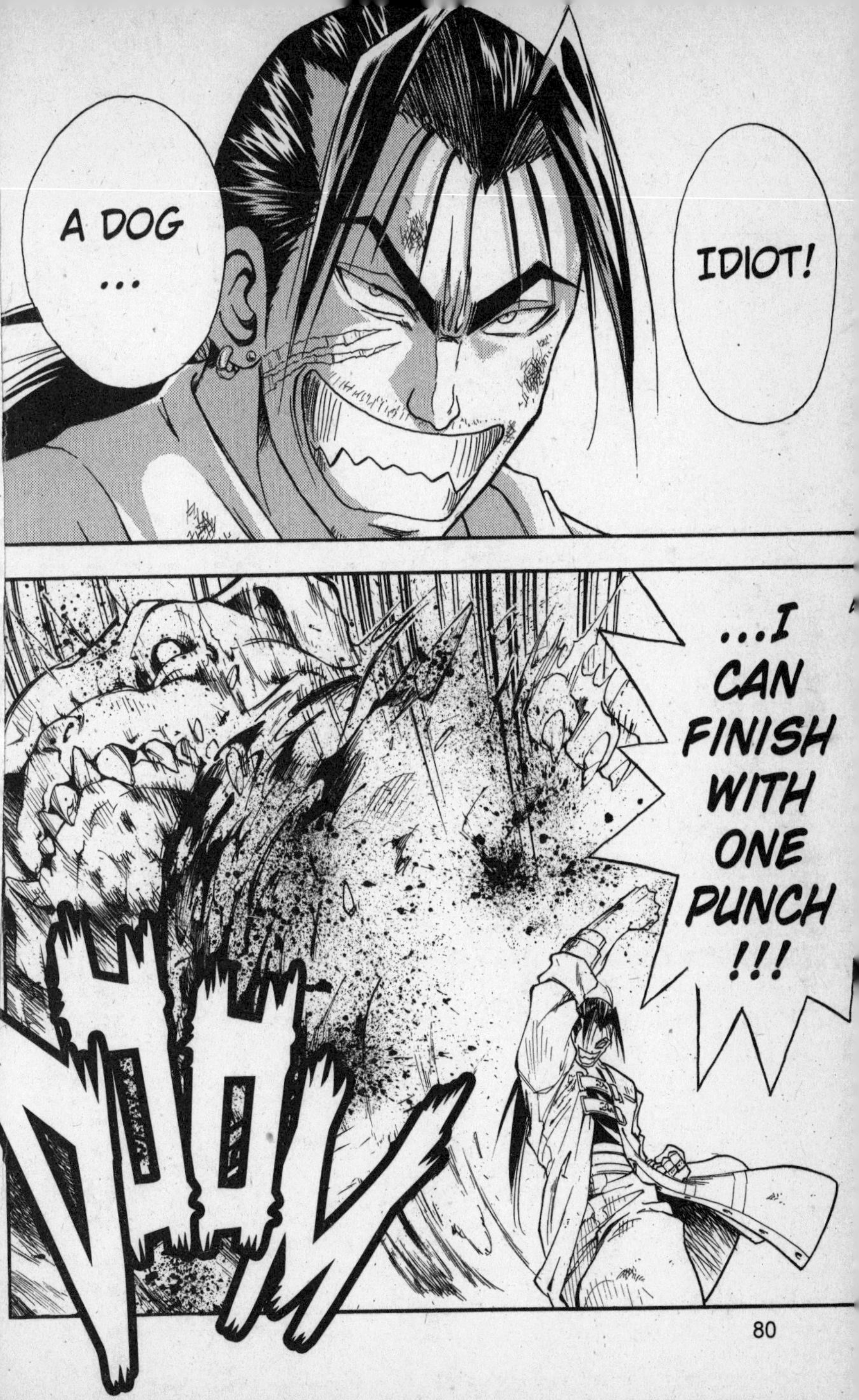
IDIOT!
A DOG ...
...I CAN FINISH WITH ONE PUNCH !!!

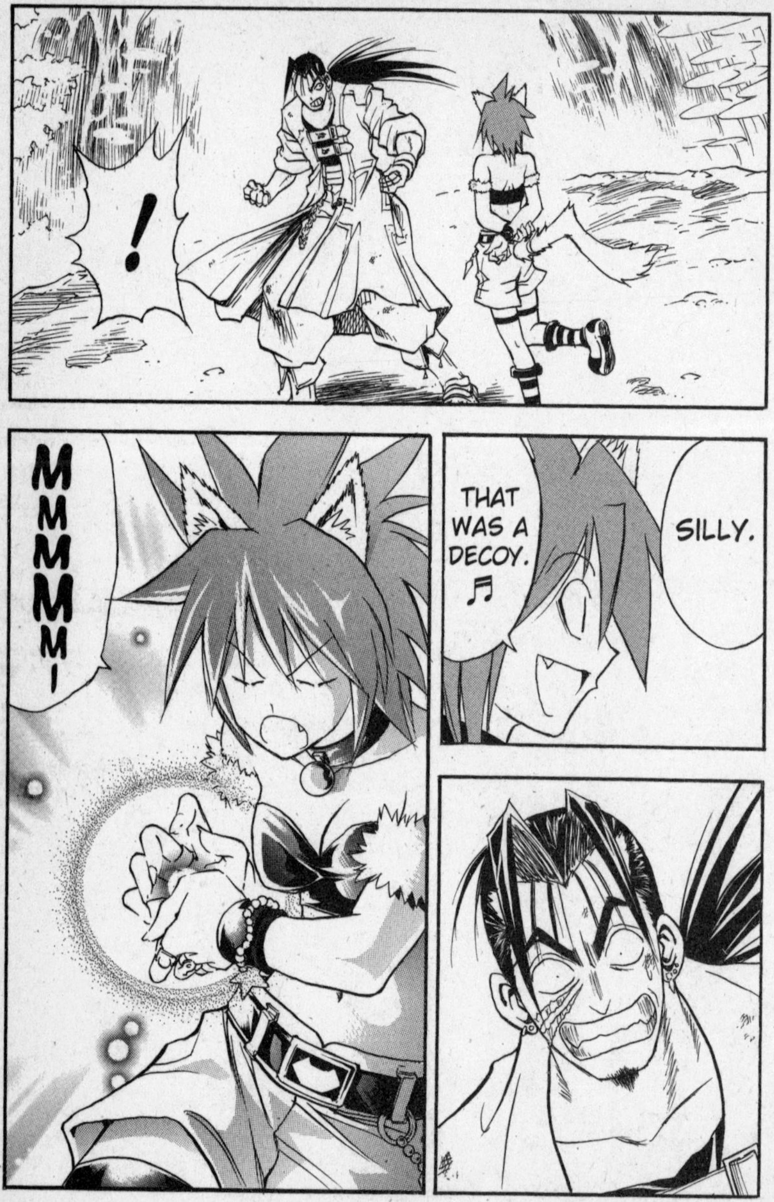
!
SILLY.
THAT WAS A DECOY. ♬
MMMMMI

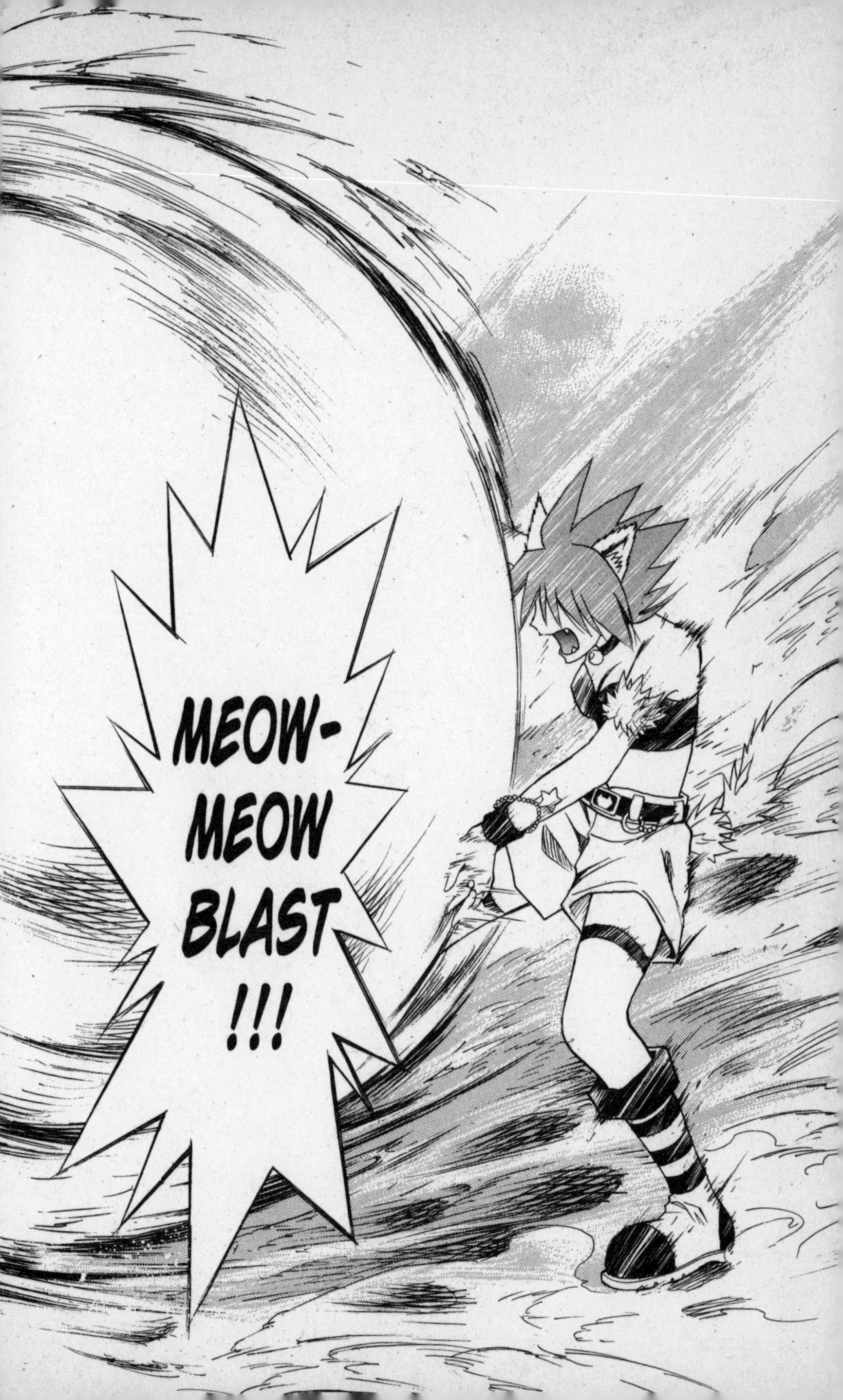
MEOW-MEOW BLAST!!!

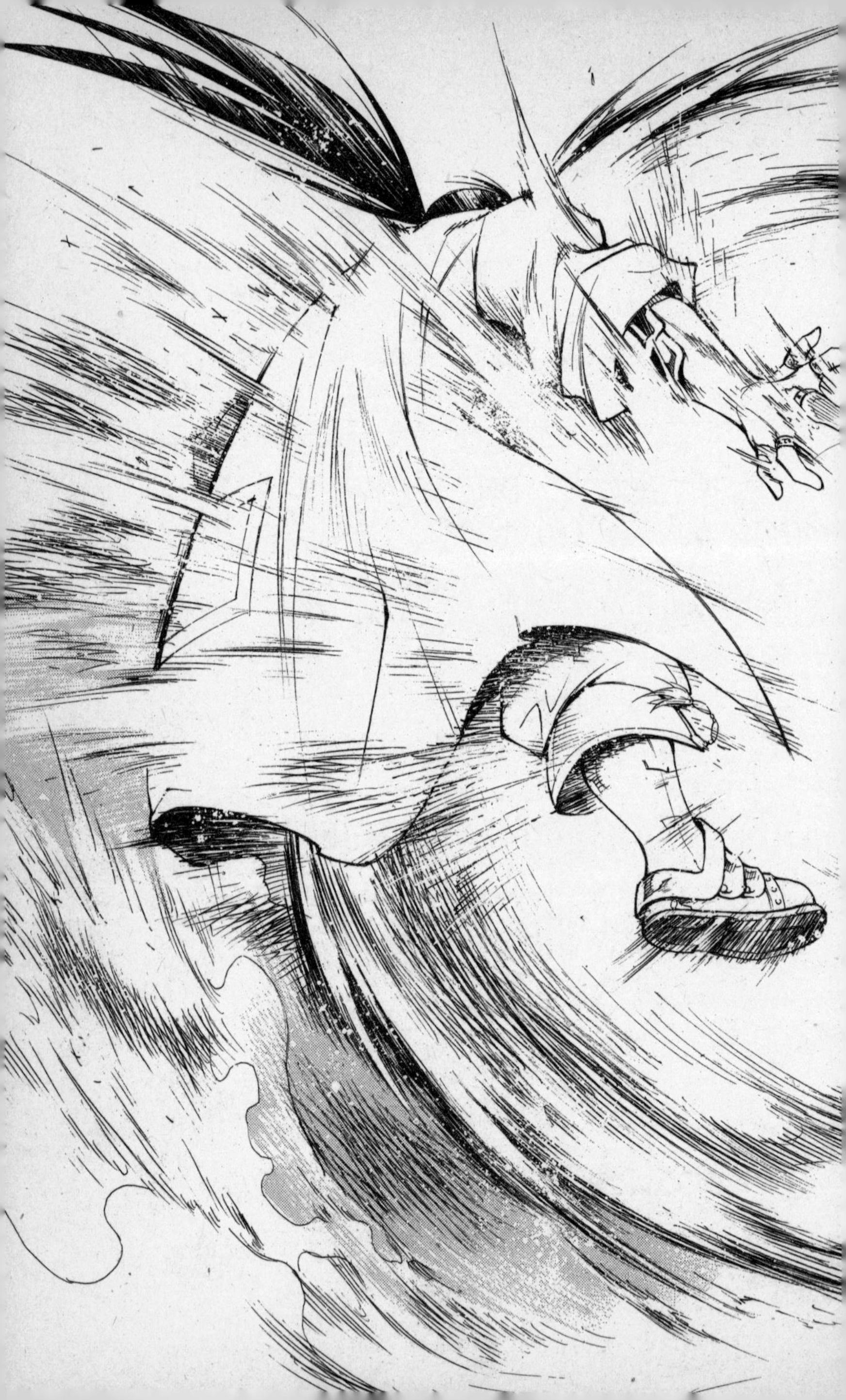

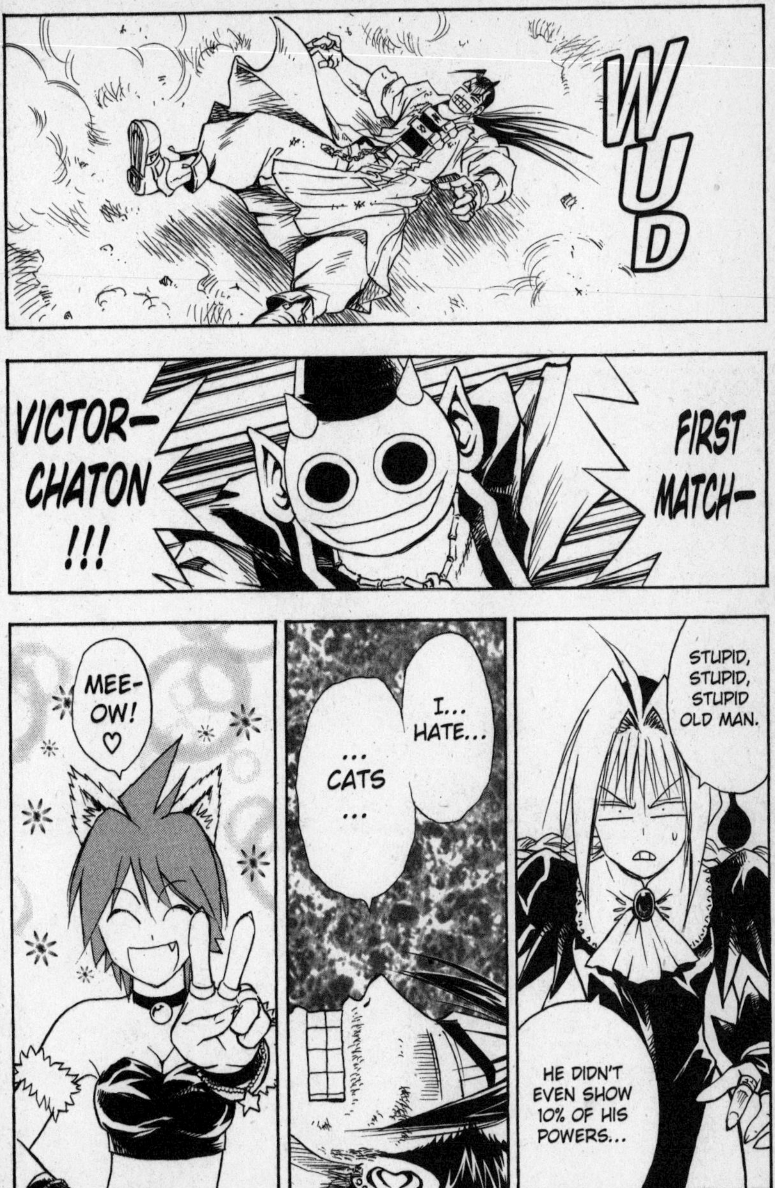
WUD
FIRST MATCH-
VICTOR-CHATON!!!
STUPID, STUPID, STUPID OLD MAN.
HE DIDN'T EVEN SHOW 10% OF HIS POWERS...
I... HATE...
... CATS ...
MEE-OW! ♡

AKT.113/ ALVISS VS. KOGA①

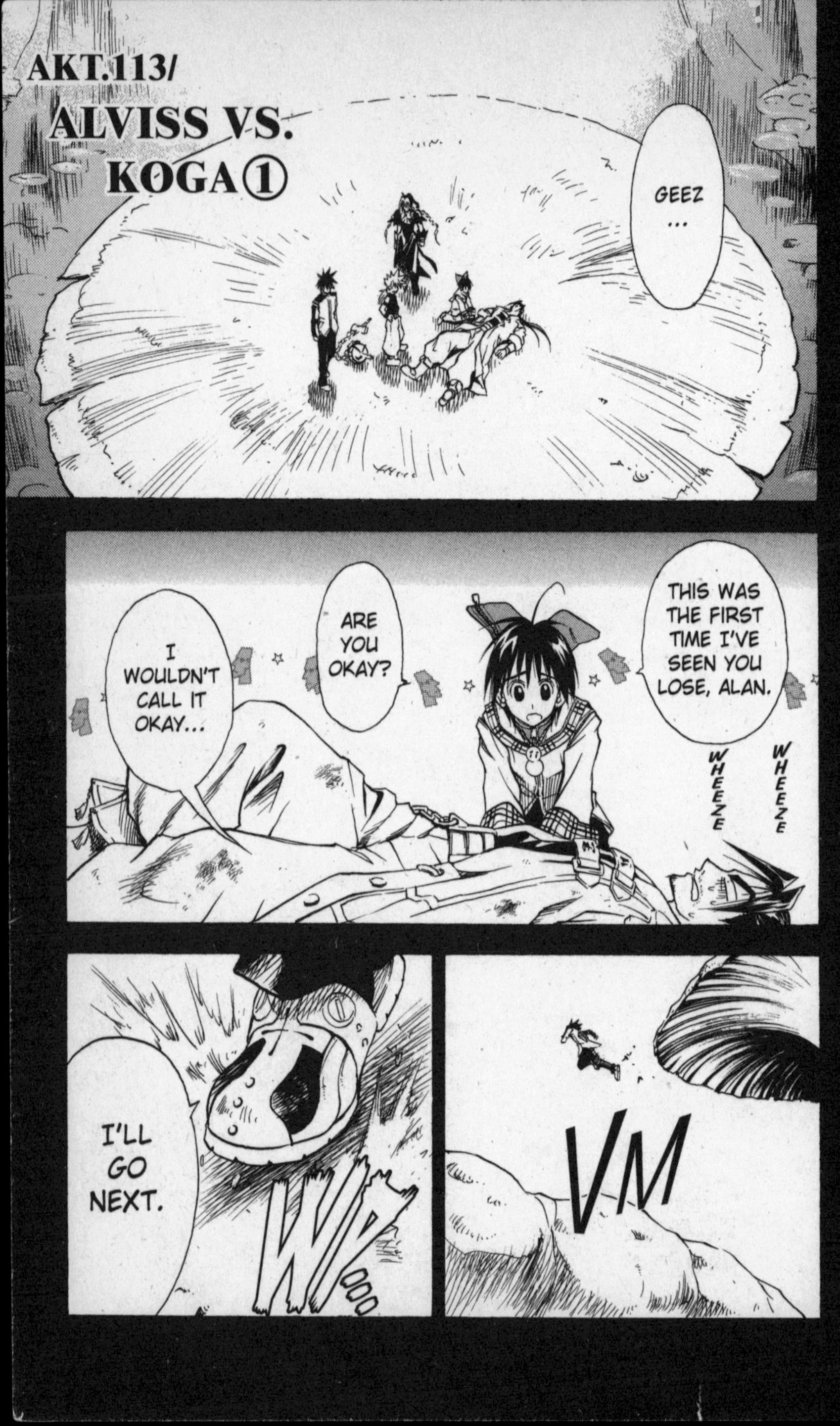
GEEZ ...
THIS WAS THE FIRST TIME I'VE SEEN YOU LOSE, ALAN.
WHEEZE
WHEEZE
ARE YOU OKAY?
I WOULDN'T CALL IT OKAY...
VM
I'LL GO NEXT.

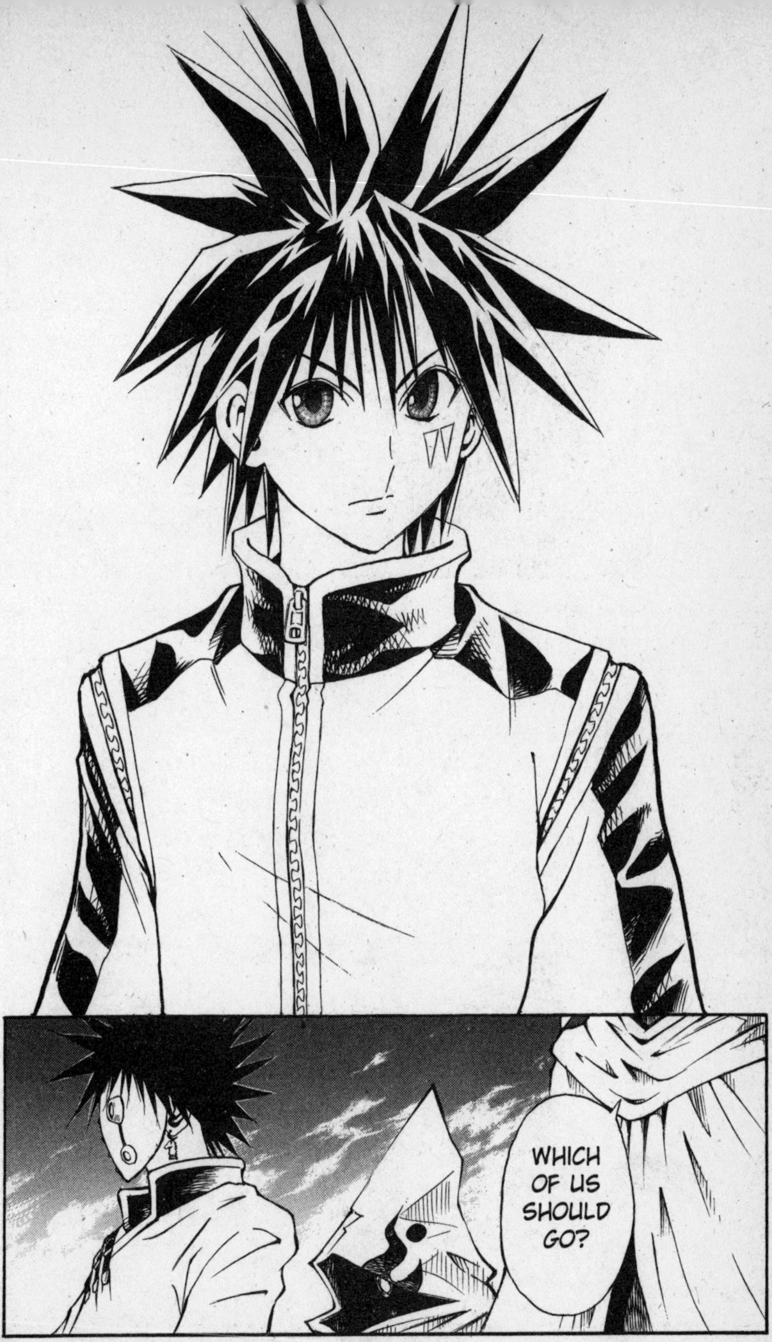
WHICH OF US SHOULD GO?

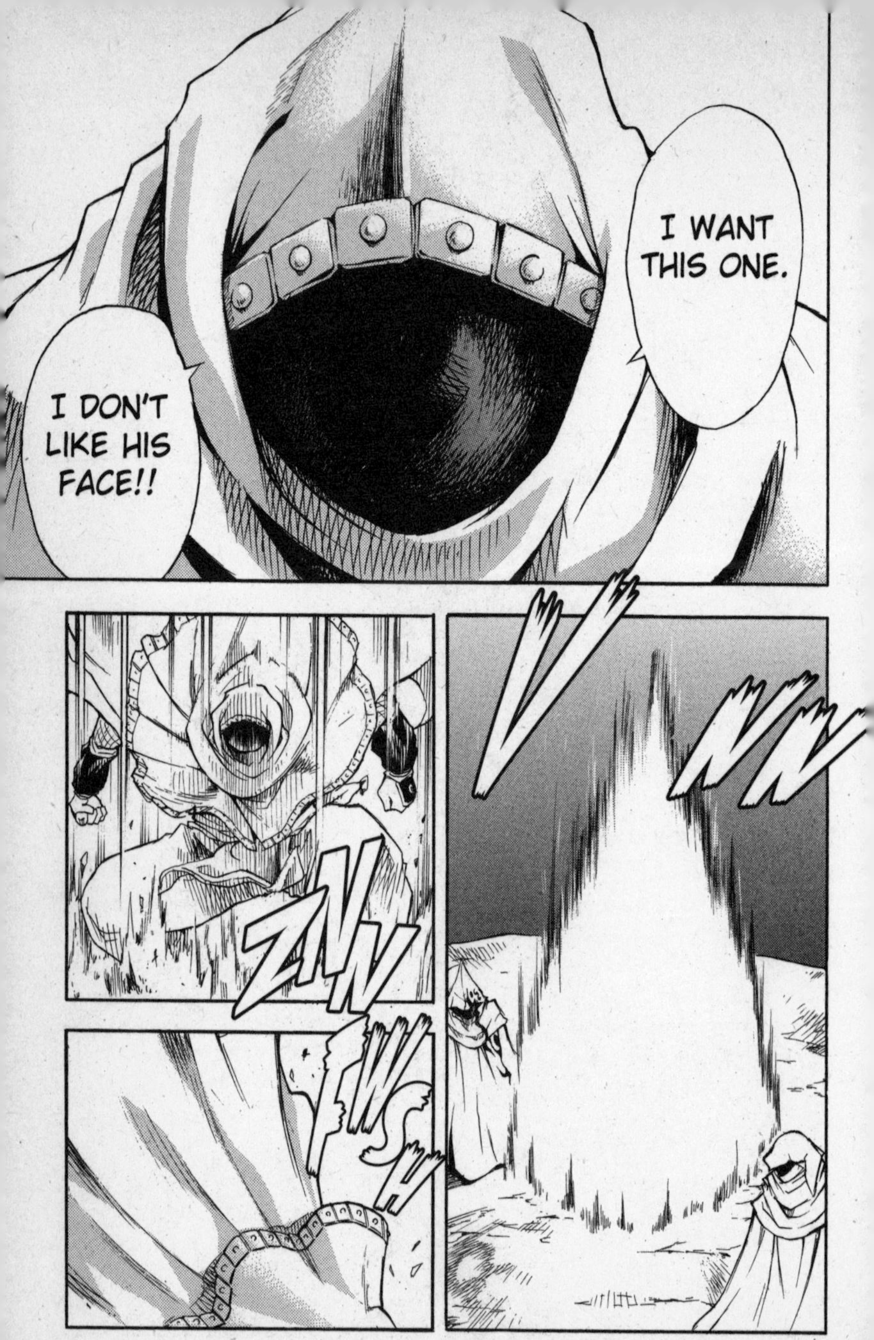
I WANT THIS ONE.
I DON'T LIKE HIS FACE!!
ZNN

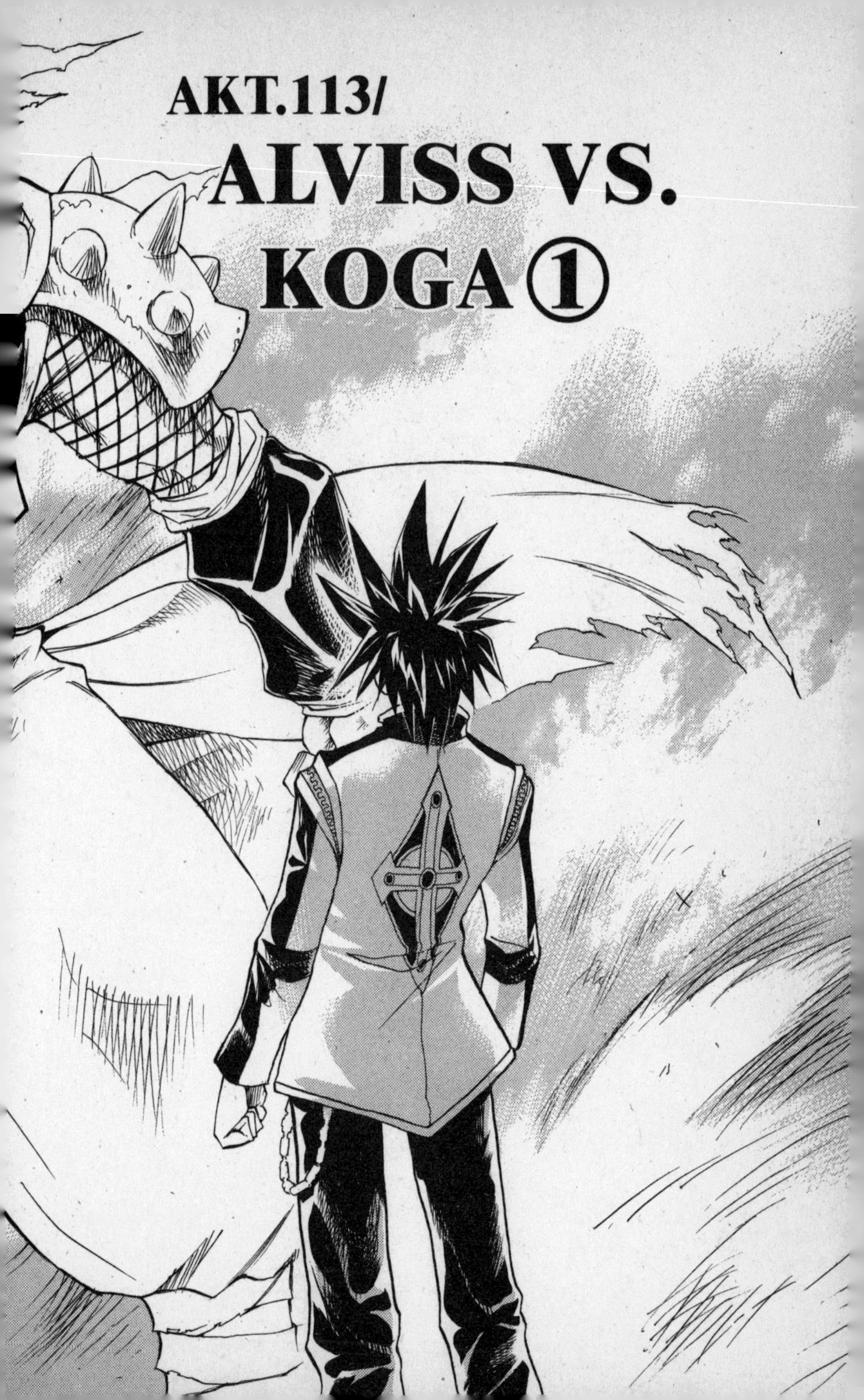
AKT.113/
ALVISS VS.
KOGA ①

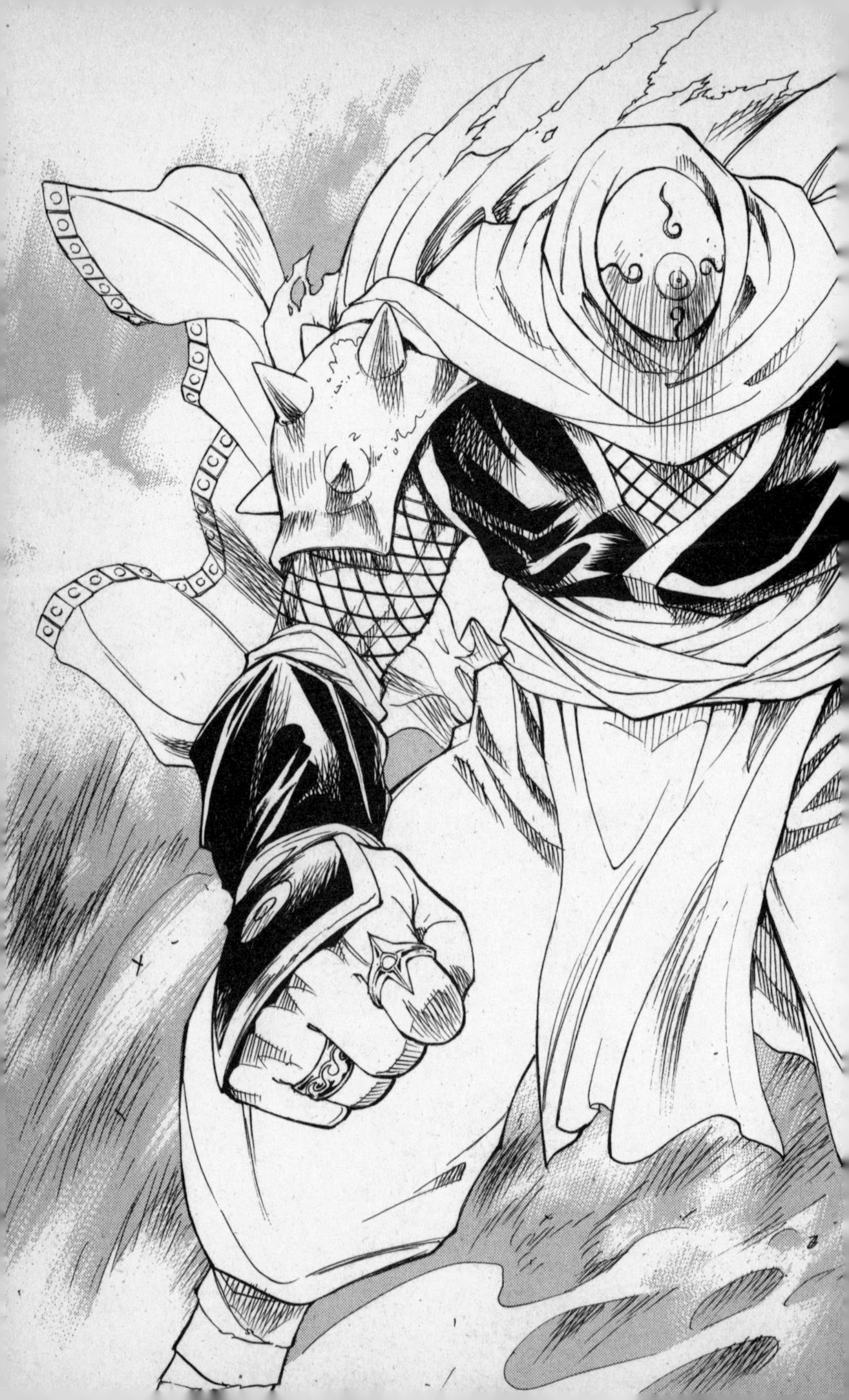

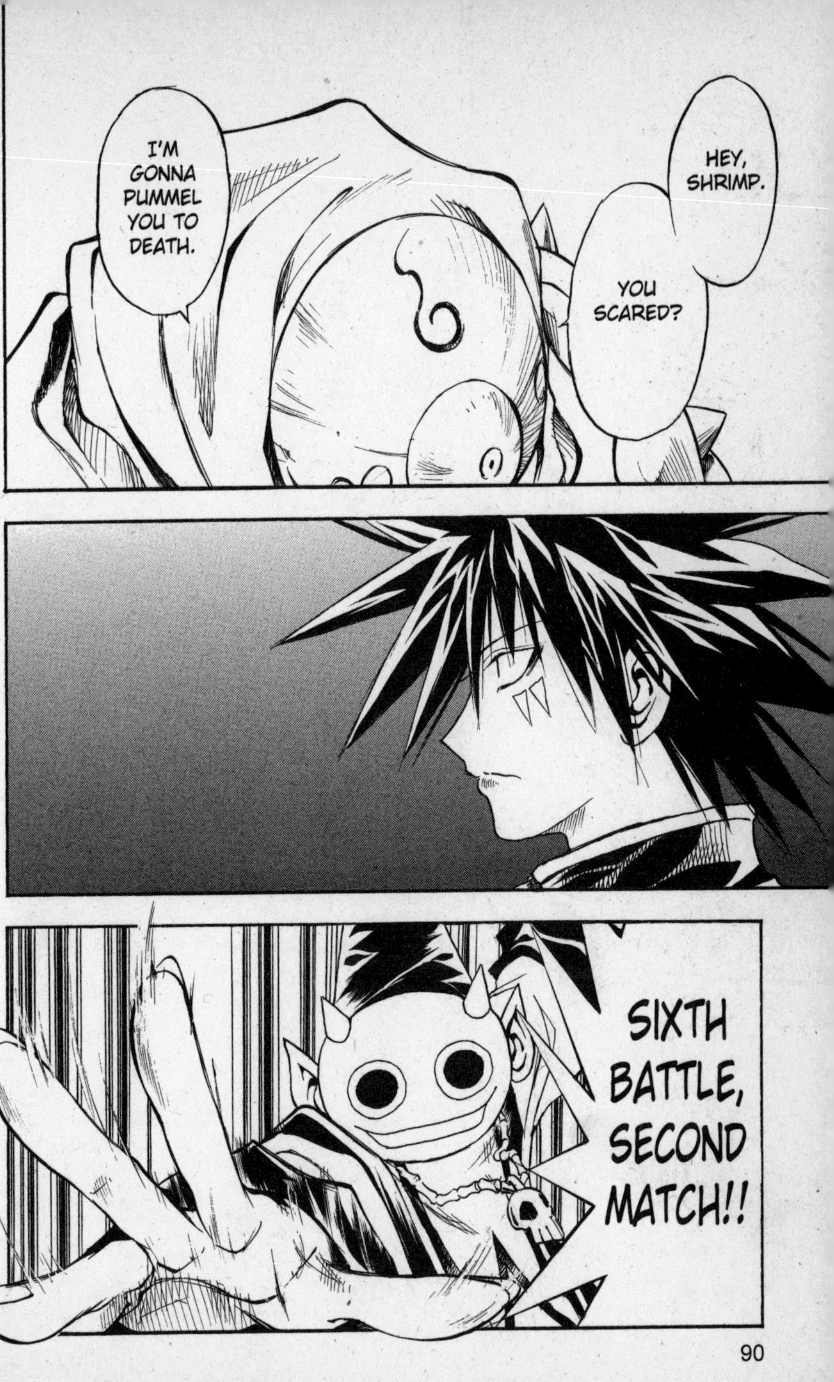
HEY, SHRIMP.
YOU SCARED?
I'M GONNA PUMMEL YOU TO DEATH.
SIXTH BATTLE, SECOND MATCH!!

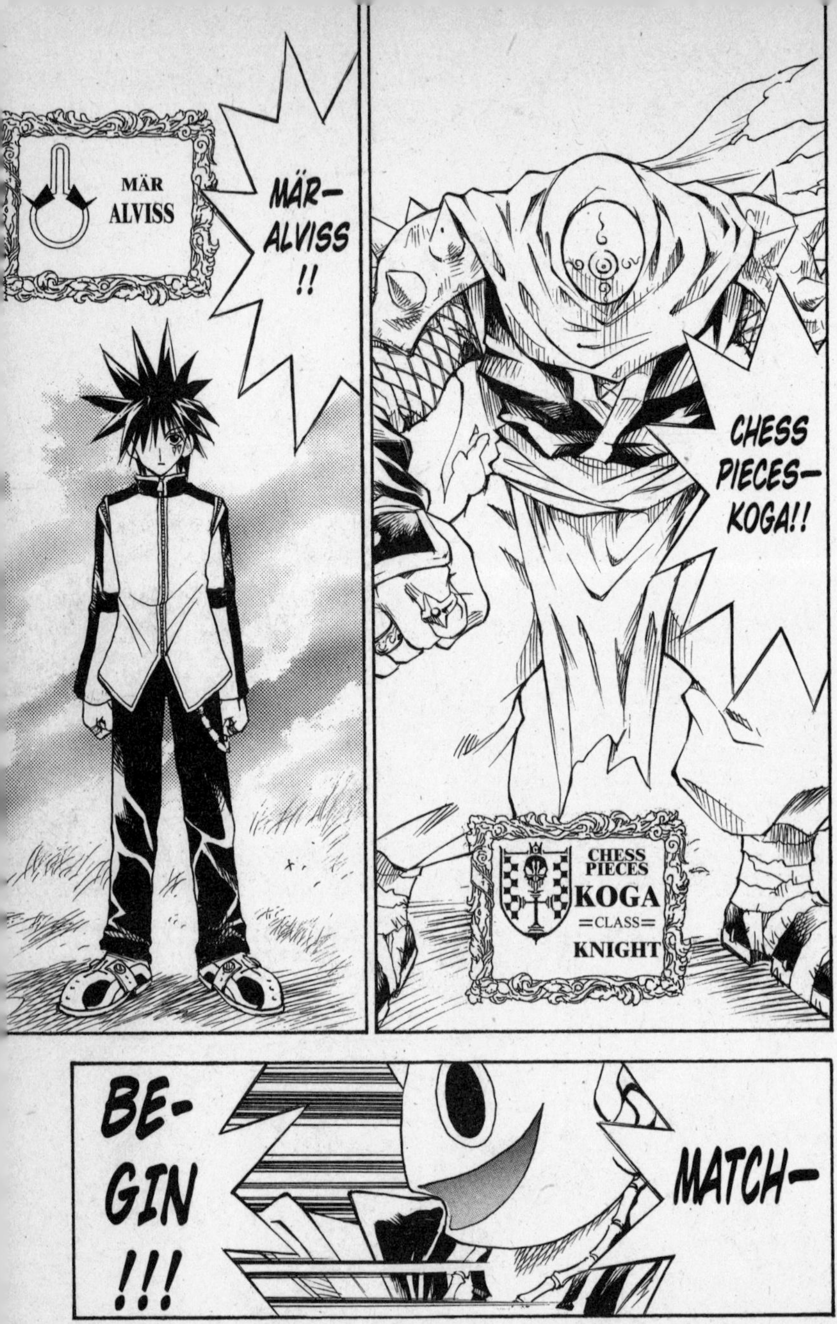
CHESS PIECES-KOGA!!
CHESS PIECES KOGA =CLASS= KNIGHT
MÄR-ALVISS!!
MÄR ALVISS
MATCH-
BE-GIN!!!

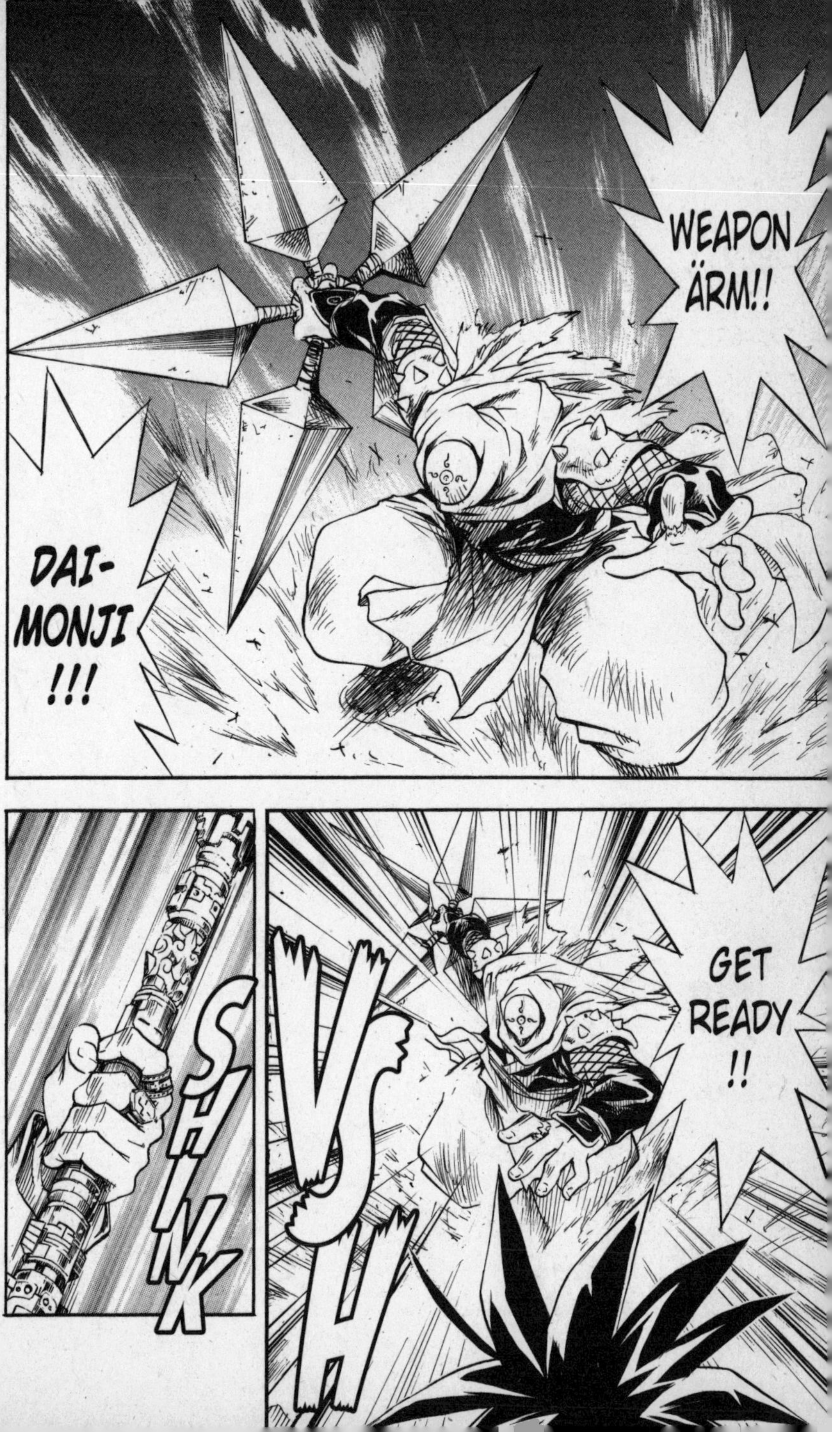
WEAPON ÄRM!!
DAI-MONJI!!!
GET READY!!
SHINK

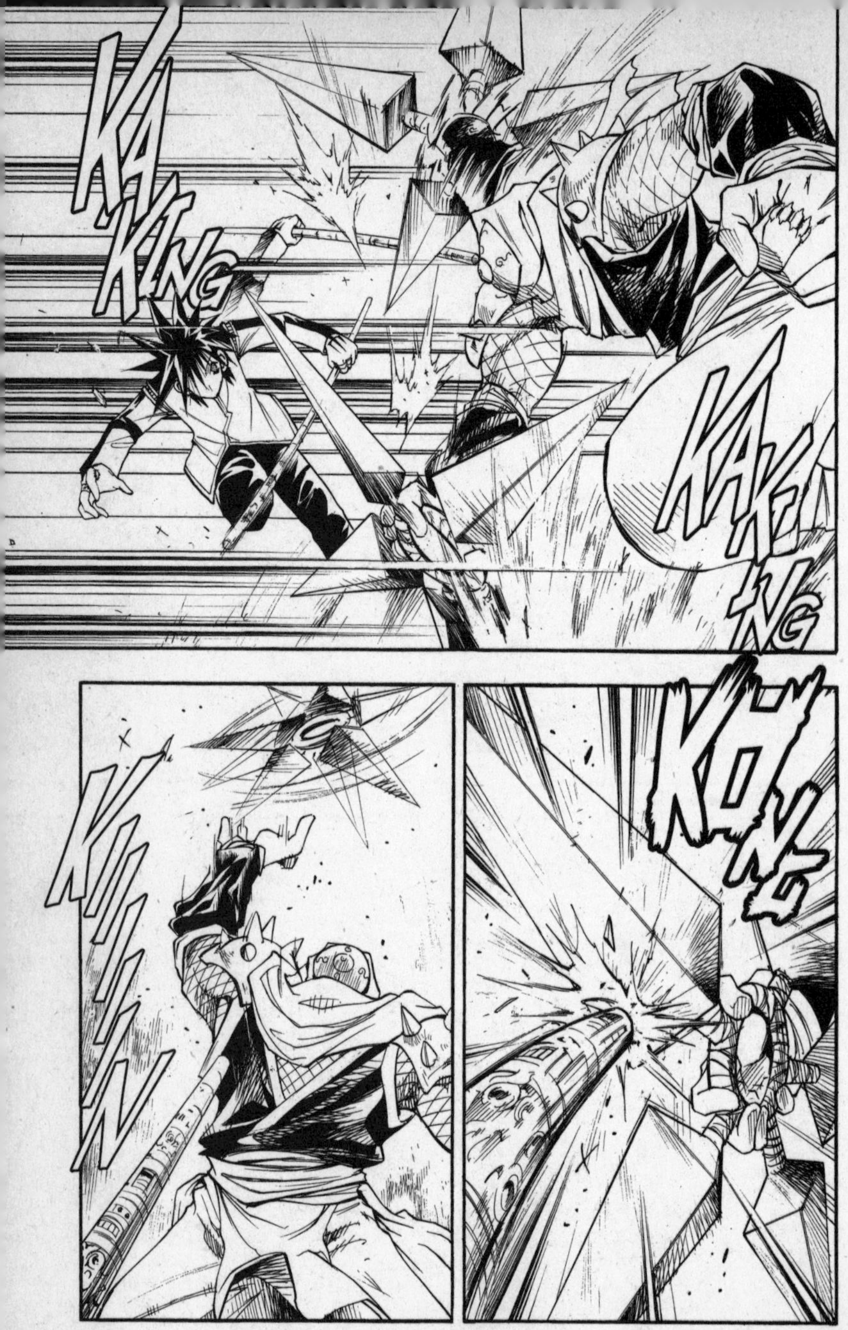
KAKING
KAKING
KONG
KIIIIIN

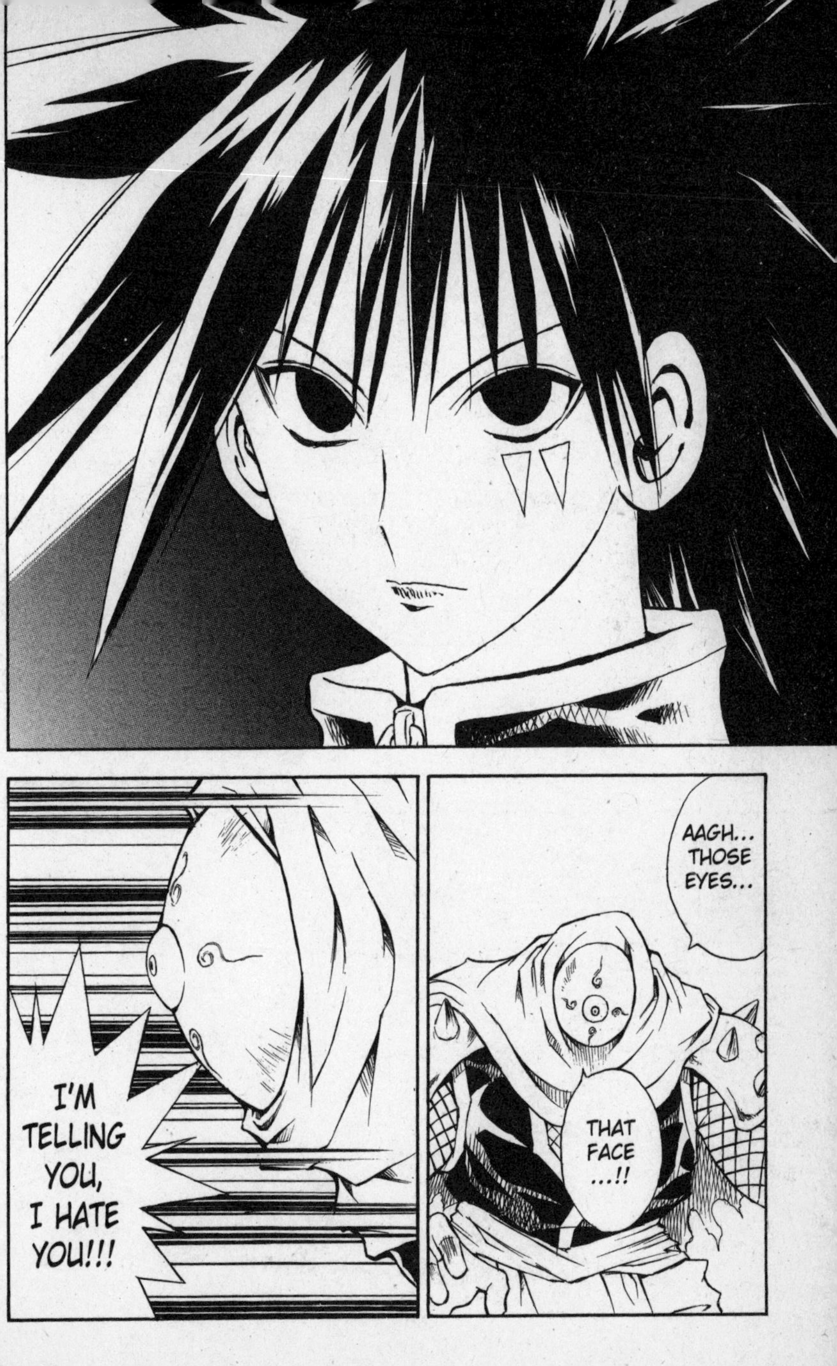
AAGH... THOSE EYES...
THAT FACE ...!!
I'M TELLING YOU, I HATE YOU!!!

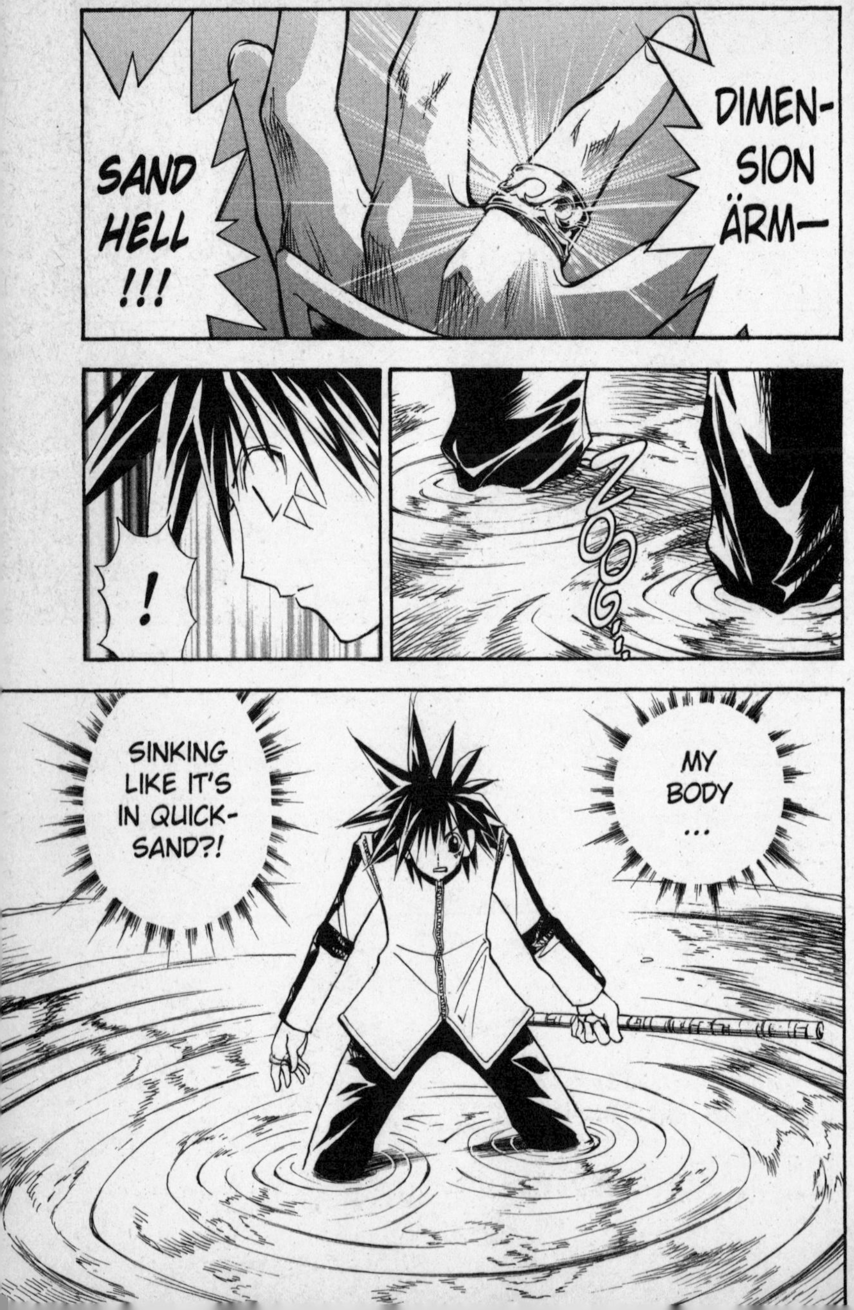
DIMEN-SION ÄRM—
SAND HELL !!!
ZOOG...
!
MY BODY ...
SINKING LIKE IT'S IN QUICK-SAND?!

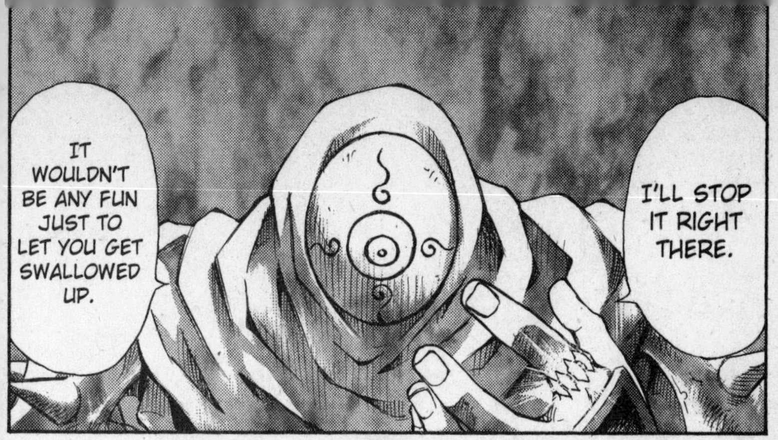
I'LL STOP IT RIGHT THERE.
IT WOULDN'T BE ANY FUN JUST TO LET YOU GET SWALLOWED UP.
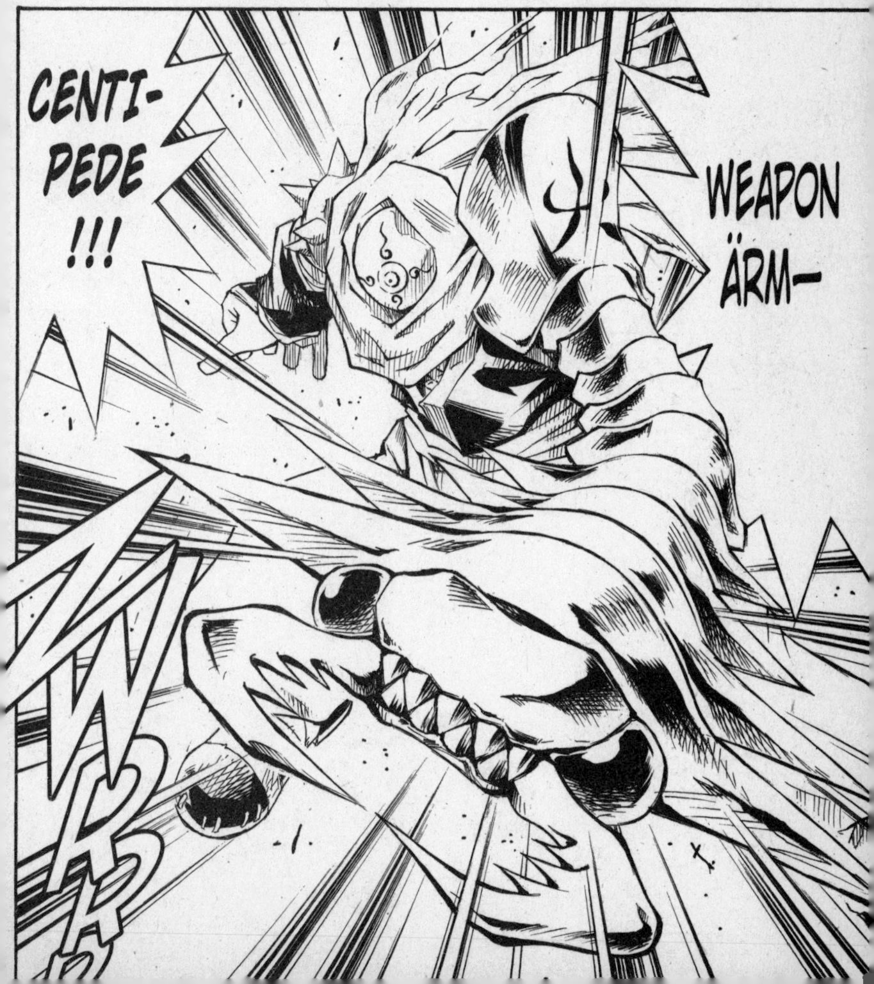
WEAPON ÄRM-
CENTI-PEDE !!!

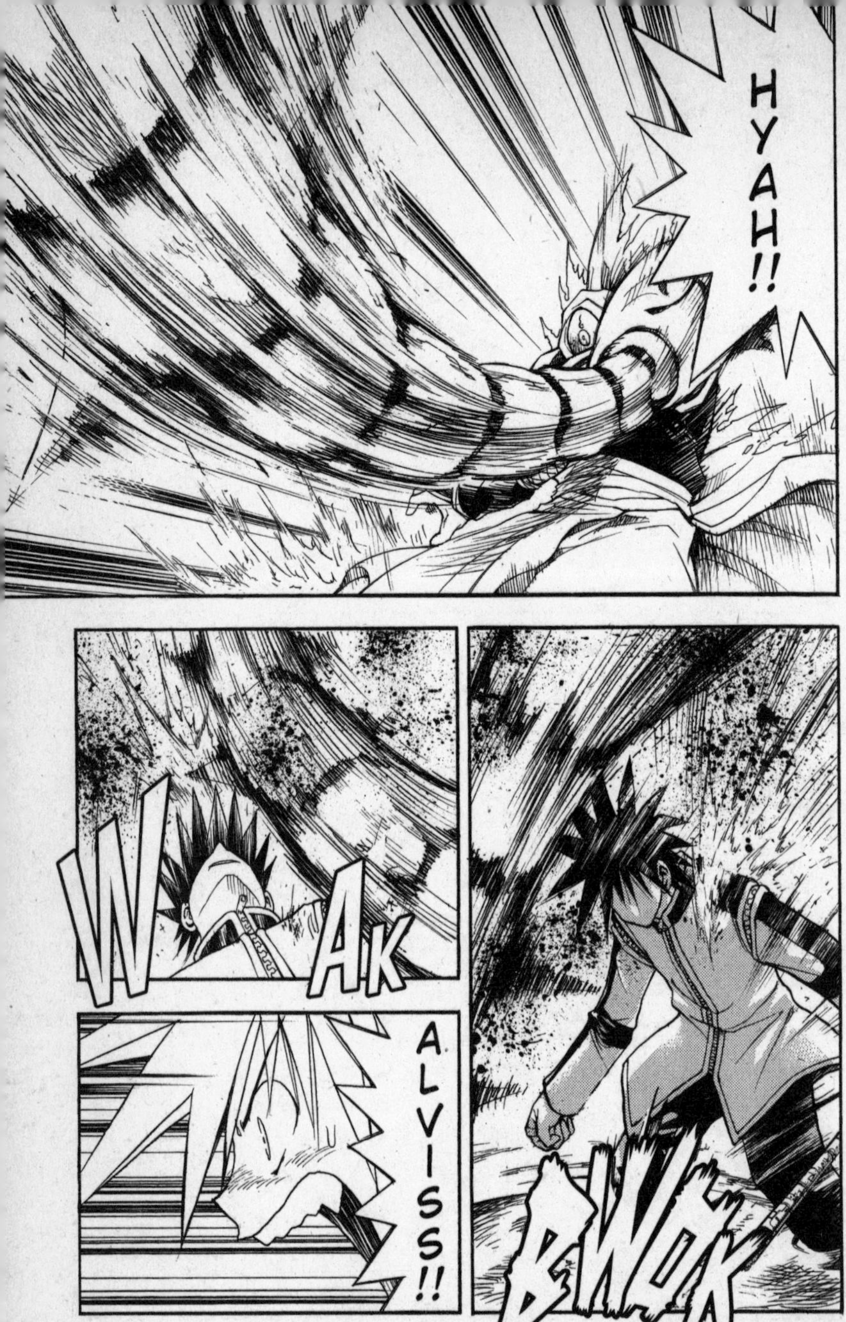
HYAH!!
BWOK
WAK
ALVISS!!

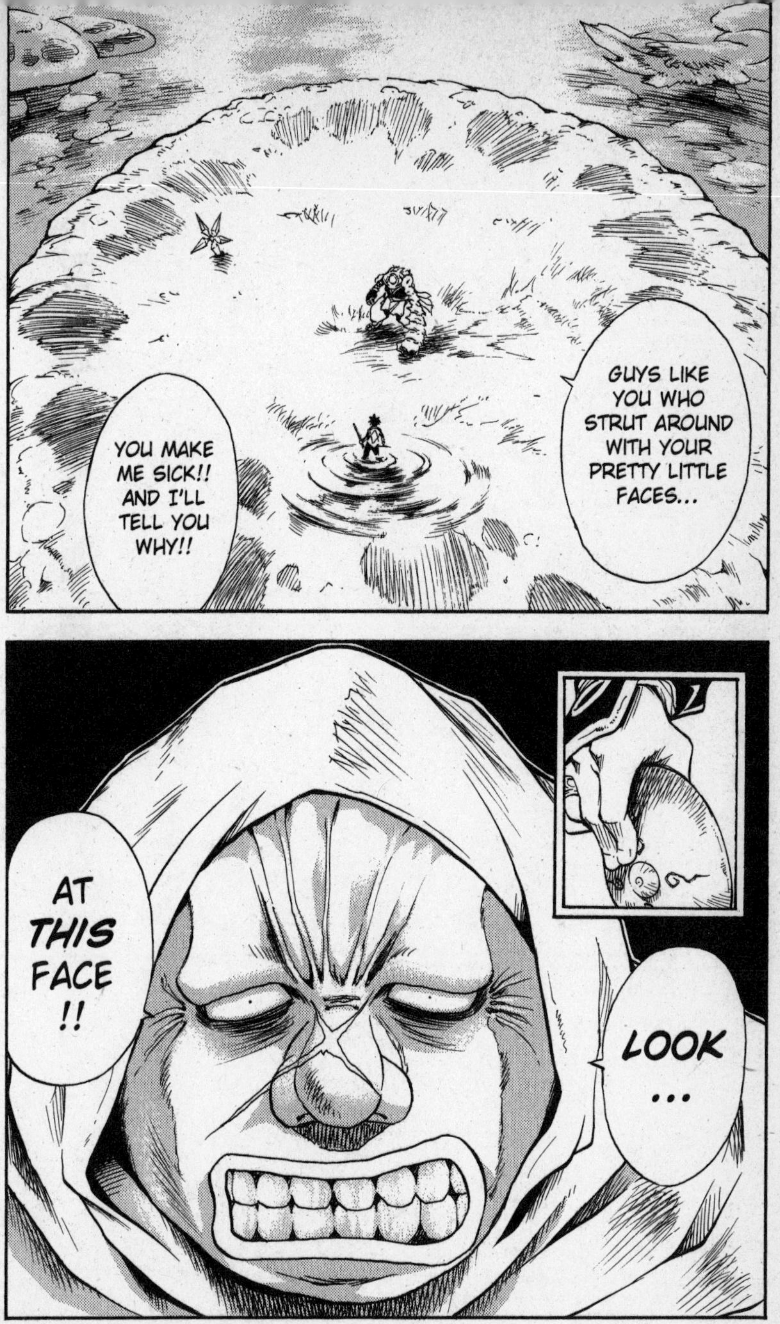
GUYS LIKE YOU WHO STRUT AROUND WITH YOUR PRETTY LITTLE FACES...
YOU MAKE ME SICK!! AND I'LL TELL YOU WHY!!
LOOK ...
AT *THIS* FACE !!

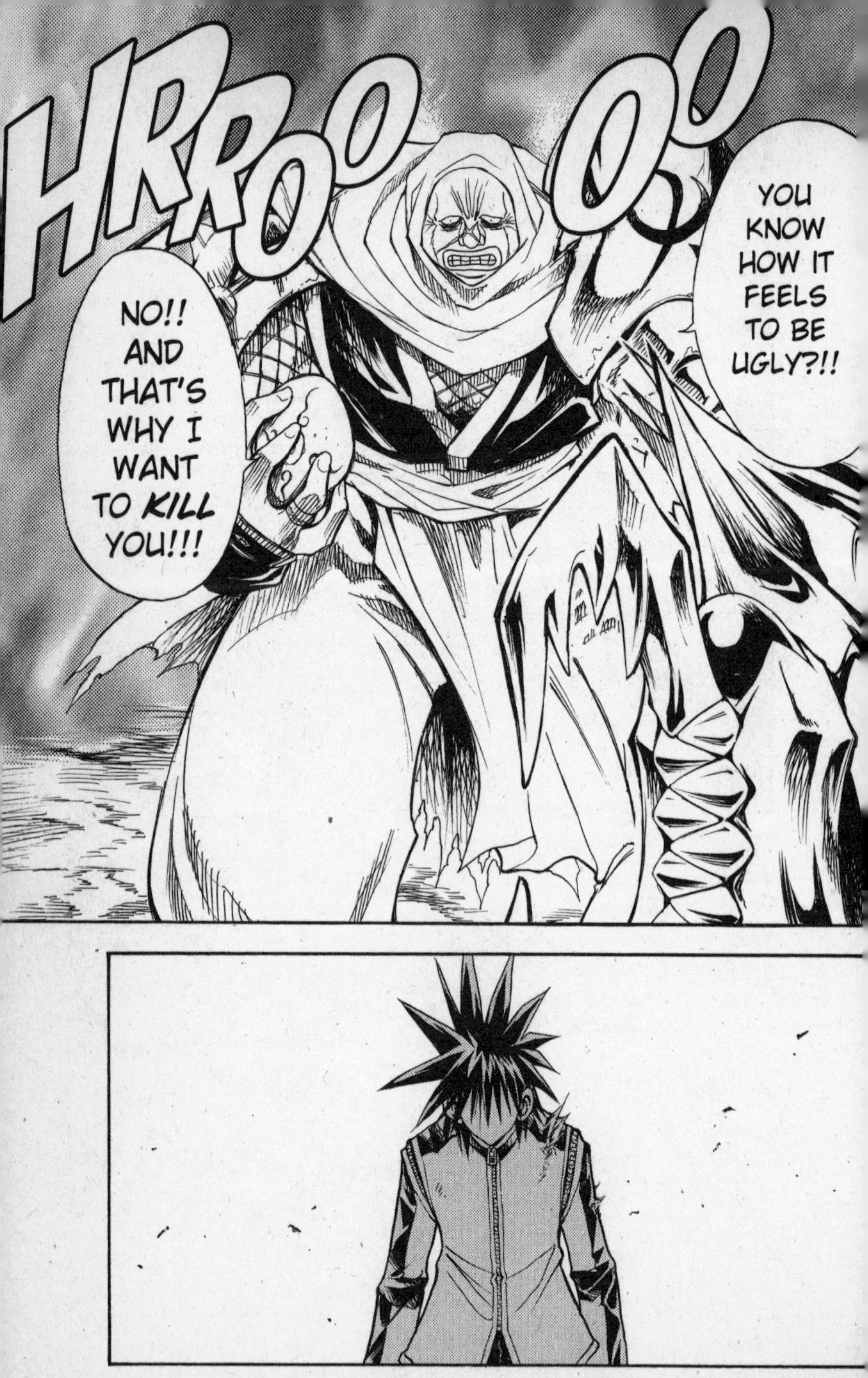
HRROOOOO
YOU KNOW HOW IT FEELS TO BE UGLY?!!
NO!! AND THAT'S WHY I WANT TO *KILL* YOU!!!

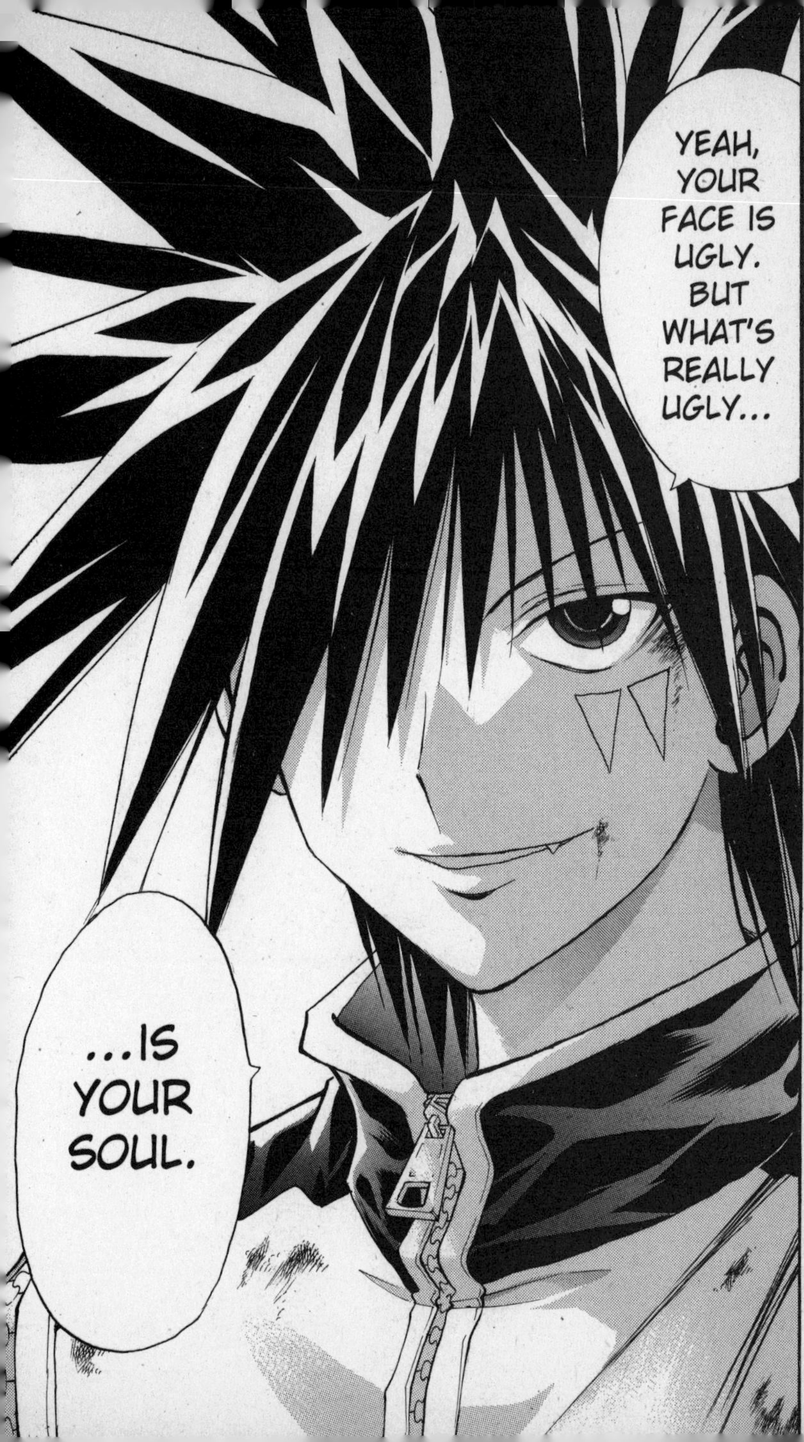
YEAH, YOUR FACE IS UGLY. BUT WHAT'S REALLY UGLY...
...IS YOUR SOUL.

AKT.114/

ALVISS
VS.
KOGA
②

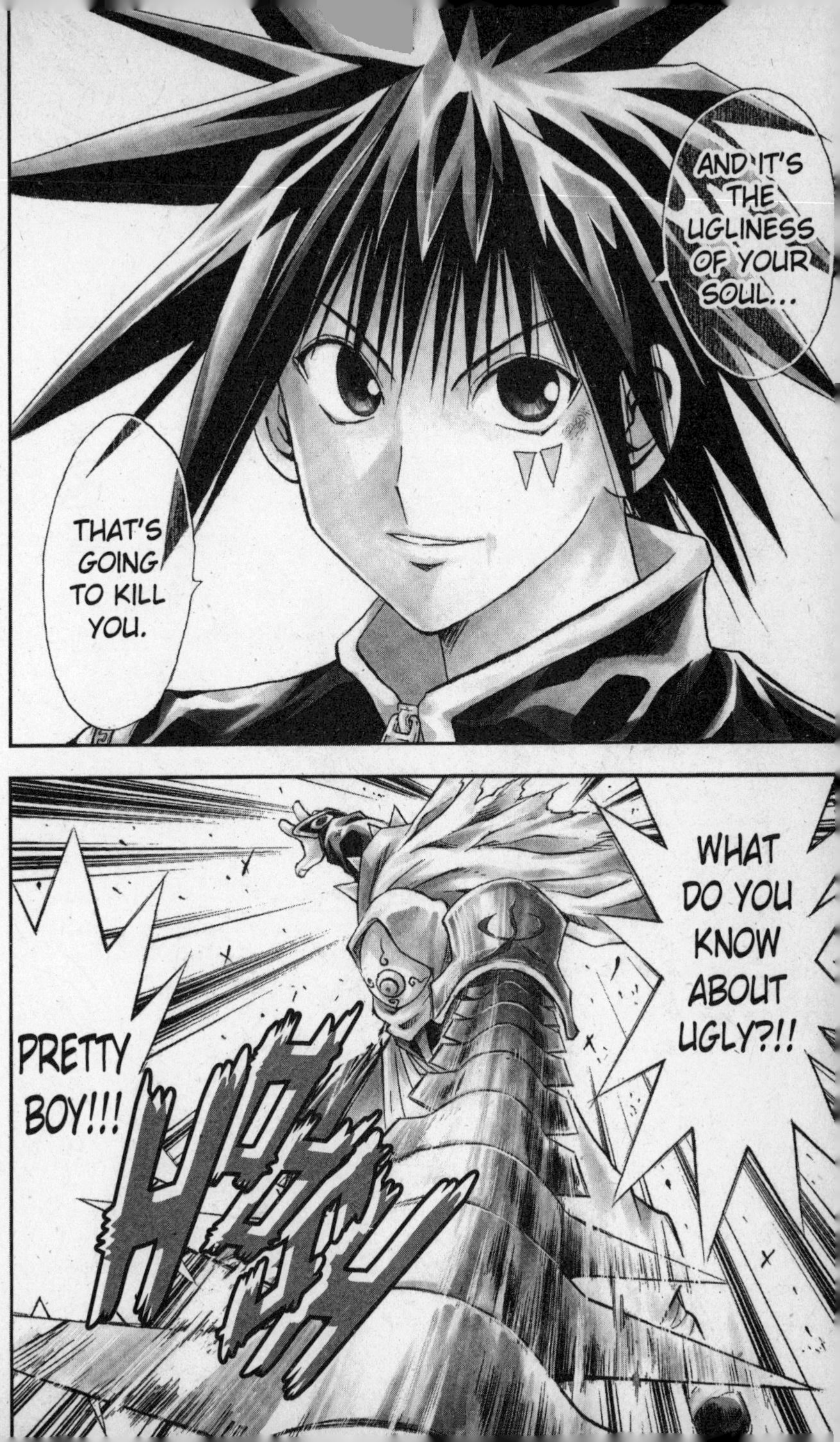
AND IT'S THE UGLINESS OF YOUR SOUL...
THAT'S GOING TO KILL YOU.
WHAT DO YOU KNOW ABOUT UGLY?!!
PRETTY BOY!!!

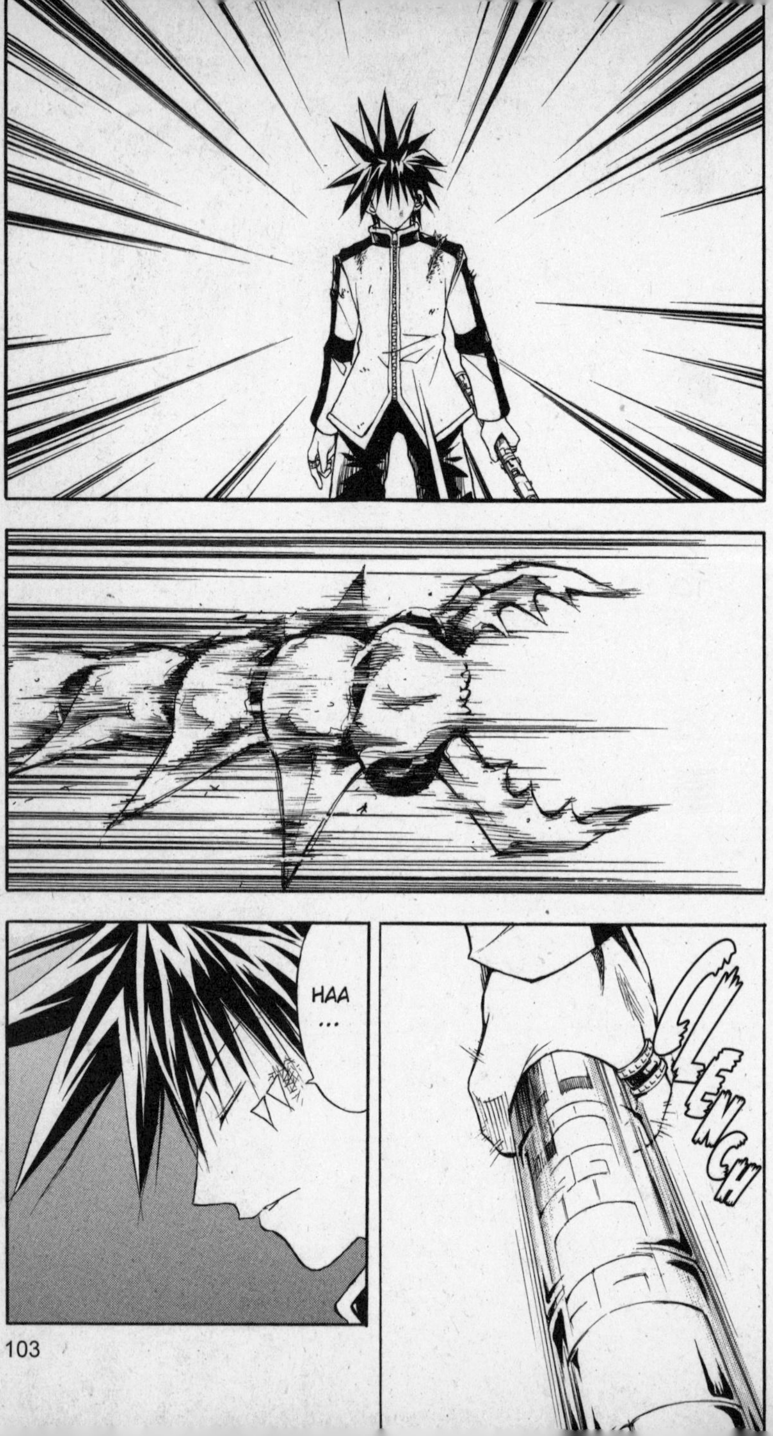
CLENCH
HAA ...

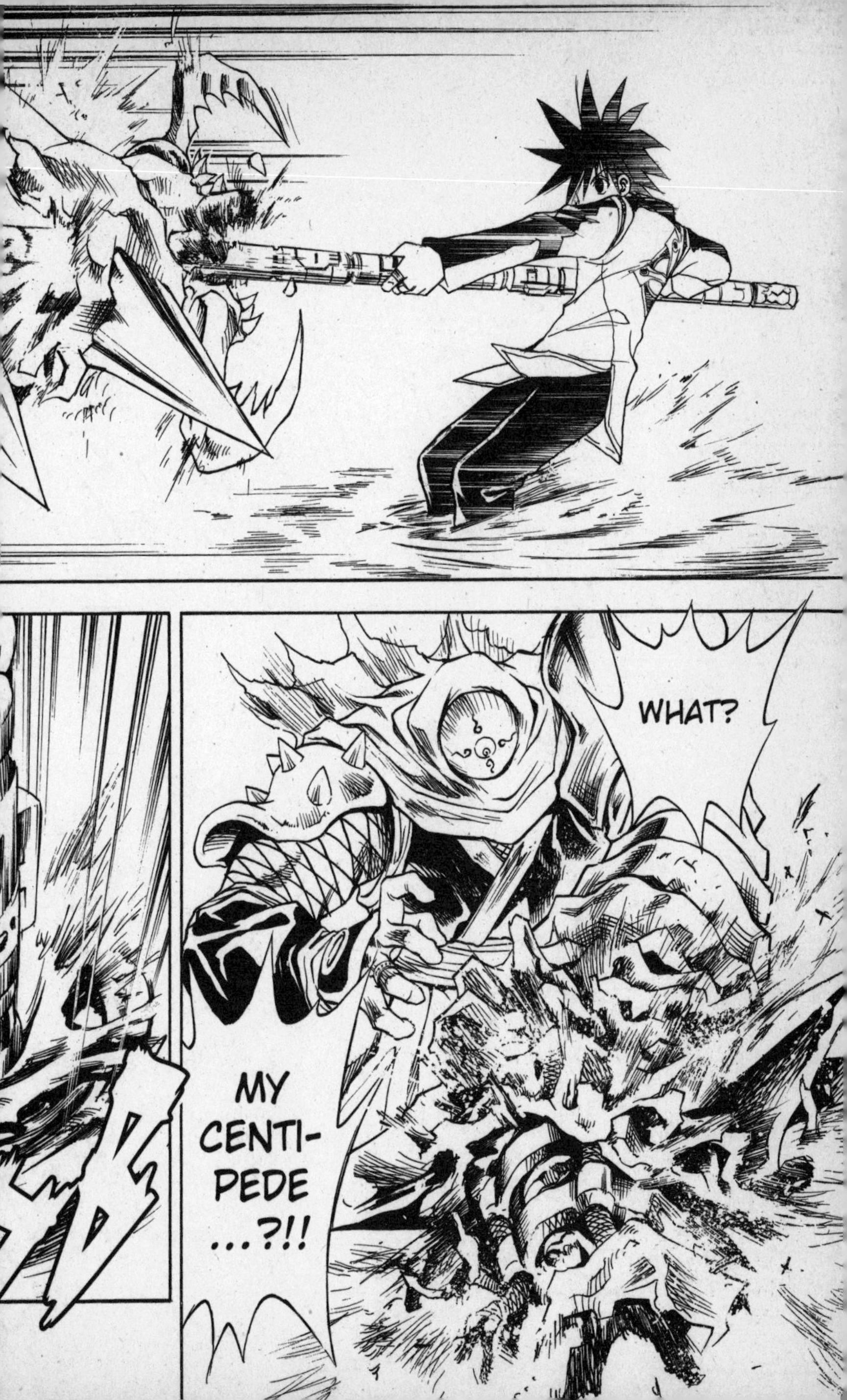
WHAT?
MY CENTI-
PEDE
...?!!

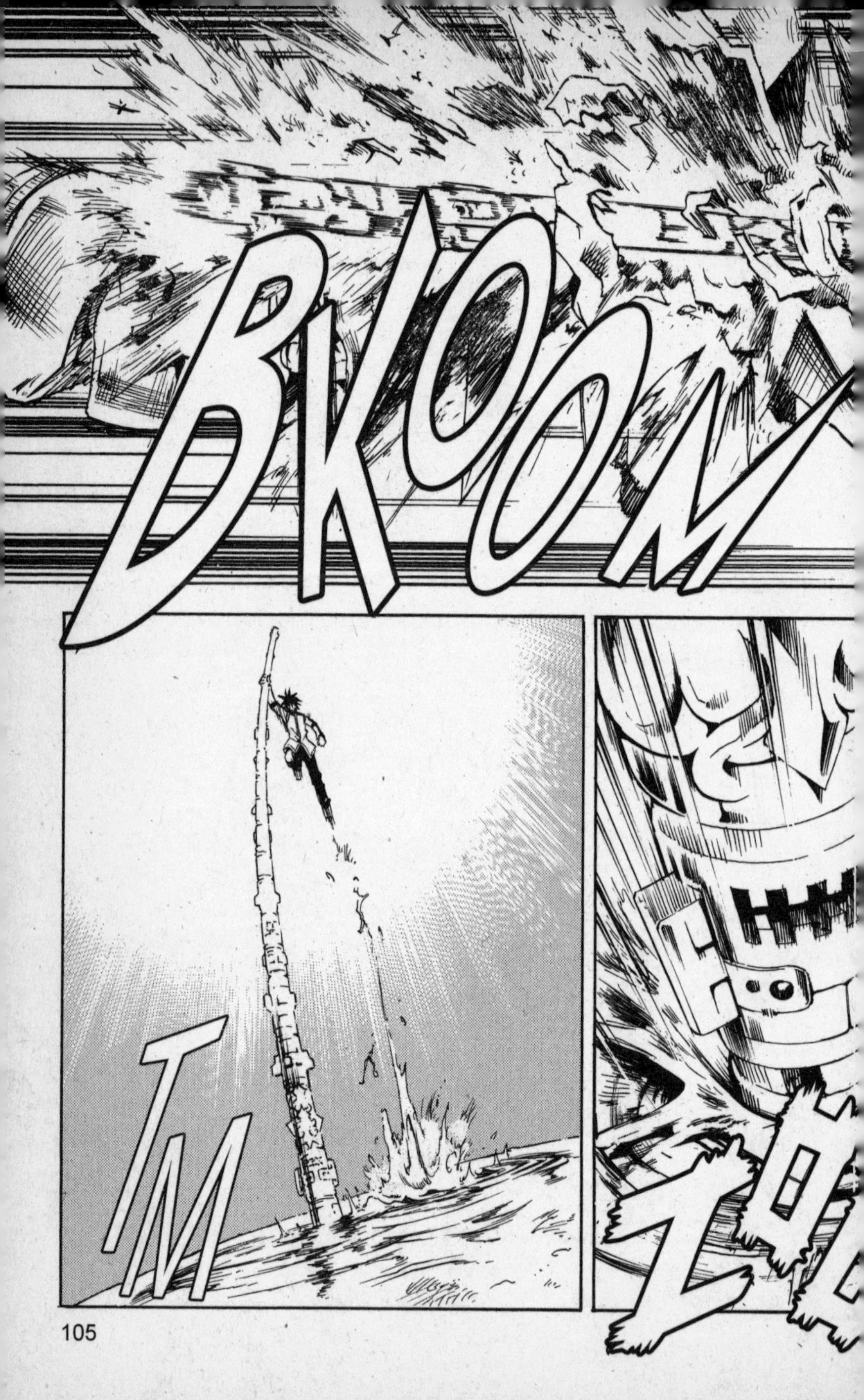
BKLOOM
TM

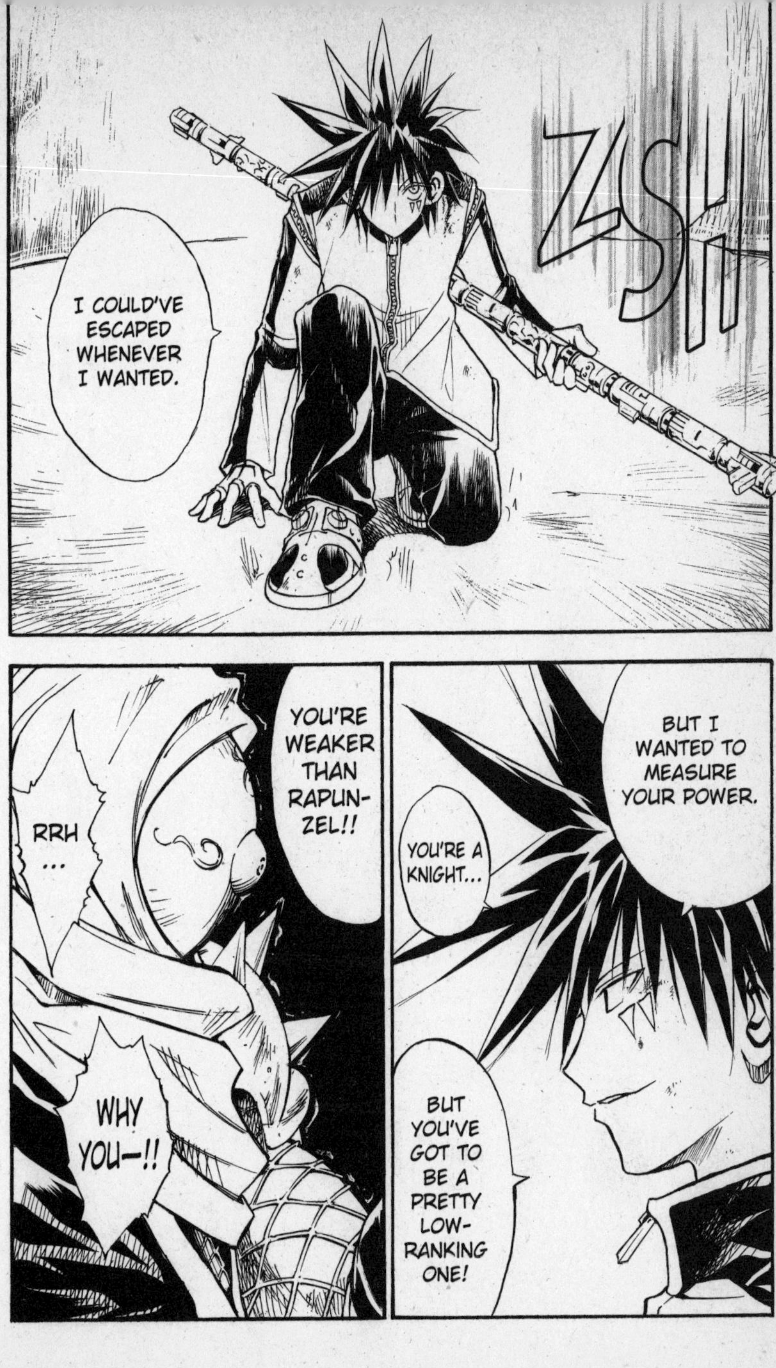
ZSH
I COULD'VE ESCAPED WHENEVER I WANTED.
BUT I WANTED TO MEASURE YOUR POWER.
YOU'RE A KNIGHT...
BUT YOU'VE GOT TO BE A PRETTY LOW-RANKING ONE!
YOU'RE WEAKER THAN RAPUNZEL!!
RRH...
WHY YOU—!!

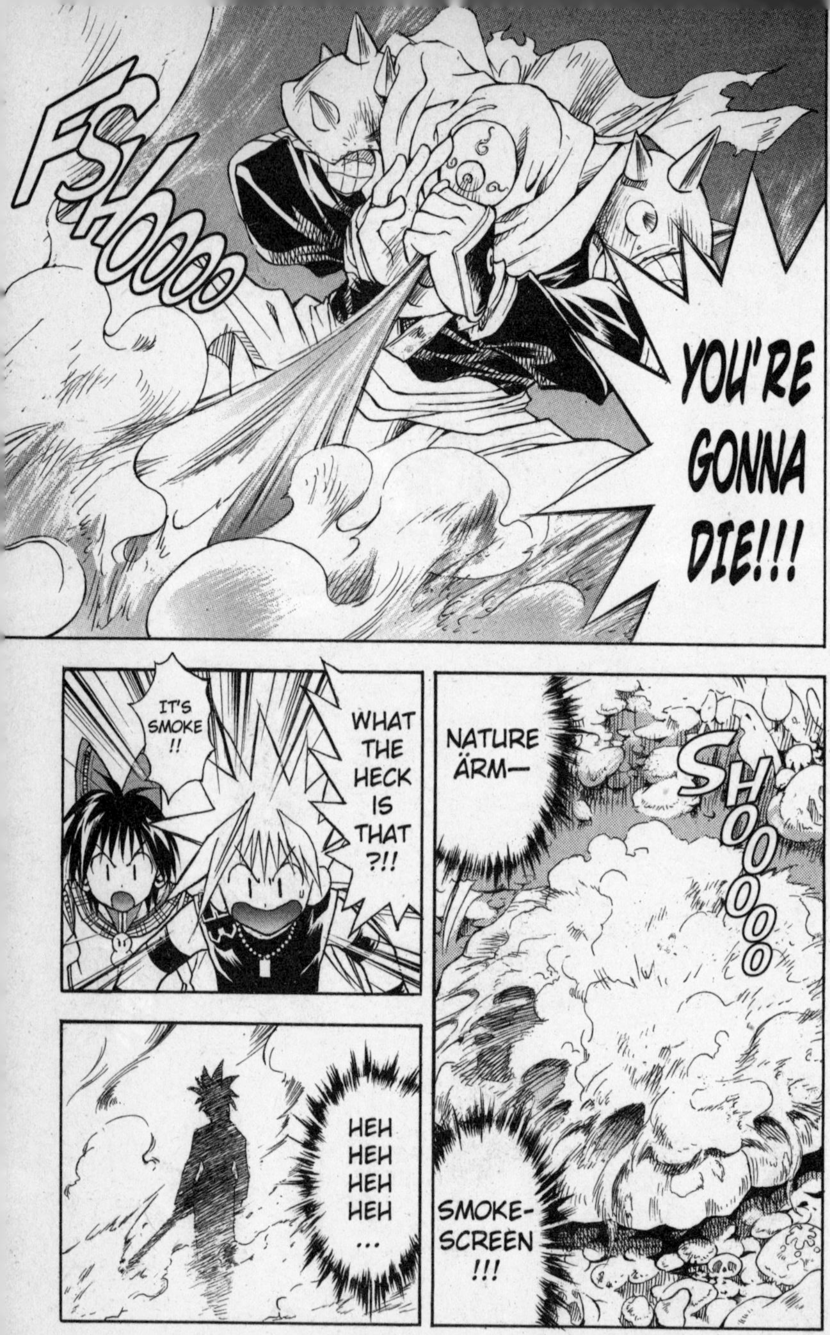
FSHOOOO
YOU'RE GONNA DIE!!!
NATURE ÄRM—
SHOOOOO
SMOKE-SCREEN!!!
WHAT THE HECK IS THAT?!!
IT'S SMOKE!!
HEH HEH HEH HEH...

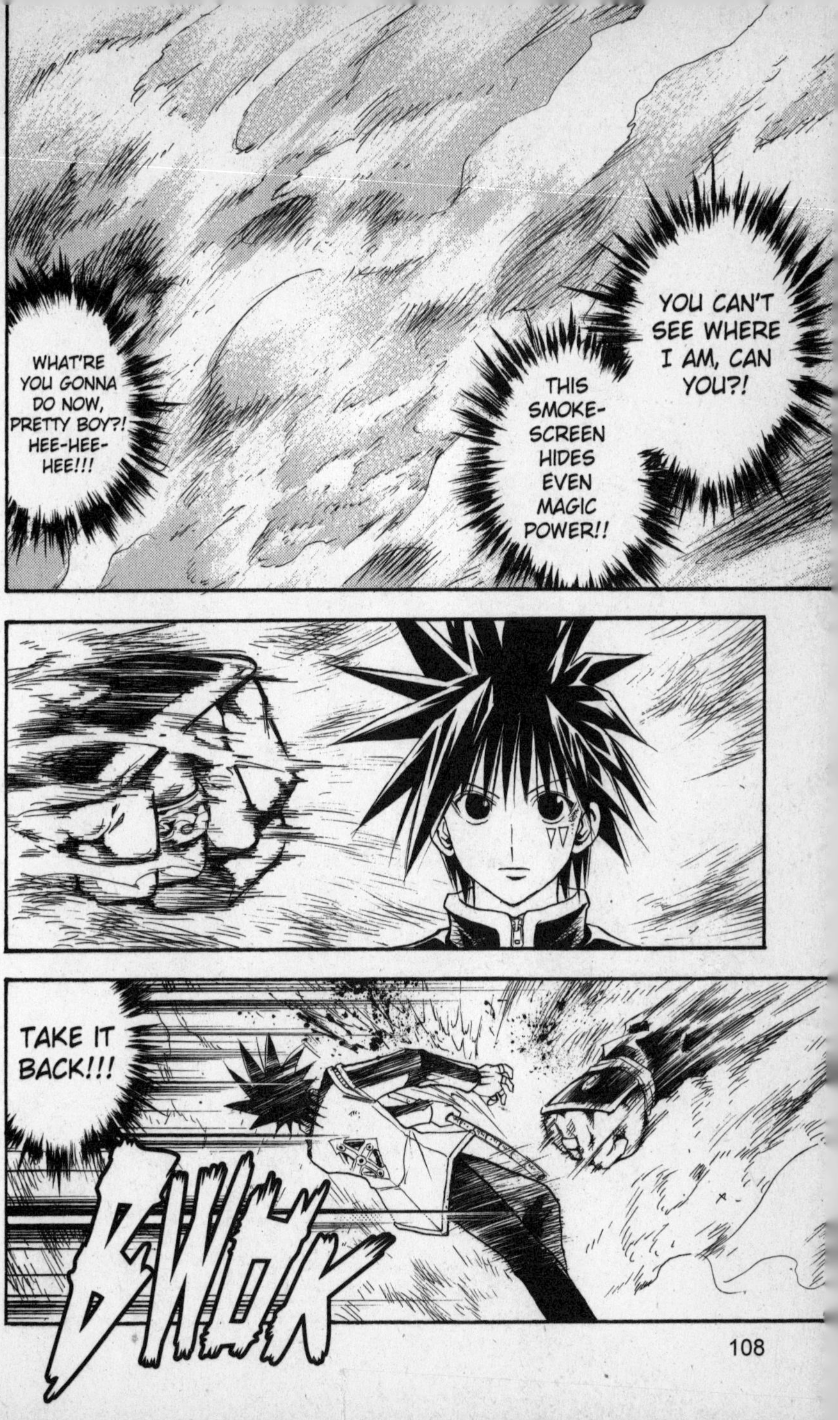
YOU CAN'T SEE WHERE I AM, CAN YOU?!
THIS SMOKE-SCREEN HIDES EVEN MAGIC POWER!!
WHAT'RE YOU GONNA DO NOW, PRETTY BOY?! HEE-HEE-HEE!!!
TAKE IT BACK!!!
BWOK

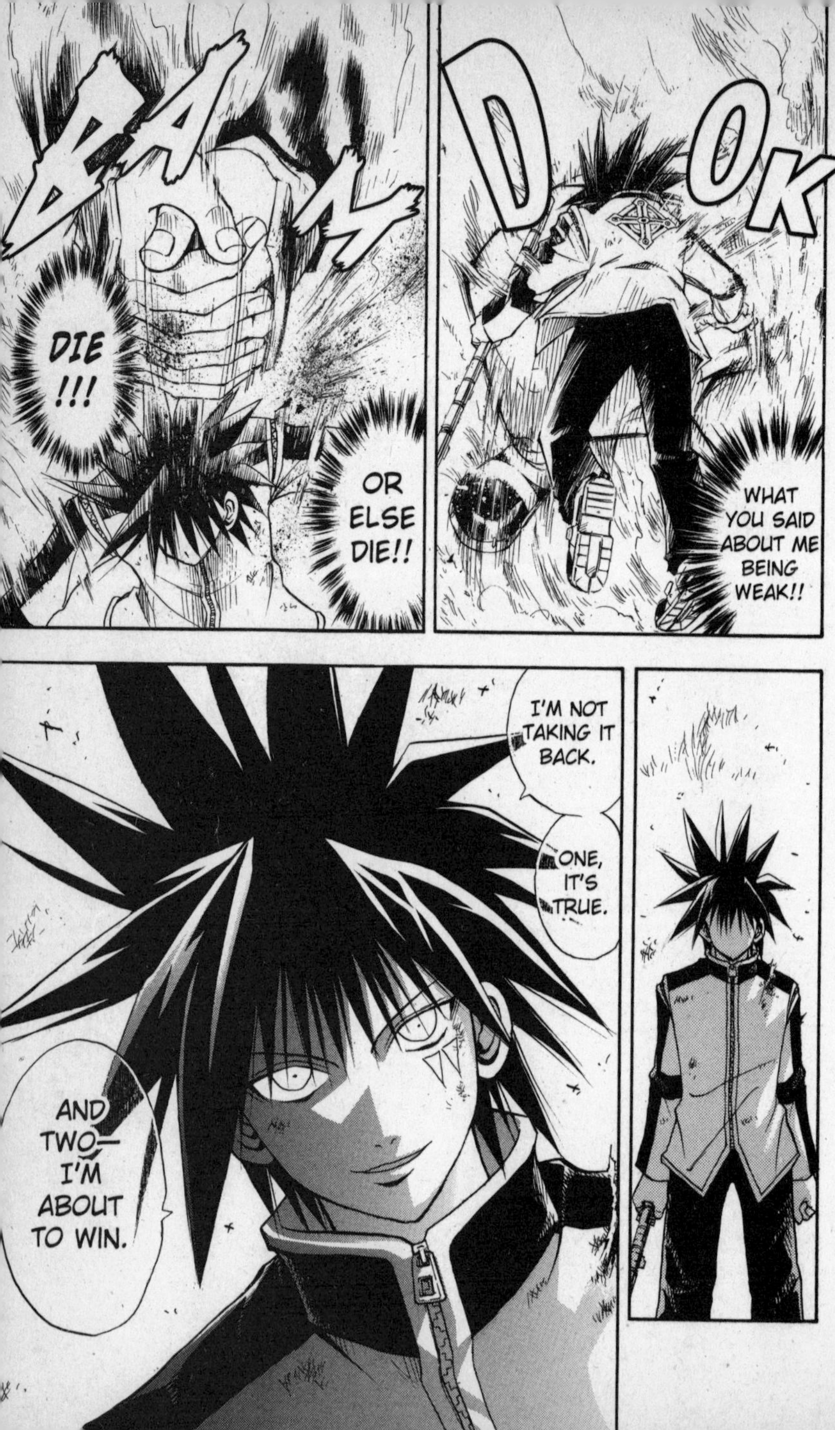
DOOK
WHAT YOU SAID ABOUT ME BEING WEAK!!
BAM
OR ELSE DIE!!
DIE !!!
I'M NOT TAKING IT BACK.
ONE, IT'S TRUE.
AND TWO— I'M ABOUT TO WIN.

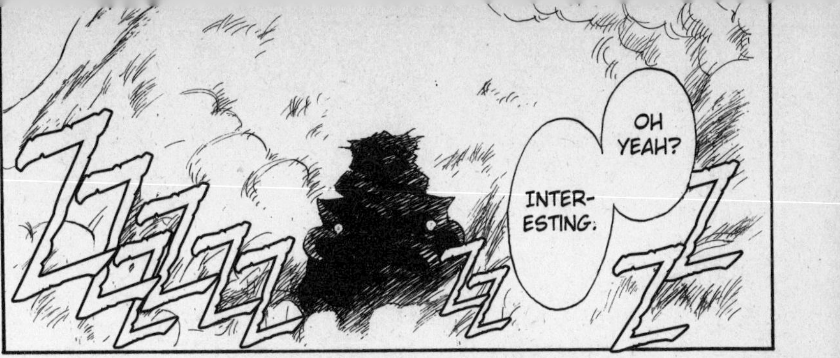
OH YEAH?
INTER-ESTING.

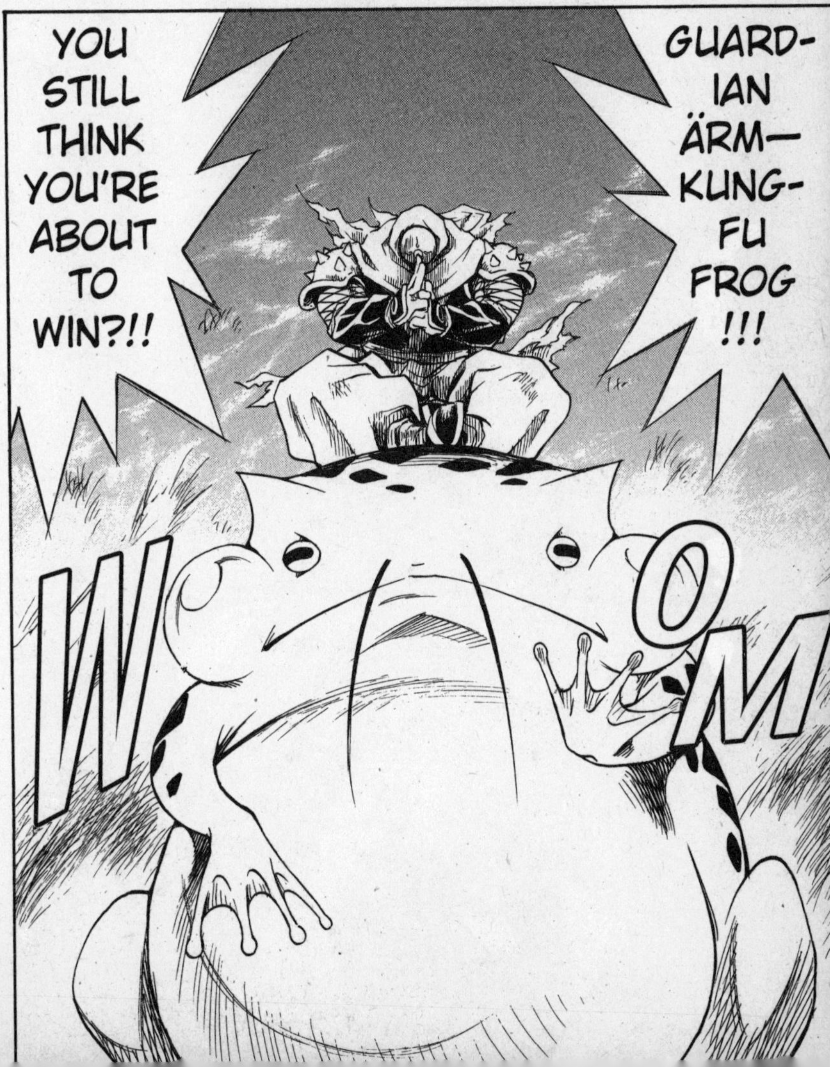
GUARD-IAN ÄRM-KUNG-FU FROG!!!
YOU STILL THINK YOU'RE ABOUT TO WIN?!!
WOM

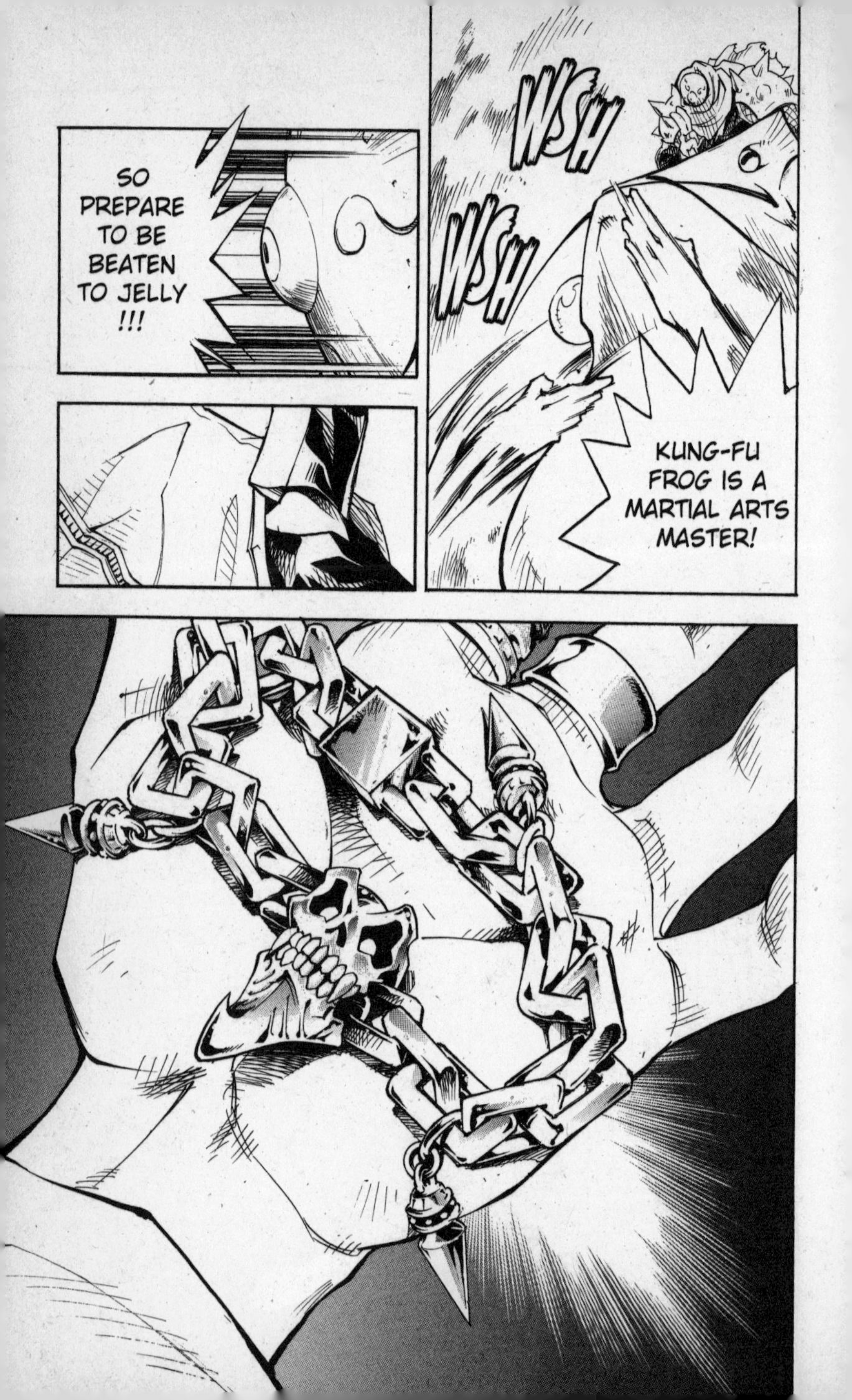
WSH
WSH
KUNG-FU FROG IS A MARTIAL ARTS MASTER!
SO PREPARE TO BE BEATEN TO JELLY !!!

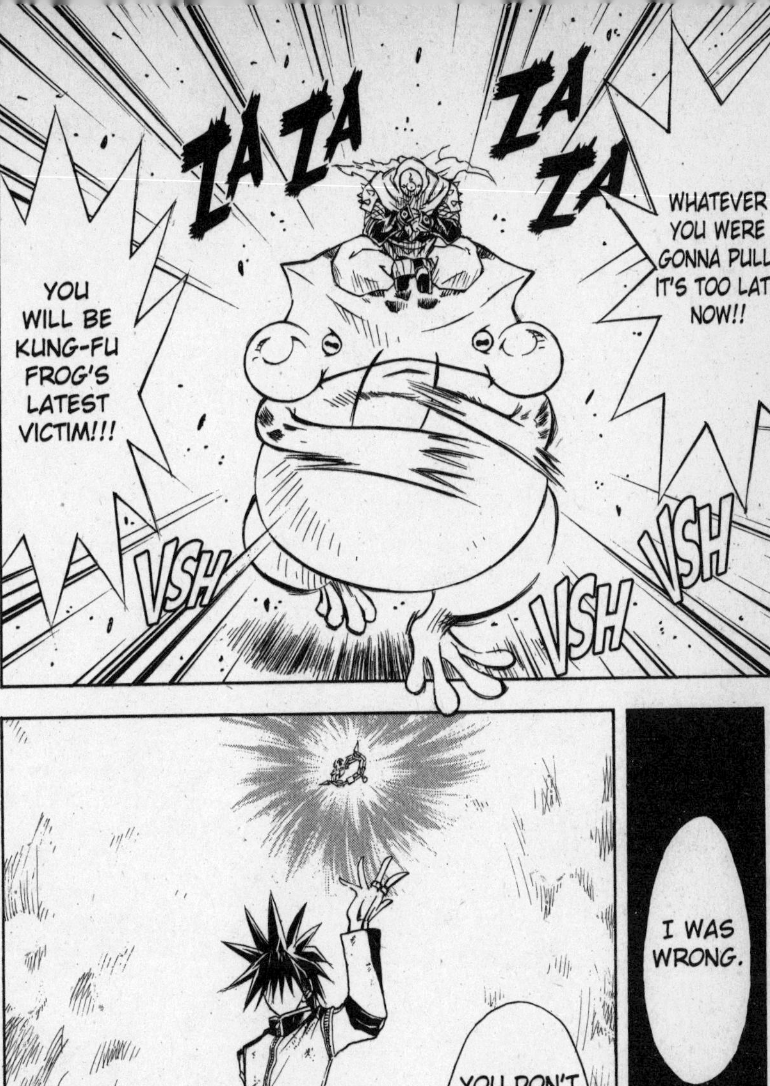
ZA ZA
ZA ZA
WHATEVER YOU WERE GONNA PULL, IT'S TOO LATE NOW!!
YOU WILL BE KUNG-FU FROG'S LATEST VICTIM!!!
VSH
VSH
VSH
I WAS WRONG.
YOU DON'T EVEN DESERVE TO BE A KNIGHT.

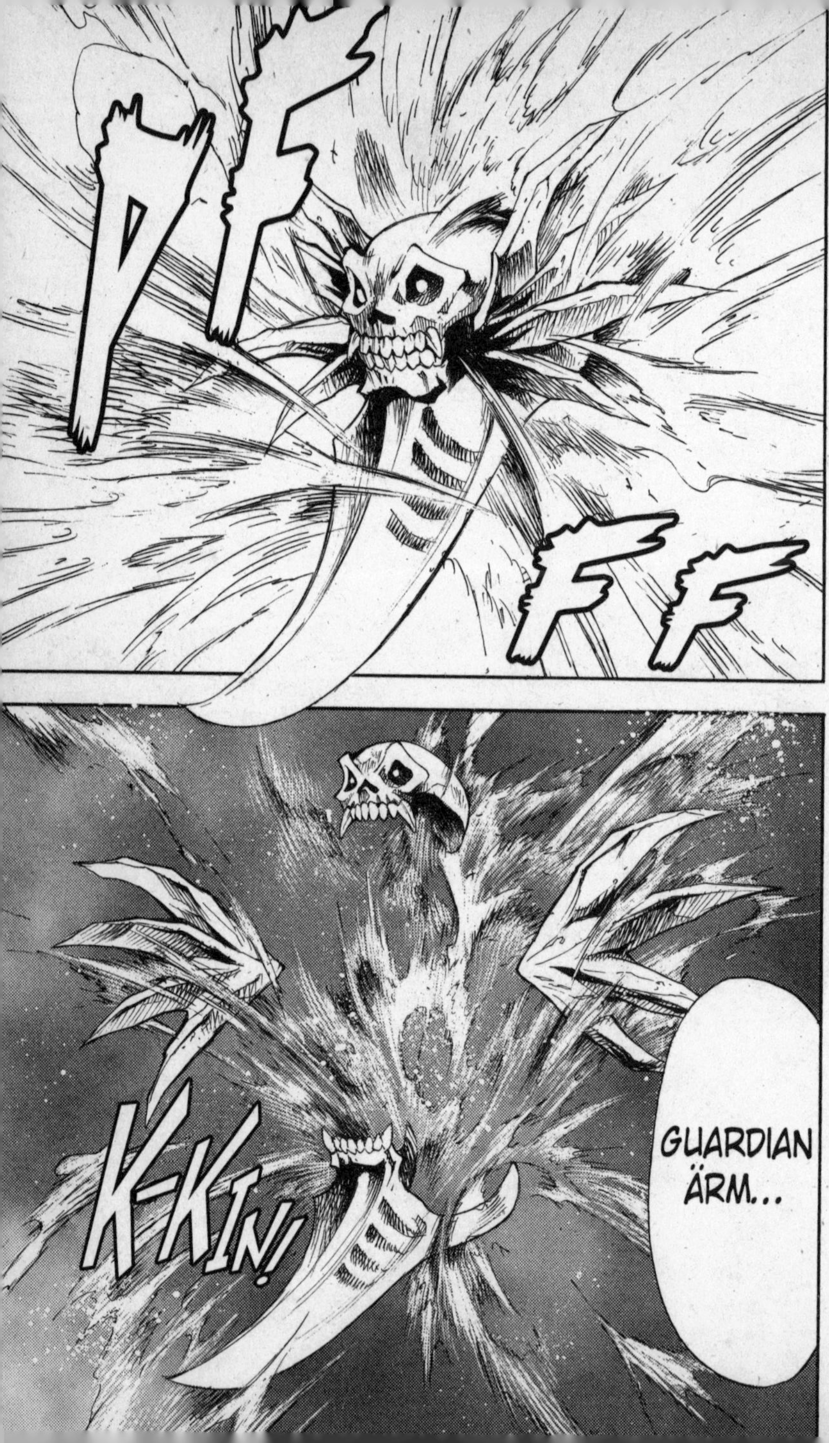
FF
GUARDIAN ÄRM...
K-KIN!

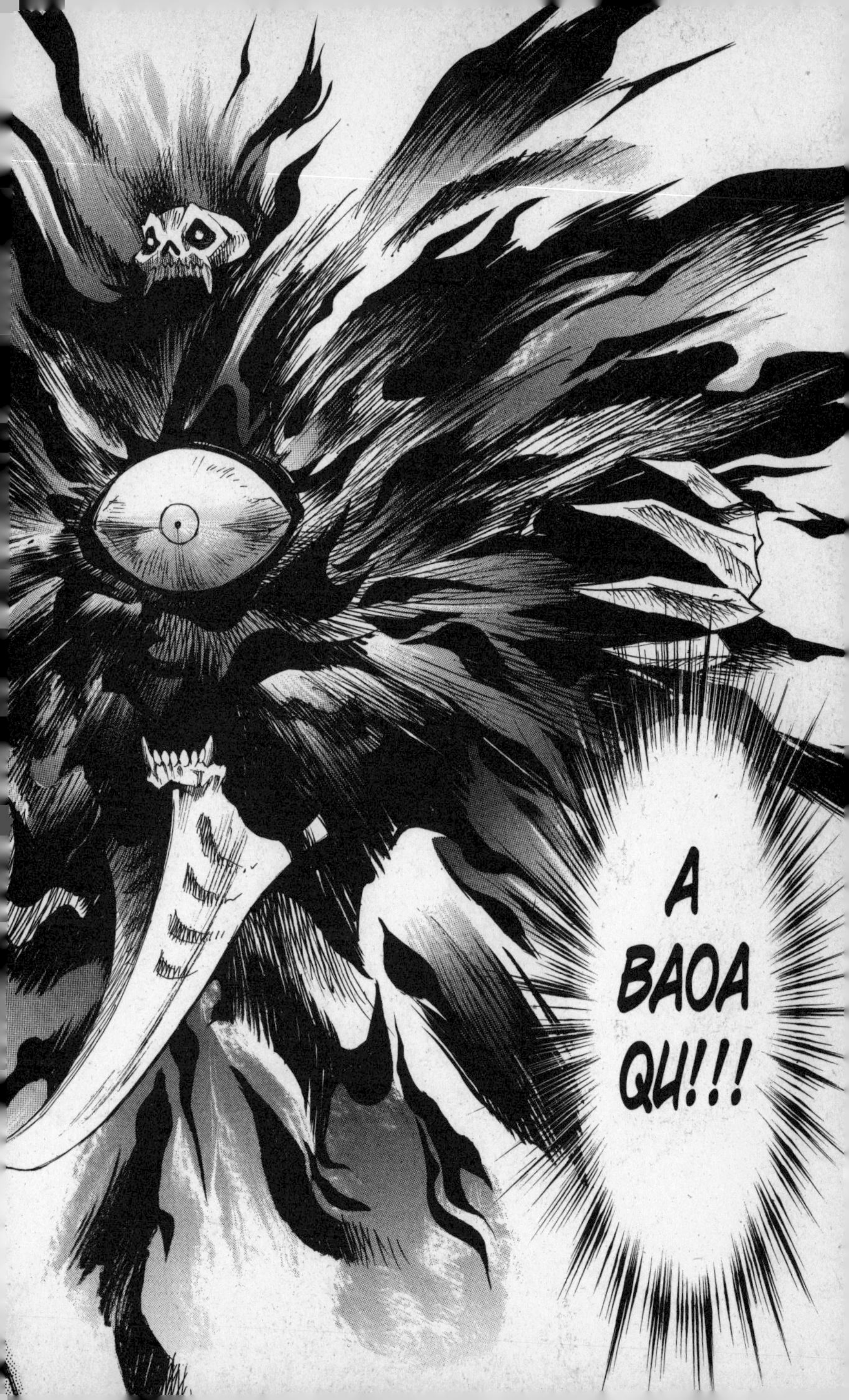
A BAOA QU!!!

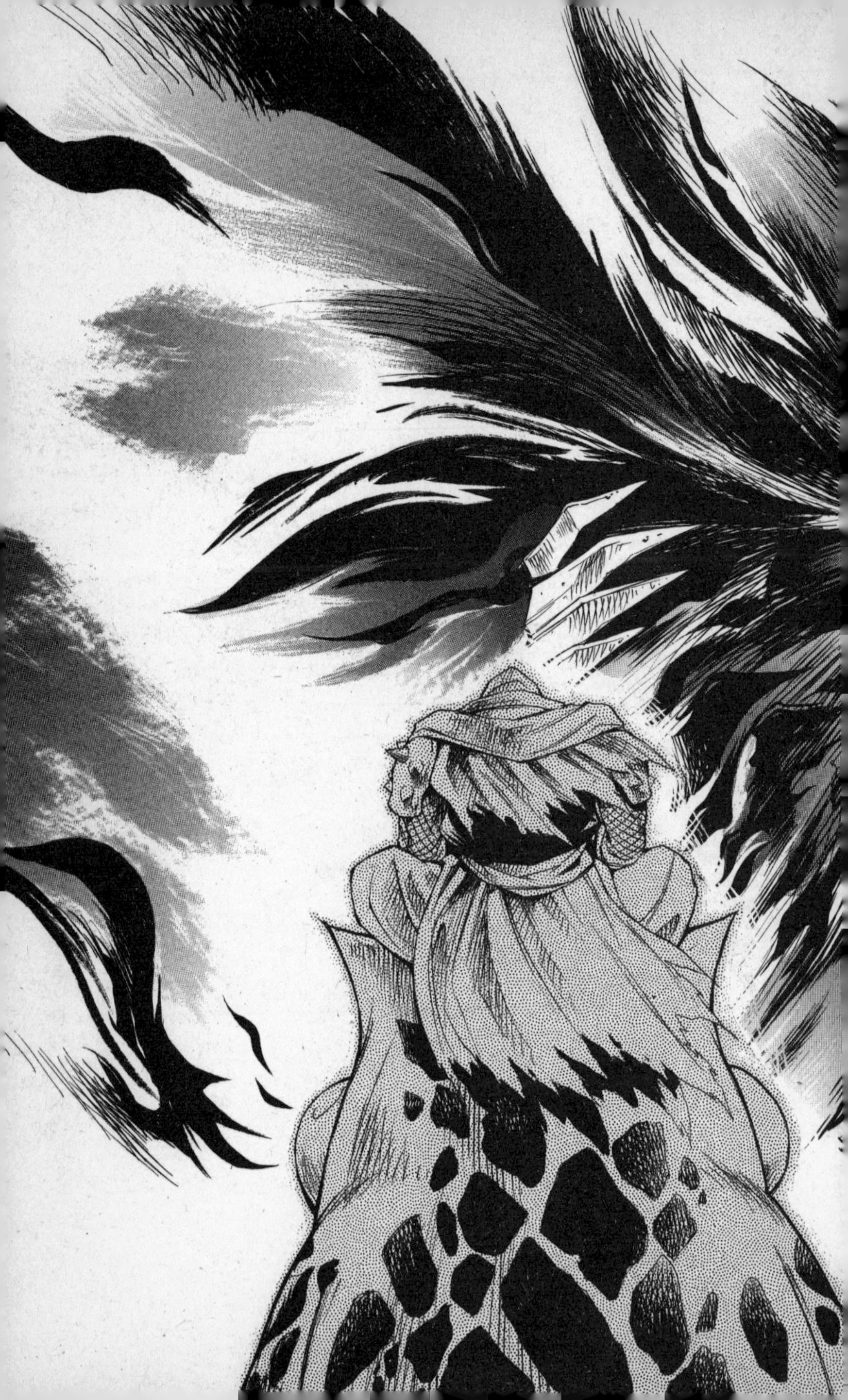

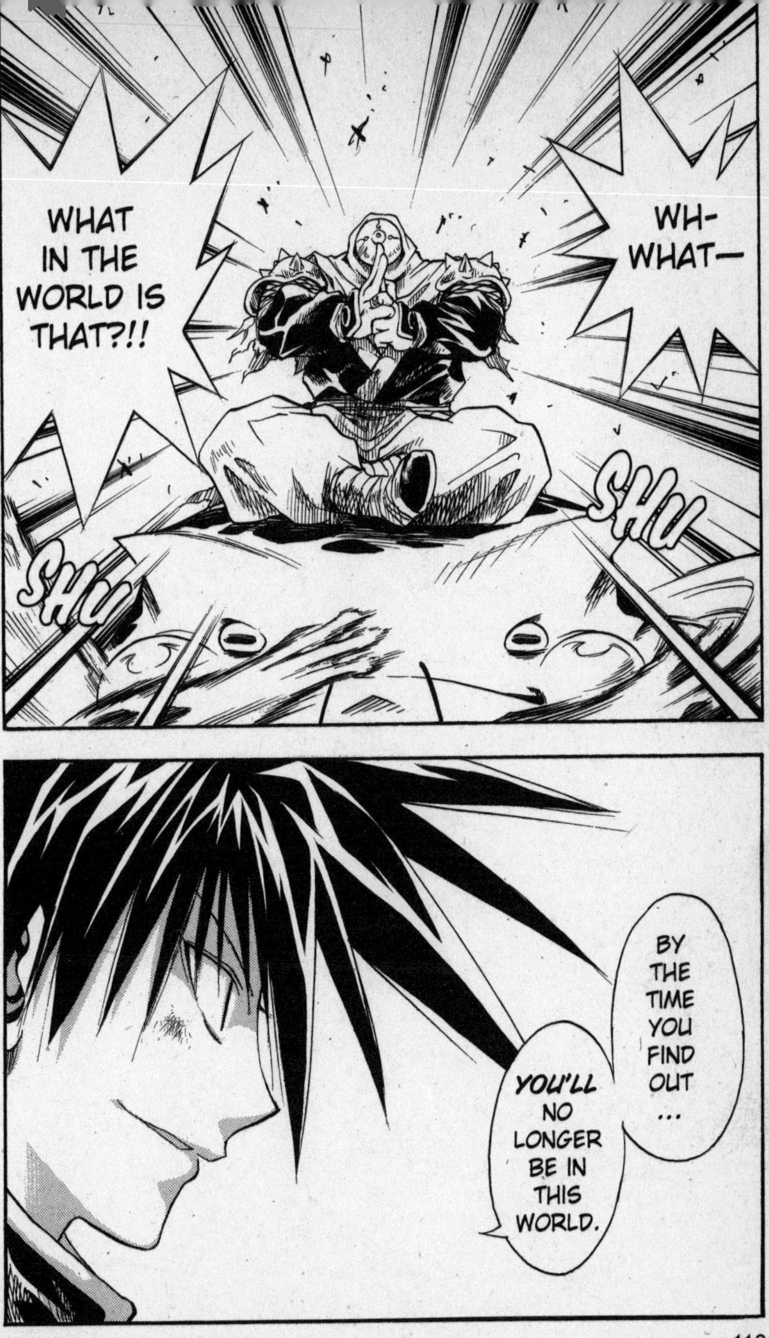
WH-WHAT—
WHAT IN THE WORLD IS THAT?!!
SHU
SHU
BY THE TIME YOU FIND OUT...
YOU'LL NO LONGER BE IN THIS WORLD.

AKT.115/ ALVISS VS. KOGA③

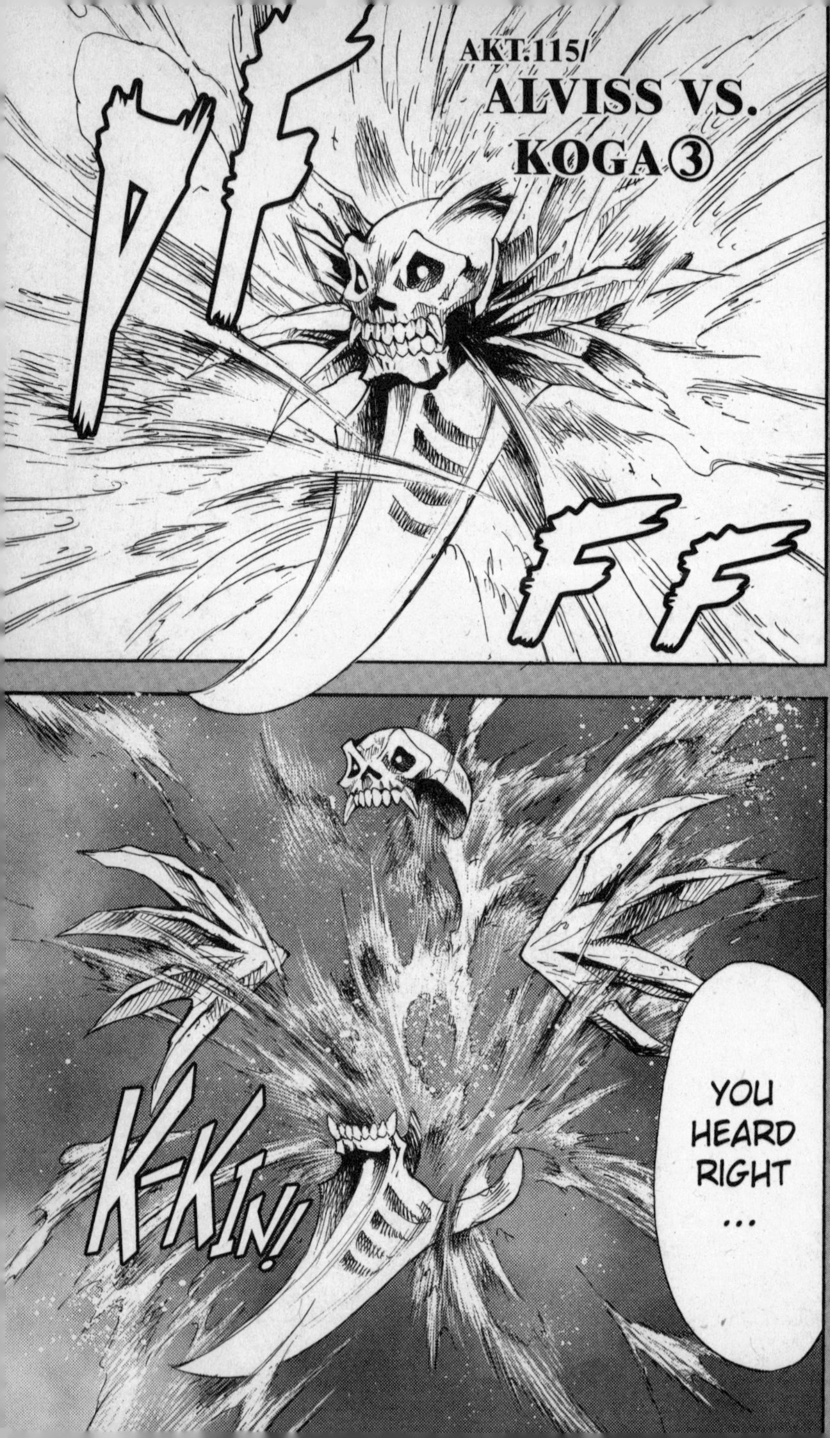
DIFF
K-KIN!
YOU HEARD RIGHT ...

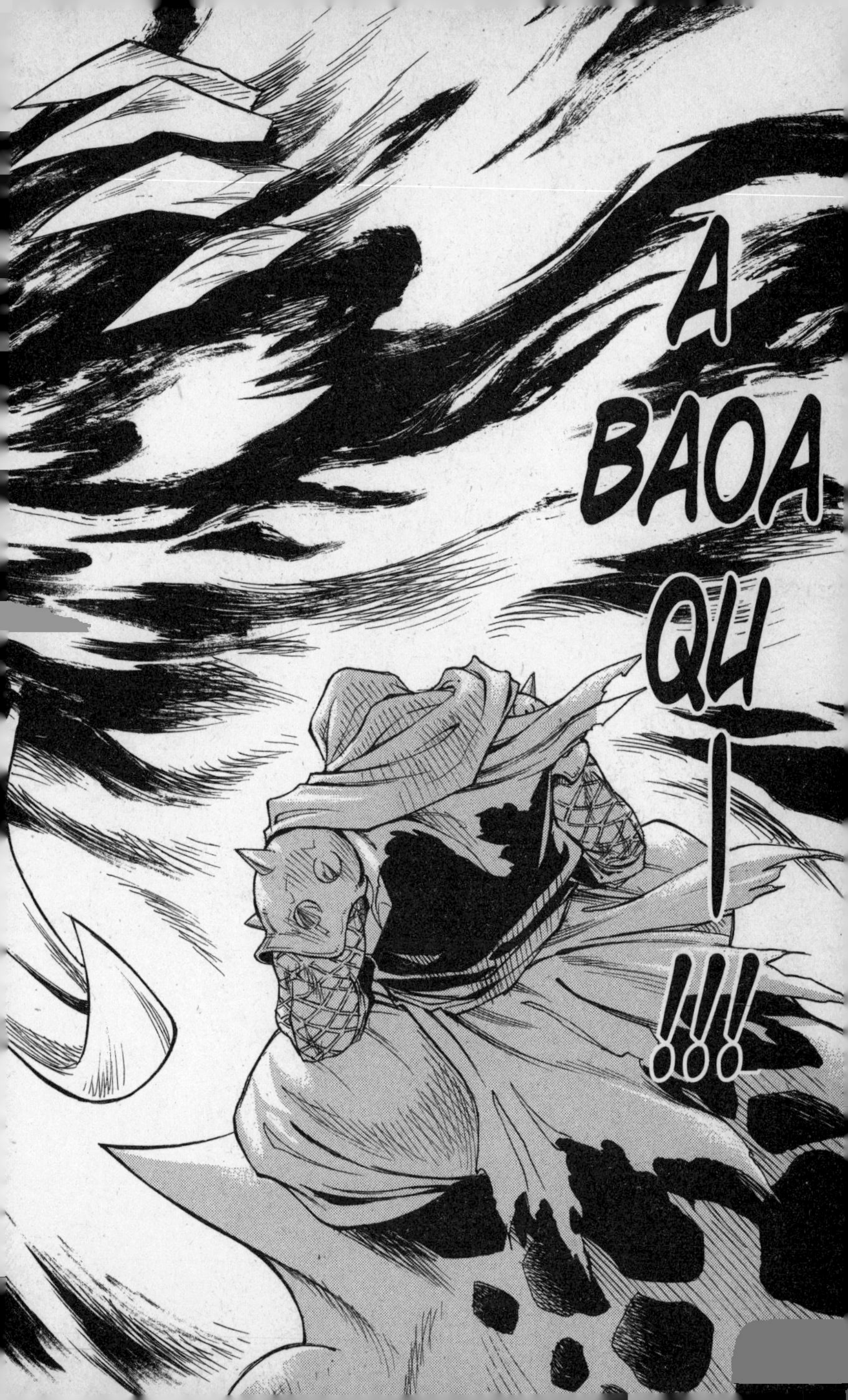
A BAOA QUI!!!!

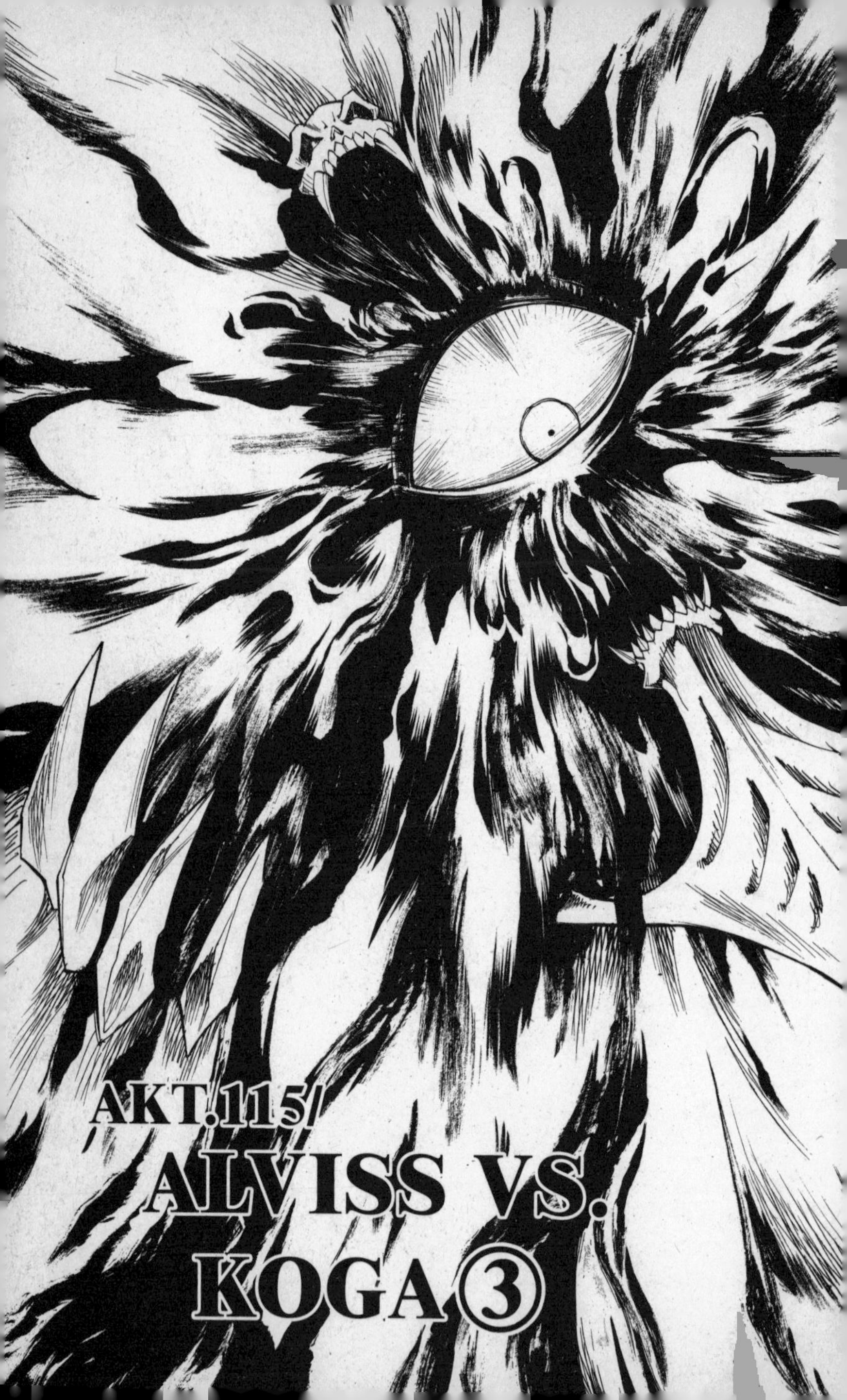
AKT.115/
ALVISS VS.
KOGA ③

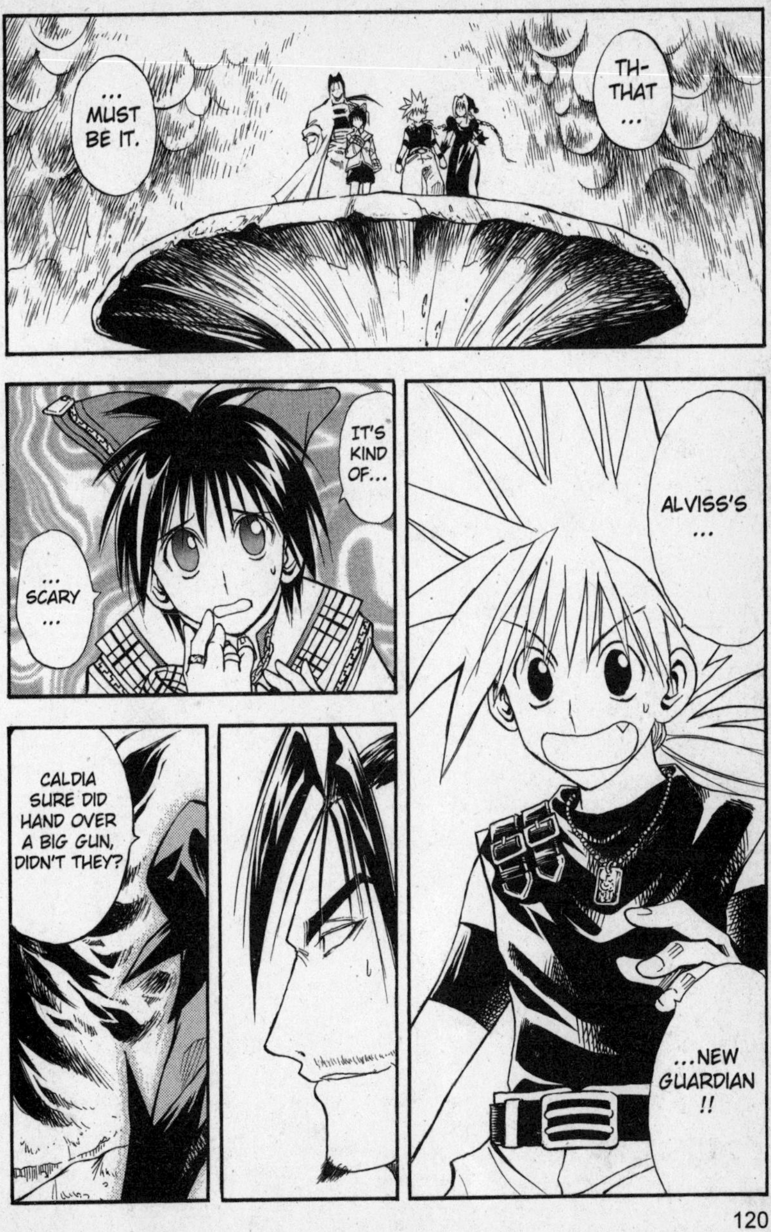
TH-THAT ...
... MUST BE IT.
ALVISS'S ...
...NEW GUARDIAN !!
IT'S KIND OF...
... SCARY ...
CALDIA SURE DID HAND OVER A BIG GUN, DIDN'T THEY?

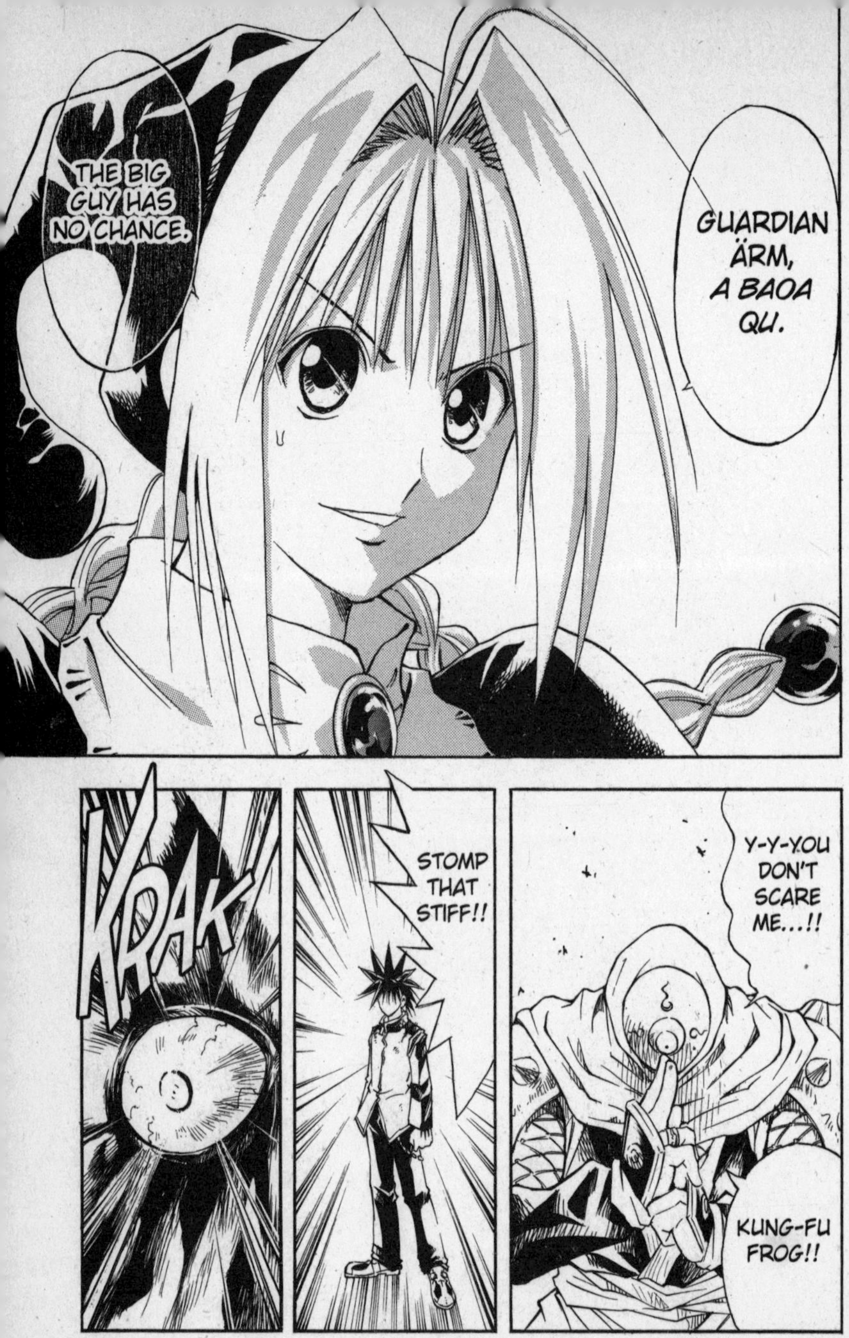
GUARDIAN ÄRM, A BAOA QU.
THE BIG GUY HAS NO CHANCE.
Y-Y-YOU DON'T SCARE ME...!!
KUNG-FU FROG!!
STOMP THAT STIFF!!
KRAK

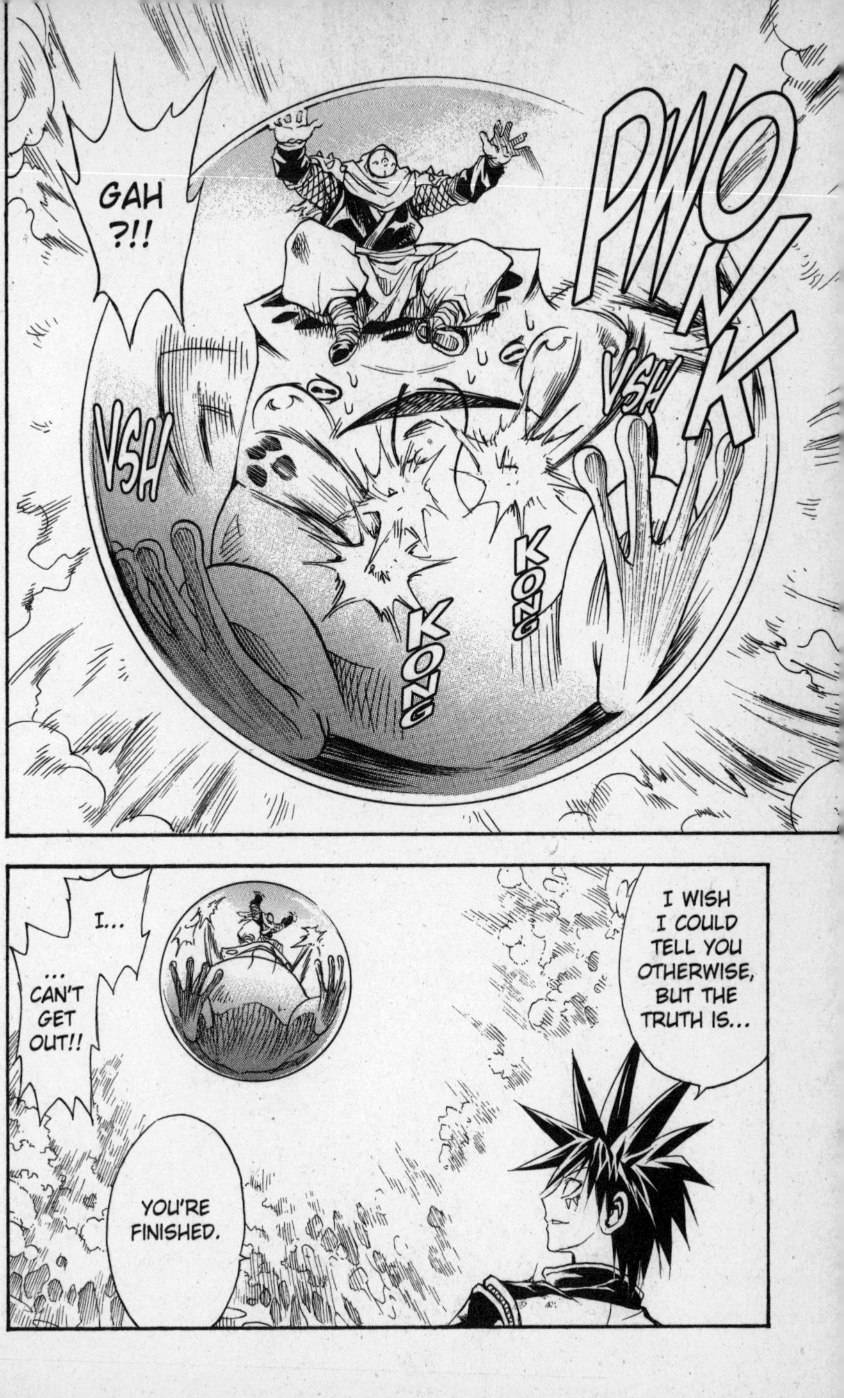
PWONK!
GAH ?!!
VSH
VSH
KONG
KONG
I WISH I COULD TELL YOU OTHERWISE, BUT THE TRUTH IS...
I...
...CAN'T GET OUT!!
YOU'RE FINISHED.

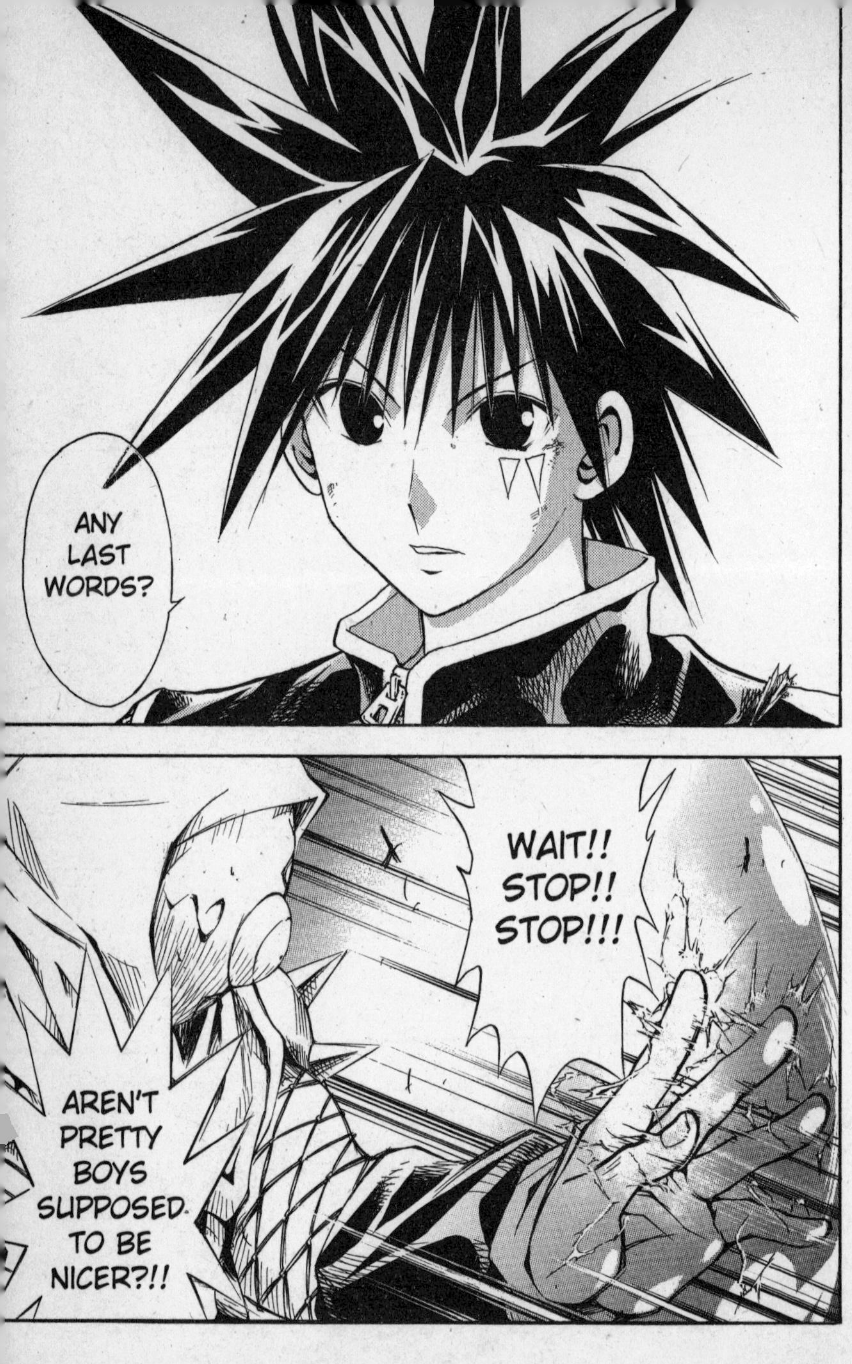
ANY LAST WORDS?
WAIT!! STOP!! STOP!!!
AREN'T PRETTY BOYS SUPPOSED TO BE NICER?!!

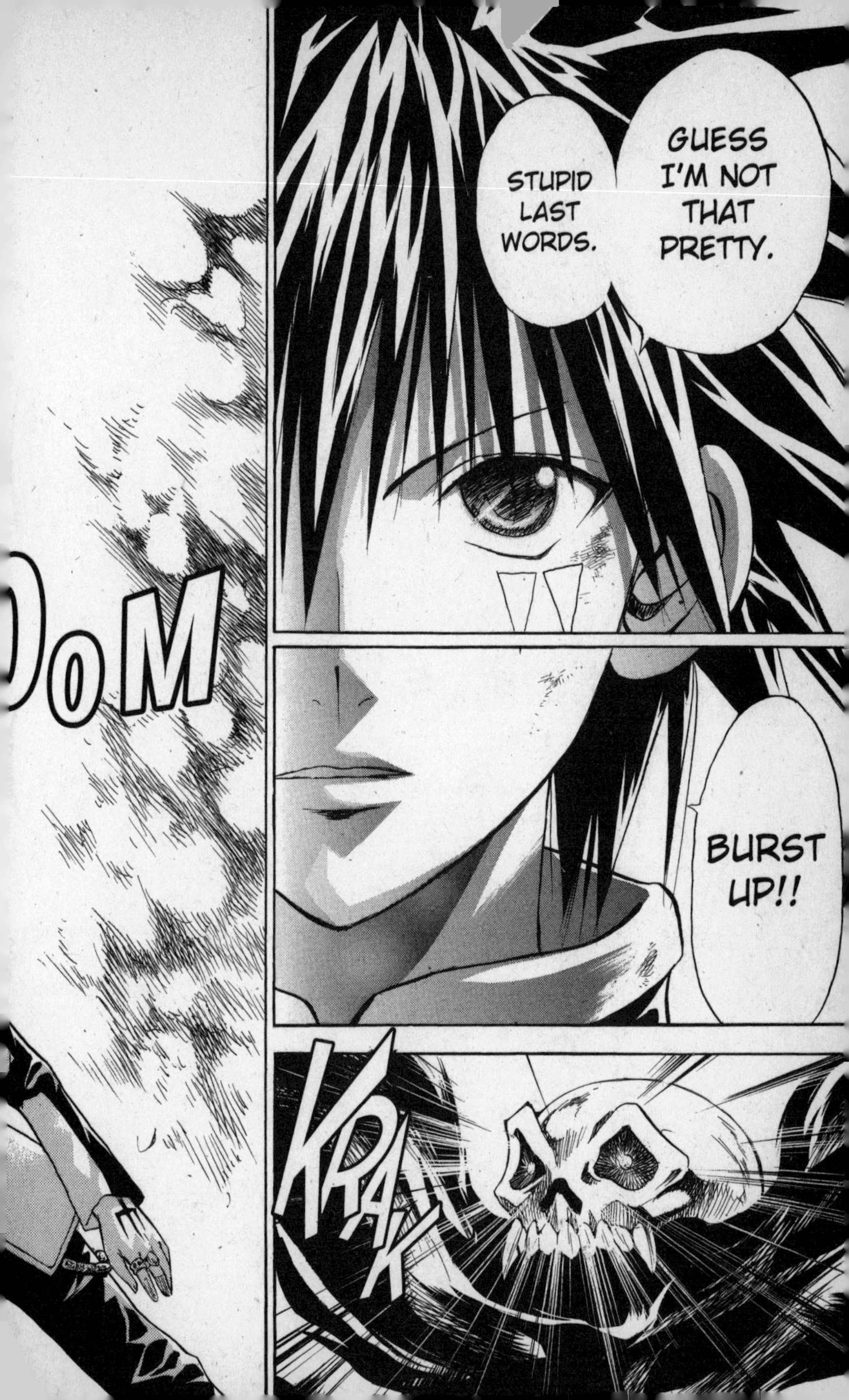
GUESS I'M NOT THAT PRETTY.
STUPID LAST WORDS.
BURST UP!!
KRAK
DOM

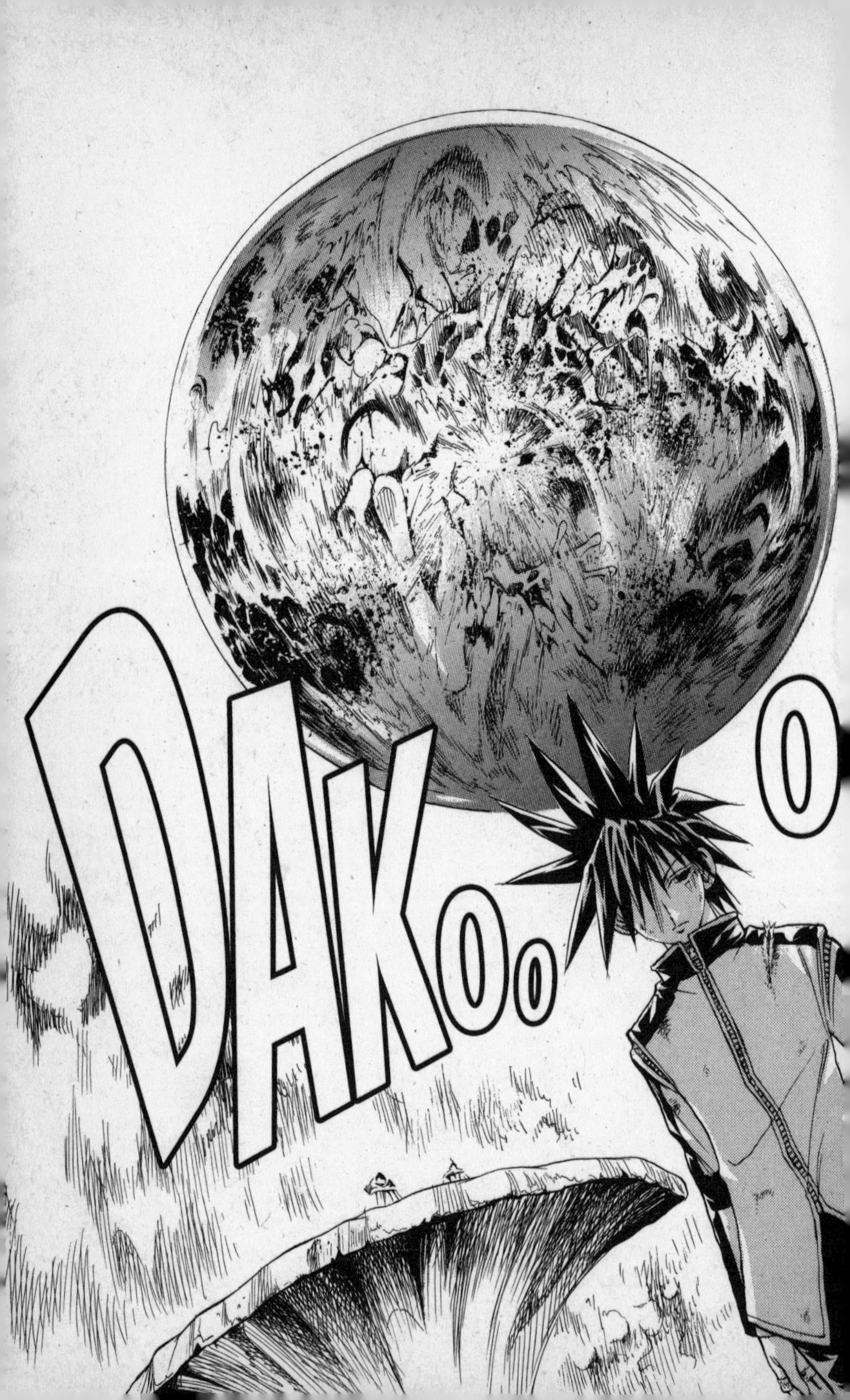
DAKOOO

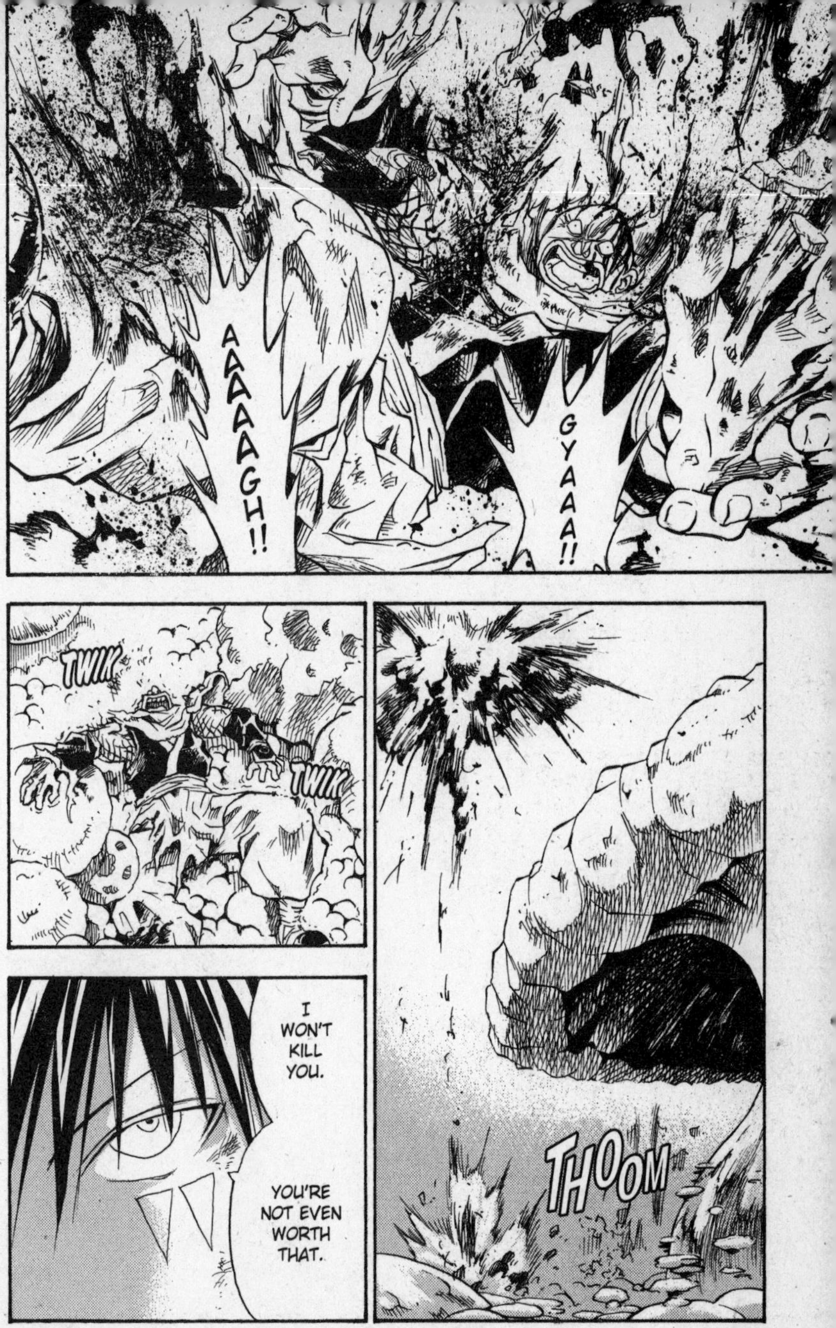
GYAAAA!!
AAAAAGH!!
THOOM
TWIK
TWIK
I WON'T KILL YOU.
YOU'RE NOT EVEN WORTH THAT.

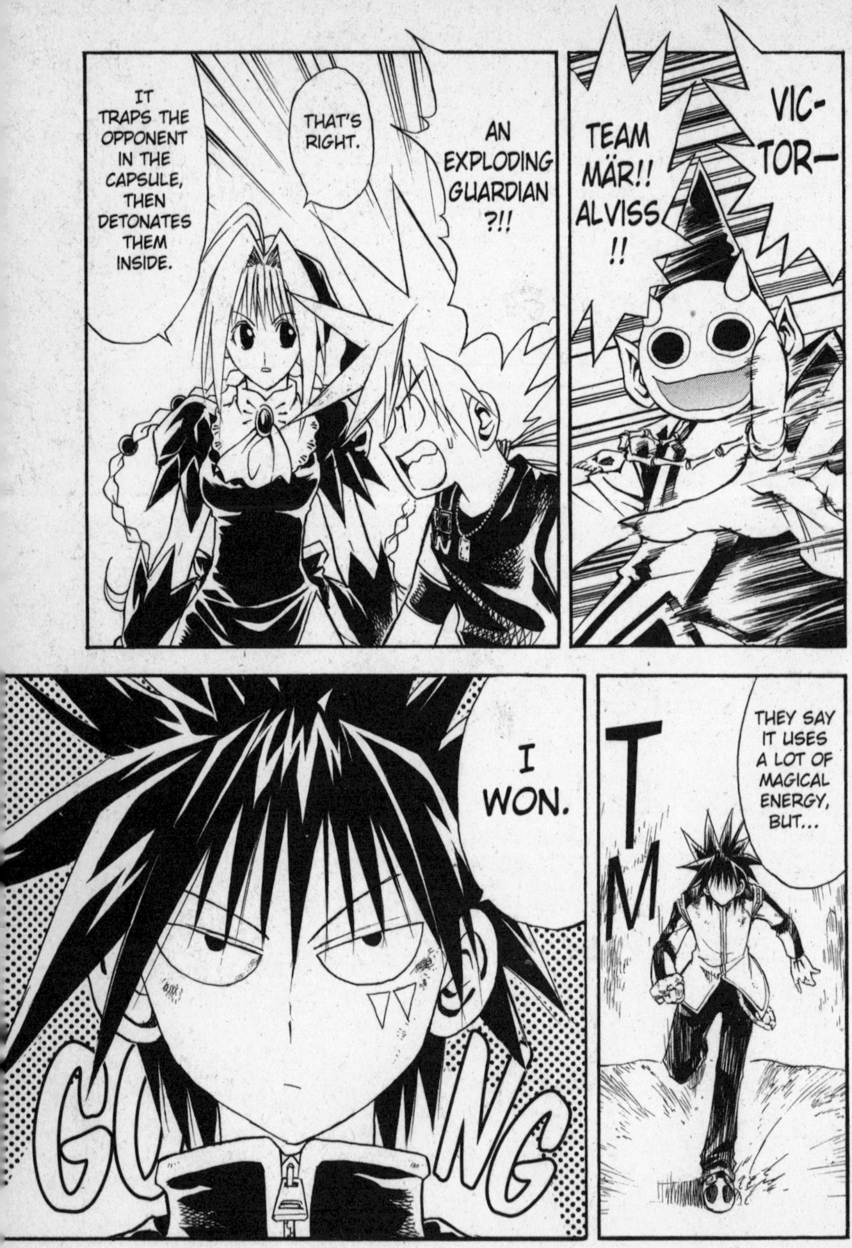
VIC-TOR—
TEAM MÄR!! ALVISS!!
AN EXPLODING GUARDIAN?!!
THAT'S RIGHT.
IT TRAPS THE OPPONENT IN THE CAPSULE, THEN DETONATES THEM INSIDE.
THEY SAY IT USES A LOT OF MAGICAL ENERGY, BUT...
TM
I WON.
GONG

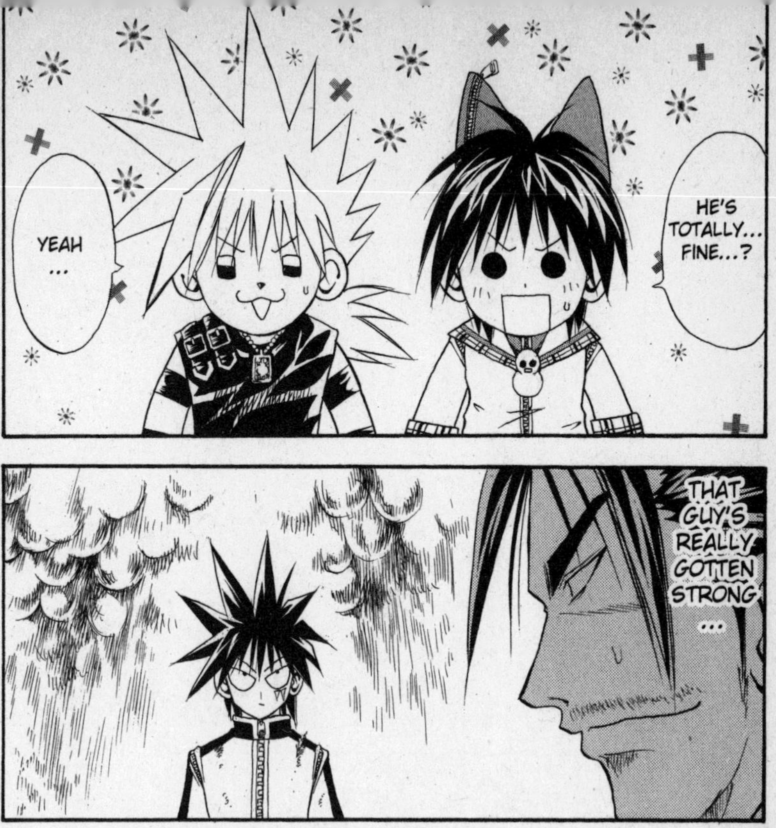
HE'S TOTALLY... FINE...?
YEAH ...
THAT GUY'S REALLY GOTTEN STRONG ...

...POSSIBLY SURPASSING EVEN...*ME*.

IS THAT POSSIBLE?

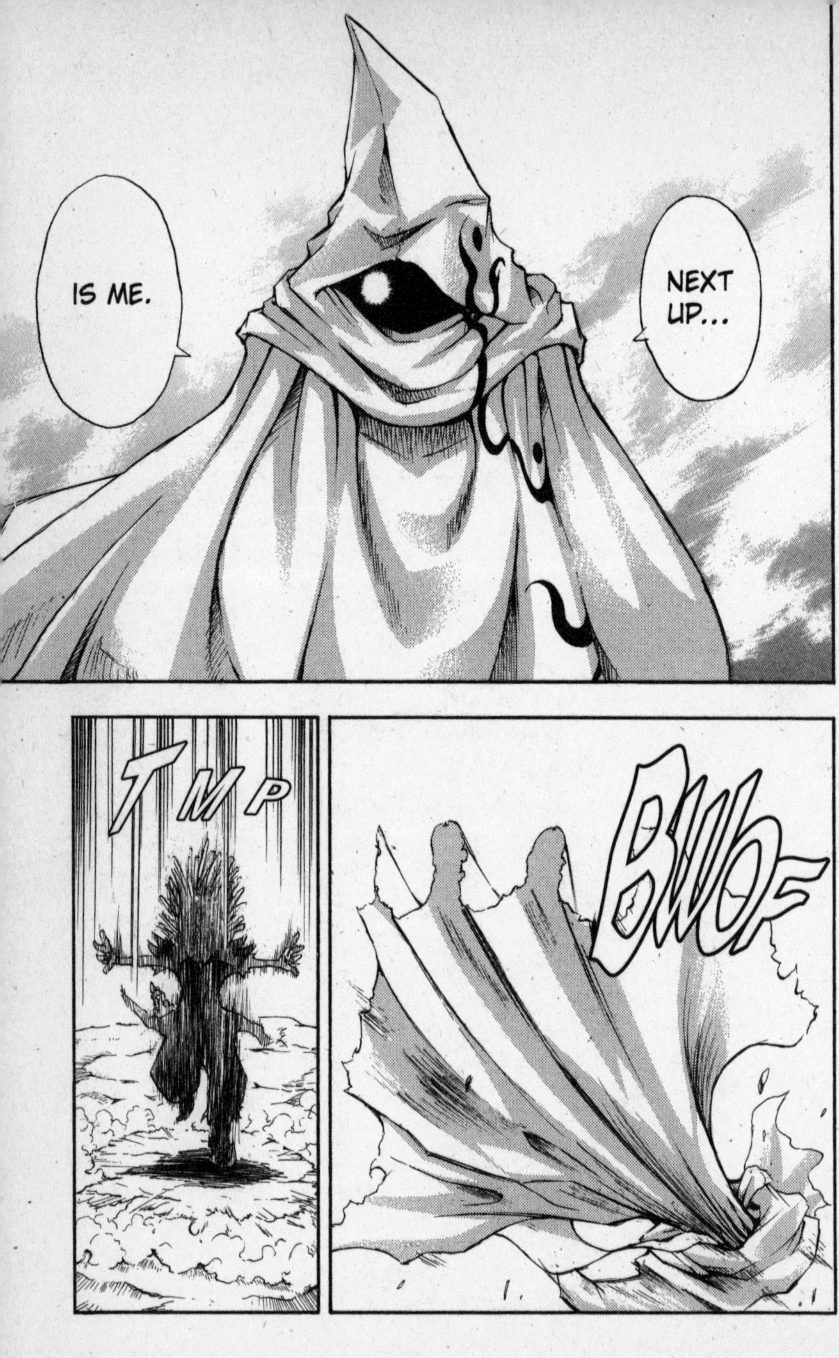
NEXT UP...
IS ME.
BWOF
TMP

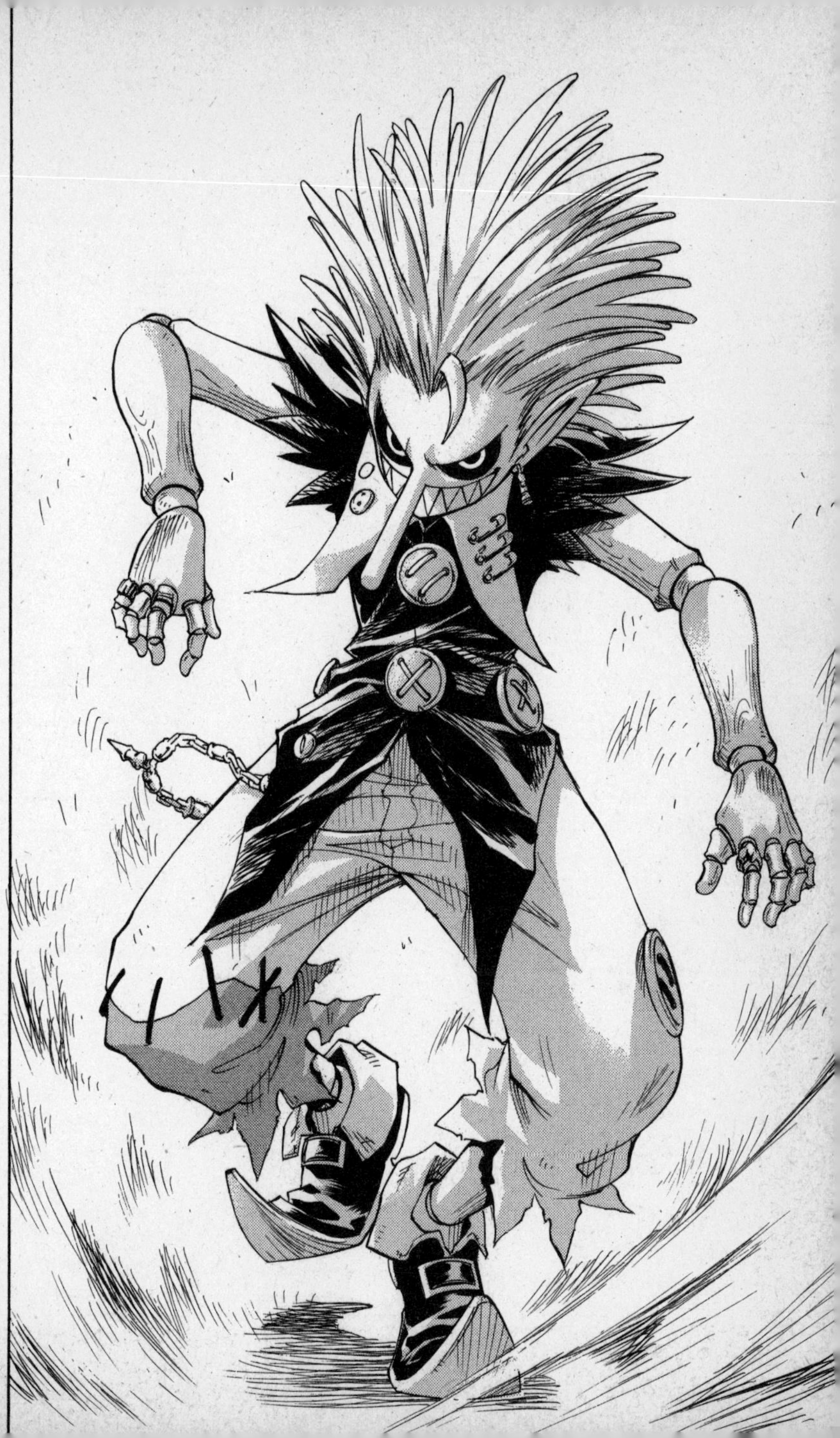

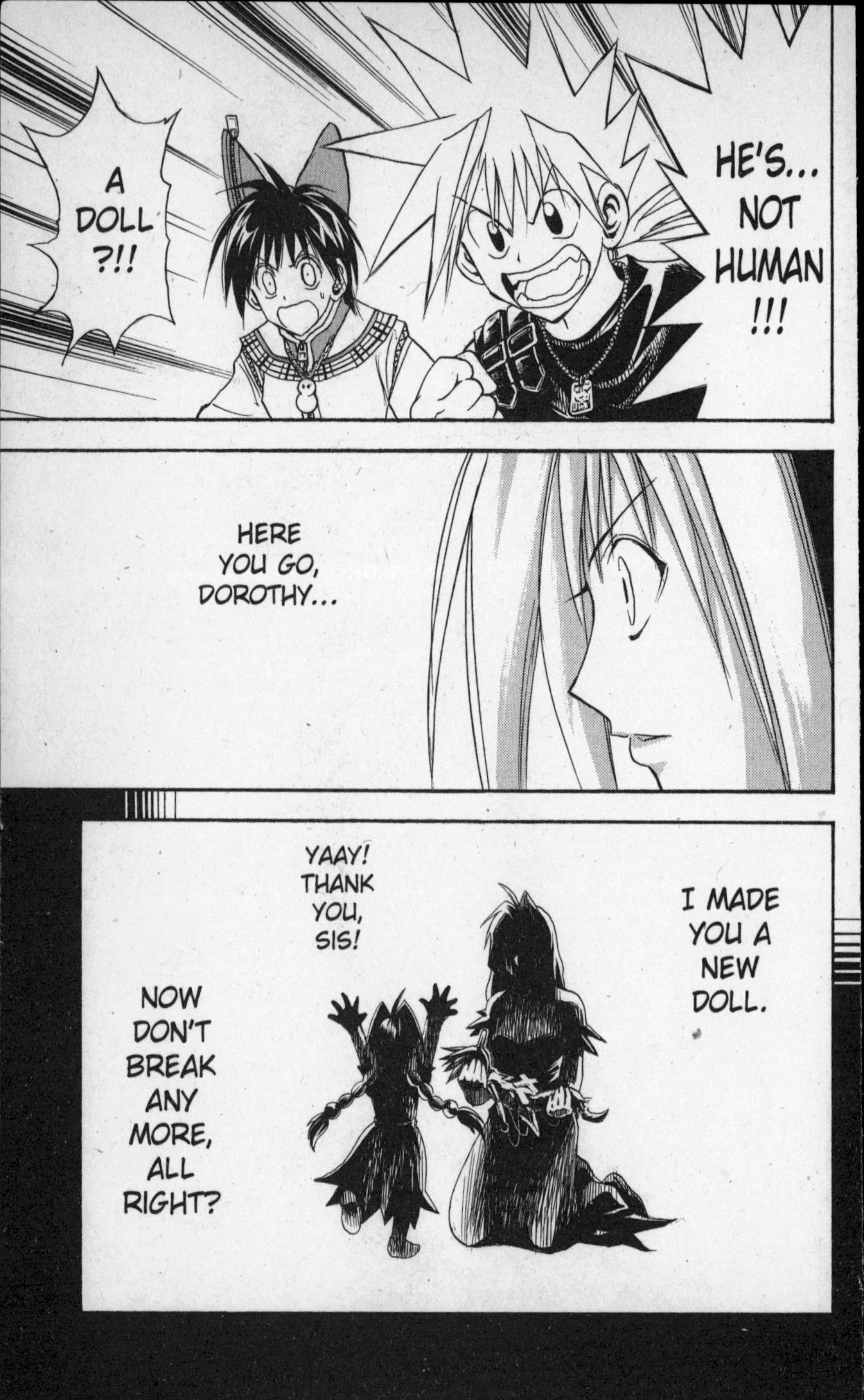
HE'S... NOT HUMAN!!!
A DOLL?!!
HERE YOU GO, DOROTHY...
I MADE YOU A NEW DOLL.
YAAY! THANK YOU, SIS!
NOW DON'T BREAK ANY MORE, ALL RIGHT?

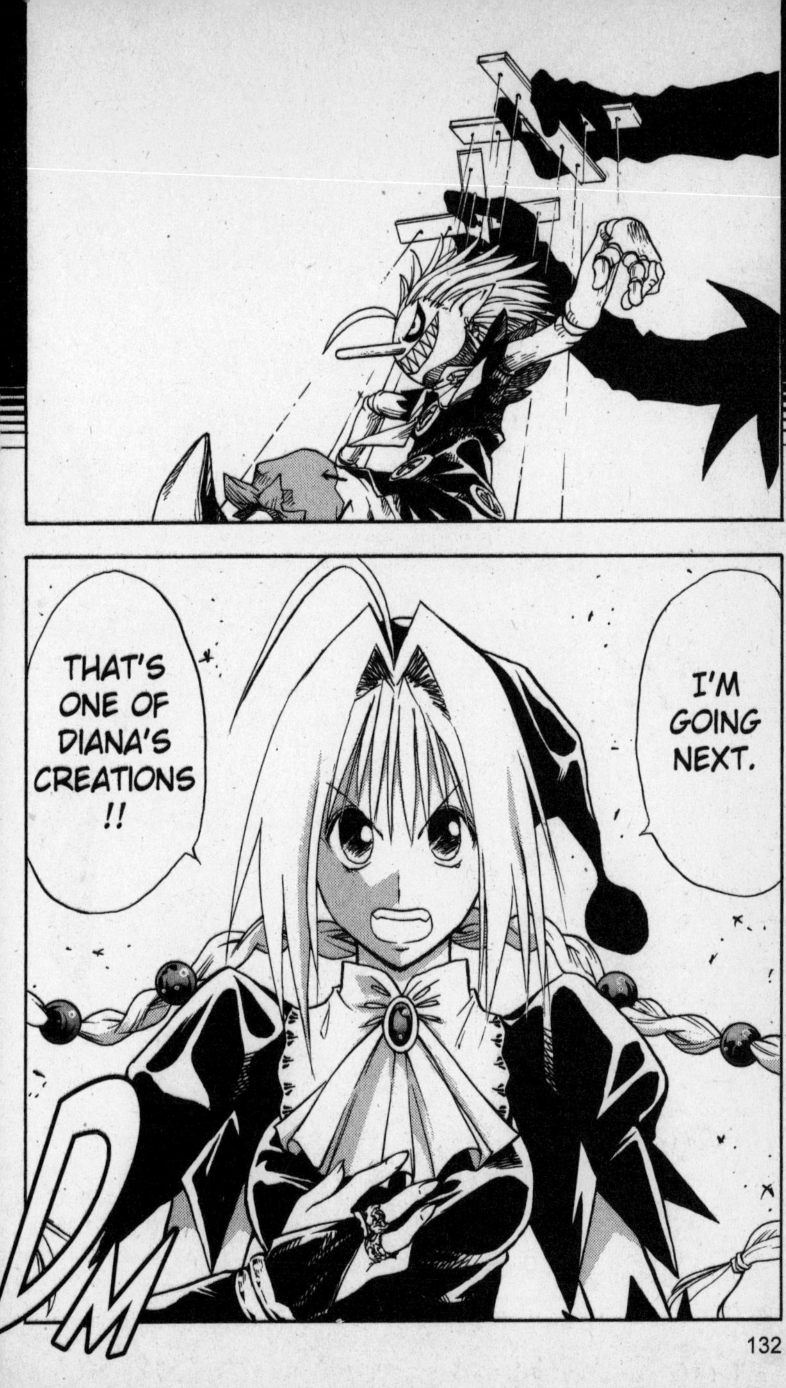
I'M GOING NEXT.
THAT'S ONE OF DIANA'S CREATIONS !!
DM

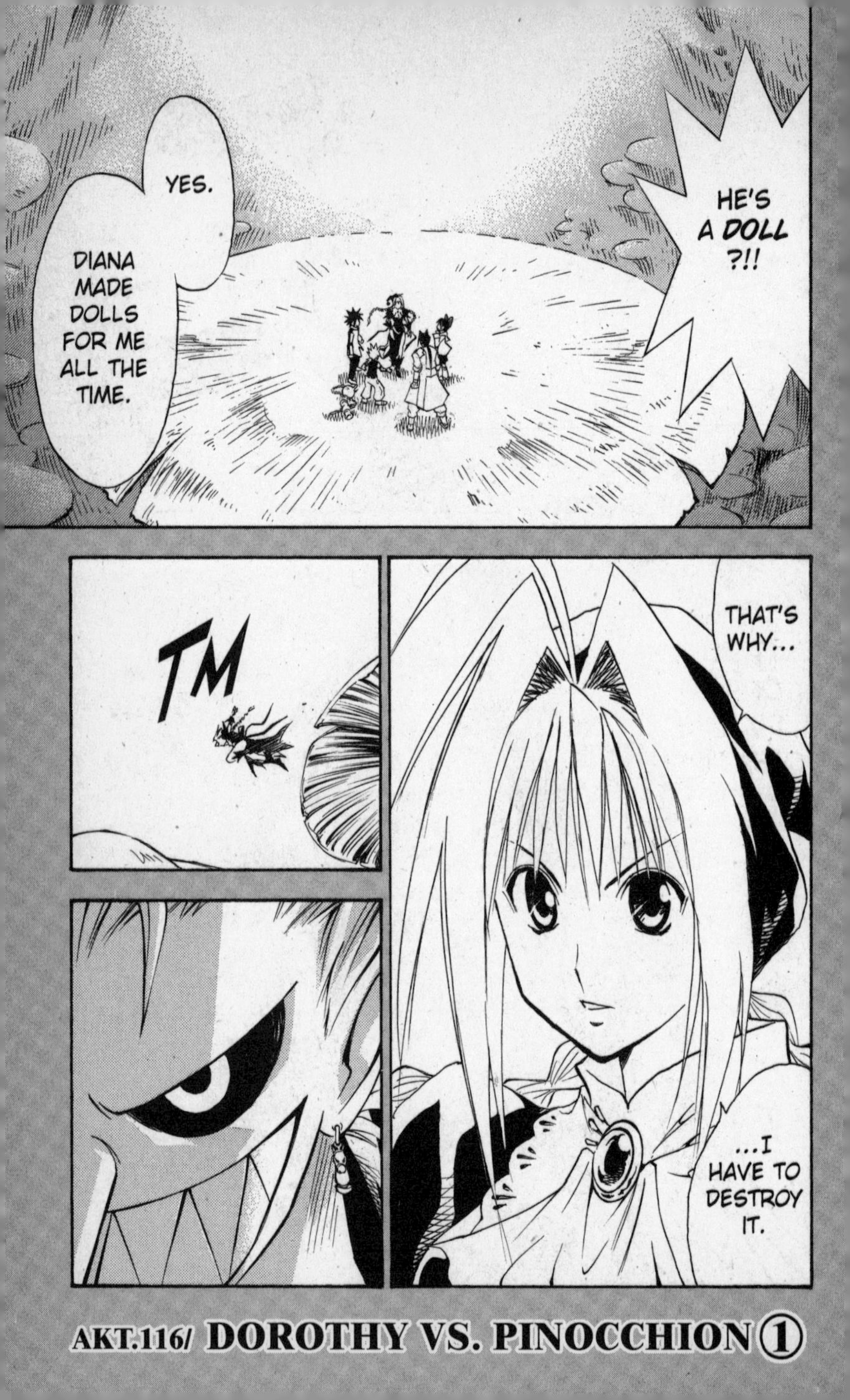
HE'S A DOLL ?!!
YES.
DIANA MADE DOLLS FOR ME ALL THE TIME.
THAT'S WHY...
...I HAVE TO DESTROY IT.
TM

AKT.116/ DOROTHY VS. PINOCCHION ①

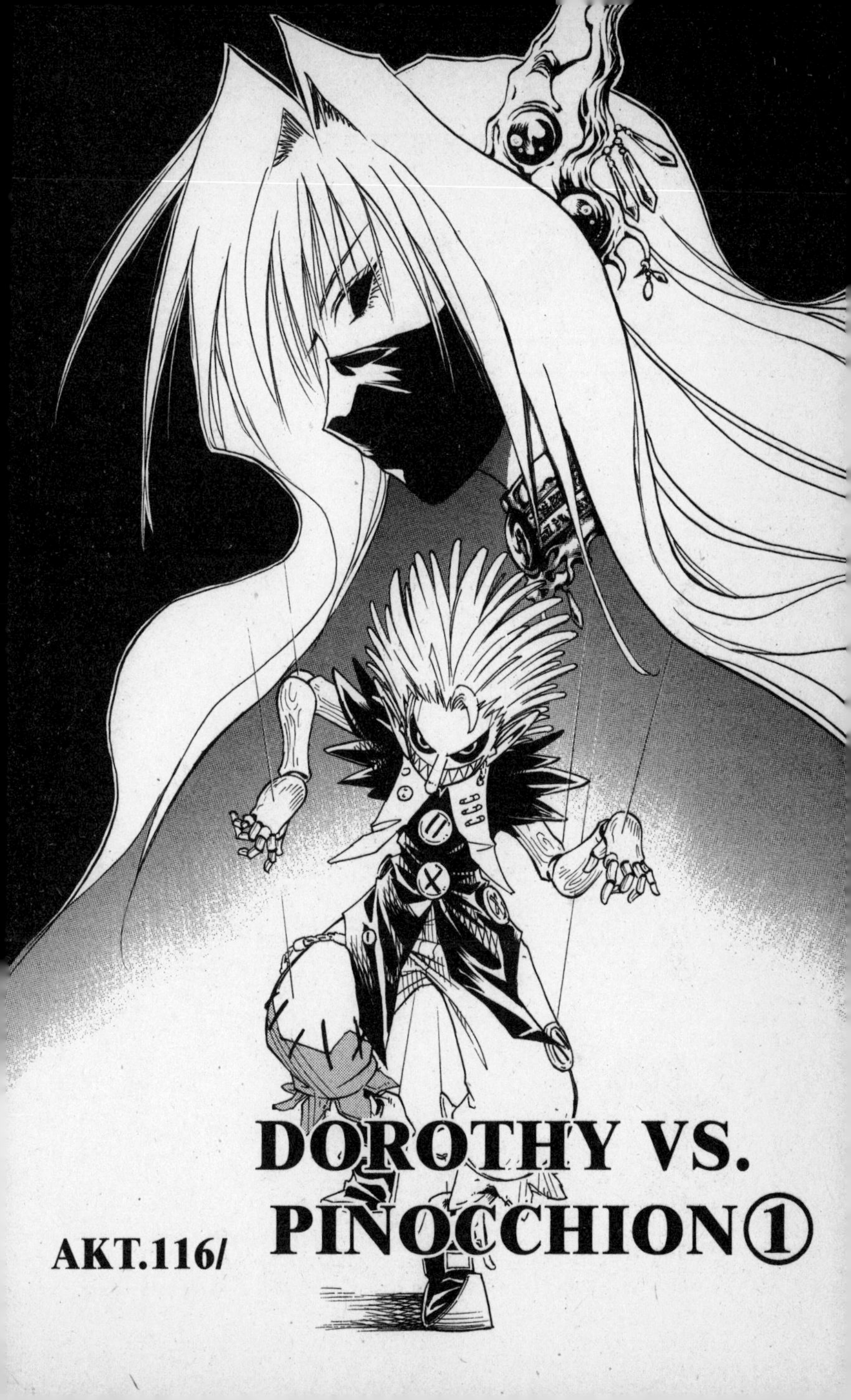

AKT.116/ DOROTHY VS. PINOCCHION①

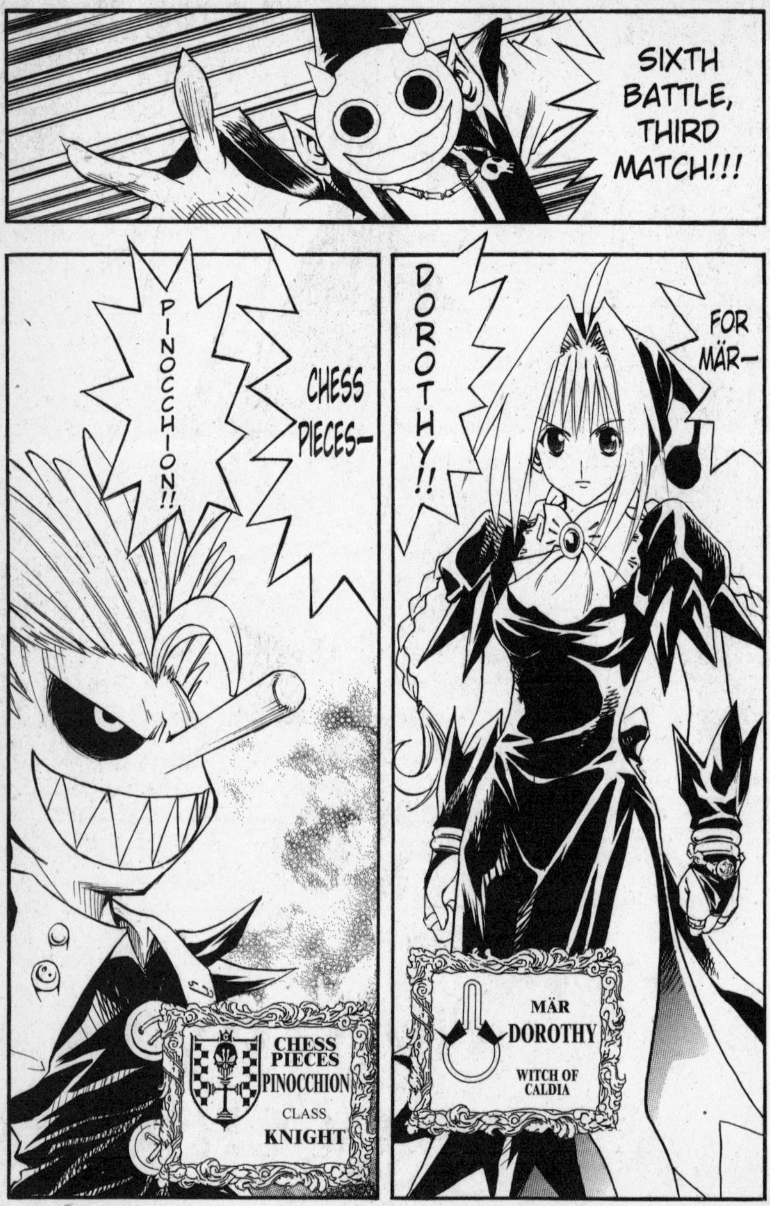
SIXTH BATTLE, THIRD MATCH!!!
FOR MÄR—
DOROTHY!!
MÄR
DOROTHY
WITCH OF CALDIA
CHESS PIECES—
PINOCCHION!!
CHESS PIECES
PINOCCHION
CLASS
KNIGHT

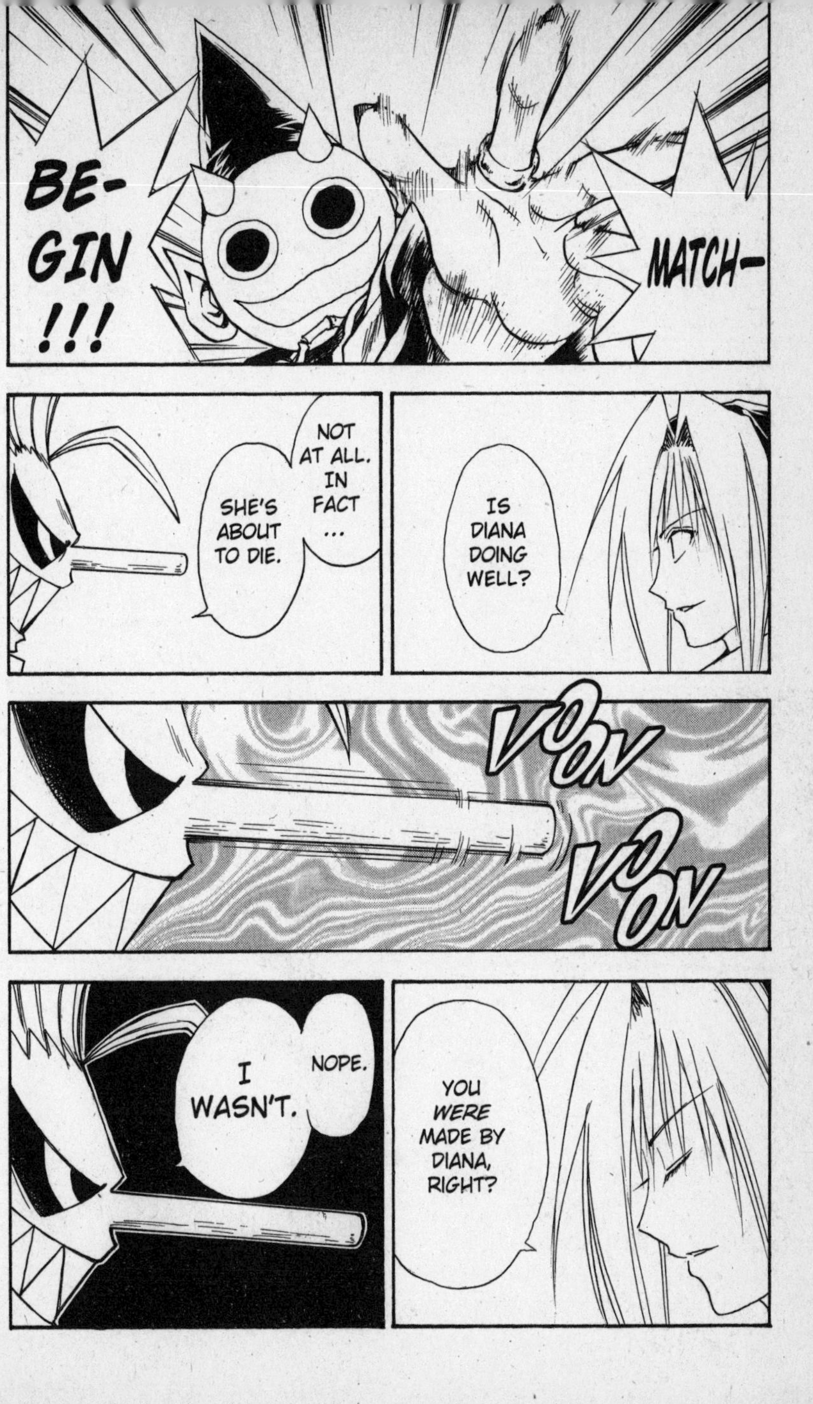
MATCH-
BE-GIN!!!
IS DIANA DOING WELL?
NOT AT ALL. IN FACT...
SHE'S ABOUT TO DIE.
VOON
VOON
YOU *WERE* MADE BY DIANA, RIGHT?
NOPE.
I WASN'T.

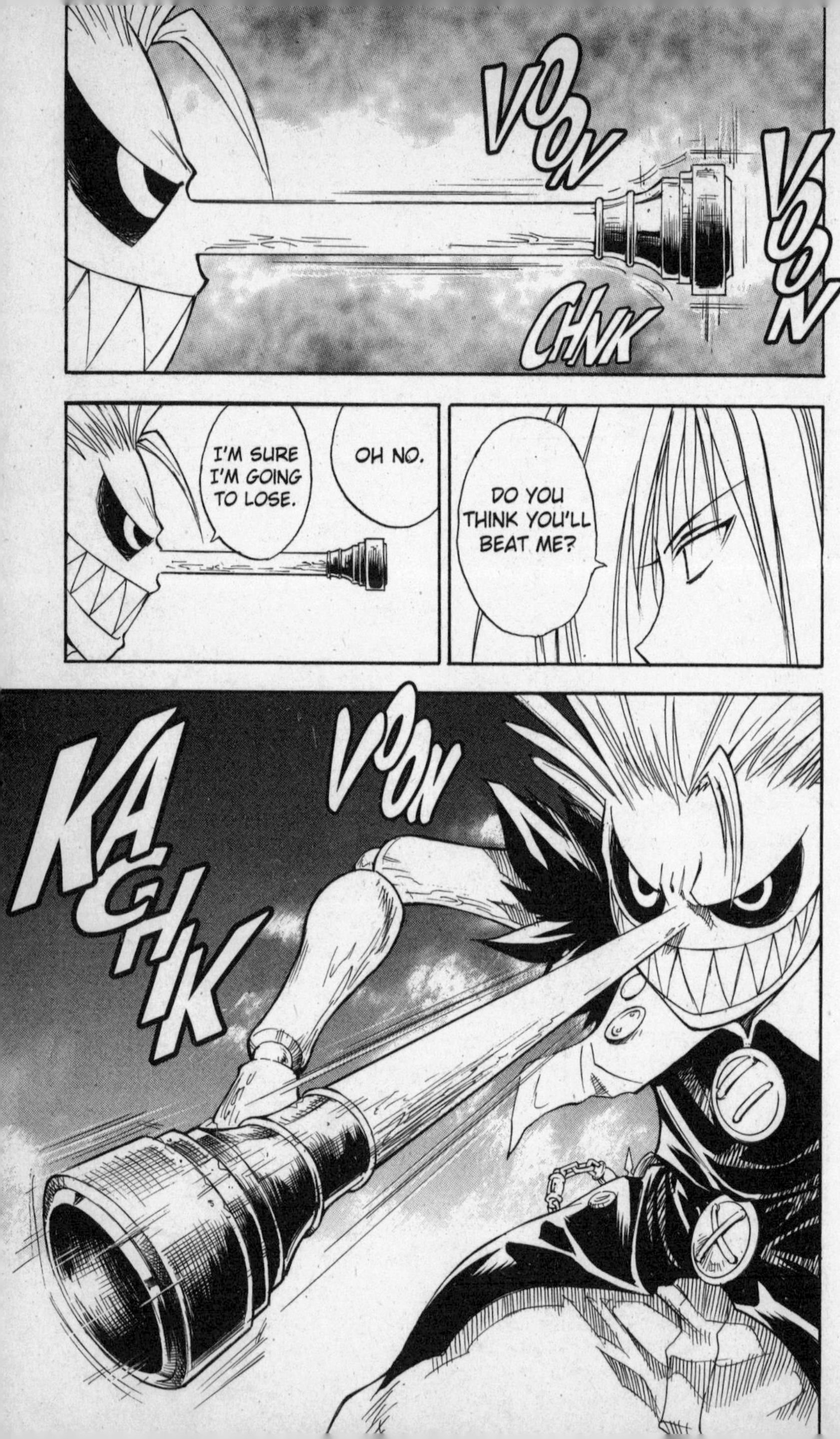
VOOON
VOOON
CHNK
DO YOU THINK YOU'LL BEAT ME?
OH NO.
I'M SURE I'M GOING TO LOSE.
VOOON
KACHK

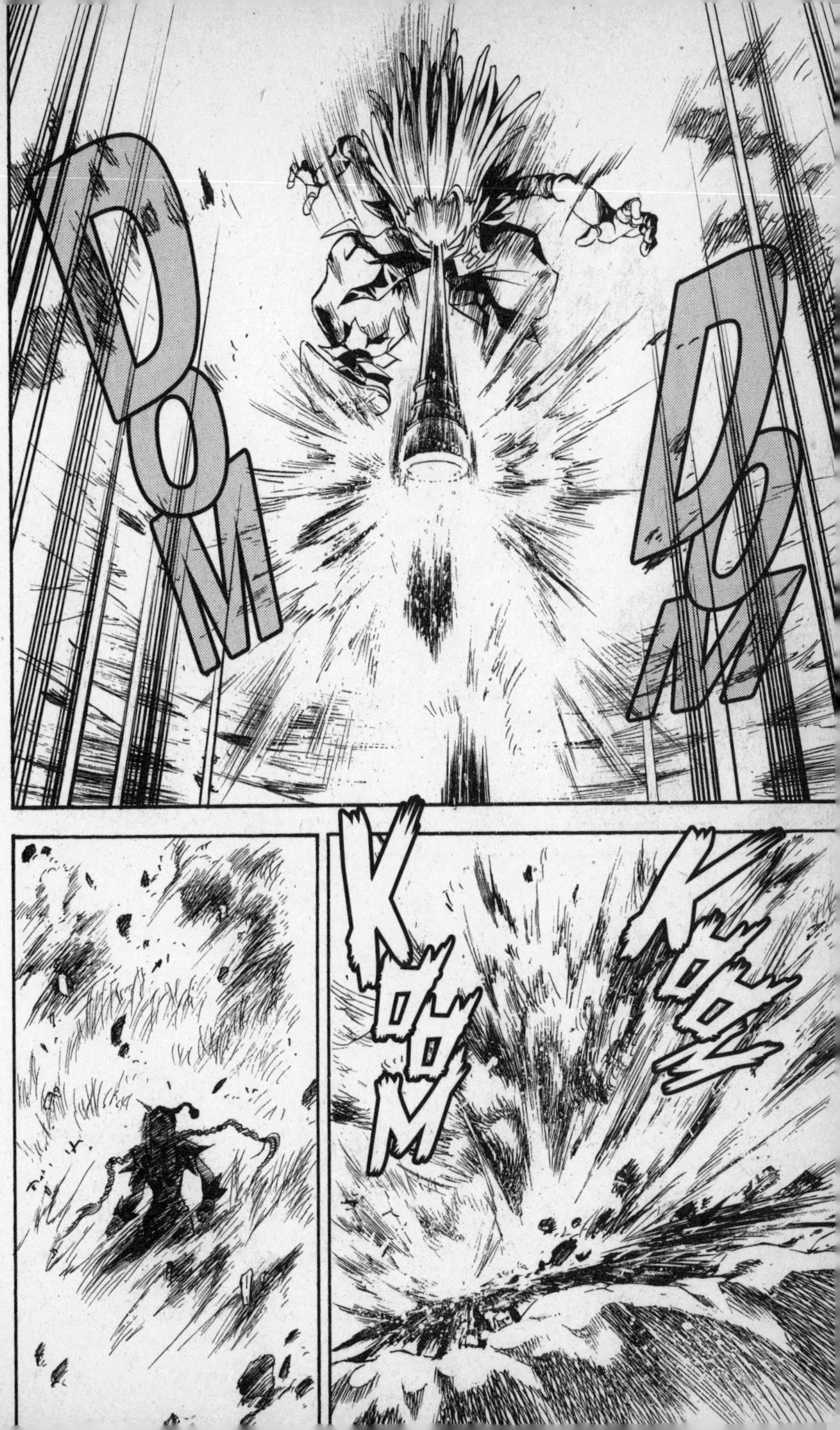
DOOM
DOOM
KOOM
KOOM

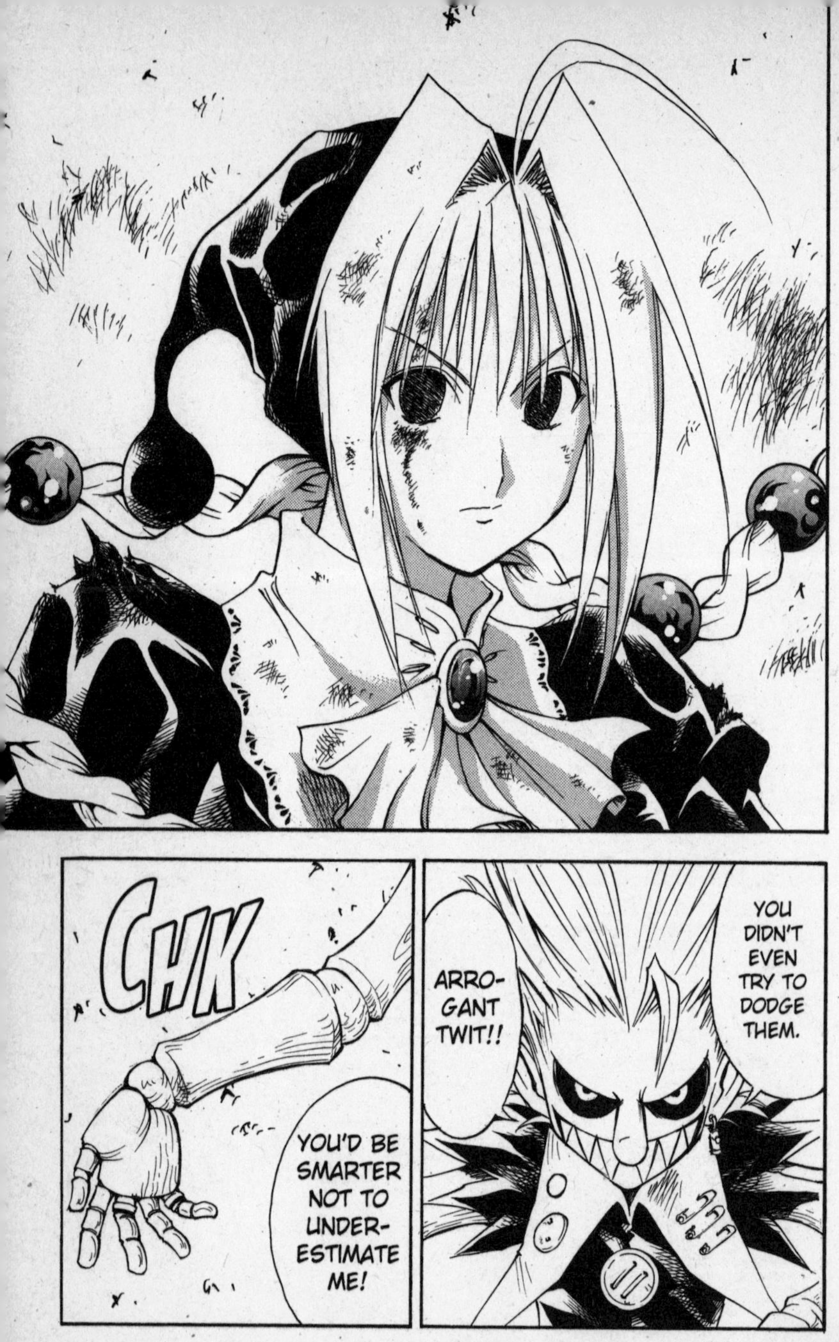
YOU DIDN'T EVEN TRY TO DODGE THEM.
ARRO-GANT TWIT!!
CHK
YOU'D BE SMARTER NOT TO UNDER-ESTIMATE ME!

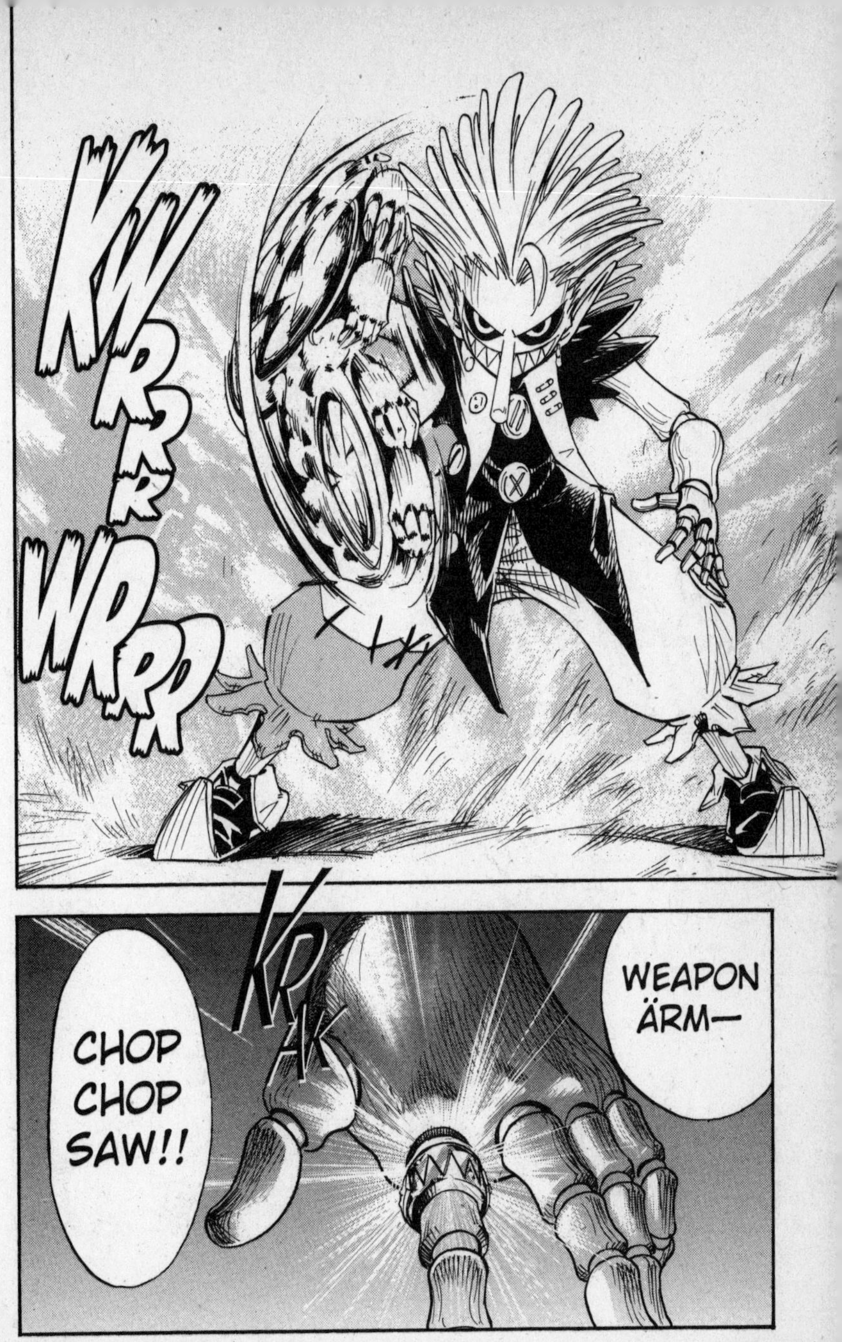

KWRRR
WRRR
WEAPON ÄRM—
KRAK
CHOP CHOP SAW!!

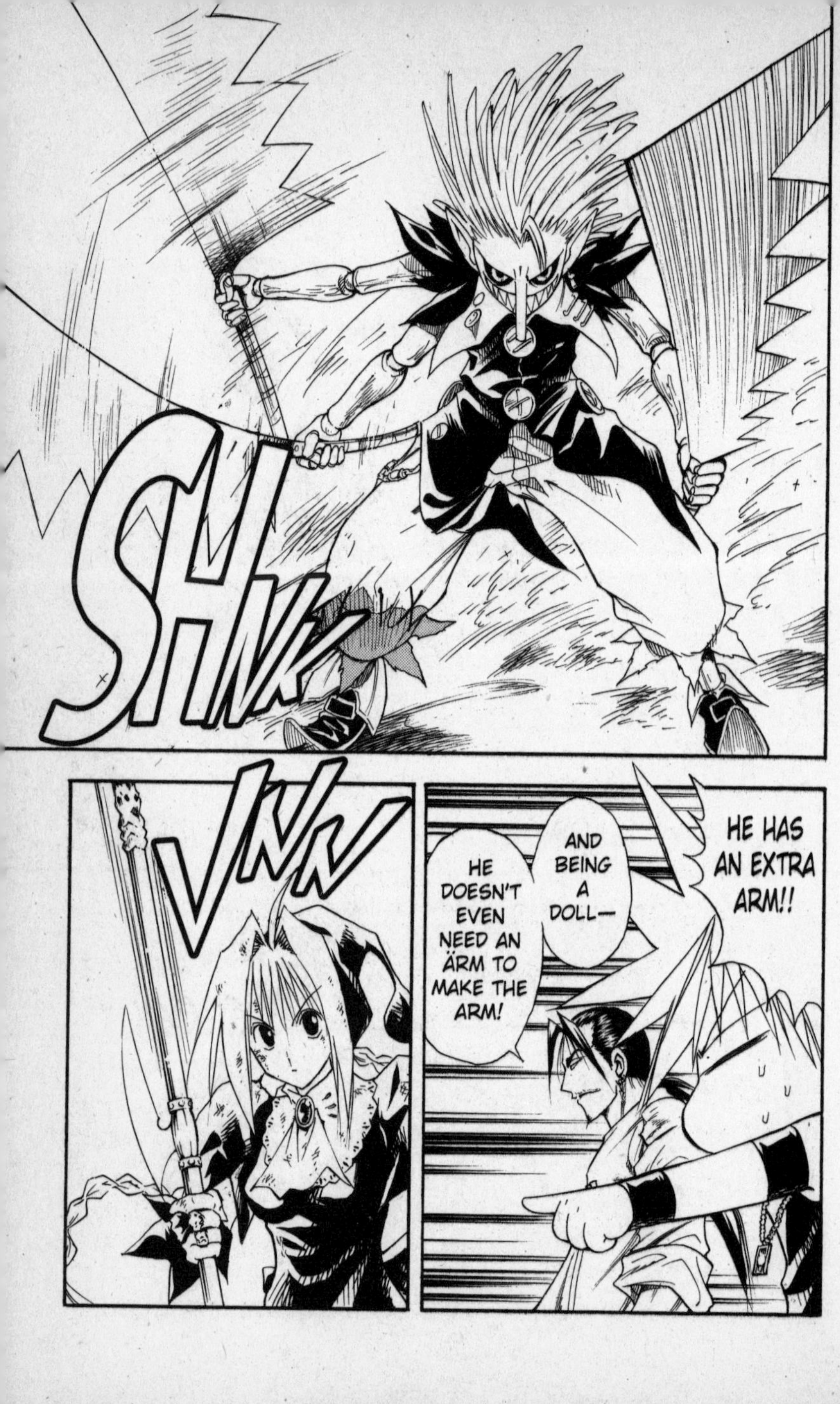
SHNK
HE HAS AN EXTRA ARM!!
AND BEING A DOLL—
HE DOESN'T EVEN NEED AN ÄRM TO MAKE THE ARM!
VNN

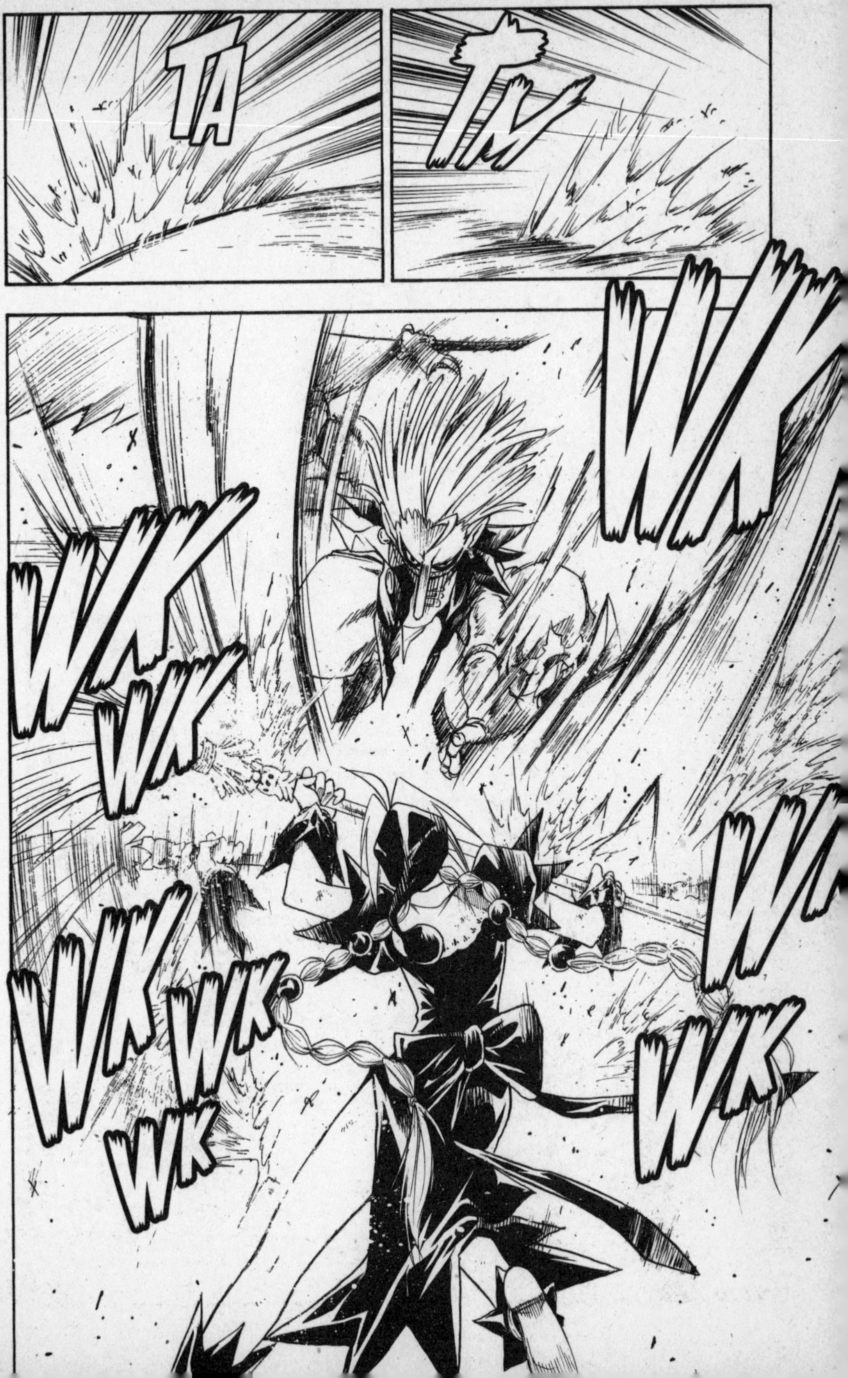
TA
TA
WK
WK
WK
WK
WK
WK
WK
WK

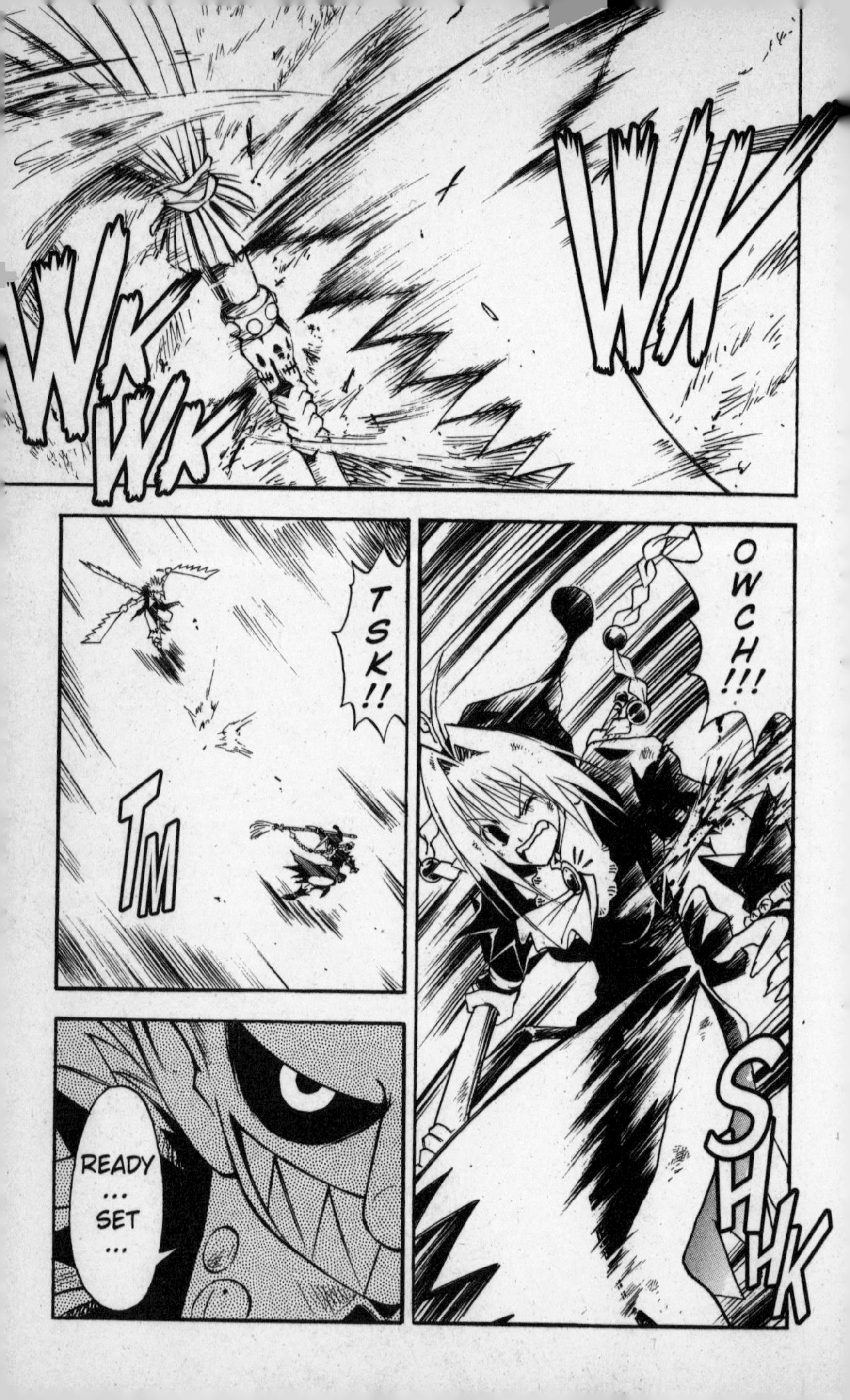
WK
WK
OWCH!!!
SHHK
TSK!!
TM
READY ... SET ...

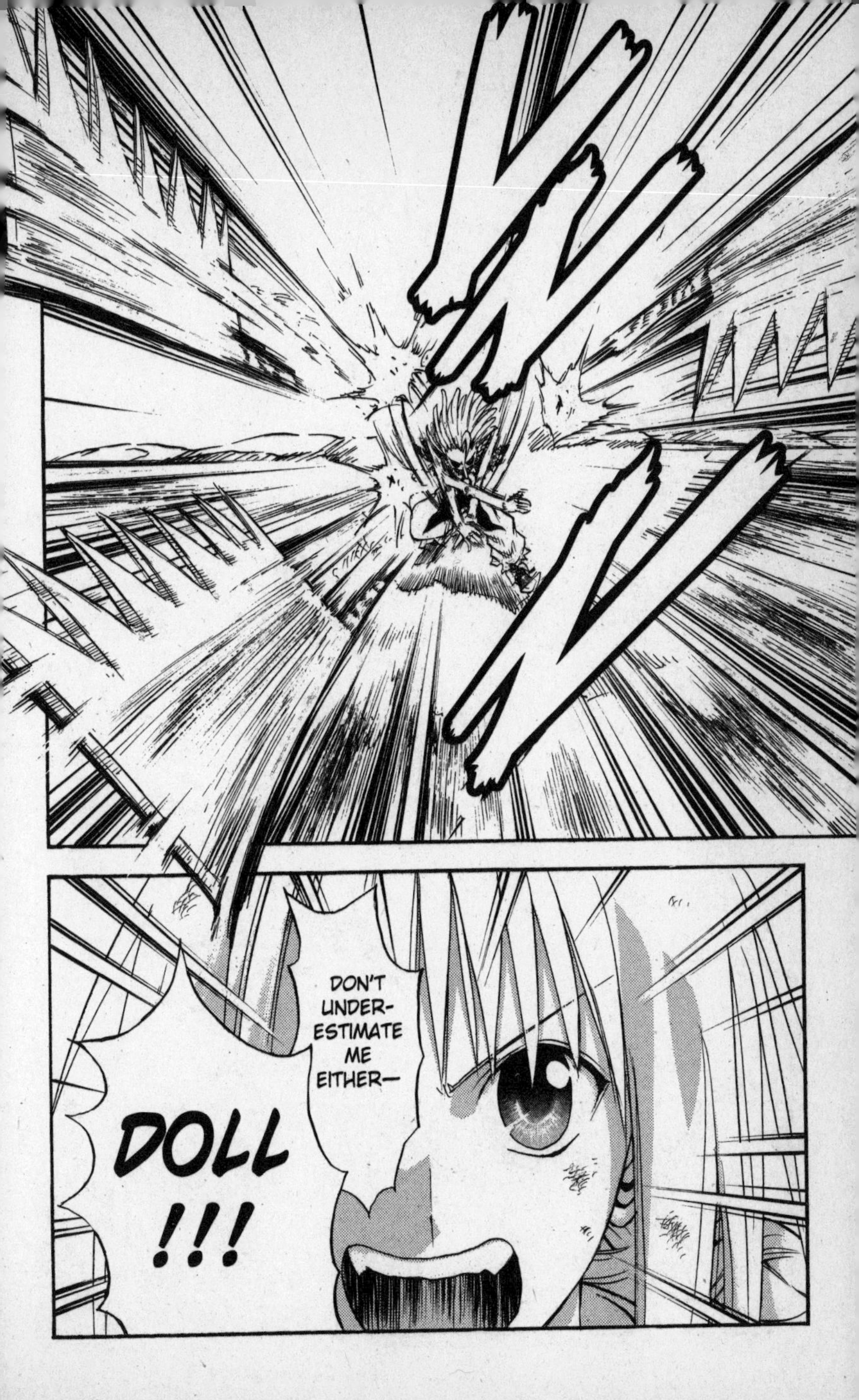
DON'T UNDER-ESTIMATE ME EITHER—
DOLL !!!

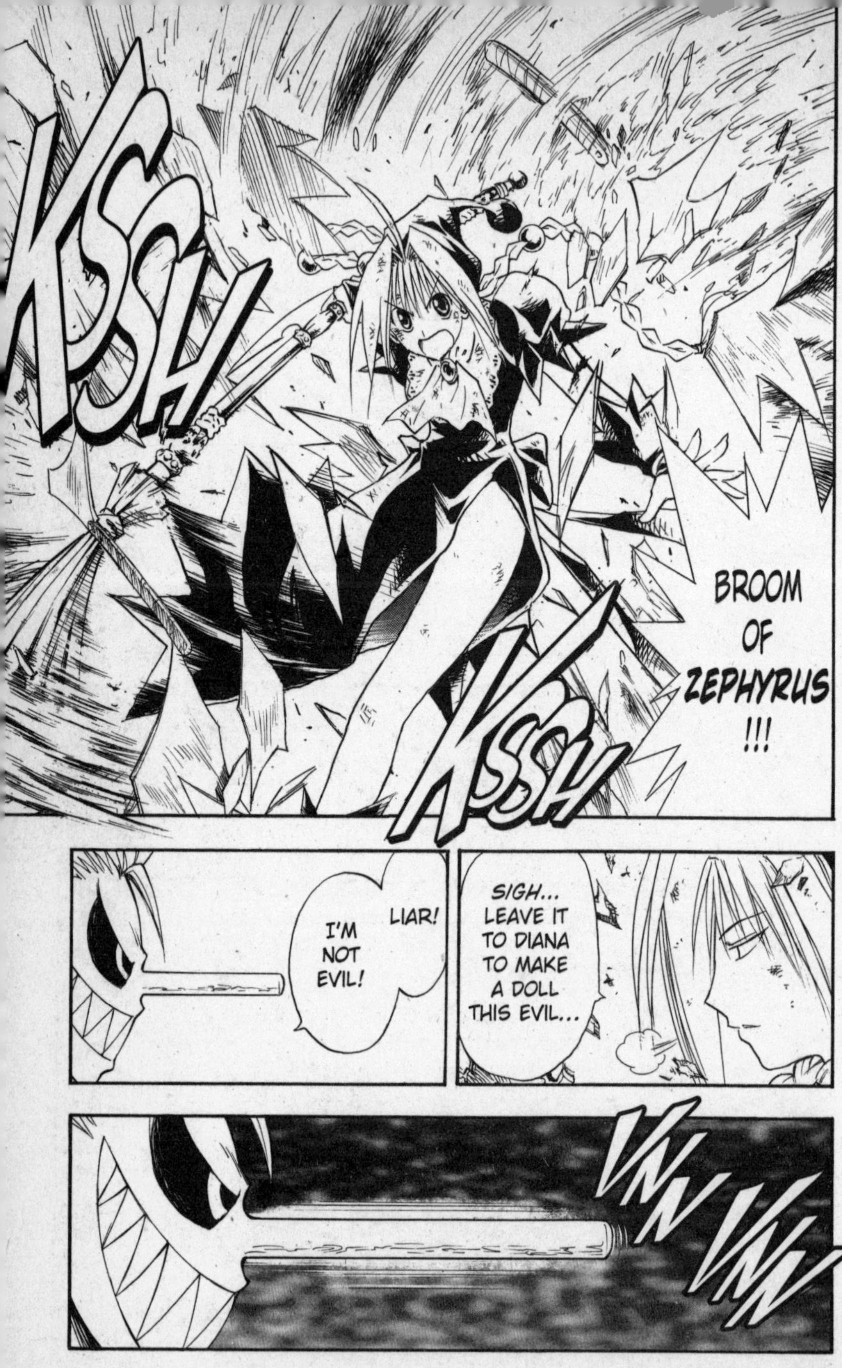
BROOM OF ZEPHYRUS !!!
KSSH
KSSH
SIGH... LEAVE IT TO DIANA TO MAKE A DOLL THIS EVIL...
LIAR! I'M NOT EVIL!
VNN VNN

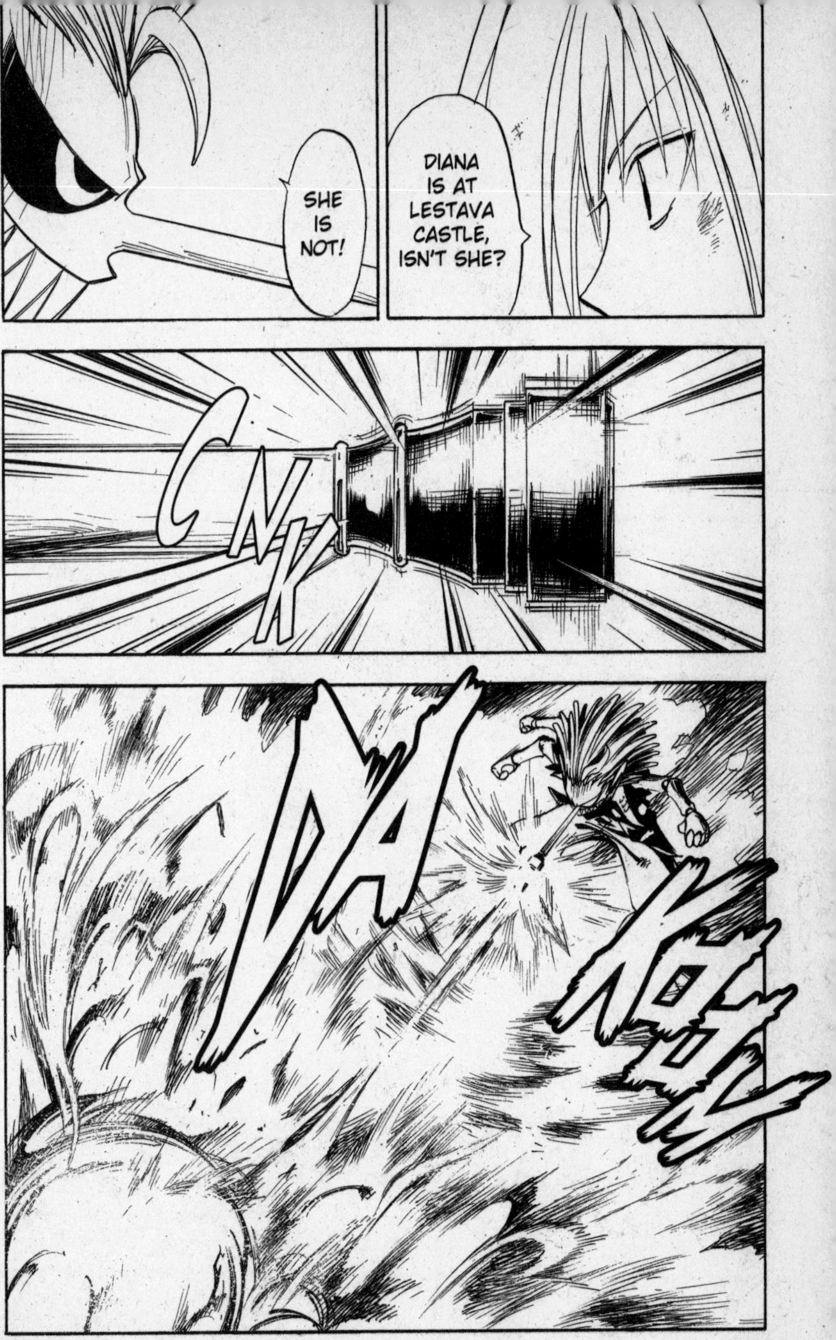

DIANA IS AT LESTAVA CASTLE, ISN'T SHE?
SHE IS NOT!
CNK
DA
KOON

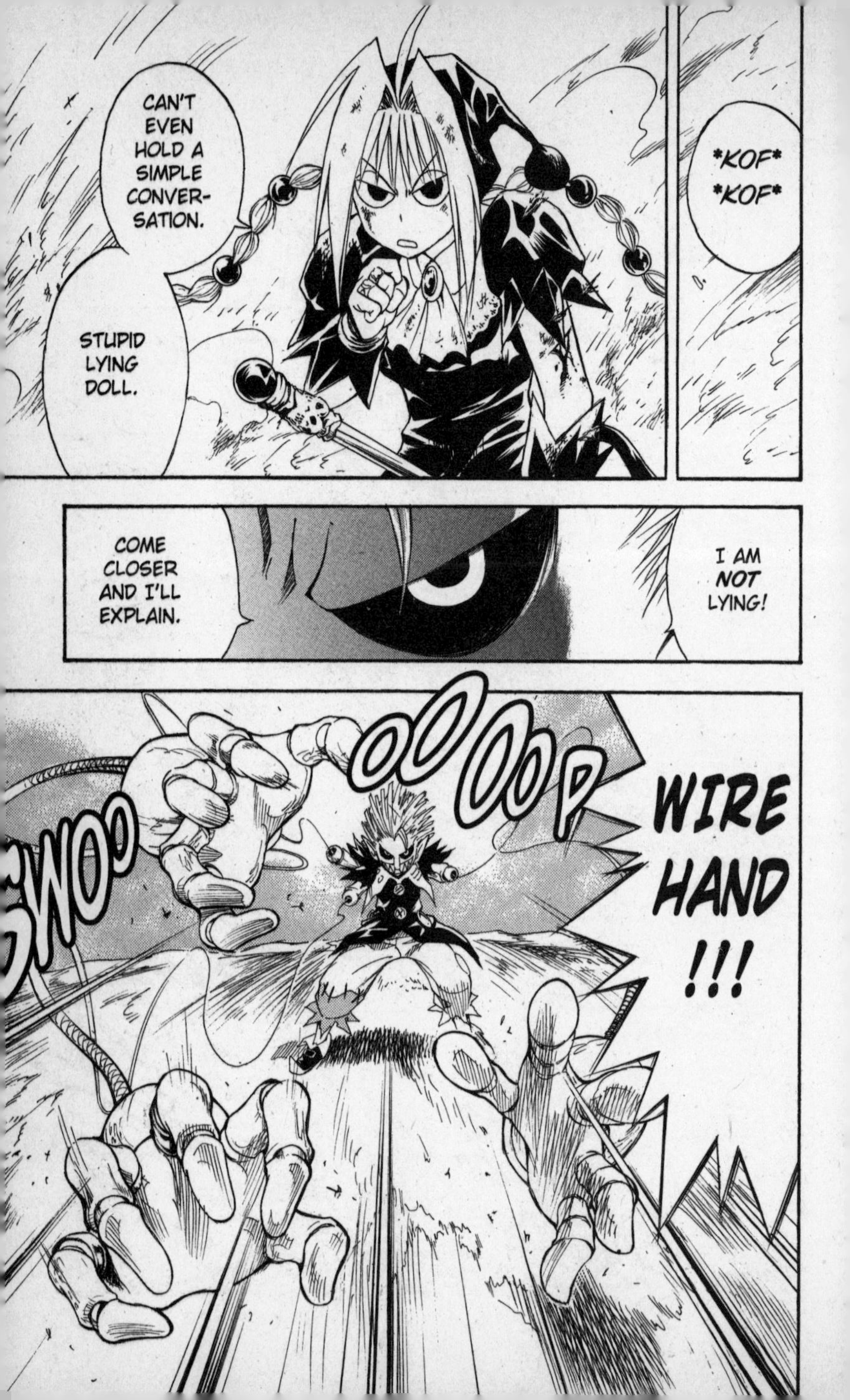
KOF *KOF*
CAN'T EVEN HOLD A SIMPLE CONVERSATION.
STUPID LYING DOLL.
I AM NOT LYING!
COME CLOSER AND I'LL EXPLAIN.
WIRE HAND!!!
SWOOOOOP

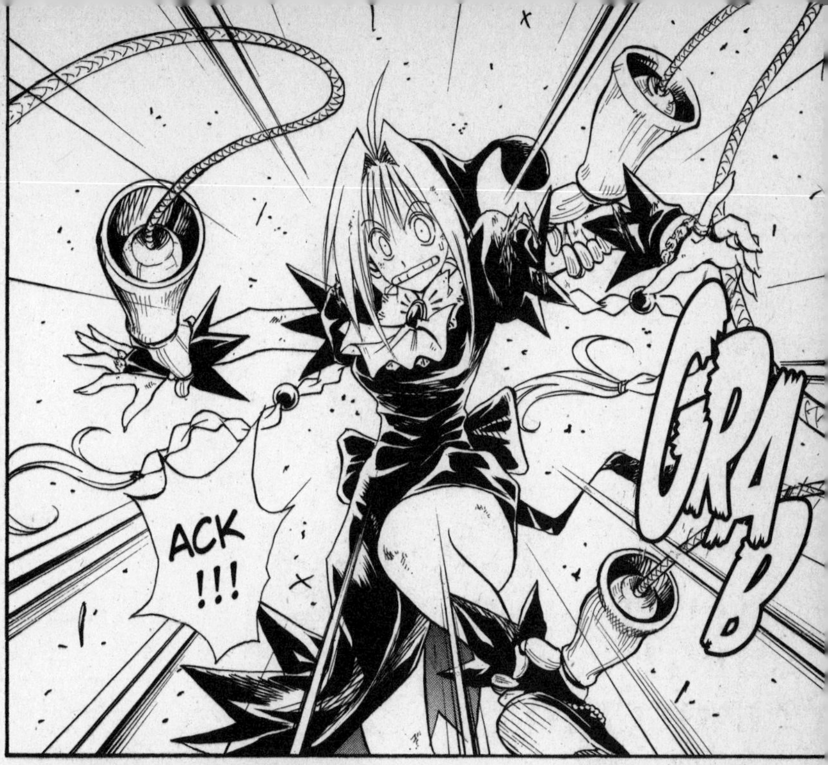
GRAB
ACK!!!

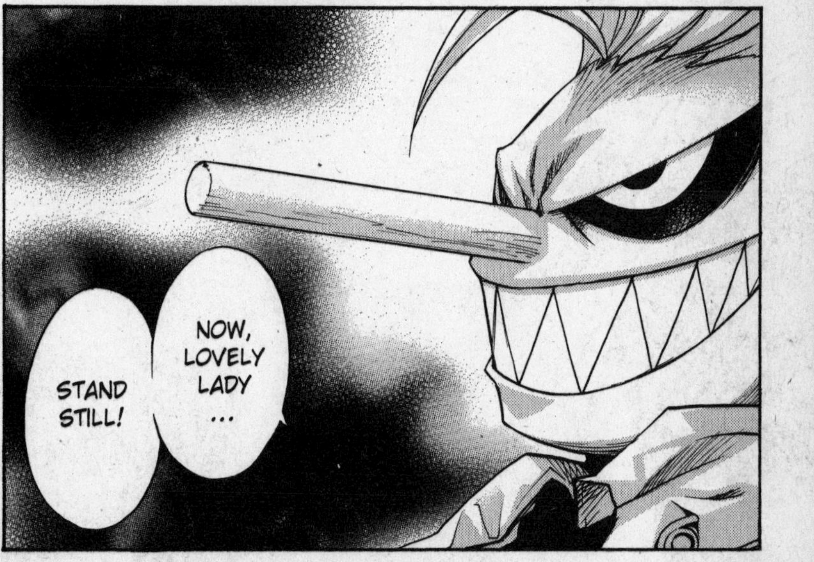
NOW, LOVELY LADY...
STAND STILL!

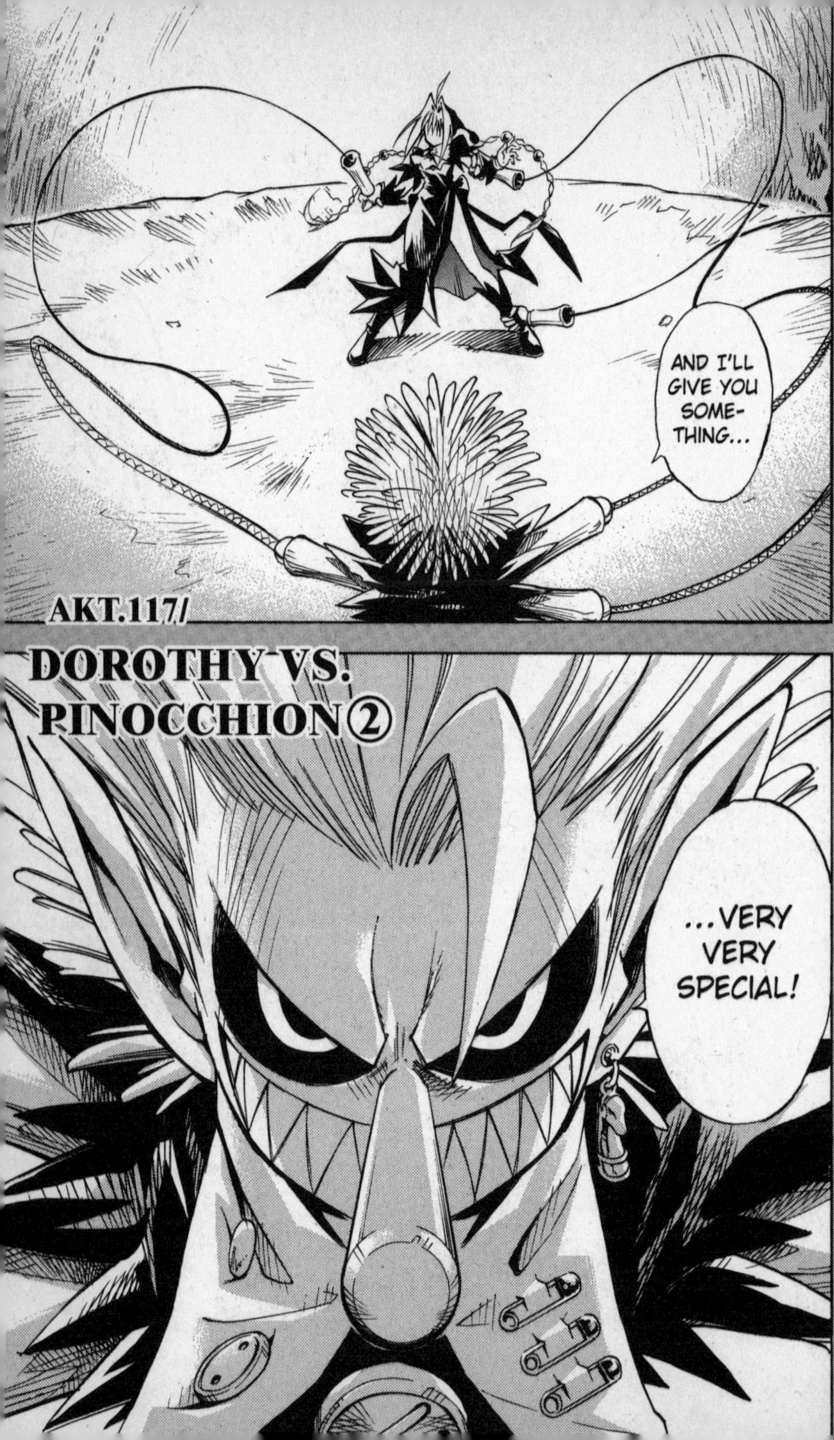
AND I'LL GIVE YOU SOME-THING...
AKT.117/
DOROTHY VS. PINOCCHION②
...VERY VERY SPECIAL!

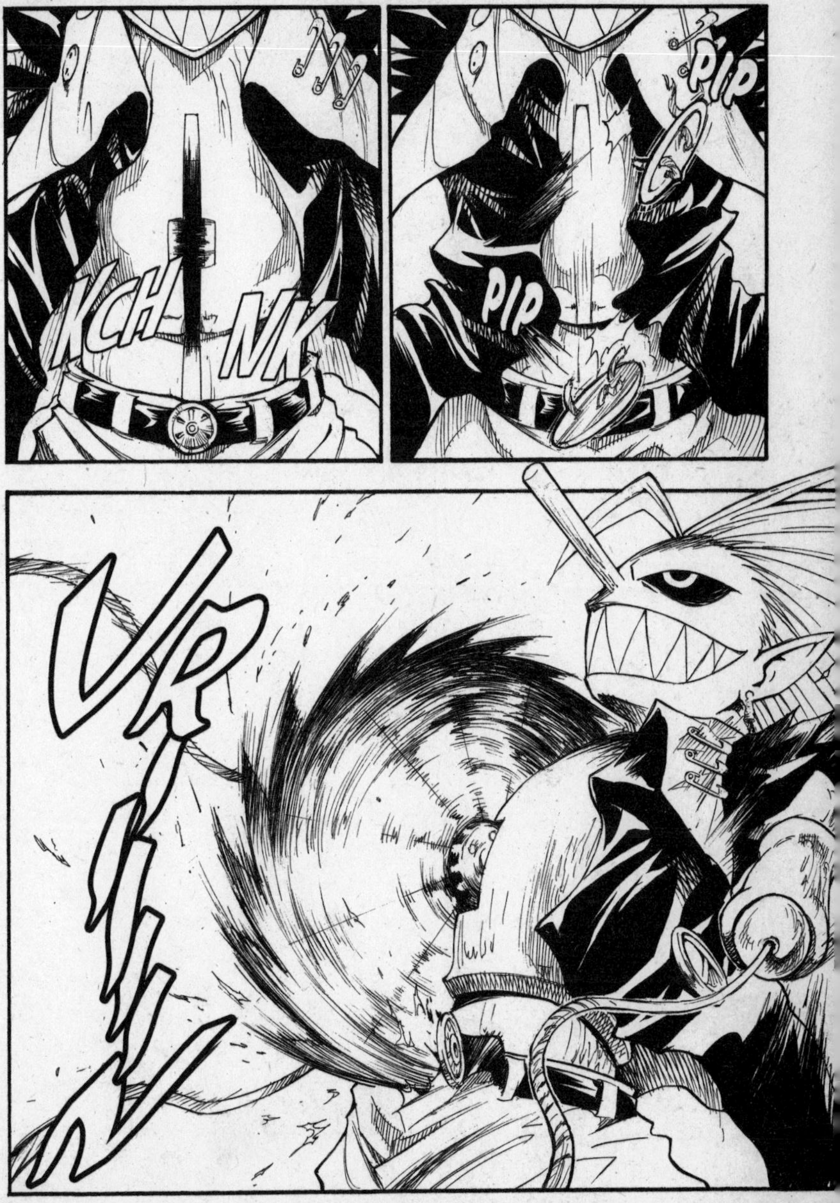
PIP
PIP
KCH NK

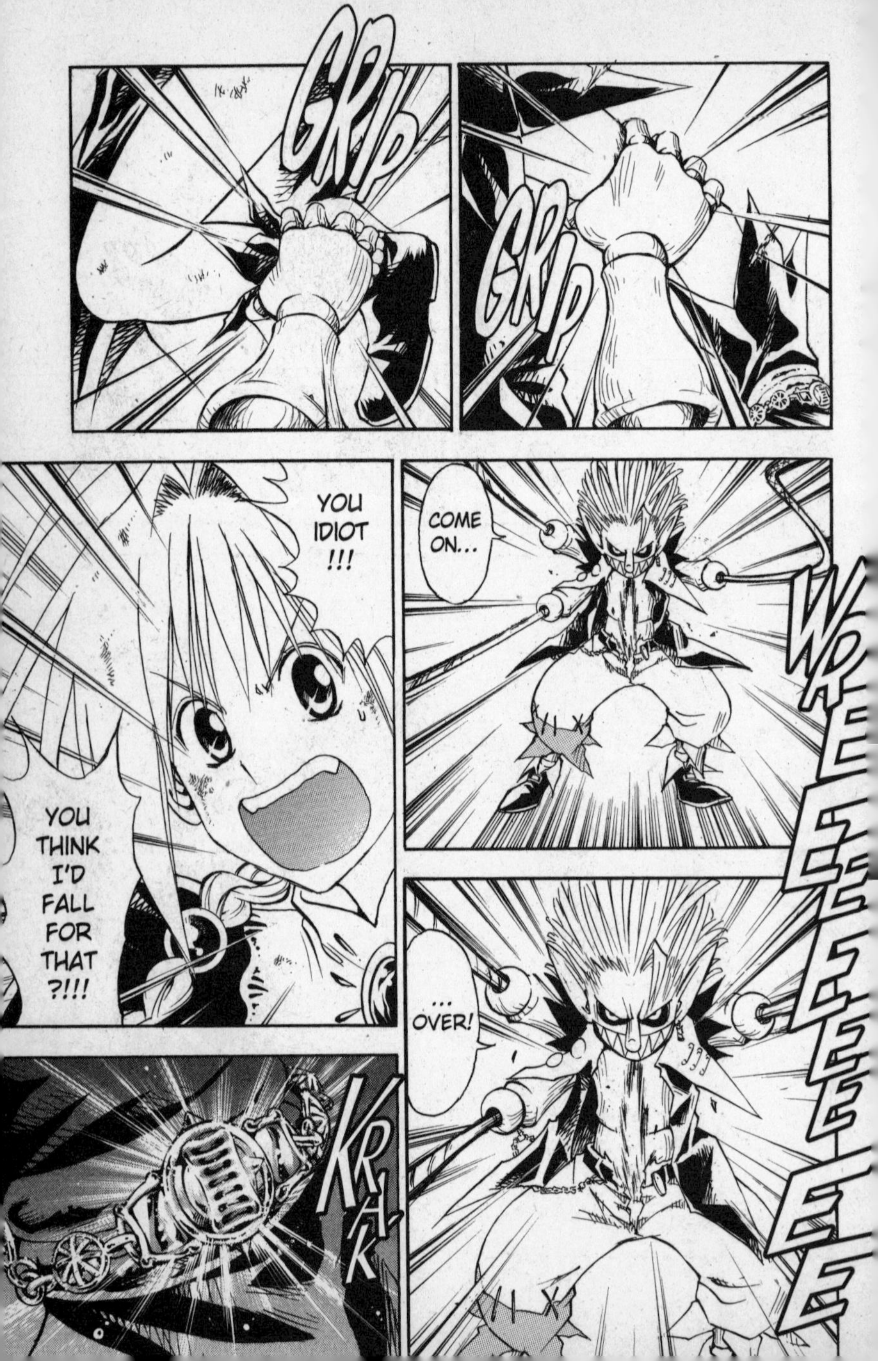
GRIP
GRIP
COME ON...
WREEEEEEEEEE
... OVER!
YOU IDIOT !!!
YOU THINK I'D FALL FOR THAT ?!!!
KRAHK

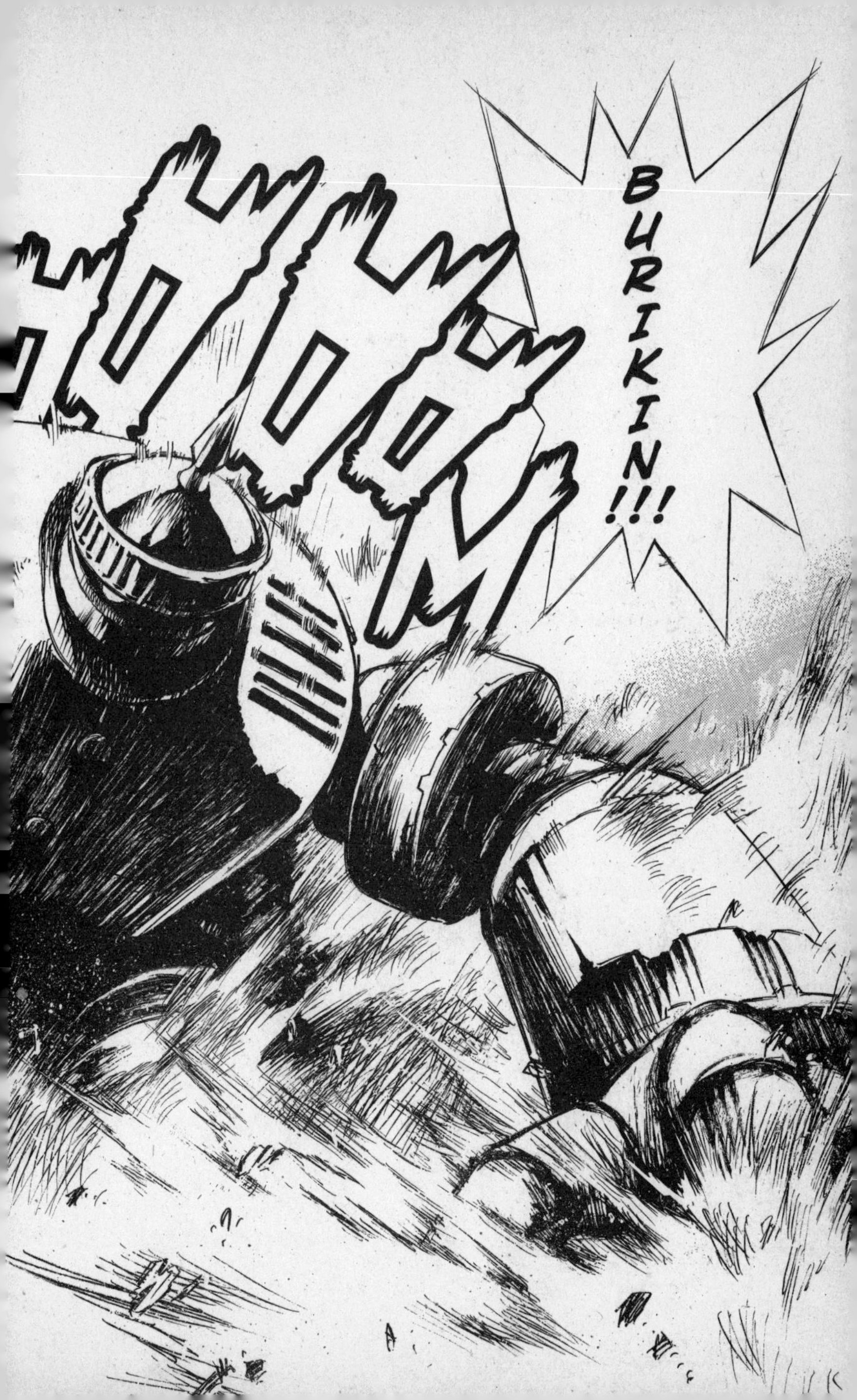
BURIKIN!!!

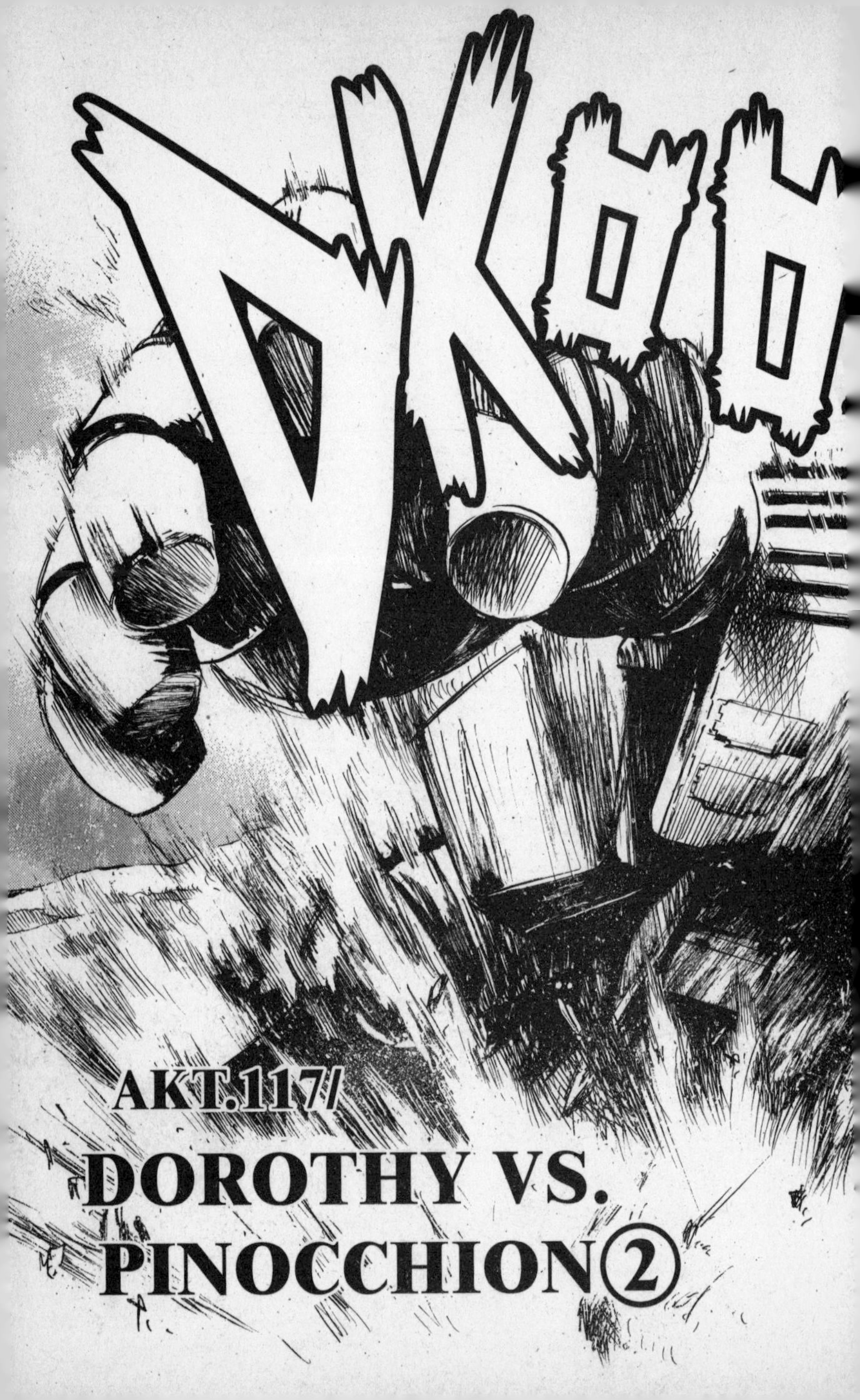
AKT.117/
DOROTHY VS.
PINOCCHION②

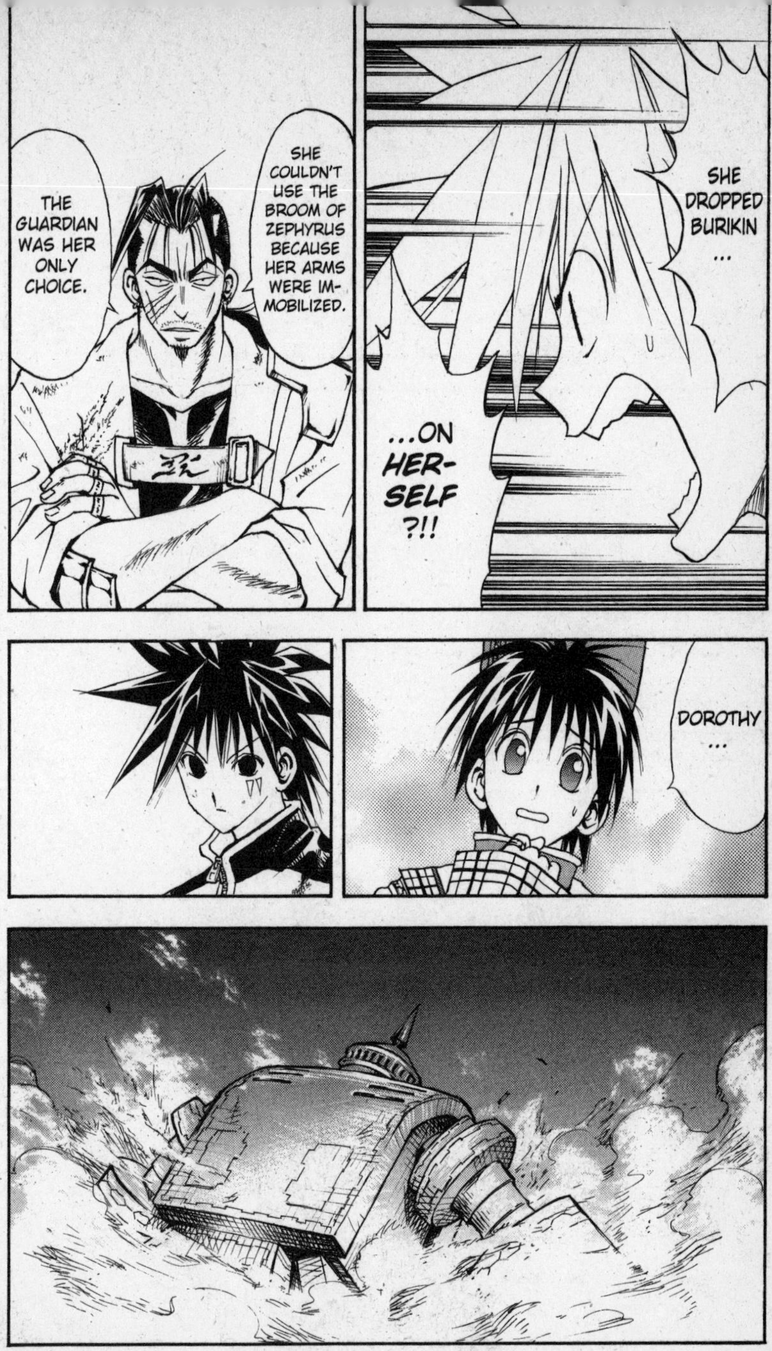
SHE DROPPED BURIKIN ...
...ON HER-SELF ?!!
SHE COULDN'T USE THE BROOM OF ZEPHYRUS BECAUSE HER ARMS WERE IM-MOBILIZED.
THE GUARDIAN WAS HER ONLY CHOICE.
DOROTHY ...

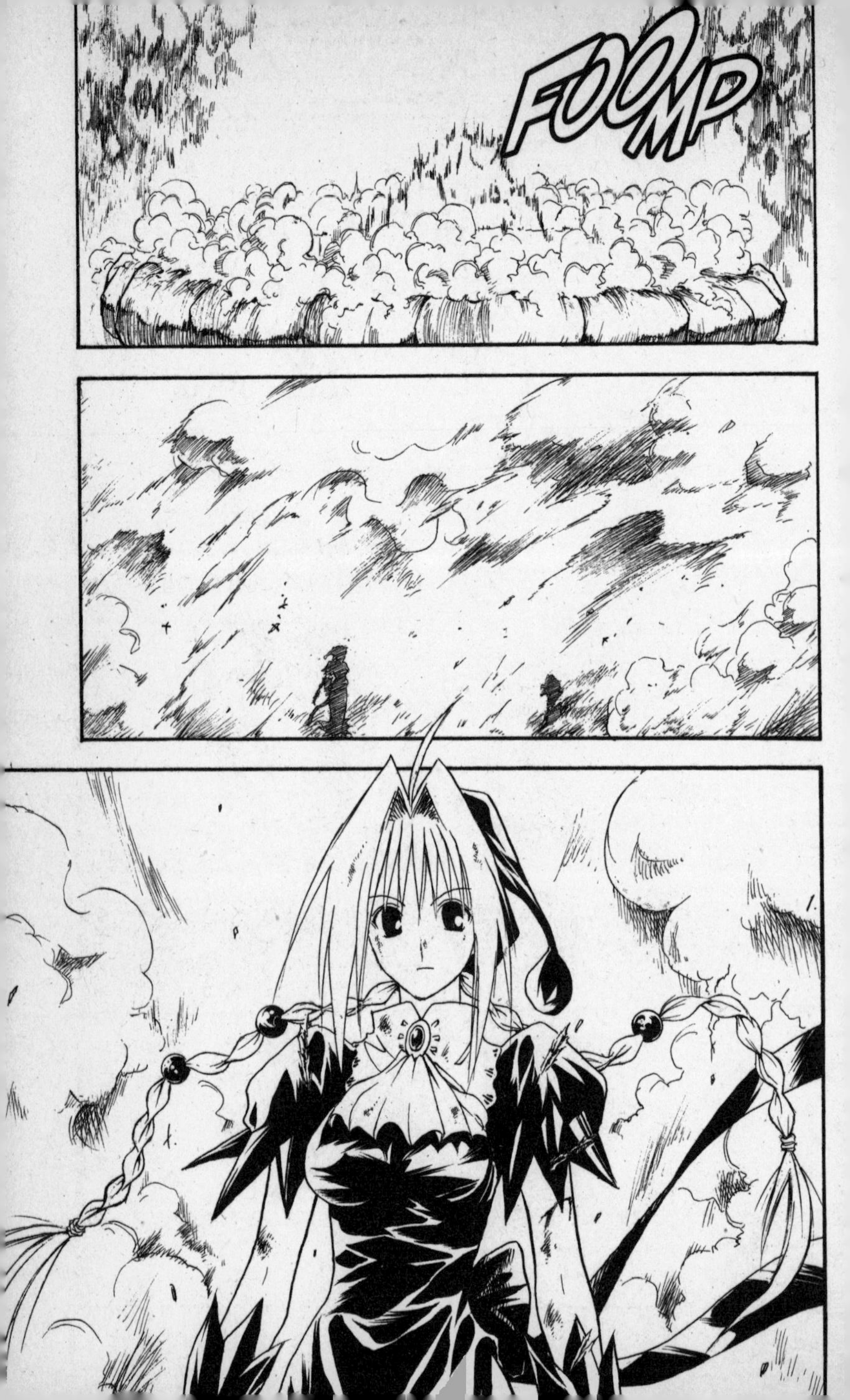
FOOOMP

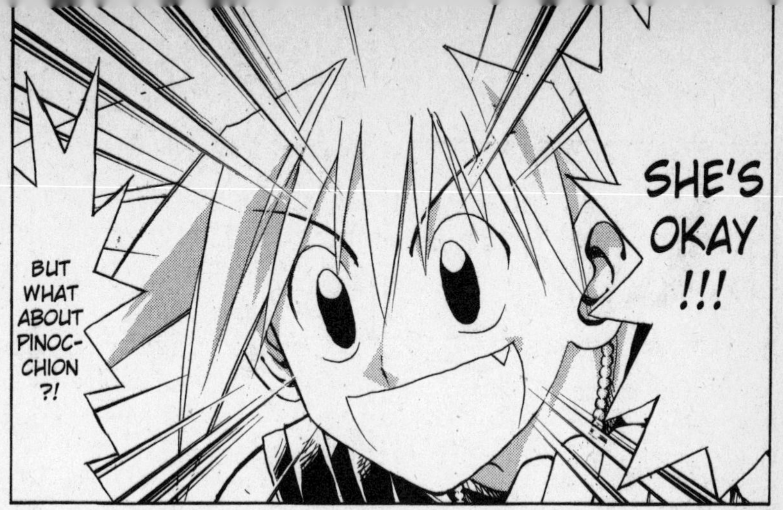
SHE'S OKAY !!!
BUT WHAT ABOUT PINOCCHION ?!

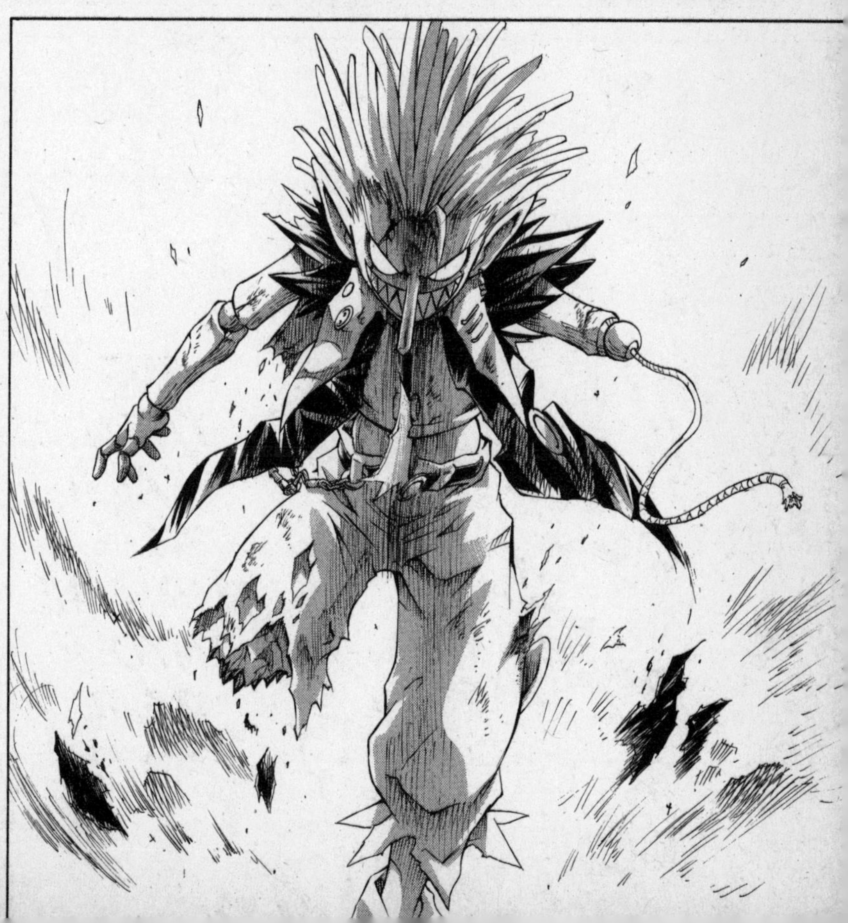

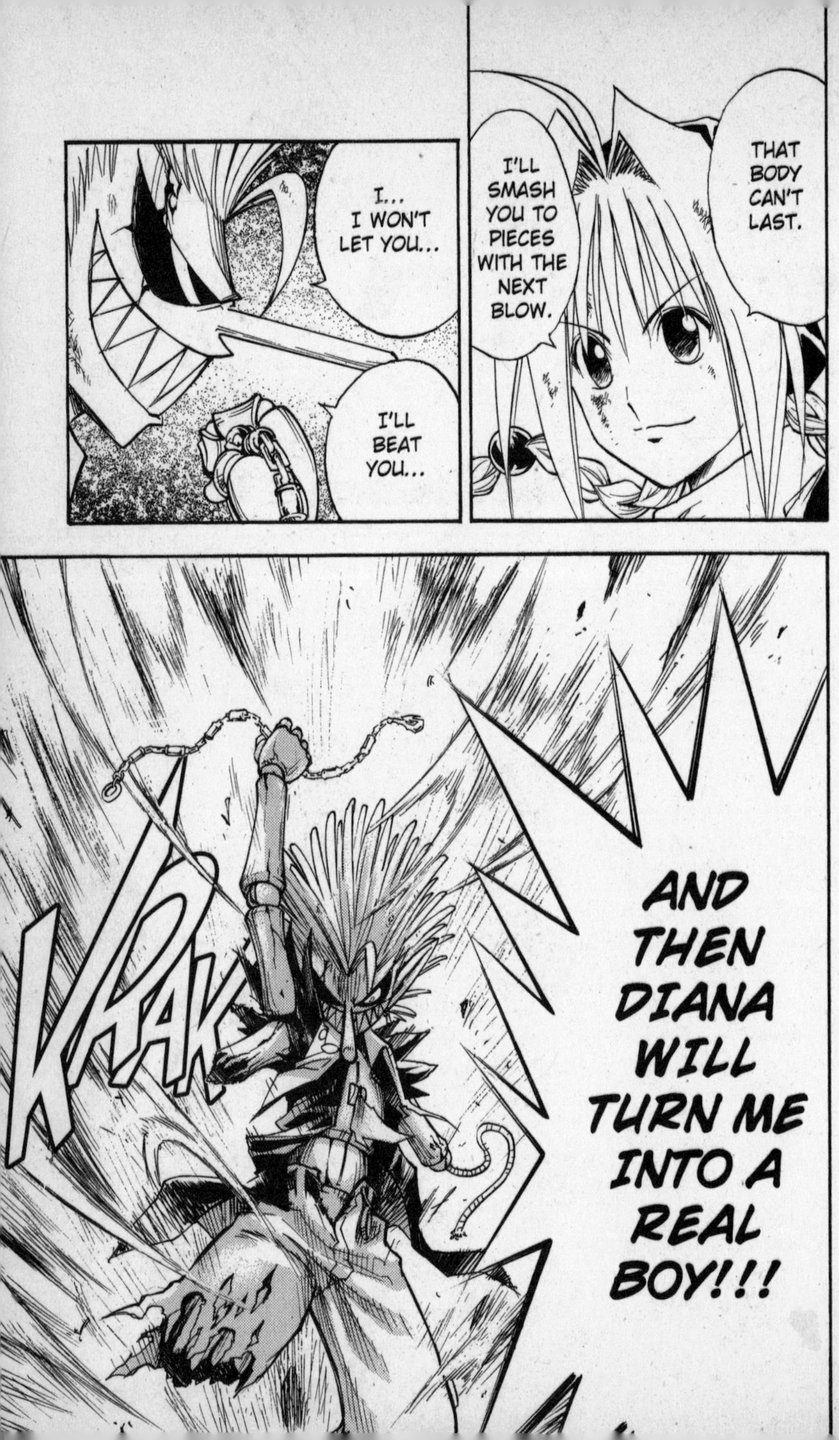
THAT BODY CAN'T LAST.
I'LL SMASH YOU TO PIECES WITH THE NEXT BLOW.
I... I WON'T LET YOU...
I'LL BEAT YOU...
AND THEN DIANA WILL TURN ME INTO A REAL BOY!!!
KAK

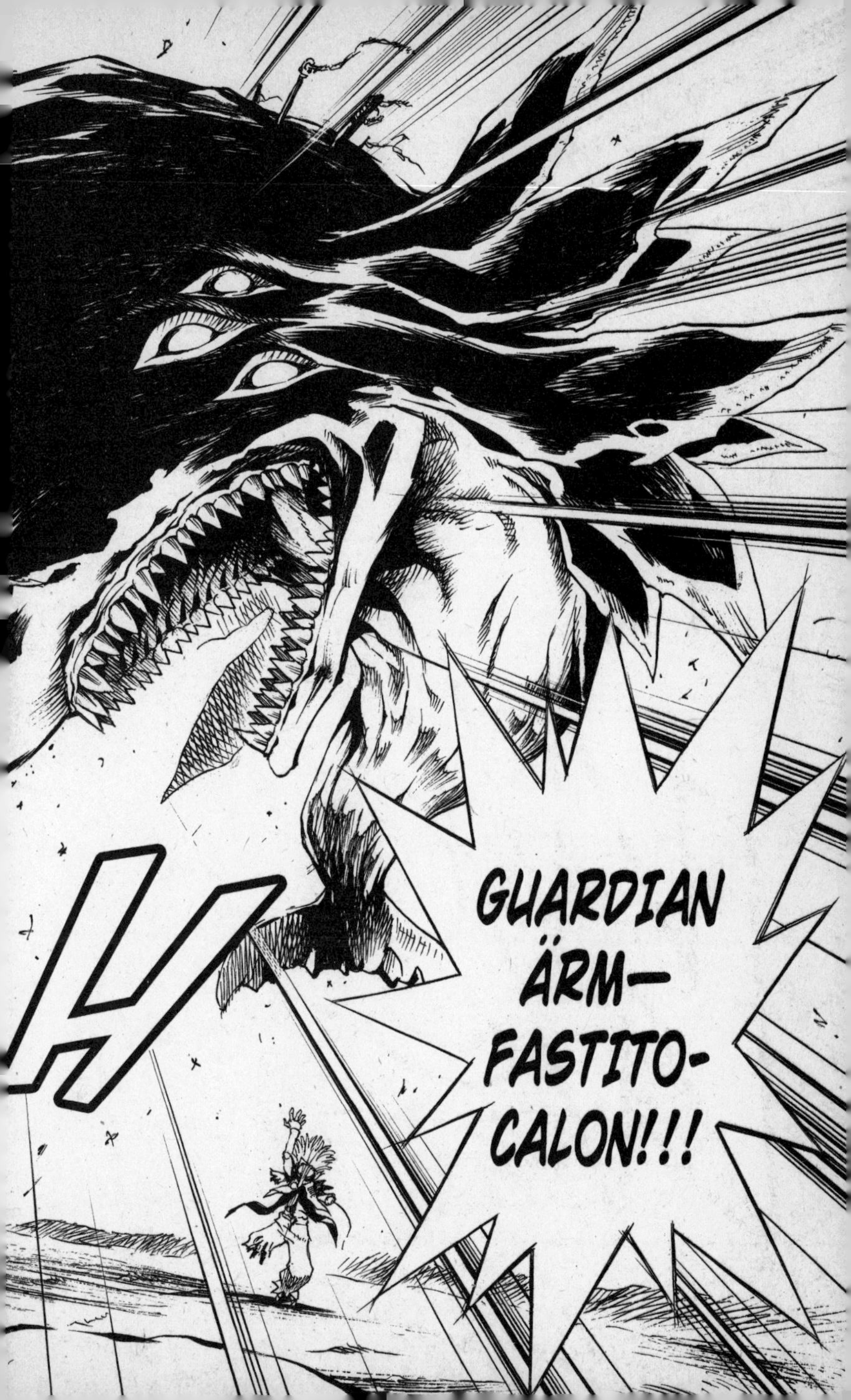
GUARDIAN ÄRM— FASTITO- CALON!!!

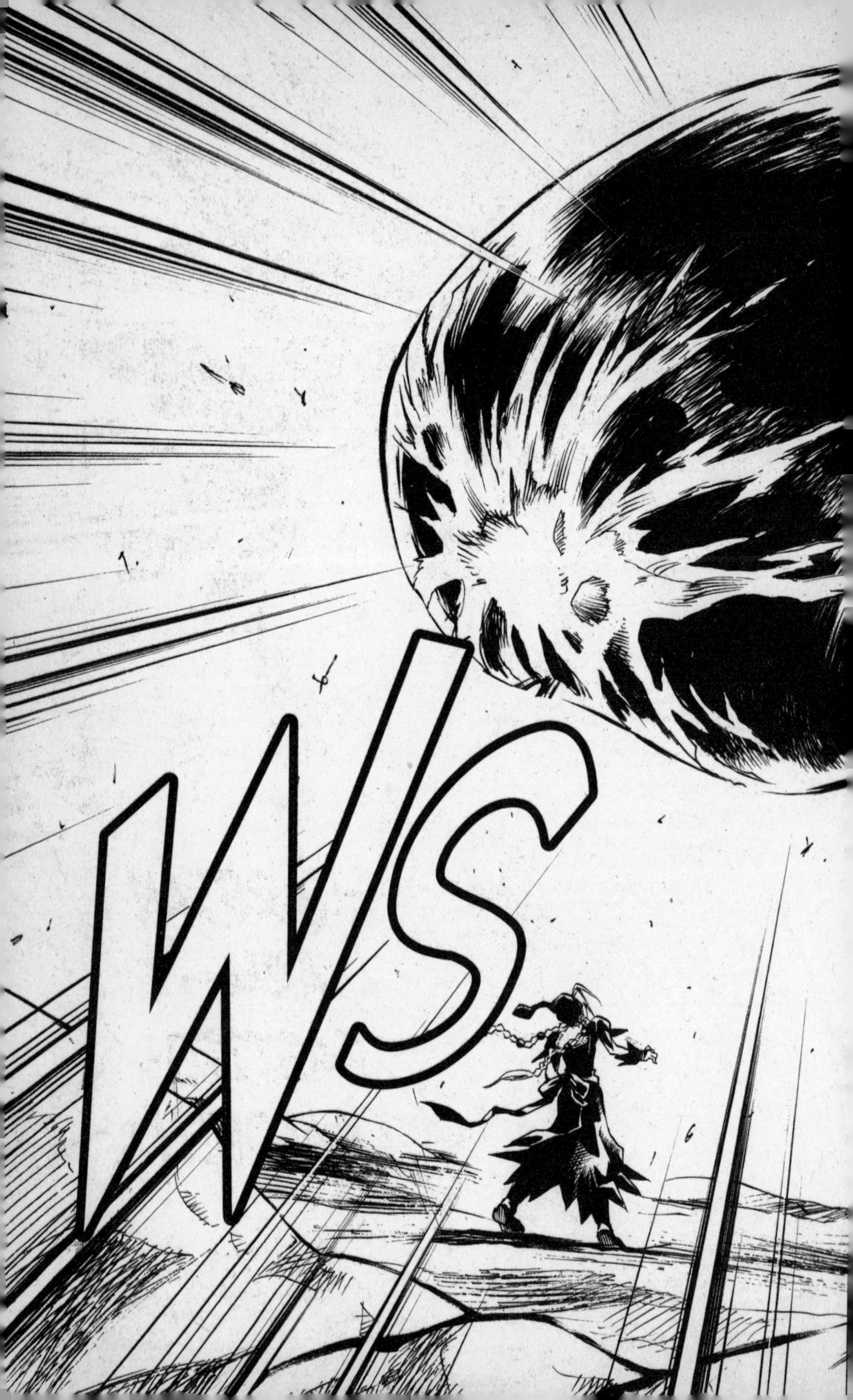
WS

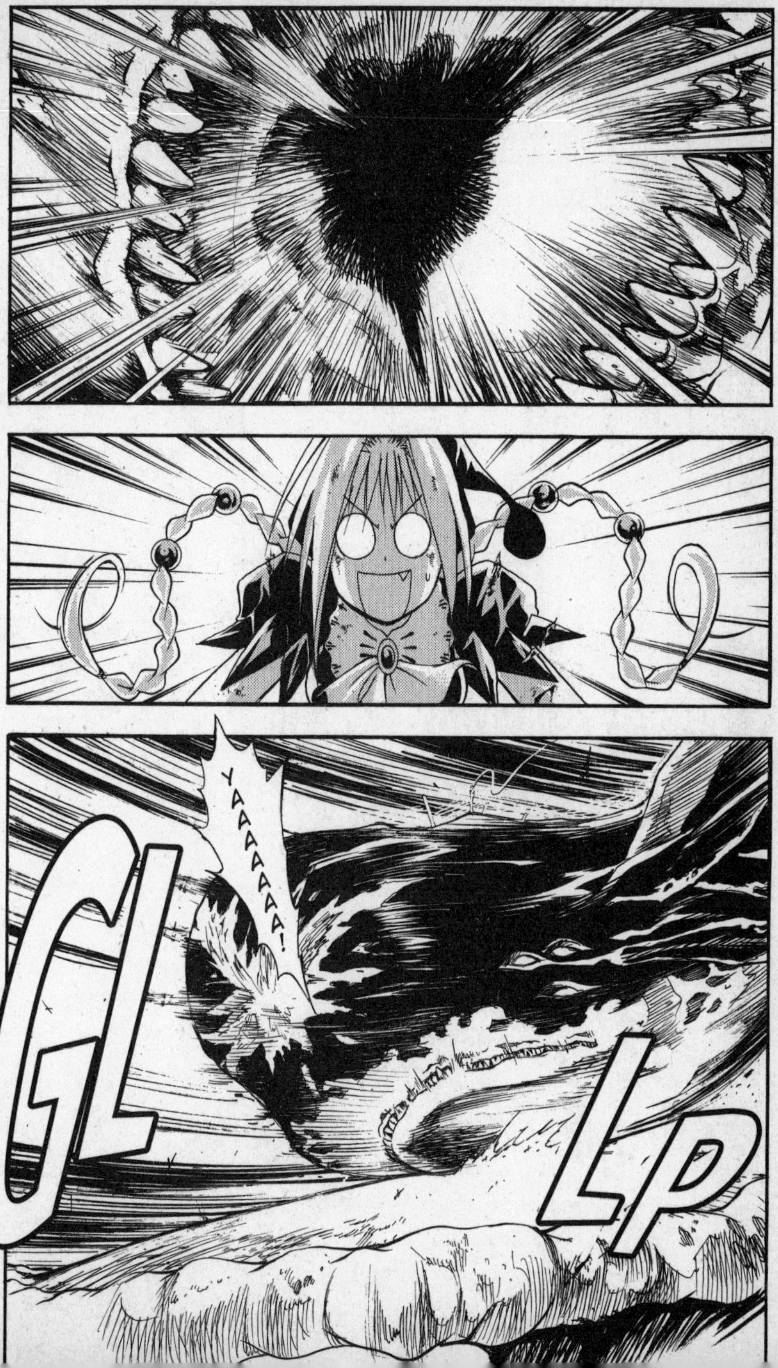
YAAAAAAAA!
GL
LP

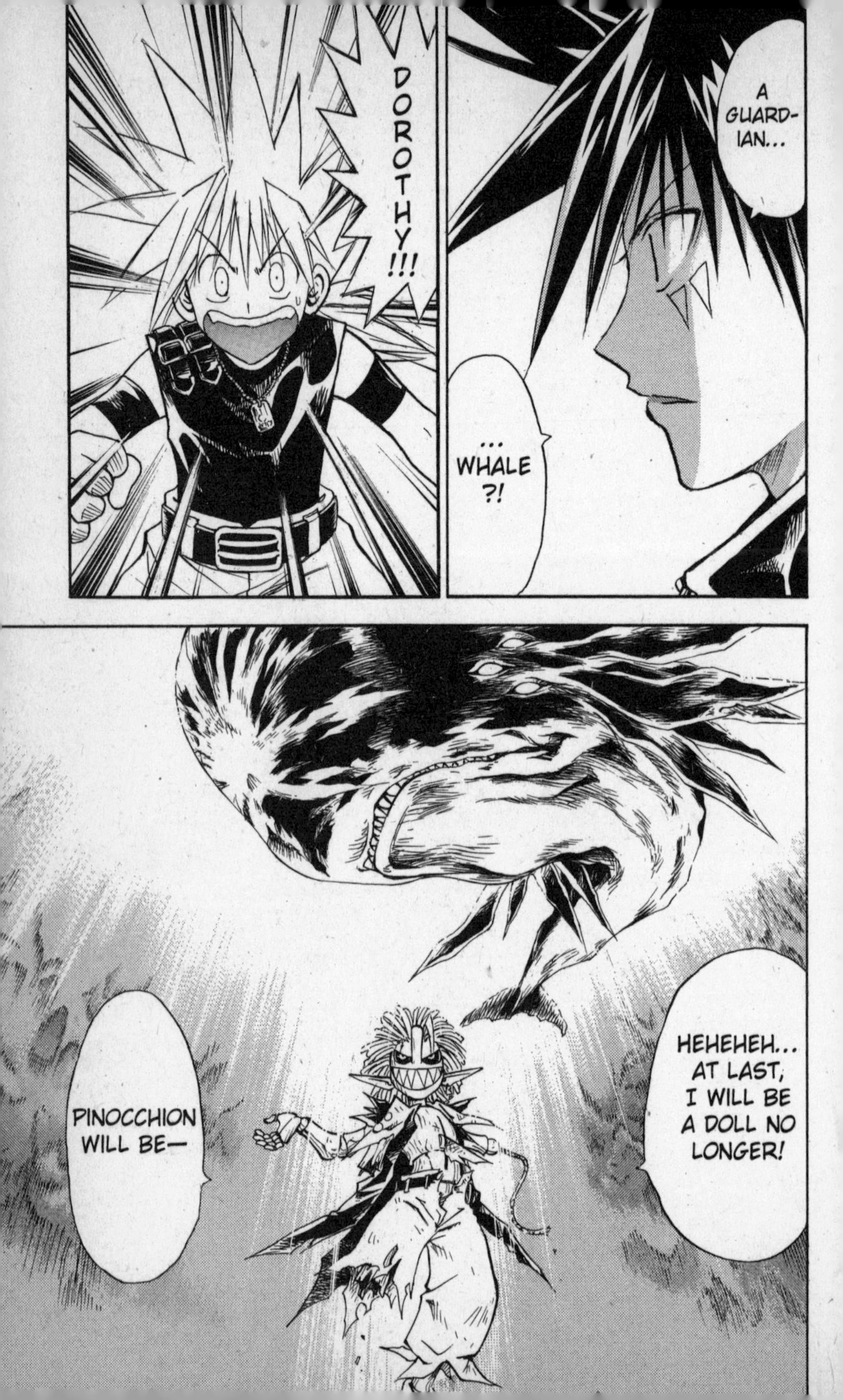
A GUARDIAN...
...WHALE?!
DOROTHY!!!
HEHEHEH... AT LAST, I WILL BE A DOLL NO LONGER!
PINOCCHION WILL BE—

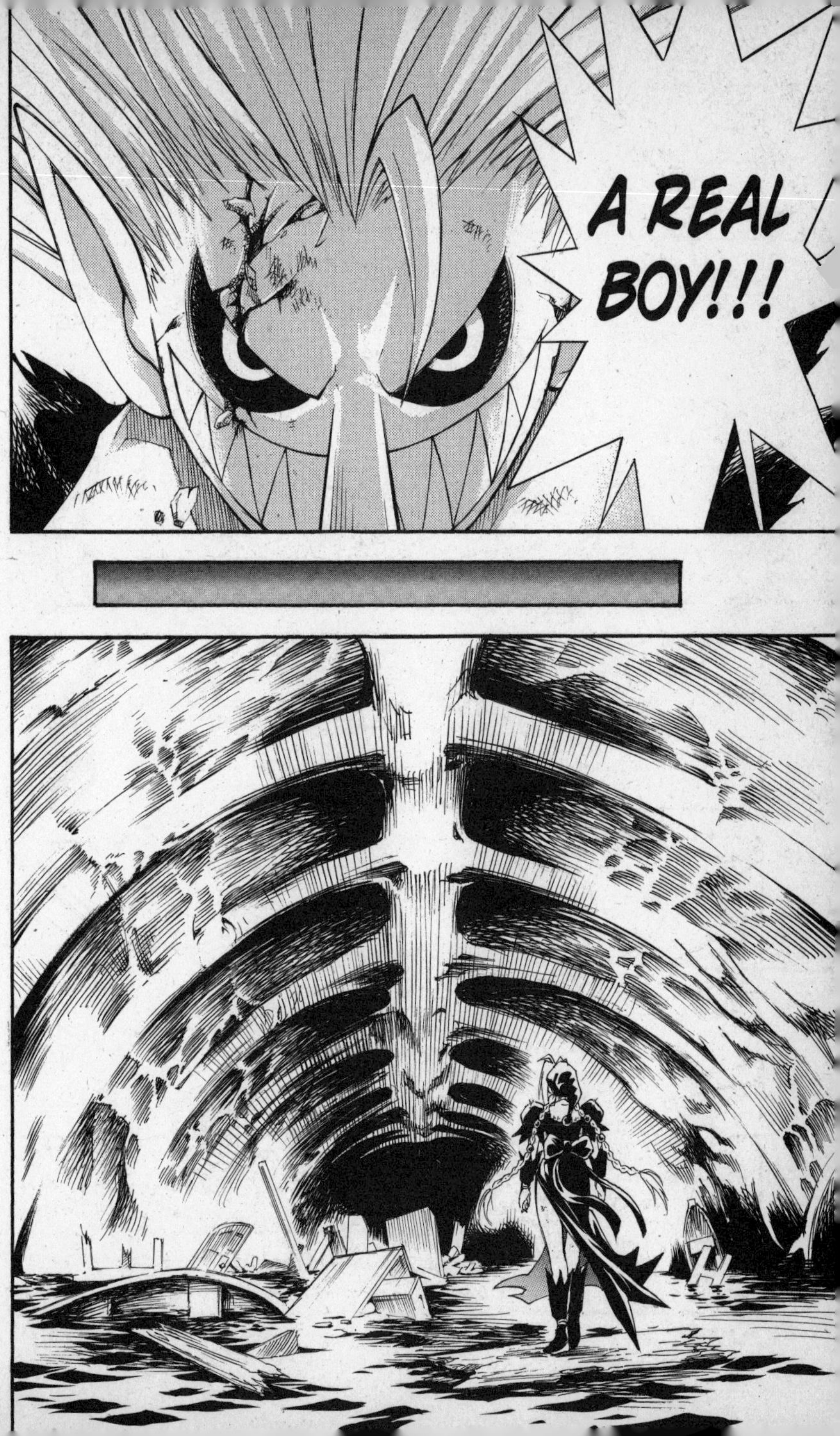
A REAL BOY!!!

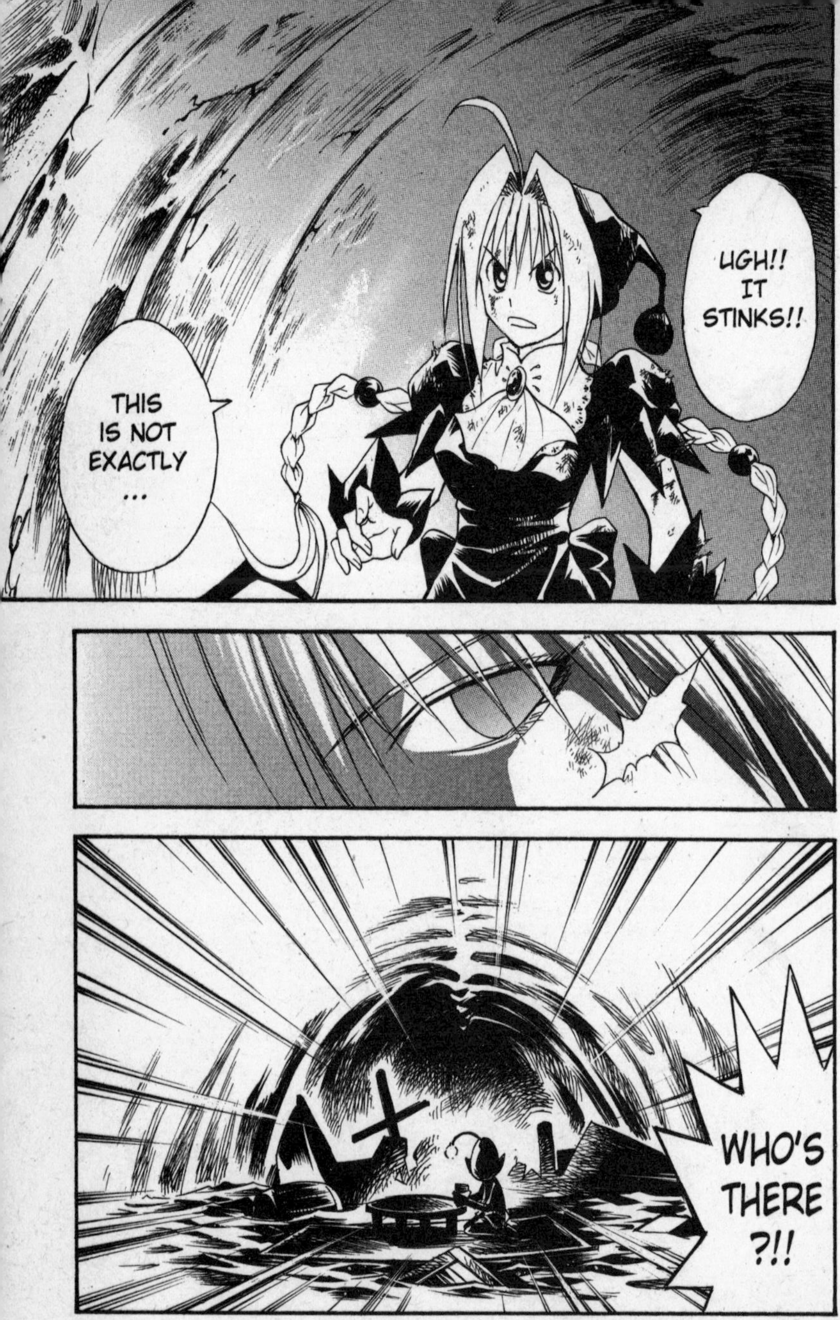
UGH!! IT STINKS!!
THIS IS NOT EXACTLY ...
WHO'S THERE ?!!

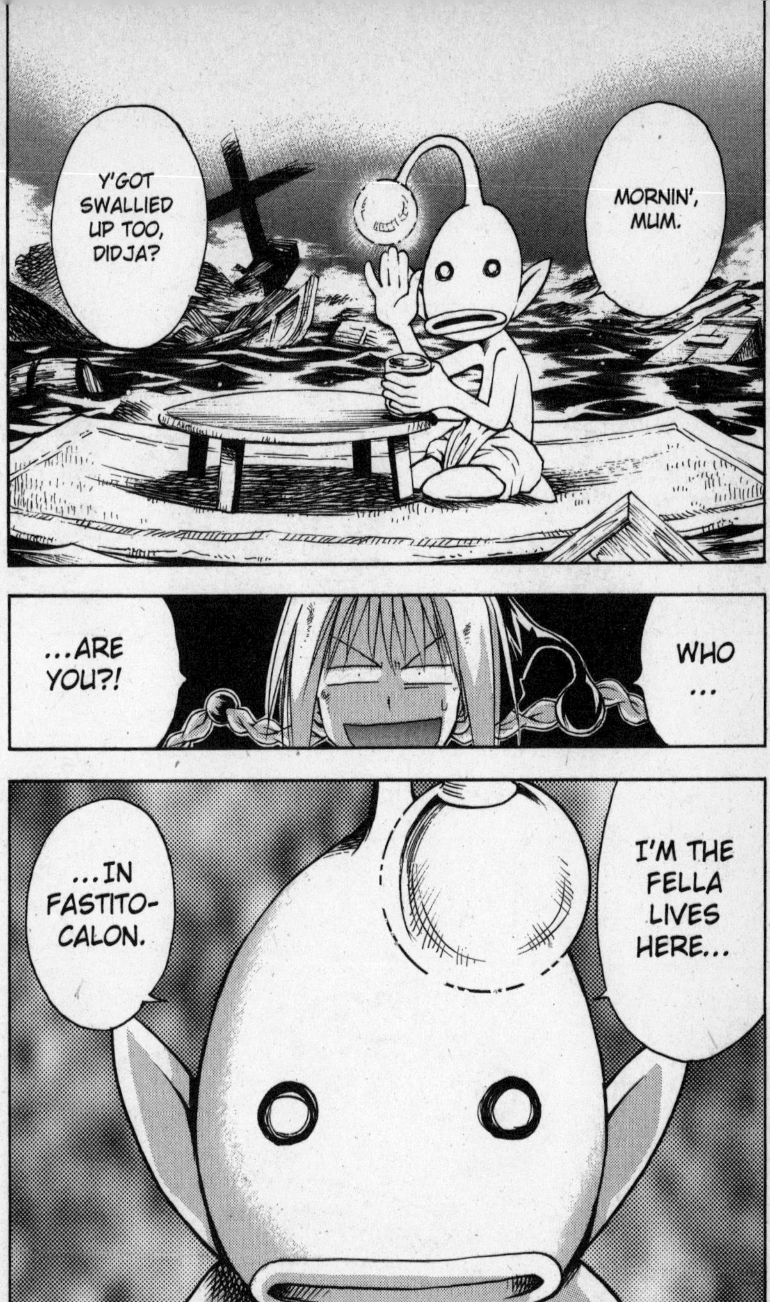
MORNIN', MUM.
Y'GOT SWALLIED UP TOO, DIDJA?
WHO ...
...ARE YOU?!
I'M THE FELLA LIVES HERE...
...IN FASTITO-CALON.

AKT.118/ DOROTHY VS. PINOCCHION③

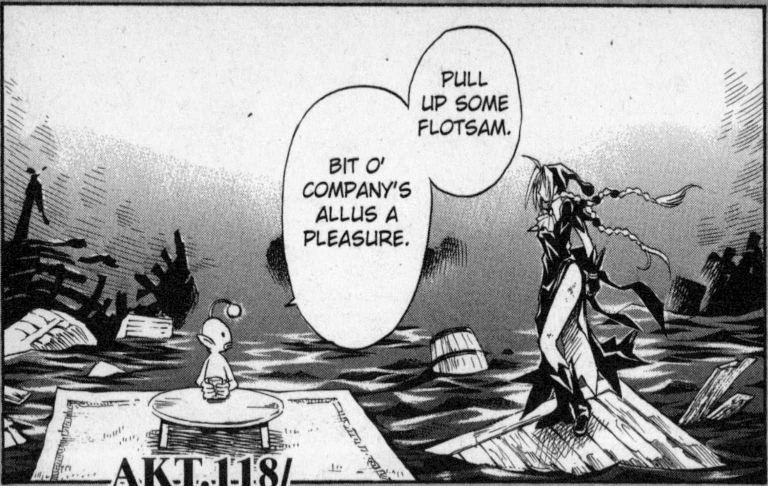
PULL UP SOME FLOTSAM.
BIT O' COMPANY'S ALLUS A PLEASURE.

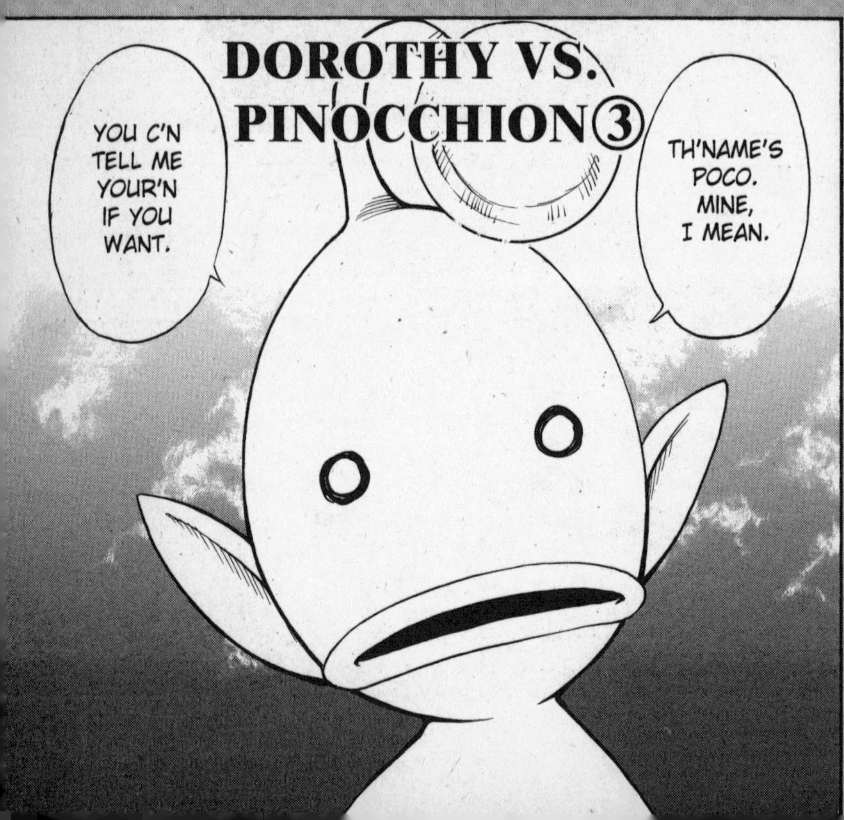
TH'NAME'S POCO. MINE, I MEAN.
YOU C'N TELL ME YOUR'N IF YOU WANT.

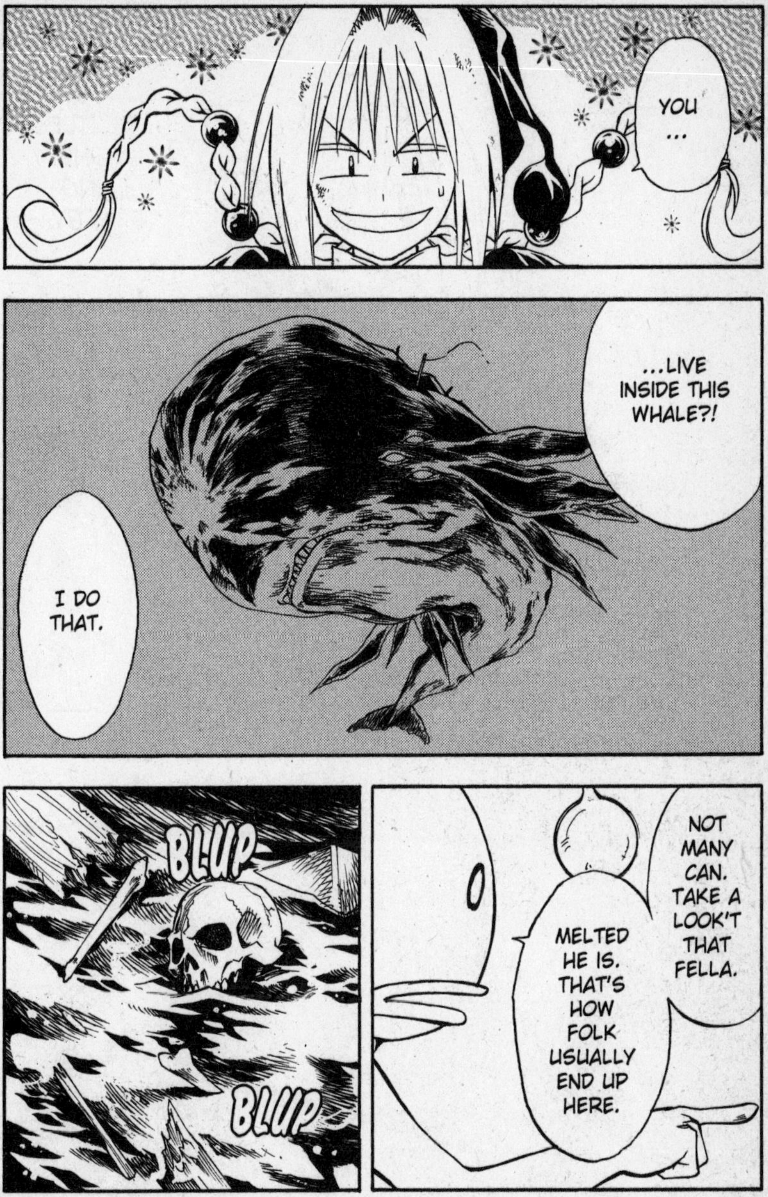
YOU ...
...LIVE INSIDE THIS WHALE?!
I DO THAT.
NOT MANY CAN. TAKE A LOOK'T THAT FELLA.
MELTED HE IS. THAT'S HOW FOLK USUALLY END UP HERE.
BLUP
BLUP

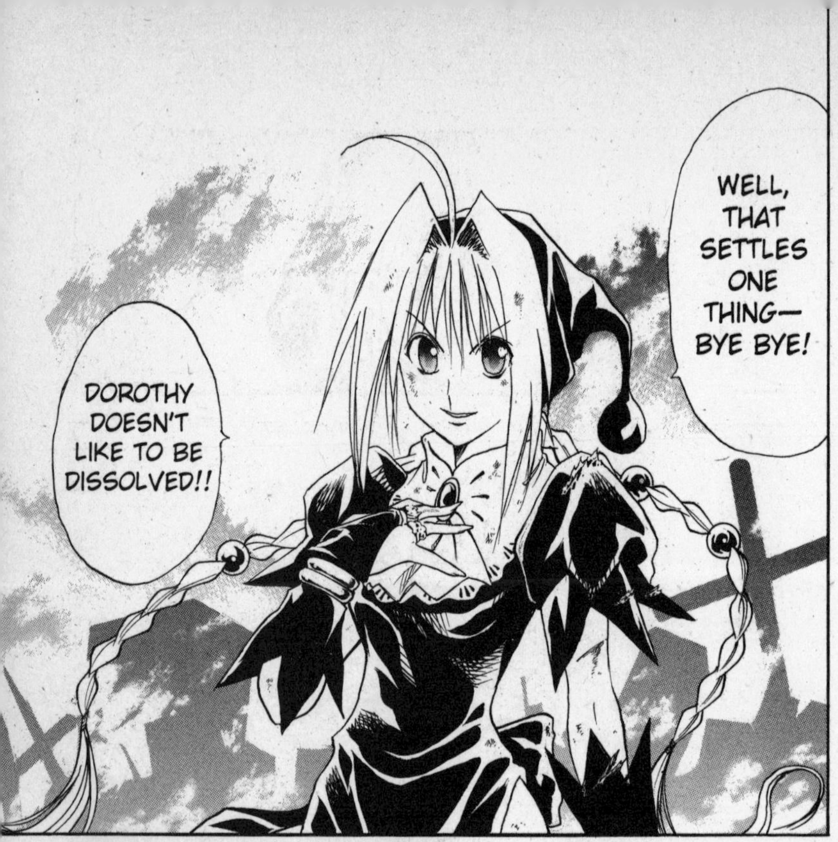
WELL, THAT SETTLES ONE THING— BYE BYE!
DOROTHY DOESN'T LIKE TO BE DISSOLVED!!
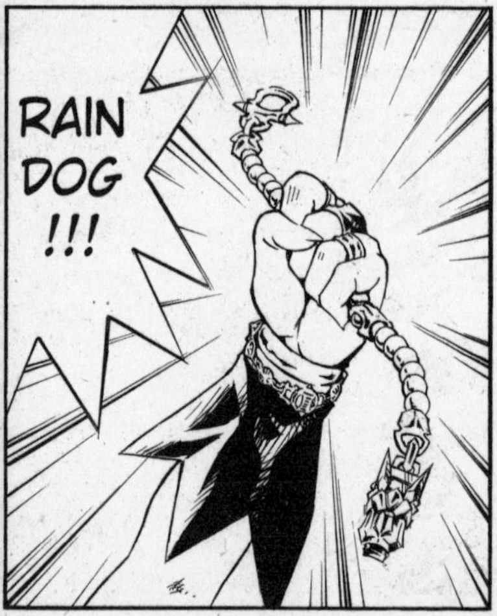
RAIN DOG !!!
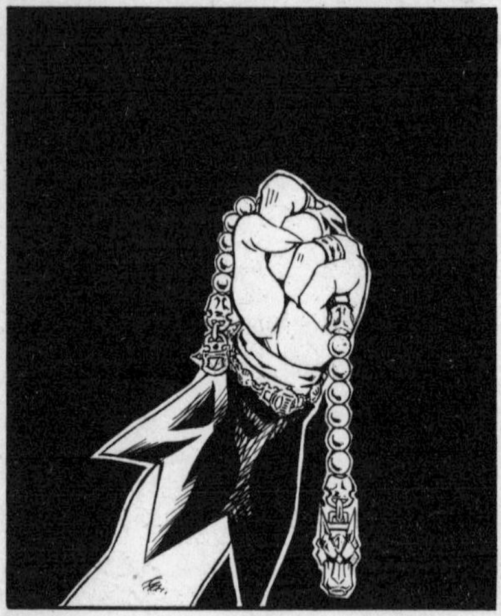

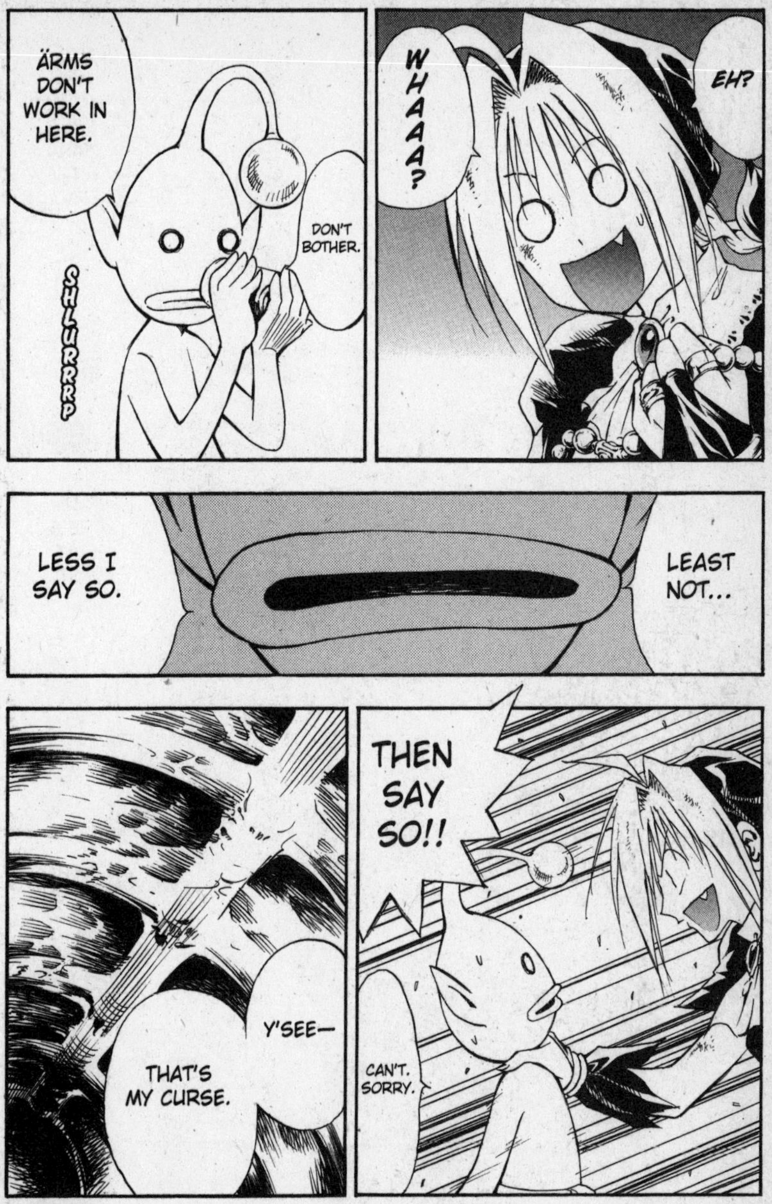
EH?
WHAAAA?
DON'T BOTHER.
ÄRMS DON'T WORK IN HERE.
SHLURRRP
LEAST NOT...
LESS I SAY SO.
THEN SAY SO!!
CAN'T. SORRY.
Y'SEE—
THAT'S MY CURSE.

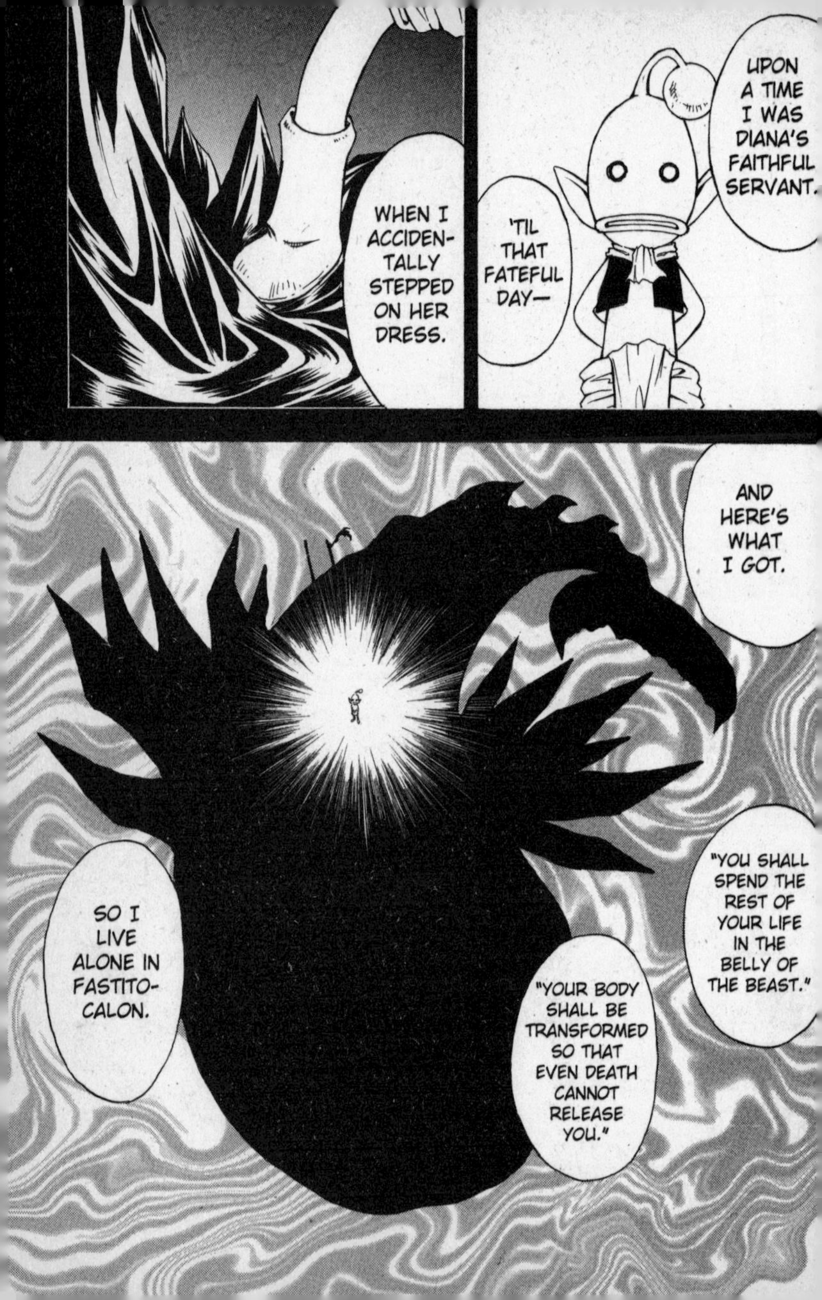
UPON A TIME I WAS DIANA'S FAITHFUL SERVANT.
'TIL THAT FATEFUL DAY—
WHEN I ACCIDEN-TALLY STEPPED ON HER DRESS.
AND HERE'S WHAT I GOT.
"YOU SHALL SPEND THE REST OF YOUR LIFE IN THE BELLY OF THE BEAST."
"YOUR BODY SHALL BE TRANSFORMED SO THAT EVEN DEATH CANNOT RELEASE YOU."
SO I LIVE ALONE IN FASTITO-CALON.

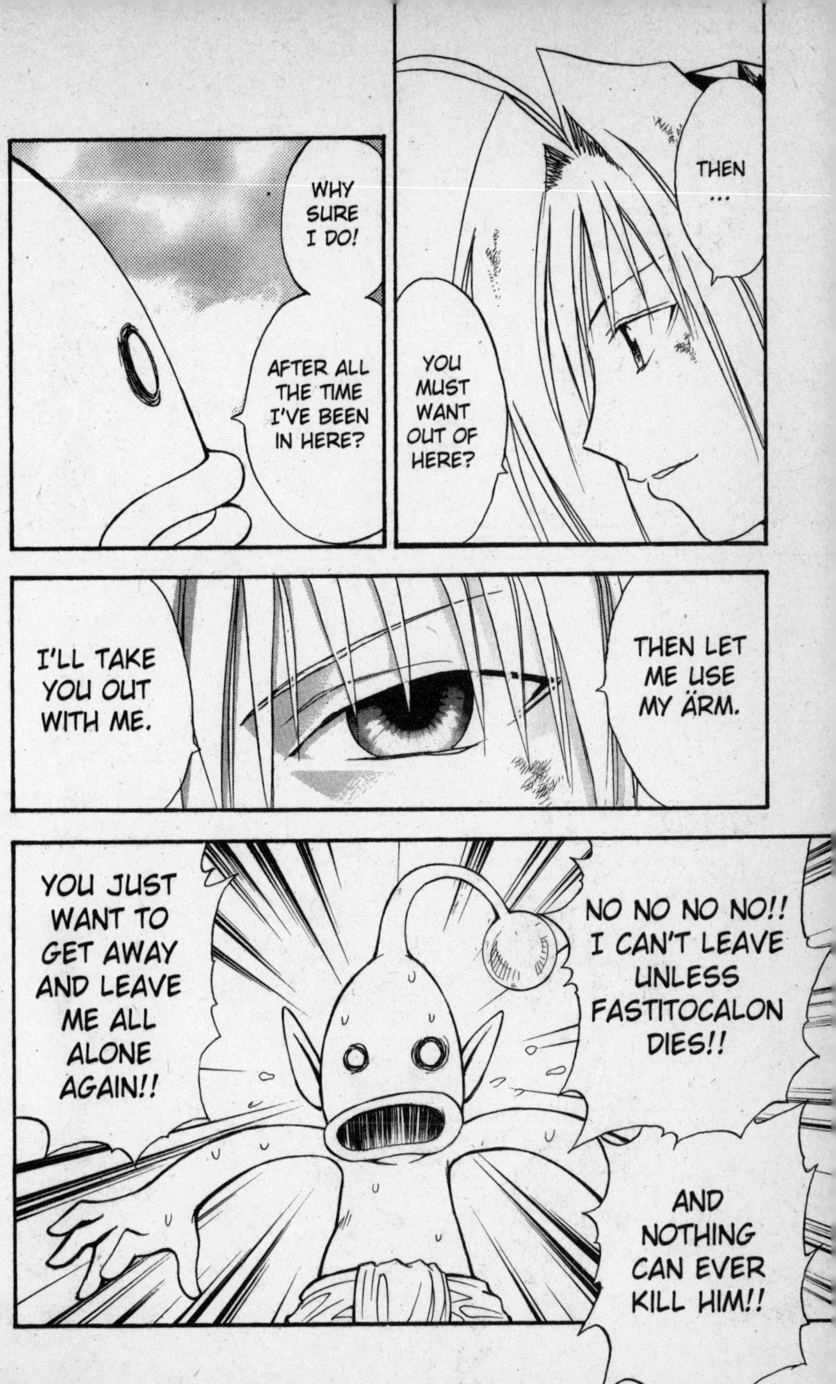
THEN ...
YOU MUST WANT OUT OF HERE?
WHY SURE I DO!
AFTER ALL THE TIME I'VE BEEN IN HERE?
THEN LET ME USE MY ÄRM.
I'LL TAKE YOU OUT WITH ME.
NO NO NO NO!! I CAN'T LEAVE UNLESS FASTITOCALON DIES!!
AND NOTHING CAN EVER KILL HIM!!
YOU JUST WANT TO GET AWAY AND LEAVE ME ALL ALONE AGAIN!!

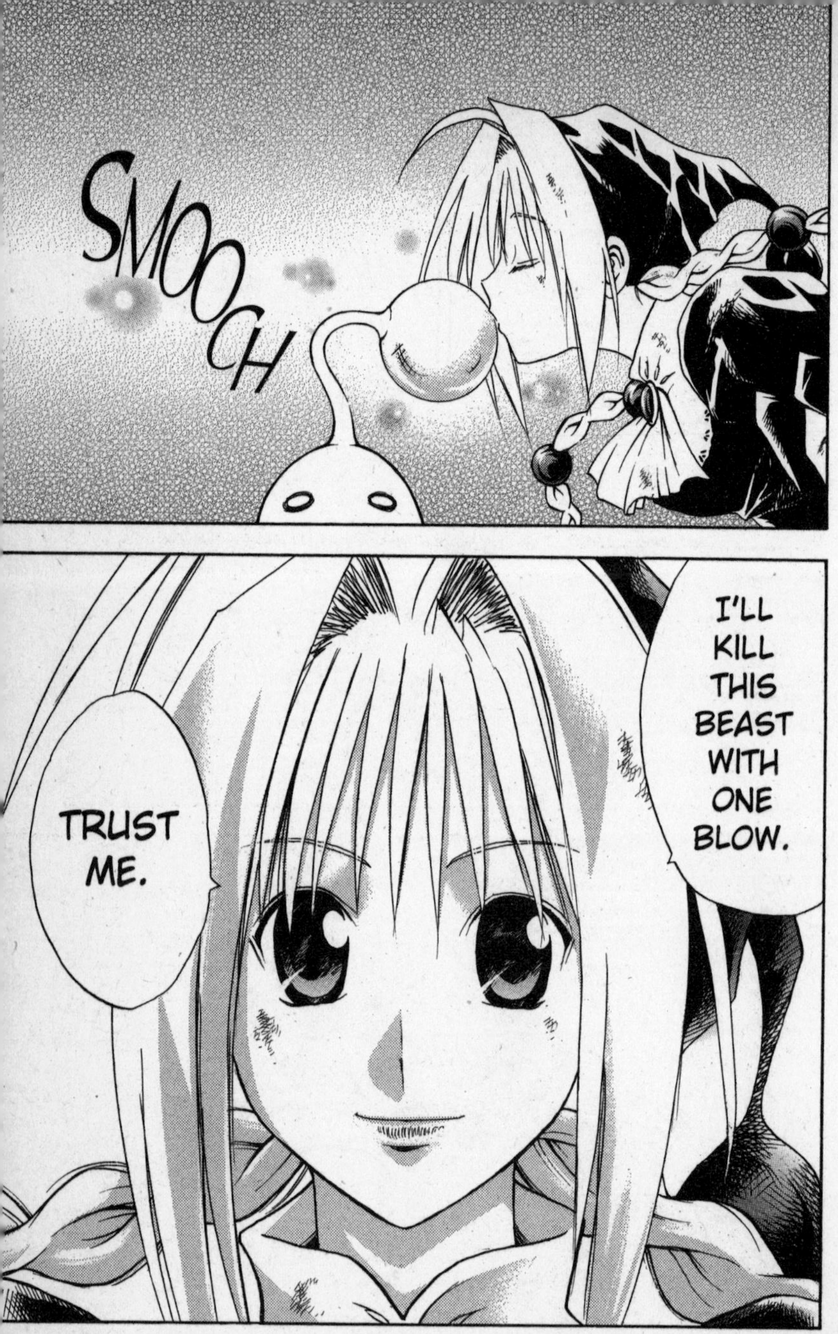
SMOOCH
I'LL KILL THIS BEAST WITH ONE BLOW.
TRUST ME.

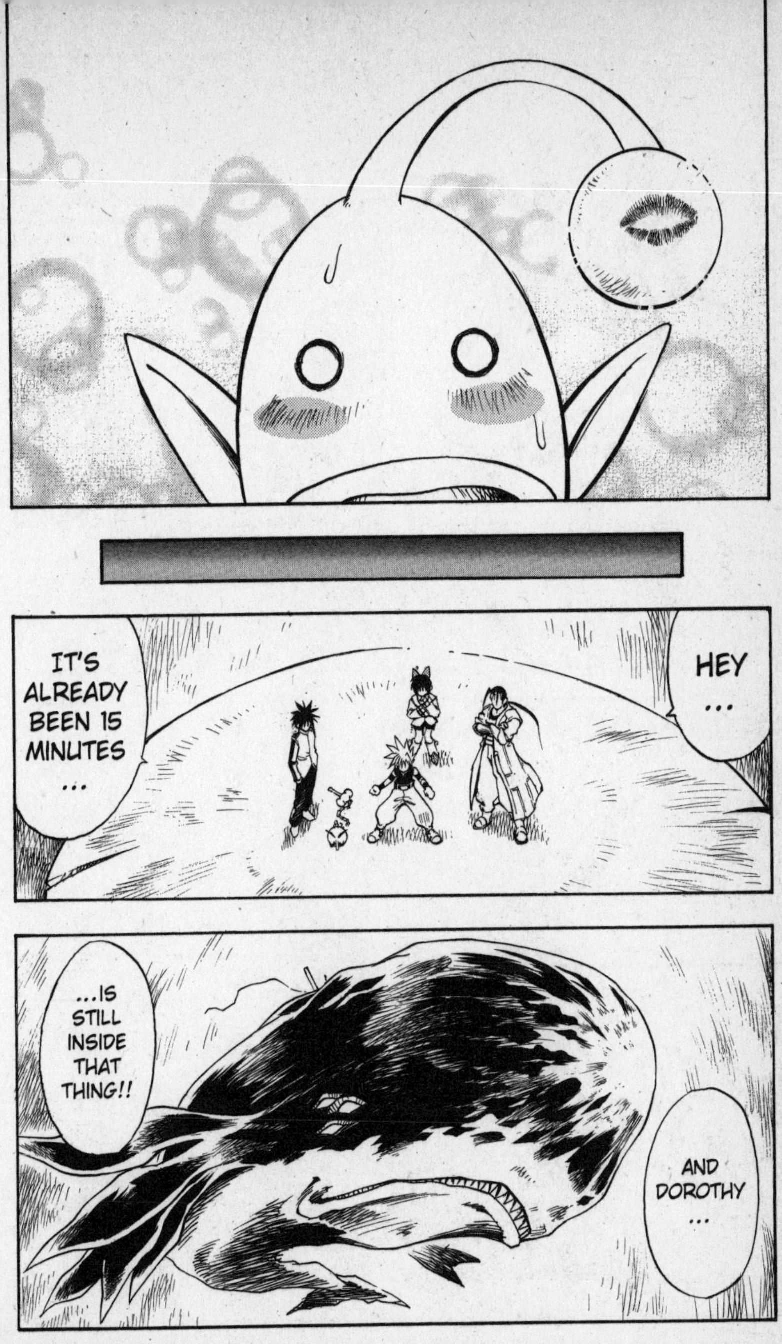
HEY ...
IT'S ALREADY BEEN 15 MINUTES ...
AND DOROTHY ...
...IS STILL INSIDE THAT THING!!

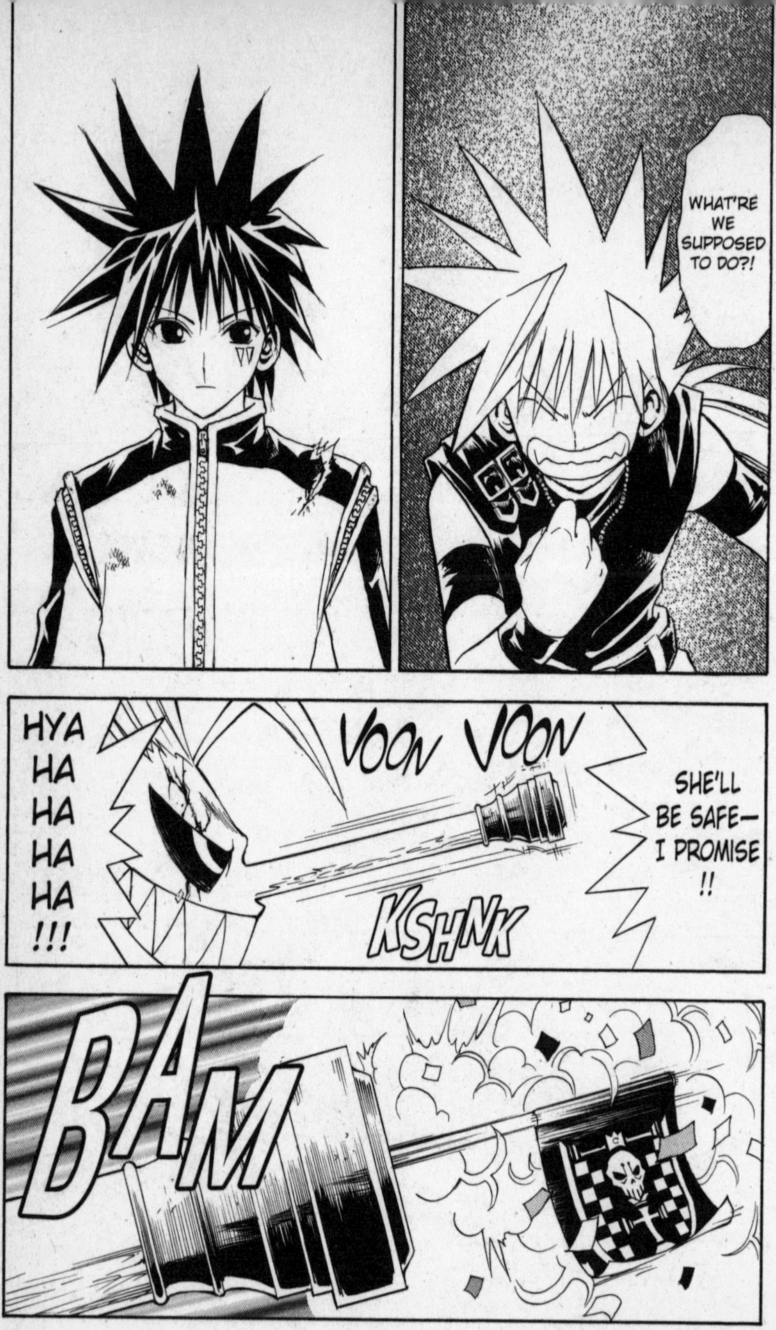
WHAT'RE WE SUPPOSED TO DO?!
SHE'LL BE SAFE— I PROMISE !!
VOON VOON
HYA HA HA HA HA !!!
KSHNK
BAM

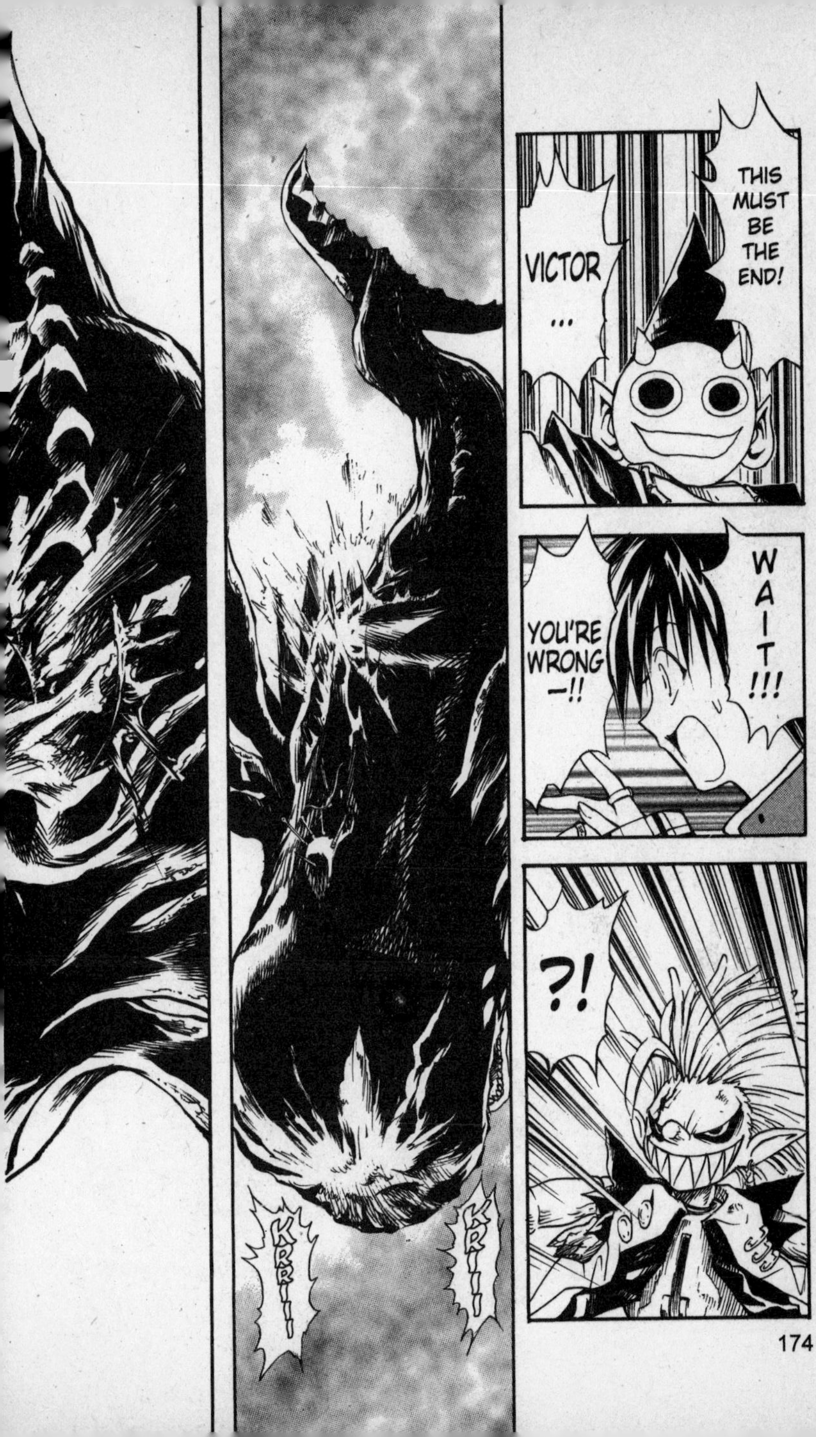
THIS MUST BE THE END!
VICTOR ...
WAIT!!!
YOU'RE WRONG—!!
?!
KRIIII
KRRIIII

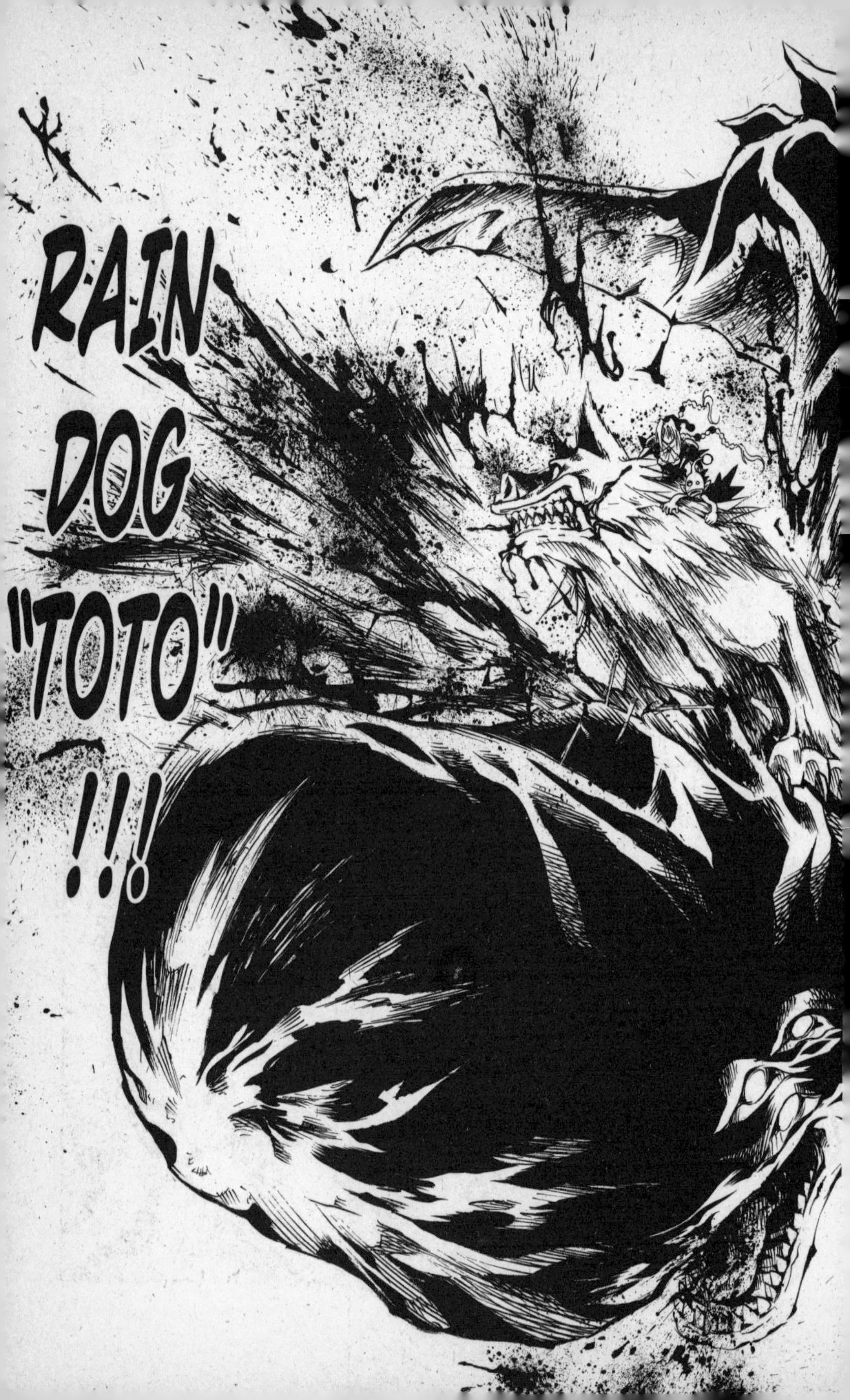
RAIN DOG "TOTO" !!!

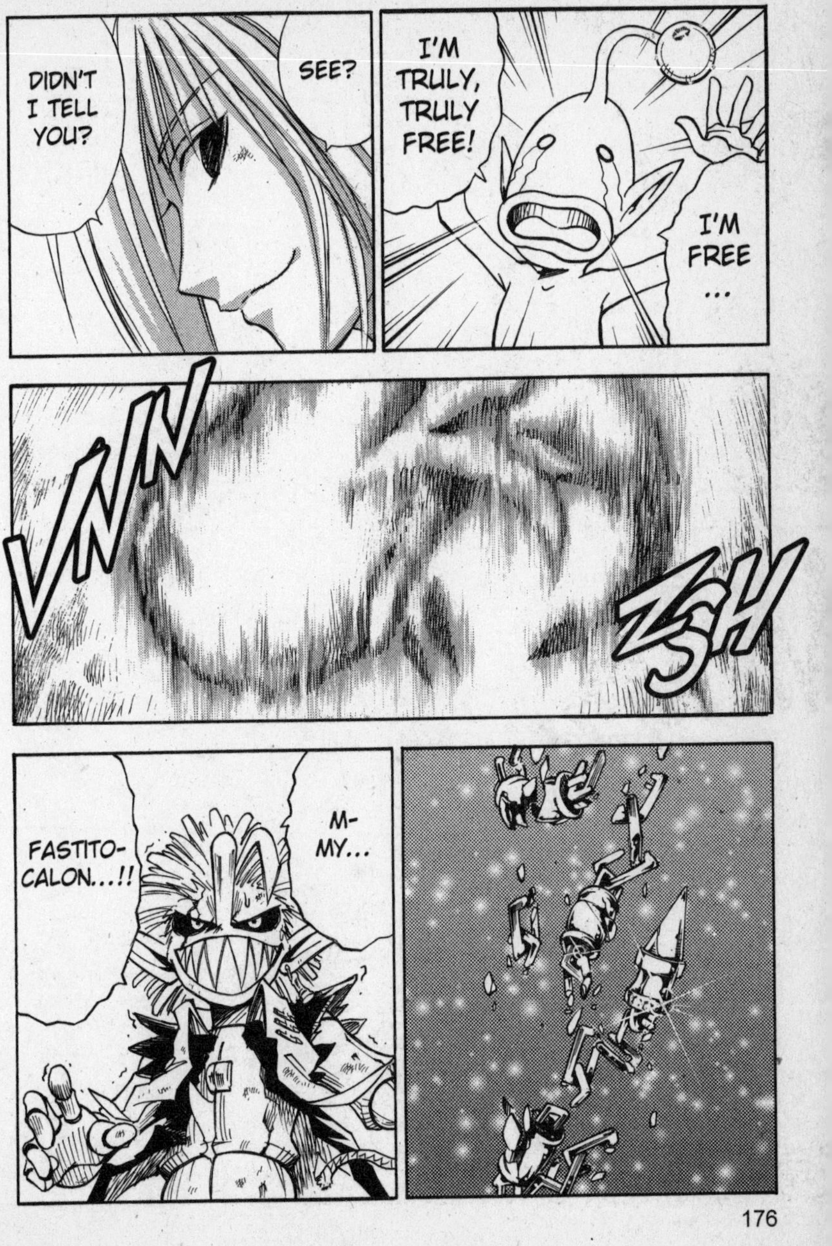
I'M FREE ...
I'M TRULY, TRULY FREE!
SEE?
DIDN'T I TELL YOU?
ZSH
VNN
M-MY...
FASTITO-CALON...!!

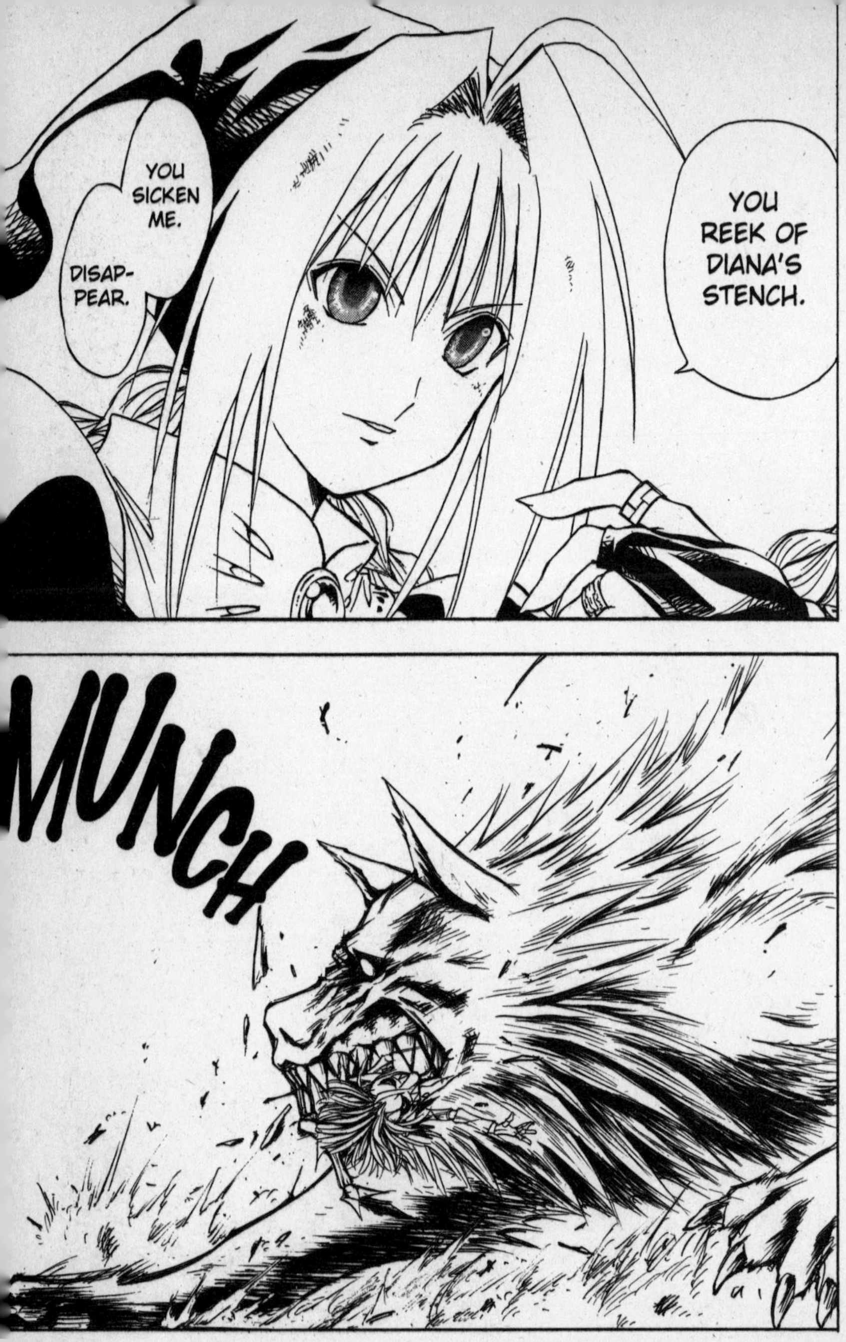
YOU REEK OF DIANA'S STENCH.
YOU SICKEN ME.
DISAP-PEAR.
MUNCH

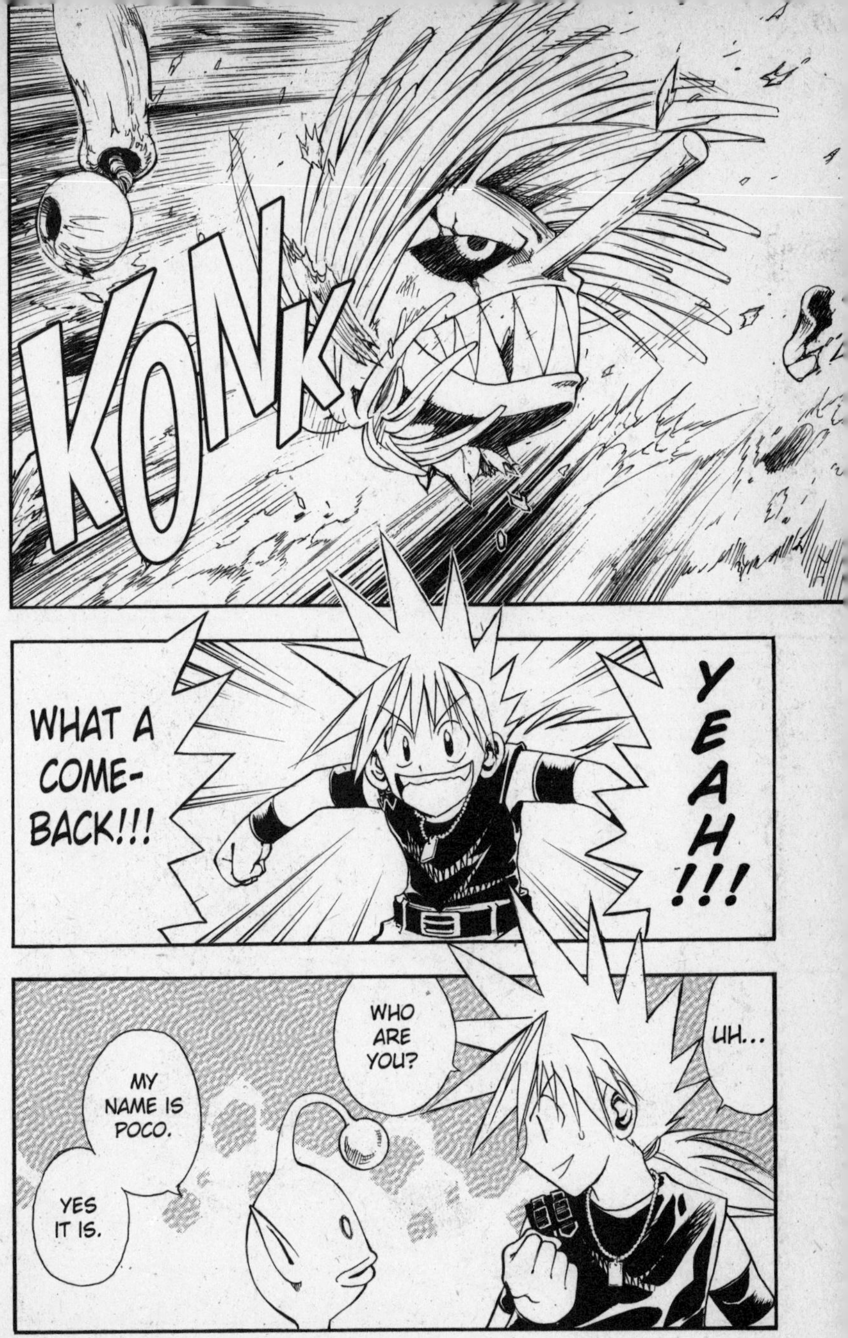
KONK
YEAH!!!
WHAT A COME-BACK!!!
UH...
WHO ARE YOU?
MY NAME IS POCO.
YES IT IS.

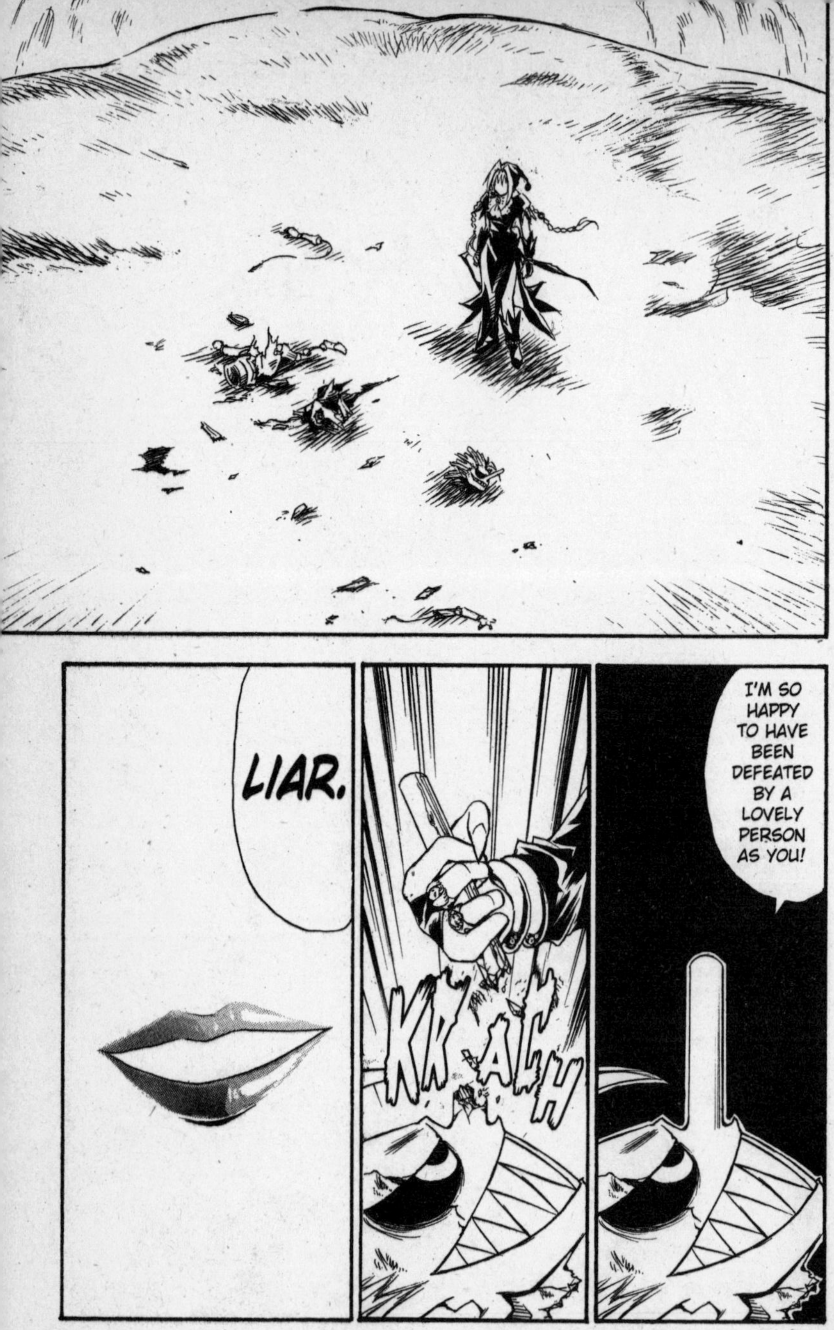
I'M SO HAPPY TO HAVE BEEN DEFEATED BY A LOVELY PERSON AS YOU!
LIAR.

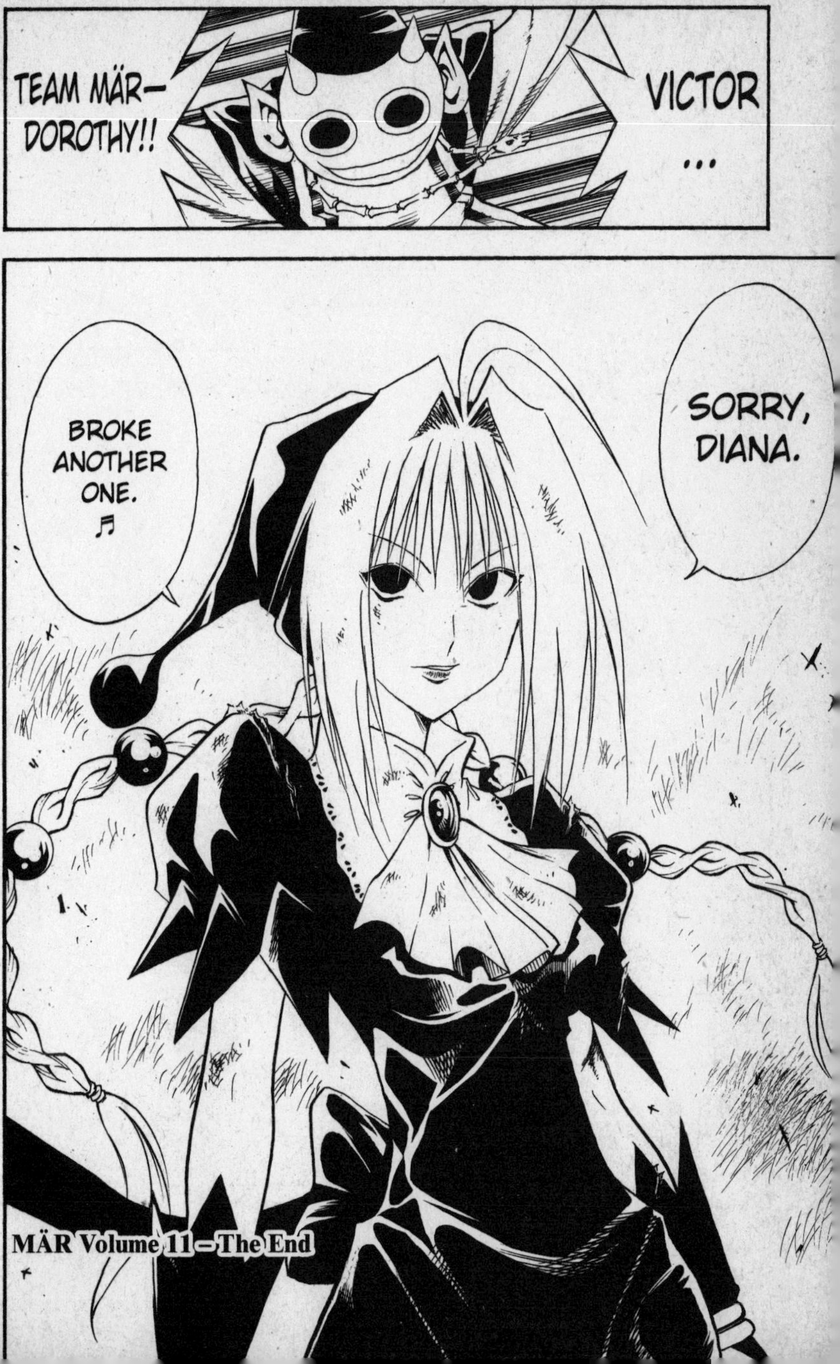
VICTOR ...
TEAM MÄR— DOROTHY!!
SORRY, DIANA.
BROKE ANOTHER ONE. ♬
MÄR Volume 11 – The End

THE EXCITEMENT BUILDS...

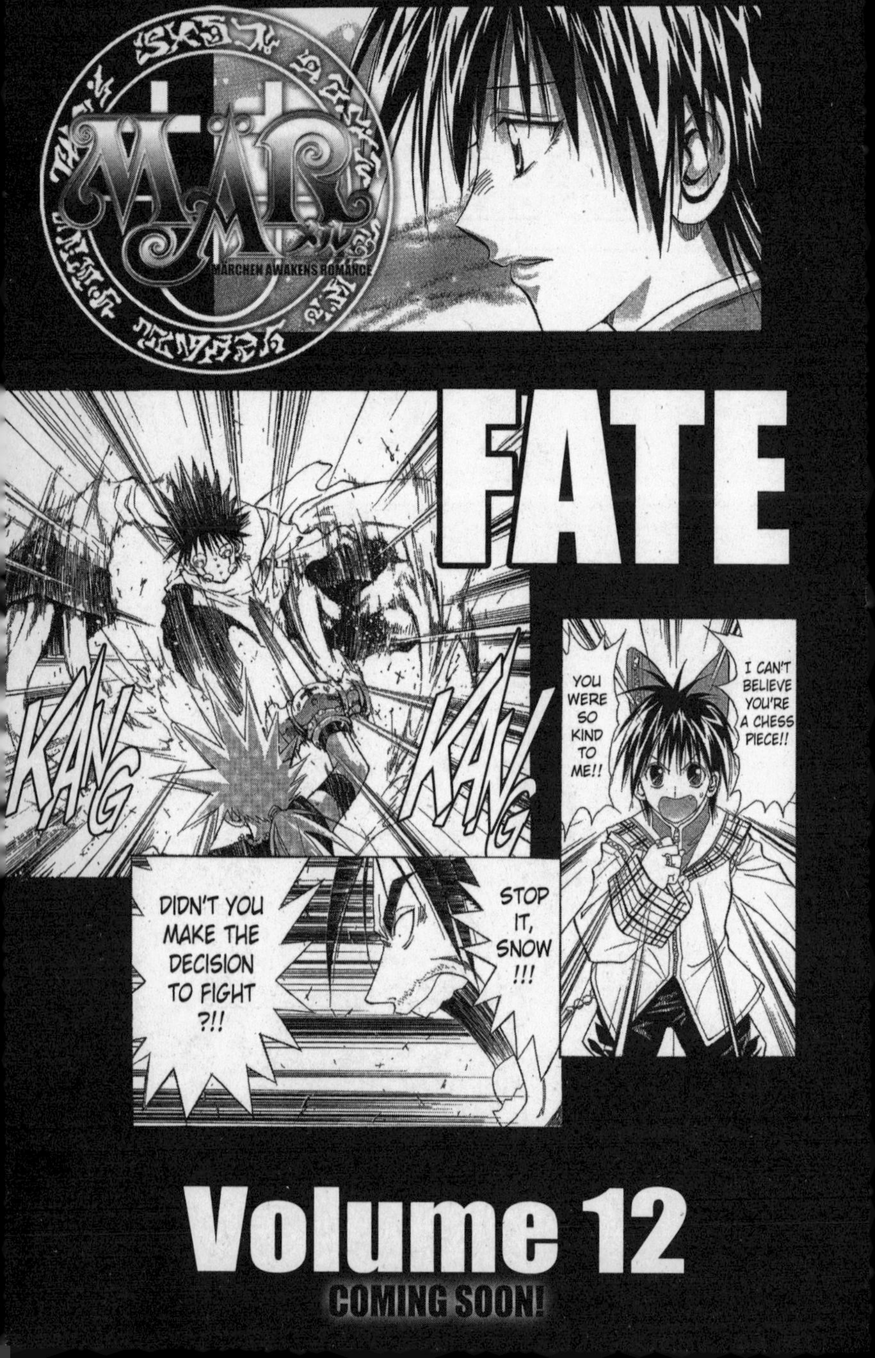
MÄR
MÄRCHEN AWAKENS ROMANCE
FATE
I CAN'T BELIEVE YOU'RE A CHESS PIECE!!
YOU WERE SO KIND TO ME!!
KANG
KANG
STOP IT, SNOW!!!
DIDN'T YOU MAKE THE DECISION TO FIGHT?!!

Volume 12

COMING SOON!

AN UNFORGETTABLE DAY

Hoshino

HAA!
ROLL
ROLL ROLL
SHWP
YEEP ?!!

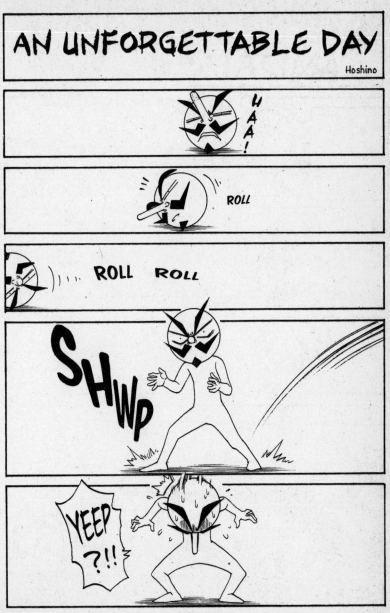

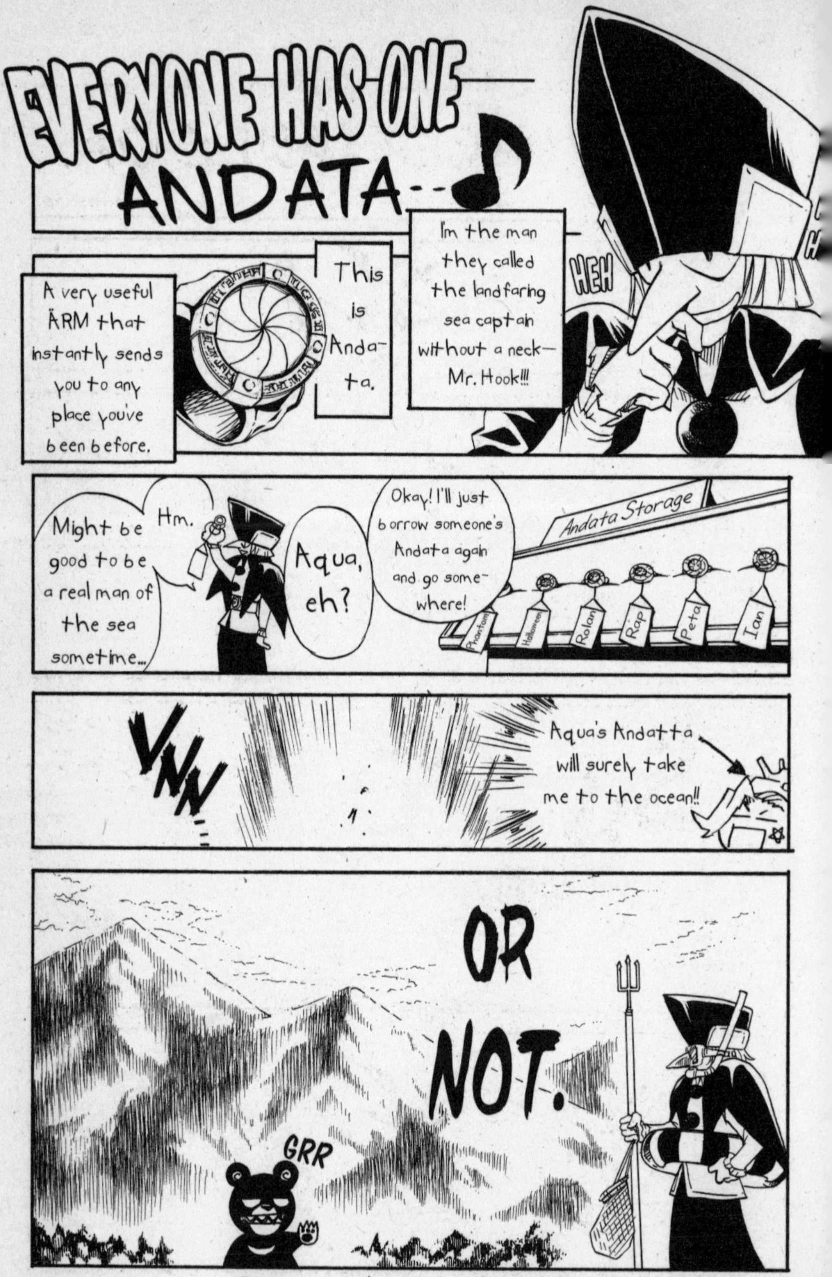
EVERYONE HAS ONE ANDATA...
HEH
I'm the man they called the landfaring sea captain without a neck— Mr. Hook!!!
This is Andata.
A very useful ÄRM that instantly sends you to any place you've been before.
Andata Storage
Ian
Peta
Rap
Rolan
Halloween
Phantom
Okay! I'll just borrow someone's Andata again and go somewhere!
Aqua, eh?
Hm.
Might be good to be a real man of the sea sometime...
Aqua's Andatta will surely take me to the ocean!!
VNN...
OR NOT.
GRR

Story and art by Koichiro Hoshino

ACID VOMIT

Title art by Anzai
Story by GB

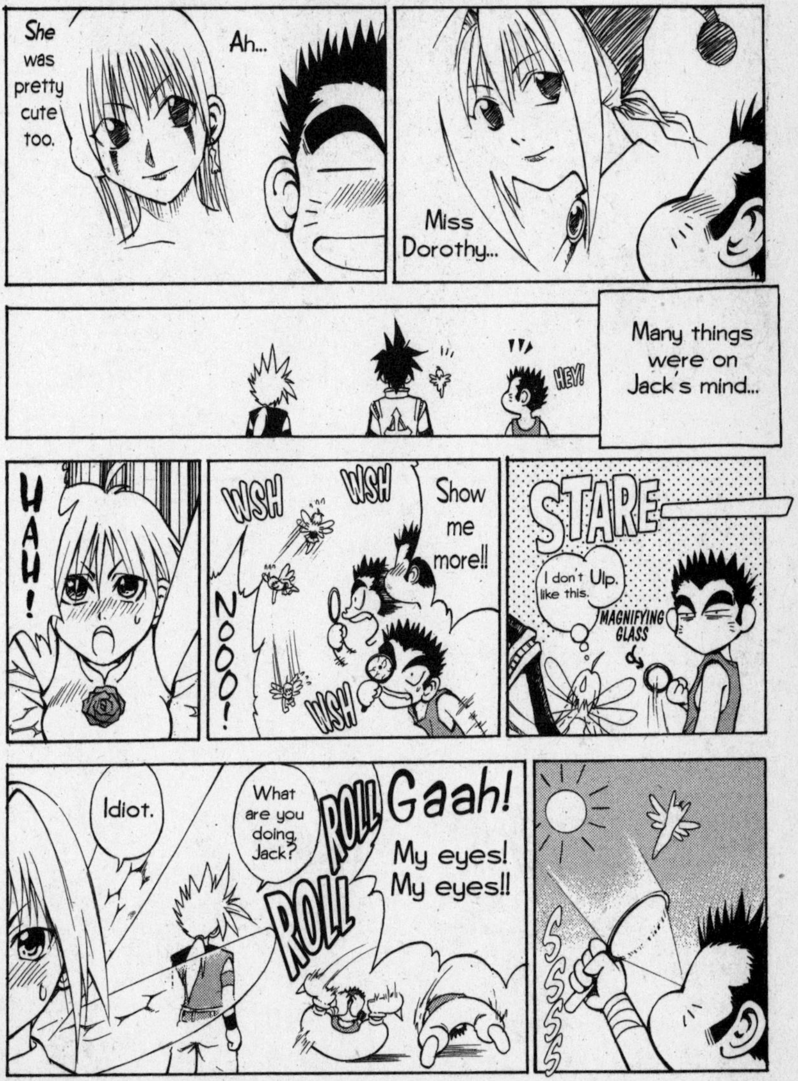
Miss Dorothy...
Ah...
She was pretty cute too.
Many things were on Jack's mind...
HEY!
STARE
Ulp.
I don't like this.
MAGNIFYING GLASS
WSH
Show me more!!
WSH
NOOO!
WSH
HAAH!
SSSS
Gaah!
My eyes! My eyes!!
ROLL
ROLL
What are you doing, Jack?
Idiot.

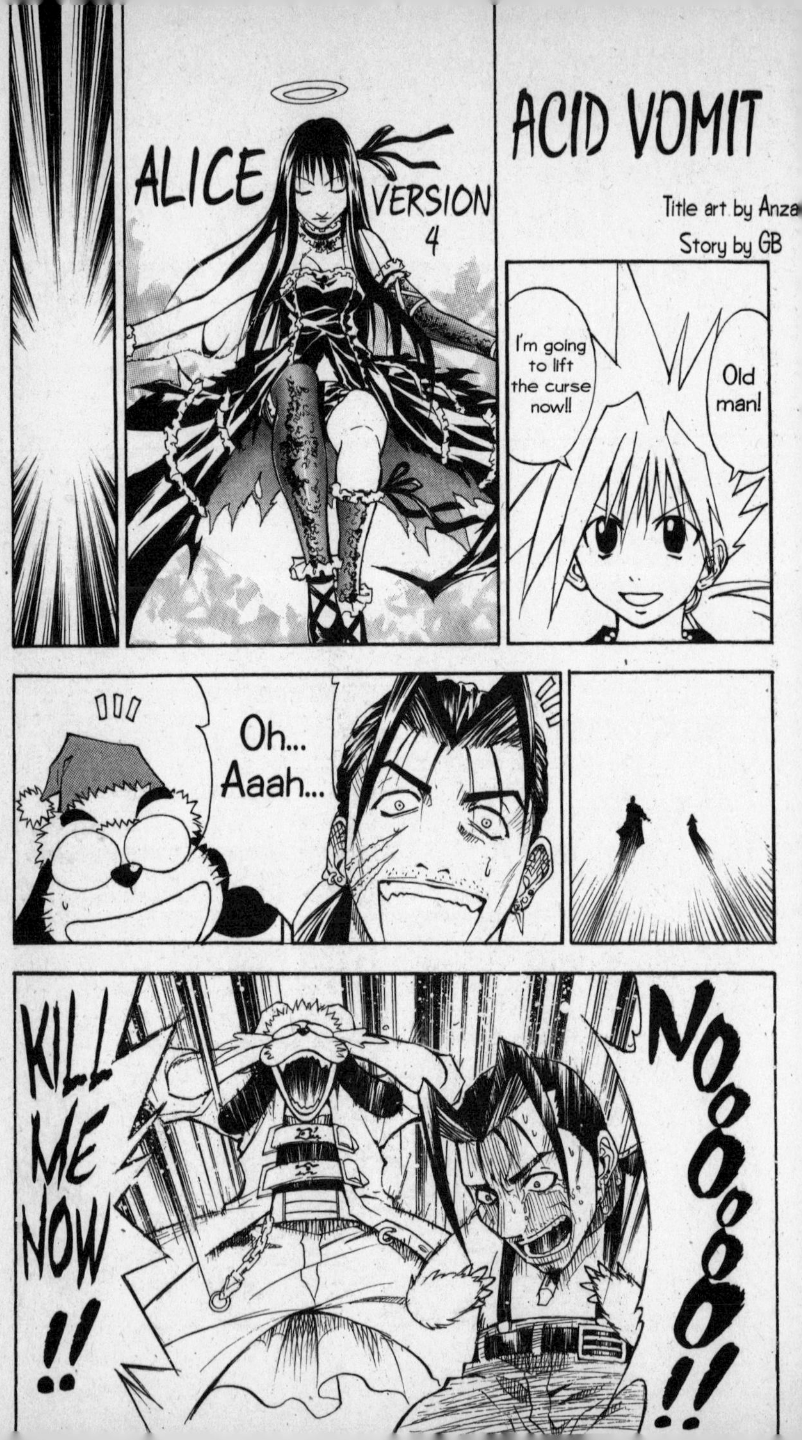
ACID VOMIT
Title art by Anza
Story by GB
Old man!
I'm going to lift the curse now!!
ALICE VERSION 4
Oh... Aaah...
NOOOOOOO!!
KILL ME NOW!!

THE CHOSEN ONES

By Fuse

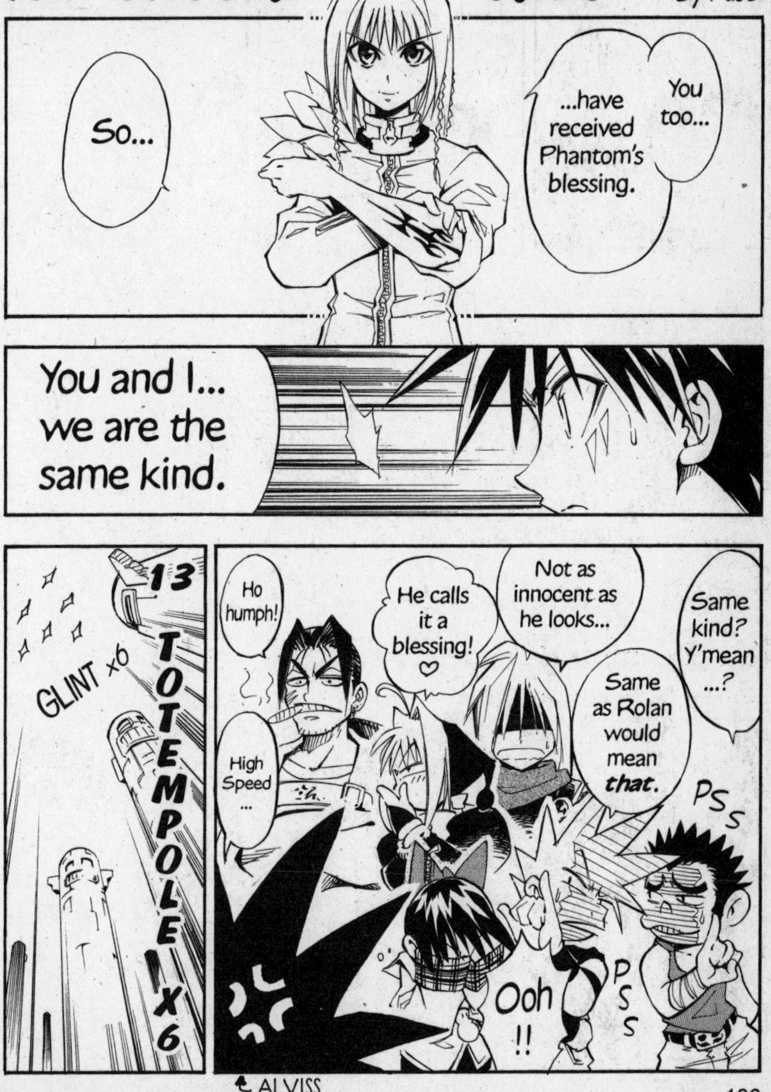

You too...
...have received Phantom's blessing.
So...
You and I... we are the same kind.
Same kind? Y'mean ...?
Not as innocent as he looks...
Same as Rolan would mean *that*.
He calls it a blessing! ♡
Ho humph!
High Speed ...
PSS
Ooh !!
PSS
13
TOTEMPOLE x6
GLINT x6
ALVISS

THOUGHTS ON SELF INTRODUCTIONS

By Masahiro Ikeno

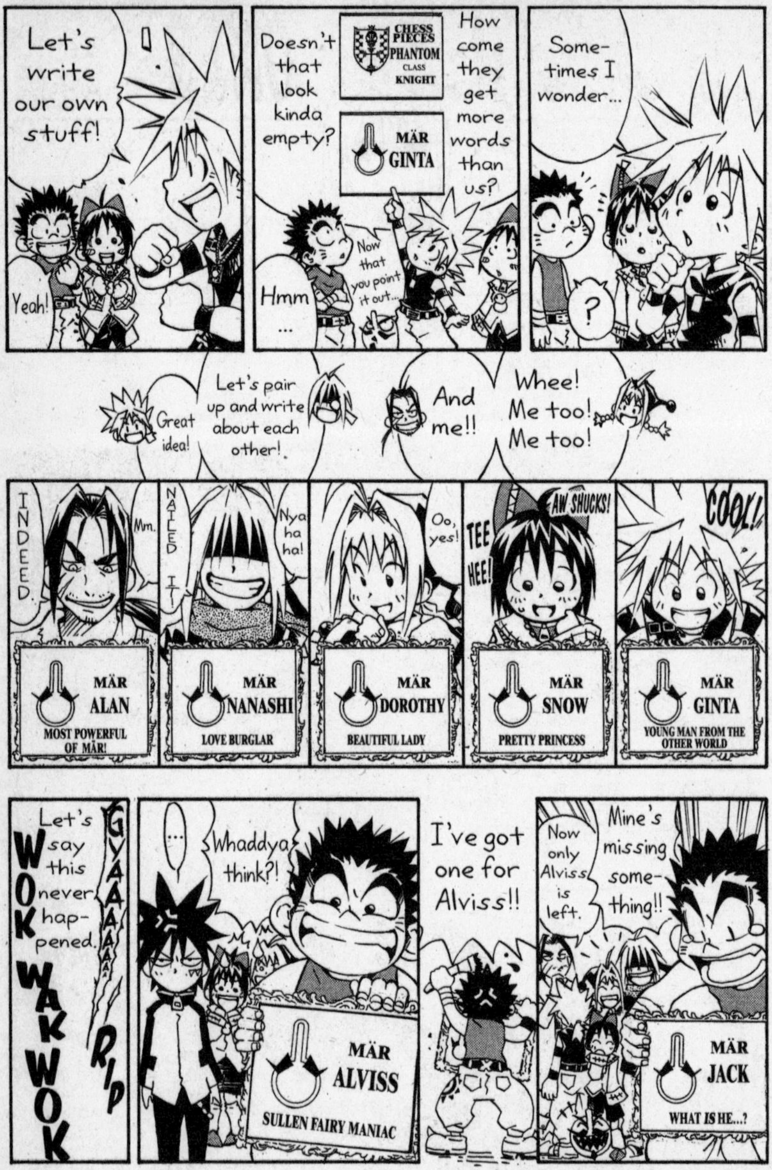
Some-times I wonder...
?
How come they get more words than us?
CHESS PIECES PHANTOM CLASS KNIGHT
MÄR GINTA
Doesn't that look kinda empty?
Now that you point it out...
Hmm...
!
Let's write our own stuff!
Yeah!
Whee! Me too! Me too!
And me!!
Let's pair up and write about each other!
Great idea!
COOL!
MÄR GINTA YOUNG MAN FROM THE OTHER WORLD
AW SHUCKS!
TEE HEE!
MÄR SNOW PRETTY PRINCESS
Oo, yes!
MÄR DOROTHY BEAUTIFUL LADY
Nya ha ha!
NAILED IT!
MÄR NANASHI LOVE BURGLAR
Mm.
INDEED.
MÄR ALAN MOST POWERFUL OF MÄR!
Mine's missing some-thing!!
Now only Alviss is left.
MÄR JACK WHAT IS HE...?
I've got one for Alviss!!
Whaddya think?!
...
MÄR ALVISS SULLEN FAIRY MANIAC
GYAAAAAA
RIP
Let's say this never hap-pened.
WOK WAK WOK

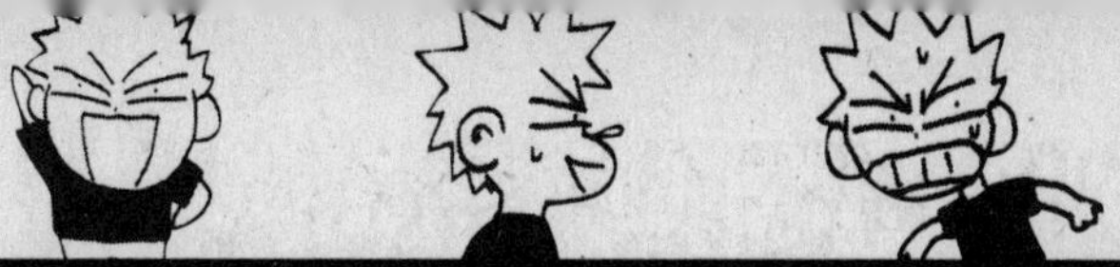

Table of Contents Pages

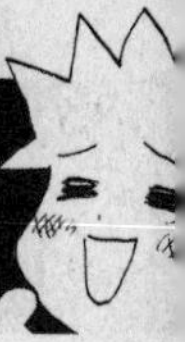

Issue 19: 19. (on sale 04/04/2005)

Anyone who has a wallet chain by the old Ash brand, lend it to me!

Issue 20: 20. (on sale 04/13/2005)

They should just cut down all the cedar.

Issue 21: 21. (on sale 04/20/2005)

When I wrote "I'm tired" here before, someone cheered me up. Thanks.

Issue 22, 23: 22 - 23. (on sale 04/27/2005)

I've been so sleepy lately.

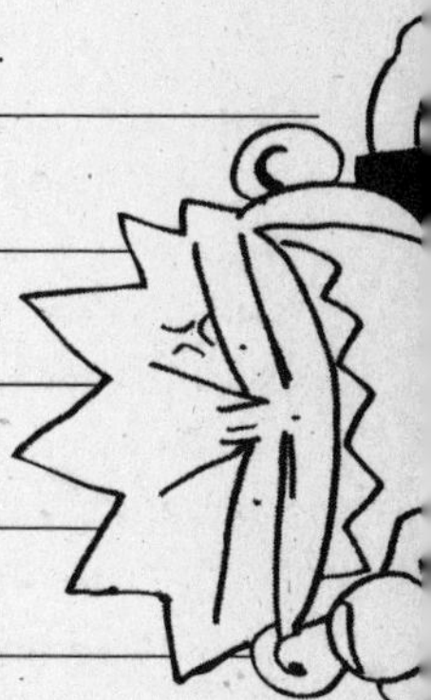

Issue 24: 24. (on sale 05/11/2005)

Recently I've been exchanging racy email with Kazuro Inoue. Heh heh.

Issue 25: 25. (on sale 05/18/2005)

Human relations are so complicated.

Issue 26: 26. (on sale 05/25/2005)

I love the theme song for MÄR. I play it a lot during work.

Issue 27: 27. (on sale 06/01/2005)

Recently I've been competing in quizzes against Katsutoshi Kawai by email.

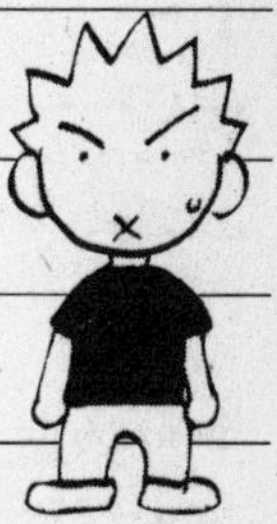

Issue 28: 28. (on sale 06/08/2005)

I just can't figure out the rules to the MÄR card game. Am I stupid?

Issue 29: 29. (on sale 06/15/2005)

I've been getting the hiccups nearly every day. It's annoying.

Issue 30: 30. (on sale 06/22/2005)

The new song for Rapsody was so-so.

Issue 31: 31. (on sale 06/29/2005)

I can't get to sleep at night. Then I can't wake up the next morning.

Issue 32: 32. (on sale 07/06/2005)

The girl in the blue skirt on that commercial is so cute. No idea what the commercial is for.

Issue 34: 34. (on sale 07/20/2005)

Nothing special has happened lately. Boring.

Issue 35: 35. (on sale 07/27/2005)

Went to a concert with lots of special effects. Kenji Ohtuski is totally cool.

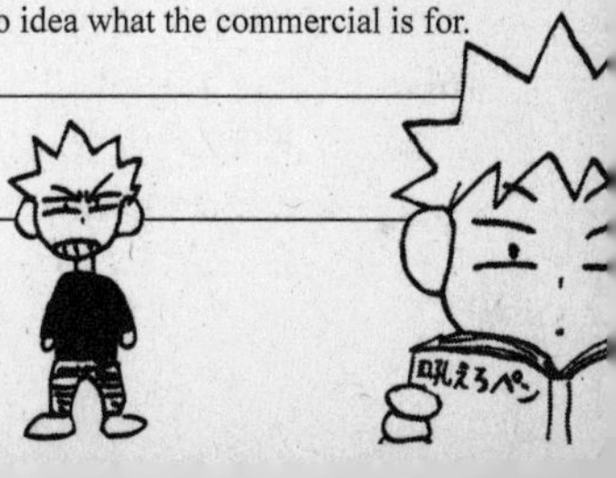
吼えろペン

2005 WEEKLY SHONEN SUNDAY

Author Comments from the

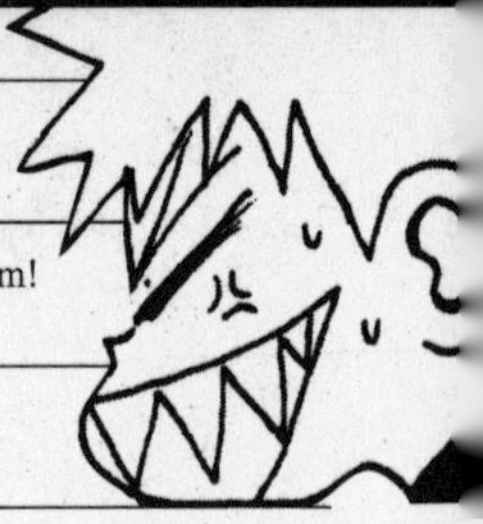

Issue 1: 1. (on sale 12/01/2004)

I've started taking care of a Welsh Corgie named Punk.

Issue 2: 2. (on sale 12/08/2004)

Whata surprise! MEGADEATH got back together to release a new album! The first song is awesome!

Issue 3: 3. (on sale 12/15/2004)

MÄR vol. 8 will be out this week. Please get it!

Issue 4, 5: 4 - 5 (on sale 12/22/2004)

I just can't get over how cute my dog is.

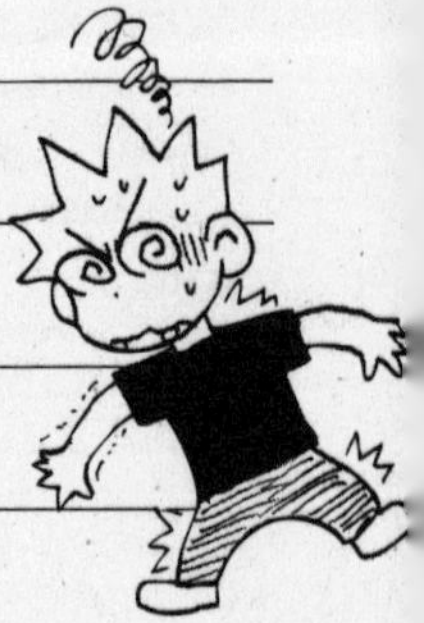

Issue 6: 6 (on sale 01/04/2005)

Happy New Year.

Issue 7: 7. (on sale 01/12/2005)

I wonder how many people actually know that I have two series out?

Issue 9: 9. (on sale 01/26/2005)

Mr. Otani from Dainoji, were you able to read MÄR?

Issue 10: 10. (on sale 02/02/2005)

My new editor will be Miyasaka. He's a dandy.

Issue 11: 11. (on sale 02/09/2005)

At our new year's party, Mizuguchi Sensei (creator of Minoru Kobayashi) thought I was scary. But I'm not.

Issue 12: 12. (on sale 02/16/2005)

I bought an 18k skull ring by Travis Walker. Feeling great.

Issue 13: 13. (on sale 02/23/2005)

I want to go to the hot springs. I want to escape.

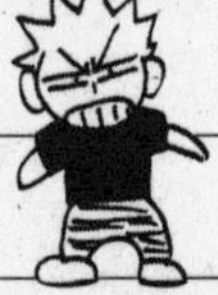

Issue 14: 14. (on sale 03/02/2005)

I'm going to the hot springs next week.

Issue 15: 15. (on sale 03/09/2005)

A million thanks to everyone who sent me Valentines chocolates.

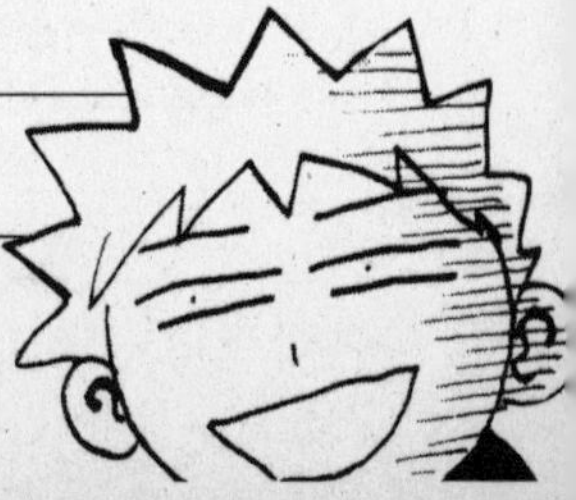

Issue 16: 16. (on sale 03/16/2005)

I'm tired.

Issue 18: 18. (on sale 03/30/2005)

For all of you who like MÄR, please check out the anime this week.

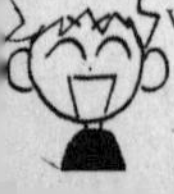

PICTURE DIARY WITH KEIJI MUTO

Nobuyuki Anzai

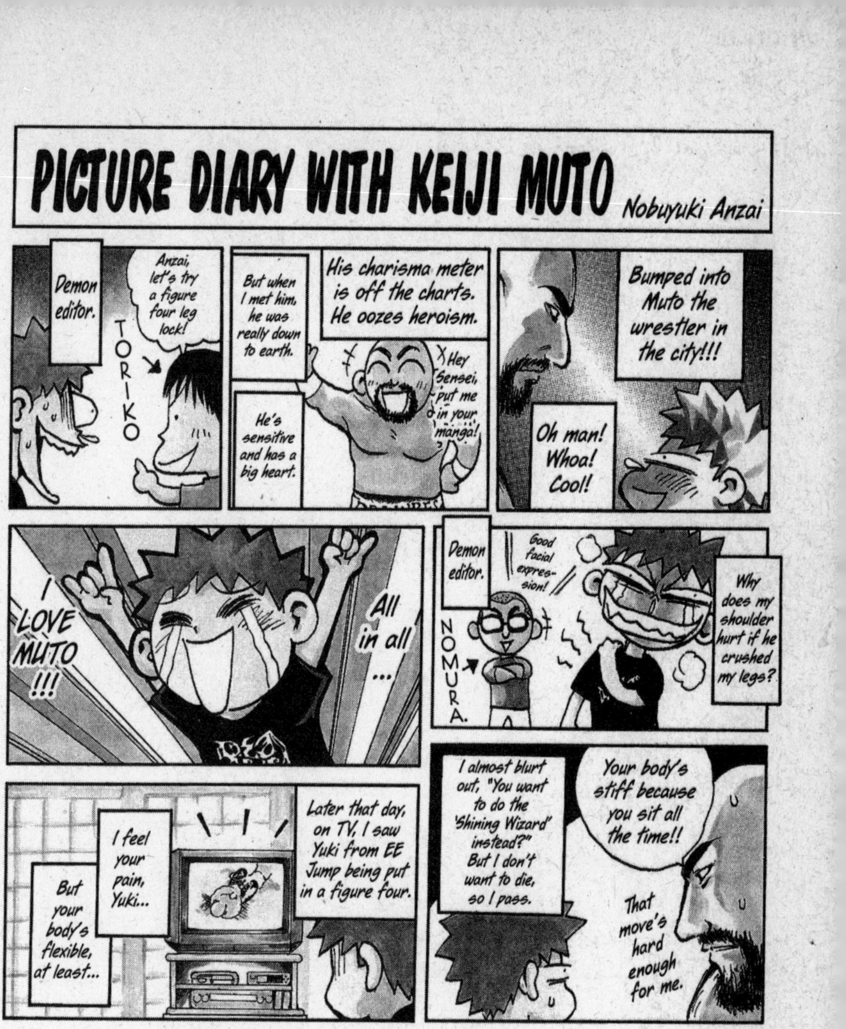
Bumped into Muto the wrestler in the city!!!
Oh man! Whoa! Cool!
His charisma meter is off the charts. He oozes heroism.
Hey Sensei, put me in your manga!
But when I met him, he was really down to earth.
He's sensitive and has a big heart.
Anzai, let's try a figure four leg lock!
TORIKO
Demon editor.
Why does my shoulder hurt if he crushed my legs?
Good facial expression!
Demon editor.
NOMURA.
All in all...
I LOVE MUTO!!!
Your body's stiff because you sit all the time!!
I almost blurt out, "You want to do the 'Shining Wizard' instead?" But I don't want to die, so I pass.
That move's hard enough for me.
Later that day, on TV, I saw Yuki from EE Jump being put in a figure four.
I feel your pain, Yuki...
But your body's flexible, at least...

This originally appeared in 2002 in Issue 20 of *Shonen Sunday*.

■ It's been three years since then, hasn't it? Guess no one remembers the pop group EE Jump anymore…

Author's
Message:

NOBUYUKI ANZAI
安西信行
PRESENTS

Punk is growing up
to be stupid.

MAR
Vol. 11
Story and Art by Nobuyuki Anzai

English Adaptation/Gerard Jones
Translation/Kaori Inoue
Touch-up Art & Lettering/James Gaubatz
Design/Izumi Evers
Editor/Andy Nakatani

Managing Editor/Annette Roman
Editorial Director/Elizabeth Kawasaki
Editor in Chief/Alvin Lu
Sr. Director of Acquisitions/Rika Inouye
Sr. VP of Marketing/Liza Coppola
Exec. VP of Sales and Marketing/John Easum
Publisher/Hyoe Narita

Printed in the U.S.A.

Published by VIZ Media, LLC
P.O. Box 77010
San Francisco, CA 94107

10 9 8 7 6 5 4 3 2 1
First printing, January 2007

www.viz.com
store.viz.com

PARENTAL ADVISORY
MÄR is rated T for Teen and is recommended for ages 13 and up. It contains fantasy violence.